THE PAUL CARUS LECTURES

Eugene Freeman, Editor

Published by the Foundation

Established in Memory of

PAUL CARUS

1852-1919

Editor of the Open Court

and the Monist

From 1888 to 1919

THE THEORY
OF
PRACTICAL REASON

Arthur E. Murphy.

1901-1962

THE PAUL CARUS LECTURES
SERIES 10
1955

THE THEORY

OF

PRACTICAL REASON

BY
ARTHUR EDWARD MURPHY

EDITED BY
A. I. MELDEN

OPEN COURT • ESTABLISHED 1887
LA SALLE • ILLINOIS • 1965

The passage from Holmes "Natural Law" Harv. L. Rev 32, (1918), 41, copyright 1918 by the Harvard Law Review Association, and reprinted by permission.

The passage from R. M. Hare *The Language of Morals* copyright 1952 by the Clarendon Press and reprinted by permission.

The passage from *The Sickness unto Death* by Soren Kierkegaard copyright 1941 by Princeton University Press and reprinted by permission.

The passage from the *Quintessence of Ibsenism* by Bernard Shaw reprinted by permission of the Society of Authors of London.

EDITOR'S ACKNOWLEDGMENTS

Professor Frederick H. Ginascol, the Executor of the Murphy Estate, and Dr. Eugene Freeman, Editor-in-chief of the Open Court Publishing Company, have been helpful at all stages in the preparation of the manuscript for publication and in the tedious work of checking the galley-proofs. I thank them for their generous assistance and good counsel on numerous matters.

A. I. Melden

INTRODUCTION

Arthur Edward Murphy began his teaching career at the University of California in 1926 immediately after receiving his doctorate from that institution. A year later he moved to Chicago and in 1931, after brief stays at Cornell and again at Chicago, he was appointed Professor of Philosophy at Brown University. In 1939 he moved to the University of Illinois as the chairman of its Department of Philosophy. Other Universities soon called upon him for his services as teacher and administrator. He returned to Cornell in 1945. In 1953 he moved to the University of Washington; and in 1958, after a visiting appointment, he joined the Department of Philosophy of the University of Texas.

The tenth series of the Carus Lectures were delivered by Murphy at the meeting of the American Philosophical Association held at the University of California, Berkeley, in December 1955. The lectures actually delivered were intended as the outline of an argument later to be worked out in detail and published in book form. However, subsequent reflection led Murphy to revise not only certain of his ideas but even the general plan and scope of the argument. He was at work on the manuscript until very shortly before his death in May, 1962. The work as it now appears is complete. Chapters I and VIII appear here precisely as

ix

they were left by their author; they were intended for publication in their present form. The remaining chapters required editorial work; but except for Chapter X, where the author left a note calling for certain changes, the revisions have been minor.

It was at Brown University that I first came to know Murphy. I recall one class in which he discussed the philosophy of Bradley, which had repelled me when first I encountered it. Murphy's exposition, and the defenses he offered in order to meet our objections, were the expression of a keen appreciation of the important philosophic perplexities that had impelled that thinker to his unusual conclusions. It is true that Murphy learned his philosophy as a student when the speculative systems of philosophy were very much alive. Alexander had recently published his *Space, Time, and Deity.* Whitehead's *Process and Reality* had yet to appear. And the philosophic temper of the time had scarcely begun to feel the full force of the attack that was to render unfashionable any metaphysics in the grand style. But while Murphy knew and understood the writings of the speculative metaphysicians of this period he understood them not merely as the audacious intellectual constructions they are but as intelligible philosophical responses to the problems of which he himself was acutely aware. It was this that enabled him to give life and significance to doctrines that might otherwise appear part of an altogether dead and eccentric past.

But sensible as he was of the problems that gave point and substance to speculative metaphysics, he was equally aware of the dangers inherent in their studied inattention to detail. A responsible and successful philosophy must keep its view fixed upon the subject-matter it is concerned to illumine—the categorial features of the world in which human beings live, and which in their varying capacities and offices, and in different ways, they discover and alter. Nor was he any more favorably disposed towards certain forms of so-called analytic philosophy in which philosophical prepossessions of yet quite a different sort could be no less mischievous than the metaphysical quest for first principles of the highest level of generality—and the farthest removed from those matters which they were designed to explain. If it is the detail to which we must attend, it is to the detail relevant to the subject-matter of our inquiry. And if, for example, we are concerned to understand the concepts of perception and knowledge, whose cogency is amply supported by the greater part of our human efforts and achievements, and avoid the philosophic confusion that surrounds and obscures them, then, as he once put it, "we shall have to know what they mean in the situations in which they have a verifiable application."[1] Murphy could be and indeed was viewed both by the traditionalist metaphysician and the rebel 'analytic' philosopher as one to whom both could turn for understanding. In every department of philosophy in which he served he functioned as a mediator in the philosophical discussions between members of divergent schools. But while he could understand the traditionalists and the innovators, he could be as critical of the one group as he was of the other for the common mistake of systematically ignoring the concrete circumstances within which philosophical problems arise and only by reference to which, in the end, they can be resolved.

For if there is any conviction that gives unity to Murphy's thought during the many years in which he wrote and taught it is that good sense can be found in the common life from which our philosophical inquiries take their departure and hence

---

[1] In "Two Versions of Critical Philosophy," *Proceedings of the Aristotelian Society*, 1937-38, p. 145. Reprinted in *Reason and the Common Good*, ed. by W. H. Hay, Marcus Singer and Arthur E. Murphy (New York: Prentice-Hall, Inc.) 1963. Included in this volume of essays is a bibliography of Murphy's writings.

that it is back to this common life, and with an increased understanding, to which our philosophy must return us. It was his
own effort, in the face of the philosophic skepticism that claimed
the authority of science itself, to make sense of the ordinary
view that the world in which we live is not "in the end" or
"really" a remote field of atoms and electrons forever cut off
from our view by the distorting data of sense, but such indeed as
sober and intelligent men take it to be, that inspired the very
first articles he wrote and which overnight won him national
attention. He himself came to recognize the unsatisfactoriness of
the "objective relativism" he had formulated and defended. But
he continued to think of his task as a philosopher first and last
to discover whatever rhyme and reason there may be in our familiar beliefs by attempting to relate the crucial concepts—to which
as philosophers we must attend—to the particular context, practical or theoretical as the case may be, in which they play their
role. The price of the failure to bear in mind clearly and firmly
that aspect of the world with which we are concerned is confusion.
And we have enough of it in the actual lives we live and no need
to compound it in our philosophy. As Murphy himself put it,
in the thirties,

> . . . the significance of signs, and of the 'concepts' which signs ex-
> press depends on the way in which they are used, and . . . such usage,
> in both ordinary life and the sciences, is a transaction in which in-
> formation is conveyed, expectations aroused, and claims tested by
> reference to the particular situation in which the communicating
> parties are concerned. And this kind and degree of validity which
> such statements have, and which it is important for philosophy to take
> account of, is that which can be tested in the situations to which they
> were intended to apply. To divorce such truth-claims from the opera-
> tions by which they can be tested and the situations in which these

operations can be performed is to invite confusion, and in most cases to get it.[2]

What we students could learn from Murphy was not a philosophical doctrine but a way of being intellectually responsible to our subject matter: he provided us with the example of one who never lost sight of the character of the world in which we live and never wavered in the conviction that there is good sense to be found in it—a world of everyday objects no less than that of hypothetical atoms and electrons, of persons with all of their hopes and aspirations no less than of causal laws and blind necessities. Both in his teaching and his publications his sense of the way things are, and his unshaken conviction that good sense could be found in it, were argued and conveyed with an earnest wisdom that contrasted sharply with the merely clever efforts of others.

The present work is the fruition of an inquiry conducted over a period of many years into the conditions and the character of the application of reason to human affairs. Like the aptly titled *The Uses of Reason* written two decades earlier during the most uncertain days of World War II, the present work was composed during times no less trying to the confidence of men in their ability to achieve a world worth living in. Here, as in the earlier work, we find a defense of the claims of reason relevantly and properly employed in conduct. But here we have a general theory of practical reason enriched by a much clearer sense of the complexity of detail to which a work of this magnitude must direct our attention. And here, too, we find the recognition of the contribution to the understanding thus achieved of the philosophical investigations of others during the intervening years.

The phrase "reason relevantly and properly employed in conduct" is intended, in part at least, as a reminder of a subject-

---

[2] *Op. cit.*, p. 145.

matter all too easily obscured by philosophical preconceptions. It is neither empty rhetoric nor an accident of the author's own interest in people that explains the frequent reference in these Carus Lectures to persons, to the transactions in which they engage with one another in the communities of which they are members, and to the actions that reflect the way of life they share with one another. Murphy never lost sight of the fact that it is persons, the full-blooded beings with whom we deal in the concrete and complex situations of ordinary life, not immaterial egos related in problematic ways to bodies they inhabit, or centers of consciousness enjoying some sort of ultimate good, with whom in morals we deal, and to whom our moral reasons are addressed. Reasons, as he put it, are addressed to whom they may concern, to human beings as we find them who are concerned to justify themselves and to achieve and to maintain adequate moral relations with one another. By the same token, the conduct in question is to be distinguished from the twitches of muscles or the movements of limbs. Nor are omissions and abstentions which also may come under our moral review to be identified with the static states of the relevant bodily parts. Equally, the actions and abstentions for which reasons are demanded and supplied are not the idle and meaningless doings in which on occasion each of us engages and for which no doubt explanations, of how and in some way they came to pass, are possible. They are, rather, the actions and the abstentions and omissions in which persons reveal their desires, their hopes and intentions during the course of their activities and in their traffic with one another.

But so to locate the scene in which reason can do its work is surely to reveal something of the conceptual character of our understanding of persons and their actions. This is the point of Murphy's frequent use of examples: these are designed to bring into clear focus the features of a subject-matter which, inevitably,

INTRODUCTION

are obscured if we succumb to the temptation to search for high-level generalities. For a reason that is relevantly and properly employed in matters of human action addresses itself to human events freighted with the intentions of agents who are concerned to do what is right and proper in the achievement of worthwhile ends. So understood actions, unlike events in the so-called external or physical world, are appraisable in principle, however deficient in particular cases they may be, in terms of the standards appropriate to them in the particular kinds of situations in which they are performed. So too with persons, the moral agents with whom we carry on our daily affairs. Our understanding of persons is not achieved by engaging in inductive inferences concerning the nature of their inner mental states or the causes of the bodily movements involved in the actions they perform. 'Action' and 'agent' are logically related terms. A reason that provides us with an understanding of the one, by means of the essentially normative concepts it employs, does so just to the extent that it grasps the no less normative character of the concepts in terms of which it makes sense of the other. As Murphy himself puts the matter in a statement he addresses to the reader early in his essay in order to indicate the general line of his argument,

> Actions . . . are not just events that happen in the world. They are deeds done by someone—Smith, Jones, Robinson, or myself. They are the actions of selves, *their* actions or mine, the expression and embodiment of what as practical agents we are and try to be. And they are imputed to such agents not as qualities to a substance that supports them or as a subject in which they inhere, or as effects of prior wants in human bodies or minds, but as doings for which they are personally responsible because it is as persons that they do them. The person thus acting is the whole man—a bodily being living here and now, or there and then, in a world he never made, and called on to act, in situations for which he is never wholly responsible, *as* a responsible being with a mind and will of his own. But it is the whole

man considered in a certain light, in his role or status as a person, and it is only insofar as we can practically understand and deal with him as such that the categories of practical action are practically applicable to his conduct. To be—or to become—in this way a self or person is a practical achievement, and in much of his behavior as Kierkegaard has observed, 'man is not yet a self.' If his conduct never reached this level, there would be no sense in so considering him, and our talk of practical reason as grounds for action, whether for others or ourselves, would be in fact as idle as in some current accounts of conduct it appears to be. Our present purpose is not to 'justify' the categories of practical action by some external standard ... but to see clearly what they are and to determine how far, in their terms, we can understand each other and ourselves. The point made here is simply that *within* this way of understanding, the conceptions of practical action and of personal agency are so intertwined that neither makes useable sense without the other.

What is here being asserted is not the empty tautology that morally successful action and agency are achievements, and that as such they enjoy a status that is irreducibly normative. Nor is it the old and familiar truism that men will do what is right and proper just to the extent to which, by being reasonable in the dealings with one another, they achieve a moral understanding with each other. What is here adumbrated, and supported in these Carus Lectures by a wealth of detailed argument, is the philosophical thesis that it would make no sense to speak of right or wrong conduct except for those who in some measure have achieved the normative status of morally concerned and accountable selves in the practical context of their everyday dealings with each other. For a reason that is relevantly and properly employed in determining the moral worth of actions or agents—a reason that can deal competently and relevantly with the distinctively normative features of moral action and agency—is a reason that is logically possible only for selves whose common concerns are involved in the common way of life in which, with varying degrees of success, they achieve their moral status. But although it is back to our common moral life to which our philosophy must bid us return in order that we may grasp the distinctive features of our moral understanding and the manner in which agents who are concerned may be justified in what they do, it is to that common life only in so far as in fact it is the achievement of morally reasonable men. Unless there were this rational pattern in our common way of life, there would be no discoverable reason which we could employ in our conduct, and neither moral problems nor conduct itself in any sense in which these concern or interest us.

There is a solemn, an earnest, mood that pervades much of this work. In the best sense of the term these lectures, especially those in Part II, are philosophical sermons—and understandably so, given their author's conception of the nature of moral philosophy and of what it can do. Moral philosophy, as it is here conceived, is no mere intellectual exercise to be conducted in the classroom or study for the fun in it. Nor is it a meta-ethics the practitioners of which can proceed with complete ethical neutrality. If moral philosophy is to elucidate the character of our moral understanding of persons and their actions, its practitioners must participate in that shared understanding that is our common way of life. And they must, if they possess the requisite sensitivity to their subject-matter, be able to demonstrate uncommonly well in thought, if not always in deed, that moral understanding whose categorial features it is their task to disclose. But, further, the enterprise of moral philosophy, nourished as it is by that reason that is to be found in the lives of those who pursue it, must contribute to it. For like certain other philosophical inquiries, moral philosophy is not without its feed-back phenomenon: a successful disclosure of the rationality that is in our lives, whatever the area of human experience may be, inevitably contributes to it.

INTRODUCTION

And it is an essential part of the author's conception of moral philosophy that, by illuminating the character of our moral understanding of persons and their conduct, it contributes to the moral community in which we participate. In short, moral philosophy by clarifying our shared understanding of human affairs in which each of us is actively engaged, can and must add to that stock of wisdom that is both our subject and our only defensible recourse in the practical situations in which we are involved. Thus understood, a sound moral philosophy calls for a response that is no mere passive assent of the intellect, but, in Murphy's concluding words, "the answering judgment of the reader who will say, 'I understand. Now I can go on,' and who makes good what he says in what he does."

A. I. Melden

June 1963

Contents

CHAPTER 1

THE "WHY" OF
PRACTICAL UNDERSTANDING

HOW CAN REASON BE practical? The question is perennial and appears to be profound. That our thinking must be rational if it is to do its work as thinking would seem to be a truism, though there have been grave thinkers who denied it. But that action can or even should be rational is *prima facie* a much more problematic claim. For valid thinking, it is often said, is one thing, and successful doing quite another. And it is to the former rather than the latter that criteria of rationality seem in the first instance and primarily to apply. The gulf between theory and practice is deep and often dark, and it is not by mere thinking, however rational, that it can reliably be bridged. Hence, while we have a high and almost superstitious regard for the factual findings of objective science, we are suspicious of the "thinking man" as an arbiter of action and accord him a subordinate place in the executive order of our practical affairs. It may be that this suspicion is not unwarranted and this subordination wise. In such matters, how are we to judge? What would it be like to be reasonable here, and is it even desirable that we should be? Why?

Such questions reflect an internal division in our thinking that itself has practical effects. Our store of knowledge or correct information about the world and ourselves is increasing at a most impressive rate. Our trouble is that we do not know what to do with it, for we do not know what is worth doing or what must be done for the right attainment of a life worth living. Our knowledge, just because it is factual, objective, and "value-free" is non-committal with respect to the issues of conduct. It can be put to any use that we are wise or foolish enough to make of it, without prejudice to its own merely cognitive validity. And our commitments, being 'non-cognitive' and hence extra-rational, are often as arbitrary and unenlightened in practice as, for such a way of thinking, they are bound in principle to be. If rational thought is practically non-committal and action is intrinsically non-rational, then a union of the two can give us only a contingent linkage of essentially unrelated factors in a situation that "mere" thought cannot direct nor "mere" action understand. Yet such directive or normative understanding is surely what we need if we are to meet wisely the practical problems that so urgently confront us. It is not surprising that in such a situation men of action consult the oracles and omens of traditional belief or the latest public opinion poll while they stockpile increasingly effective instruments for incoherent and mutually destructive ends. If thinking has no more than this to give us, why should we take its rational requirements seriously when great issues are at stake?

It is clear that for human purposes there is something seriously wrong in this picture. Perhaps the trouble is with the world itself, which certainly appears "absurd" when we try in this way to understand it, and with our own irrational nature which, we are often told, was not made for understanding but for groundless action (here called freedom), and for blind belief. There is a currently popular philosophy which in this way rationalizes our practical confusion as a revelation of the inner "existential" meaning of our human situation. It thus provides a formula for frustration and a theory of the irrelevance of thought to action that seems dramatically relevant to the only sort of action which, being "ultimately" senseless, would, in such a world, make sense. Its light indeed is darkness, but in a world as obscure as this, what could be more illuminating? Its wide acceptance is an authentic sign of the times, and in such times signs are taken for wonders, and philosophies are built upon them.

There is, however, *prima facie* at least, another possibility. It may be that it is not the world, or the times, or even the constructive capacities of human nature that are essentially out of joint. Perhaps the fault lies rather in the way in which we have, in the picture thus presented, tried to understand them. How far things make sense for us, and in this way have a meaning, depends in part at least on the sense we show in our attempts to deal with them. A foolish man will always live, for practical purposes, in a senseless world and a disordered mind in one (for it) of quite insoluble contradictions. It would be premature, however, until the resources of human understanding have been exhausted, to generalize their unhappy situation as an ontologically privileged disclosure of the deeper meaning of existence. Before we commit ourselves to so sweeping a conclusion, it would be well to ask in somewhat more prosaic and specific terms just what our resources of practical understanding are, how such reason operates when it is about its appropriate business, and how, if we are willing to make proper use of it, it might in fact provide a relevant solution for our problems. We might then ask not how *can* "reason" be practical, when "reason" and "practice" are so defined as to stand in dialectical opposition to each other, but rather how can practice be reasonable, and why is it important that it should be so?

My purpose in this inquiry is to explore this alternative possibility and to try to answer the questions that it raises in terms that make both theoretical and practical sense. This sense—the only adequate answer to the quest for "meaning"—will not in the first instance be something brought in from a higher or deeper realm of "reality" to "save the appearances" of an incoherent world. It will rather be the sense that we can find in the intent of our own actions where these are adequately understood, when we know what we are doing and the good of doing it. It is in such action, I shall contend, that "reason" can be, and sometimes is, of practical importance, for it is here that the "gulf" between theory and practice, thought and conduct, is bridged not merely in philosophy but in fact. This bridge is simply practical understanding itself. And it is its structure that we must try to understand, not on our terms but on its own, if we are to make a reliable start in our investigation.

In the familiar sense in which I shall here use the term, to "understand" something is to make relevant sense of it in some context of human thought, action, or enjoyment, in which it can significantly be said to have a meaning. It is, in a useful metaphor, to see it in a certain light, a light which, as we shall see, is that of understanding itself. To understand a spoken sentence, we must hear and respond to it as a statement, or ejaculation, or command, in the practice in which it has, for those who have learned to use the language, a communicative function. To understand a painting aesthetically, we must be able to see it as a painting and have the capacity to appraise and enjoy it as such. To understand an event as an occurrence, we must be able to see it as a consequence of things past and a condition for things to come in a sequence of happenings in which it is at once an outcome and a portent. To understand a person, in the way in which we sometimes reach an understanding with those who share with us the values of a common way of life, we must see his actions *as actions,* as the embodiment of intentions that show us at once what it is that he is doing, or trying to do, and what, as the doer of such deeds, he is as a practical and moral agent.

It is with this last use of "understanding" that we shall in this inquiry be initially and primarily concerned. I shall use the term "practical" to characterize such understanding, not because it refers us to a practice—it is at least arguable that any specification of a use of "understanding" does that—but because it carries with it that sense of "practicality" in which we speak of actions that we try to understand and to appraise as practical or impractical, as right and appropriate to ends worth seeking and justifiable or unjustifiable in that context of activity in which a distinction between right and wrong with respect to actions has an examinable sense. The appropriateness of this designation can be judged as our investigation proceeds.

The best method, perhaps, of indicating in a preliminary way the locus of this kind of understanding is to say that it is that of conduct to which the question "why?" is applicable in a sense of "why?" that we must now attempt to specify and make clear. Given alternatives for action, why *should* we act in one way rather than another? What's the good of it, and how will this action serve to bring about that good? Is it, in my situation and for my purposes, the right thing for me to do? Or, when we are trying to understand the actions of others: why did he do it? What was he trying to accomplish, and did he go about it in a proper, sensible and effective way? It is evident that when we ask these questions about the behavior of others, we consider them as beings like ourselves, with needs and wants to satisfy, concerned and competent to some degree at least to conduct themselves in a manner appropriate to the requirements of the situation with which, as rational creatures, they are called upon to deal. Our appraisal of their conduct or, in retrospect, of our own, may be negative and disapproving. We all act foolishly, irresponsibly, disgracefully in some situations. But it is only in terms of some notion of what would have been sensible, responsible, and creditable that this estimate can be made. To understand a man's actions in this sense, and to understand him as a practical agent, we must know what he was trying to do and appraise his actions as an accomplishment, or a failure to accomplish, something thought to be in some assignable way worth doing. And when I ask "why should I?" it is in the same light that I try to understand the facts of my human situation as practically relevant to the action to be done.

The relevant answer to a "why?" is a "because", and a "because" is a kind of reason. Practical reasons, within this context of understanding, are grounds for action, the sort of grounds we ask for when we try to reach a decision on the merits of competing claims upon our conduct: the sort of grounds we expect from others when their actions are in question and our aim is to understand and to appraise them at their proper worth. And hence they are essentially normative or appraisive reasons. Their function is to "license" one course of action as against another as, in the circumstances, right and proper, and where they fail to do so the action, and the agent, as the doer of that act, are to that degree condemned. The judgment that an act is foolish, arbitrary, or in the widest sense "impractical", is not a practically non-committal judgment. It may be, of course, that a foolish action is in some other way approvable—it may testify to the kind heart of the man who does it—but *as* foolish it is futile, inept, inadequate to the requirements of the practical situation in which it was performed. These are terms not merely of description but also of dispraise. Nor is it at all surprising or paradoxical that this should be the case. For it is in the guidance and control of conduct that we look for this kind of practical understanding and have a use for it. The categories that guide actions are those of better and worse, good and evil, right and wrong. A cognitively neutral description of human conduct is not, as it stands, a relevantly cogent answer to the "why" of practical action. It does not meet the requirements of practical understanding. What it reports must be understood not merely as a report, but as a ground for action, as a "because" for doing one thing rather than another, if it is to have the practical import that mere thinking cannot supply. This way of understanding is, as has been said, the "bridge" between thought and action that makes sense of "practical reason", for it provides the conceptual structure of the situation within which it makes sense, and practical sense, to ask for and to offer reasons that are grounds for doing. It is here that in the first instance at least we can reasonably expect to find an answer to the "why?" of action— the why that, for practical purposes, we seek.

The whole course of our inquiry will be required to make clear this sense of practical understanding and the use and cogency of the reasons that are grounds for action. But it will be useful, at the start, to mark out some focal points of orientation within the area we shall try to explore and some central notions with which we shall operate throughout. We are dealing here not with the whole of human behavior, but primarily and specifically with *actions*, with the aspects of our conduct to which the question "why?" in the sense indicated above, is significantly and practically relevant. Much of our behavior has, *in this sense*, no "why" in it at all, though it may well have a causal explanation. And there may be a higher ontological "why" of it in the unsearchable design of the Creator. What we are here trying to understand, however, are actions that have a why *in* them in the sense that they are the doing, or trying to do, of something for which the agent can be called to account and fairly asked to give an account in terms that are designed to show the worth of what he does, and the rightness, in his situation, of his way of doing it. To understand an action in this sense, we must know not merely what is going on in the agent's body at the time and what forces were acting on it, or how he had in the past been conditioned, or what images were before his mind, but what he was trying to accomplish and why, for practical purposes, he took this way of going about it. An action, thus understood, is an intentional doing for which criteria of better and worse, right and wrong with respect both to what is achieved and the manner of its doing are required for the appraisal of its practical significance. It is a "rational" doing, not at all in the sense that what is done is always approvable as reasonable, but in the wider sense that it is a performance to which criteria of practical rationality are relevant in *either* positive *or* negative appraisal. Only the actions of a "rational" being can in this sense be foolish—the fall of a stone or the terrified twitchings of a trapped animal cannot. It might turn out to be the case that no aspect of human conduct "in the end" makes this kind of sense—that in all alike fallings and pushings and twitchings, or the blind surges of the unconscious, provide the final answer to our quest for understanding. In that case, our talk of such a "why" of action would have no application and no use, save as a peculiarly pointless form of propaganda or of self-deception. We shall consider that way of understanding human nature at a later stage in our inquiry. We do not, however, act on that kind of understanding, and could make no practical sense of human actions, including the actions of those who advance this kind of theory, if we did. Since our aim is to make sense of it, if we can, the part of wisdom is to see first what sense, on its own terms, it makes. We shall then be in a position to deal more seriously with those who, for their own purposes, would deny its pertinence to the conduct of our lives.

Actions, as thus understood, are not just events that happen in the world. They are deeds done by someone—Smith, Jones, Robinson, or myself. They are the actions of selves, *their* actions or mine, the expression and embodiment of what as practical agents we are and try to be. And they are imputed to such agents not as qualities to a substance that supports them or a subject in which they inhere, or as effects of prior wants in human bodies or minds, but as doings for which they are personally responsible because it is as persons that they do them. The person thus acting is the whole man—a bodily being living here and now, or there and then, in a world he never made, and called on to act, in situations for which he is never wholly responsible, *as* a responsible being with a mind and will of his own. But it is the whole man considered in a certain light, in his role or status as a person, and it is only insofar as we can practically understand and deal with him as such that the categories of practical action are relevantly applicable to his conduct. To be—or to become—in this way a self or person is a practical achievement, and in much of his behavior, as Kierkegaard has observed, "man is not yet a self." If his conduct never reached this level, there would be no sense in so considering him, and our talk of practical reasons as grounds for action, whether for others or ourselves, would be in fact as idle as in some current accounts of conduct it appears to be. Our present purpose is not to "justify" the categories of practical action by some external standard—that is a matter that will take care of itself at a later stage—but to see clearly what they are and to determine how far, in their terms, we can understand each other and ourselves. The point made here is simply that, *within* this way of understanding, the conceptions of practical action and of personal agency are so intertwined that neither makes usable sense without the other.

Persons are the doers of their deed, and what in this way they do shows us what in their character as practical agents they are. The world of action is a world of persons involved with each other in this shared activity that gives a practical structure and significance to their common life. It is as members of a community, as sharing and maintaining and in some cases rejecting or reconstituting the practices and standards of a way of life that men in this way act as persons. To say this is not merely to repeat the platitude that man is a social animal whose activities are conditioned and supported by the institutional environment with which, if he is to get on in the world, he has to deal. The social environment is something outside the individual. The community is inside him, not spatially, physically, or biologically, of course, but practically and morally, in the sense that it is in his responsible participation in its shared concerns that he has being as a person. Before he can use or criticize practical reasons, he must *learn* to understand considerations offered as grounds for action and acknowledge their cogency for right conduct. Training here is prior to significant argument, logically as well as temporally, since without this working basis of normative concern and competence—the concern and competence to get things right—all our talk of practical reasoning would, as Wittgenstein has put it, "hang in the air," and we should have no common ground on which to stand. Our appeal to grounds for action *might* then mean anything or nothing, as we chose for meta-ethical purposes to interpret it in one way or another. It does in fact mean something, and something of importance for our lives, not because we are uncommonly astute in such analysis, but because we have in some instances learned the difference between getting things wrong and getting them right, between failure and achievement, and are concerned and competent, to some degree at least, to act accordingly.

The communities in which we do thus learn and act are not idealized abstractions. They are the familiar, unideal, specific social groups in which we happen, without our own consent or preference, to have been born, or into which we move to make a living and to live a life. But they are social groups seen in a certain light, the light, once more—of practical understanding, as the ground and locus for those personal ties that make *moral* sense of what we do. There is a great deal more to being practically reasonable than this. We shall be extensively concerned with this "more" as we proceed. But without this basic grounding in that working understanding which is the stuff of our common lives this "more" would make no moral sense. A man who does not know, on the basis of such learning, what it is like to get things right and why it is his job to do so, will never understand the "normative force" of practical reasons because he will not *in this way* grasp their meaning, or be a master of their use. And it is in this use that they have the cogency he seeks. It must be our concern, at the beginning and throughout, to keep this *primary* fact in mind, and to steer our reasoning by the course it sets.

The language of practical reasons is a language of justification. This does not mean that it is a language of edification, or persuasive ejaculations, or transcendental probings of a noumenal realm of "values" beyond our world of space and time. The actions that we are concerned, in its terms, to understand are in the first instance at least, those of embodied human beings in a natural environment with which they must somehow come to terms if they are to survive and prosper in it. To know what he ought or to judge what others ought to do within this human situation, a man must know the relevant facts of the conditions under which actions are done and the consequences to be reliably expected from them. Such factual knowledge is essential to enlightened action and the "light" of a practical reason not thus instructed would be dim indeed. But the point of the activity in which this appeal to facts has a practical use is not just to discover and report the facts, but to understand and appraise their relevance, as grounds for doing something, to the worth of acting in one way rather than another, the worth of responsible and enlightened doing. Only for a being concerned and competent to act in this way would the question "why should I?" have a practical meaning, or the answer to it normative cogency as a guide for conduct.

"Why do you trade at the neighborhood supermarket?" "Because it is convenient, reasonably inexpensive, and gives good value for the money." If the market has in fact these merits, this would normally be accepted as a satisfactory answer to the question asked, when "because I am deeply drawn to it by its red and golden front" or "because its owner calls himself 'God's grocer'" would not. The latter sort of answer might accurately report the motivation of the buyer, but it would not show his action to be, in the circumstances, a practically sensible one. It would not justify the action *as* sensible or enhance our confidence in the good sense of the buyer as a shopper. To accept the one sort of answer as practically adequate and the other not, we should have to understand and use the standards of the way of life in which supermarket "values" and the Good Housekeeping Seal of Approval have a normatively cogent place. The action might of course be described as "sensible" in a practically non-committal way by an anthropologist who meant merely to convey the information that actions thus justified are in fact in this way approved within a given culture group. But that is not the way we use the term when we ask others to be sensible or try to determine for ourselves where we should do our buying. Here what is wanted is not information about the folkways, but grounds for action which will show it to be the right way of doing something worth achieving.

The characterization of an action as "sensible" is faint praise in comparison with the superlatives of moral approbation. Perhaps a sensible action is one that on other grounds we ought not to do and a *merely* sensible person has missed the higher goods of life. What, in the last analysis, is the good of being sensible? There is a point at which this question can be rightly asked, and will demand a reasoned answer. But unless we understand in the first instance what is good *in* being sensible, we would not know what we were talking about when we asked such a question or what a relevant answer to it would be like. For to understand the "why" of justification, we must use—though often on a larger scale—the same concern and competence that are embodied here in a familiar and mundane example. To call an action "sensible" is perhaps faint praise, but it is praise nonetheless, an authentic embodiment and expression of the operative discriminations and approvals by which we understand and appraise the issues of our common life. To act sensibly is so far to behave well in the situations in which good sense is called for in the conduct of our practical affairs, while to be careless, gullible, or stupid, is to fail to meet adequately the requirements and responsibilities of such action. To see an action as sensible or foolish is to see it as in this way meeting or failing to meet such requirements, and as justified or unjustified accordingly. And it is insofar as we do see it in this light that the language of practical reasons has a normative bearing on our conduct.

Justification is not of actions only, but of persons. A man who can be relied on to act sensibly is, for practical purposes, a sensible man—a man on whose good sense we can depend in those shared undertakings in which such sense is called for. As such he bears a certain responsibility and, when he bears it well, has earned a title to respect from others, and to self-respect. To achieve and to maintain this status is important to us, so important that we often go to great lengths to present ourselves and our actions in this light when our actual behavior gives but little ground for it. The process of giving the reasons for one's action is often, though not always, one of self-justification, and when we hear the words "I want you to understand why I acted as I did," we normally expect that what follows will be a plea for the acceptance of the action as right and of the agent as having played his part well in the activity in which right action is properly expected of him. The need for such acceptance is perennial and profound, and it is in practical understanding that it is sought and sometimes achieved. Sometimes, of course, a man does not try to justify himself in this way. He may admit the folly of his action and offer excuses for it, or ask for a chance to do better next time. Or he may reject the demand for justification and say, "So I was foolish—so what?" These are "moves" within the game of practical justification that have a point in special cases. But the point of the activity in which they have a point is to maintain a level of working understanding in which such acceptance is sometimes achieved and men can act together in the light of it, in mutual confidence and respect. This, in Wittgenstein's terms, is the importance of being justified.

The reasons a man offers are not always good reasons, and where good, not always his actual reasons for behaving as he did. The man who acted selfishly would like to have his action understood as one of impartial justice and will frequently offer reasons that present it in that light. His aim may be not merely to deceive others but to deceive himself as well, for there is no one in whose eyes a man more needs to cut a creditable figure than himself. There is endless room for deception and for "bad faith" here. But if men never acted for good reasons, if all self-justification were a deception, what would be the point of the deception? Who could possibly be fooled by it? By what criteria could it be detected and condemned? More realistically, how is it in fact detected? When a selfish man gives an account of his act as one of justice, he asks us to understand it in this way. And then the question is whether we can in this way make sense of what he does. This is not a matter of guessing what was going on in his inner experience when he did the deed, or what gnawings of greed were at that time occurring. We ask rather: was this the kind of act a man practically concerned to pursue his own interests without regard for the relevant claims and needs of others would do if the opportunity were presented? Can it be "rationalized" as just only by reasons so far-fetched that only an individual thus biased could be imposed on by them? In a particular case it may be difficult to judge, for some actions are both personally advantageous and just. But in the longer run of conduct there will be cases in which an action thus advantageous is not just and a just act not in this way to a man's advantage. The man whose action in such cases is well calculated to advance his own interests at the expense of justice shows himself thereby to be a selfish man. His "real" reasons are those that in this way account for what he does, and it is what in this way he does that shows us what, as a practical agent, he is. If he is so self-centered as to fail to make the distinctions that a fair-minded man would make in this matter, that is not at all a reason for saying that he is not "really" selfish. It is only further evidence of what it is, in practice, to be a thoroughly selfish man. Here actions do indeed speak louder than words, and the words we use in the practical appraisal of conduct make justifying sense only as they discoverably elucidate and articulate the meaning of such action.

Here, then, in a preliminary first look, is the subject matter of our inquiry, described in the categories that seem *prima facie* to be appropriate to its structure and intent. Our aim is to find in it if we can, the answer to a question at once of philosophical and practical importance—the question of the connection between thought and action in which thinking can be practical in its import and action enlightened and made fruitful by the work of rationally cogent thought. It is a quite familiar subject matter; there is nothing esoteric or hidden about it. The light in which we shall try to understand it is the light of common day, for it is just that light of understanding in which, as human selves, we live our days in common. And the language used is that which we all employ, with some degree of understanding, in the quite ordinary conduct of our practical affairs. In the course of the discussion I shall frequently observe that "we" do this and "we" say that in one sort of situation or another. And the critically-minded reader will no doubt be inclined to ask "who are the 'we' thus confidently referred to?" The answer is quite simple: "you and I." Unless we shared such a working basis in practical understanding, there would be no common ground on which our minds could meet in any inquiry into the sense or meaning of practical reasons, and the question of the "why" of action would, for us, have no discoverable sense. The fact is, however, that we do have such a basis, which only a fool or an advanced thinker (as Bradley put it) could deny—the fool because in fact he lacked it and the advanced thinker because, in the interests of some theory of his own, he was unwilling to admit it. And while we all aspire, in philosophy, to be advanced thinkers, we should be foolish indeed if we did not see that the only reliable basis on which thinking can advance is that which starts with something we can understand and carries with it and fulfils the intent of that activity in which, on the basis of such understanding, significant questions can be asked and sometimes adequately answered. Such, in any case, will be our procedure here, and the reader is warned of it in advance. An unfriendly critic has said of philosophy that it is a way of talking about things that everybody knows in terms that nobody can understand. The first clause of the allegation is true. We shall be talking, in the first instance, about things that every practical agent knows, but our aim will be to understand them better, and to this end, to talk about them in terms conceptually and practically adequate to the nature and intent of the activity in which they make a kind of practically reasonable sense.

This task will not be easy. For it is one thing to use this language meaningfully in familiar situations and another to think wisely about the nature, cogency, and limits of its use. But for practical as well as theoretical purposes we often need to think about it, to make sense not merely *with* but *of* it, to be clear

THE "WHY" OF PRACTICAL UNDERSTANDING

about its implications in the hard cases with which our training and habitual acceptances have not prepared us adequately to deal. In the moral chaos of the contemporary world, this fact is too obvious to require reiteration. Our theoretical scepticism about the cogency of practical reason is in large part a reflection of this practical disorientation. In large part, but not wholly. For while it is practical confusion that calls for conceptual elucidation, the elucidators or analysts of "meaning" have often added to the confusion by conceptual mistakes—quite natural in the circumstances—that *make* nonsense of our situation by trying to impose upon it the categories of a language, logically "simple", epistemologically "basic", or ontologically "ultimate", in whose terms we cannot say what practically we mean or mean what we appear to say. This is the way we reach the language nobody but the professionally indoctrinated can understand, and theirs is not a practical but only a verbally manipulated understanding, which too frequently carries with it a trained incapacity to make relevant practical distinctions. To avoid the pitfalls of this kind of learned misunderstanding, and to keep the categories of our language relevant to the practice in which such language can have a practically important sense is a formidable undertaking. Our thinking must be accurate and subtle and broadly wise if, in these hard cases, it is to fulfil the intent of the activities in which it has a discoverably cogent use and our language adequate to the requirements of such thinking. To make and keep it so we shall be obliged, at times, to engage in some high level verbal haggling with those whose prescriptions as to what we must or cannot mean would strip our language of the practical sense that, for enlightened action, we require. This haggling, however, will never be engaged in for its own sake or carried further than in the contemporary state of philosophical discussion seems necessary for the avoidance of probable misunderstanding. Our primary concern is not with analytic mistakes, but with practical understanding, and our hope is that by starting with such understanding as we already have and working out its structure and implications for conduct in the precarious world in which today we live, we may reach that better understanding which can show its authenticity not in dialectical virtuosity, but in the conduct of our lives. The proper business of the elucidation of meaning is an enhancement of understanding and of the analysis of practical reasons, the enhancement of our understanding of the worth of action and of persons, when, where, and as such understanding is just now, too frequently, in short supply.

In its preoccupation with "understanding", and in some of its methods of investigation, this inquiry resembles what is now called "conceptual analysis" or "language analysis" in philosophy. And how much it owes to Wittgenstein's *Philosophical Investigations* a reader familiar with that great work will have no trouble in discerning. If analysis is the elucidation of meaning, and philosophical analysis the making clear of the conceptual or categorial structure of language as we use it, then we shall, especially in the earlier stages of our inquiry, be "doing" a good deal of conceptual analysis. We shall look for the meaning of such concepts in their use in the language in which, within a common way of life, we sometimes do in practice understand what we and those with whom we work, are doing. But differences will be as frequent and, on the whole, as fundamental as resemblances. For the "linguistic" meaning that concerns us here is that discoverable in a practice whose point is a certain kind of justification, and the way of life in which it is embodied is one in which men learn not merely to "behave" correctly according to the rules of the game, but to respect each other as persons—as, in Kant's lofty language, "legislating members of a kingdom of ends." Hence the positivistic bias that current "conceptual analysis" carries over from its earlier entanglement in an atomistic logic and epistemology will have no place in our investiga-

THE "WHY" OF PRACTICAL UNDERSTANDING   19

tion. It is the normatively cogent use of language in the guidance and appraisal of actions that we shall try to understand, when to understand it is to make sense of it in its own practical terms, not in those imported from valuationally non-committal enquiries of a different sort. Our aim is not to make conceptual analogies almost a science, or a branch of formal logic, but to understand, in conceptually relevant and adequate terms, what practical understanding is when it is about its own distinctive business. Those who refuse, on methodological grounds, to think in practical terms and still profess to analyze the "meaning" of practical discourse will never find the sense they seek. They could not understand it if they met it.

Nor is our purpose merely to report and describe existing linguistic uses and to insist that their conceptual structure be respected. That is a useful but for us only a preliminary work. For our ordinary use of normative language is often confused, short-sighted, and radically inadequte to our present need for practical understanding. For practical purposes it is *not* "in perfect order" as it stands. The root of the matter is in it, but it takes more than roots to make a fruitful harvest. If we are to meet adequately the requirements for enlightened action in our present human situation, we must grow in understanding, and such growth does not leave unaltered the structure of the organism in which it takes place. Hence, as our inquiry proceeds, we shall increasingly point out ways in which the concepts embodied in ordinary language must be altered and developed if they are to meet well the requirements of the practices in which they have a normative use. The point of a better understanding of the use of practical discourse is to use it better for its own practical purposes so that men, in the light of it, may know better how to live. Hence its place is not above or beyond the often controversial work of practical decision-making, but explicitly and constructively inside it. This is enough to distinguish it sharply and basically from the purportedly normatively non-committal "analysis" of the meta-ethicists who disclaim such normative pretensions and describe themselves as scientific or *nearly* scientific in their "cognitive" detachment. They go their way, we ours. At times our paths will cross, and we shall have to try to come to terms with what they say. Meanwhile our business is to know what we, at least, are doing, and the point of doing it, and to keep our thinking clearly relevant to this task.

In its explicitly normative intent and in its concern for the specifically practical meaning of the categories of practical reasoning our account is closer to the classics of traditional moral philosophy than to the logical exercises of contemporary analysis. In some fundamental ways, the Socratic dialogues of Plato and Aristotle's *Ethics* are still the best accounts of practical wisdom that we have. The British moralists are a perennial source of moral understanding. And Kant's *Critique of Practical Reason* brought the subject into a focus which no discussion of the subject that pretends to adequacy can neglect with impunity. But here, again, the differences are fundamental. What is "Practical Reason" and from what standpoint is a critique of its validity to be made? For Reason as a transcendent agency from beyond the world of space and time issuing categorical imperatives to a noumenally free will, we shall find no evidence and, for moral purposes, no use. What we shall find are practically cogent reasons inside our spatio-temporal world, and reliable procedures for the understanding and justification of human actions on the terms they set. Nor shall we seek for any other justification of the categories of such practical reasoning than that which is found *in* its appropriate and effective use and *for* conduct that makes no sense without them. Whether the world of practical action, seen in the light that their proper use supplies is "appearance" merely or "Reality", and how far the demands of Reason correspond to the theoretically unknowable structure of things in themselves are further questions which must be answered, if at all, by a different use of reason. Practical reason, as we shall understand it, does not issue edicts or lay down laws; it offers grounds for action, and it is in the world in which, in our human condition, we live and act, that such reasons have normative sense for men concerned and competent to act responsibly, as selves or persons, in the fulfilment of the shared aspirations of their common life. Whatever more "Reality" may be than this, it cannot well be less if it is to be relevant to the right living our lives. It may be that the light that guides us here can lead us further toward the speculative heights to which philosophers have traditionally aspired. If so, so much the better. When we have got our bearings where we are we shall be in a better position to judge how far we can go. But to try to reach the heights in one presumptuous (or postulational) leap and then "criticize" the findings of practical reasoning about its mundane business from the precarious pinnacle thus questionably attained would be a use of practical reason neither reasonable nor practical nor philosophically wise. Hence, while we shall respect the grandeur of Kant's speculative intentions we shall not follow his procedure.

There will, in consequence, be those who will refuse to accept our undertaking as truly "philosophical" at all. For they identify philosophy with the quest for "ultimate" truth and "final" justification and they look for such finality in some description of the world as "Being", "Reality", or "the Good", or all of these at once, in which the qualified, conditioned truths of practical experience are transcended and only the *Ultimate* remains on as a final norm for practice. We, on the other hand, shall find *in* just such qualifications and conditions the structure that gives human reason a practical sense and a reliable and effective use. We shall have a good deal to say about the language of normative action and shall try to find in its rightly understood employment an answer to problems of practical and moral import. They will want to know, however, how such language is connected with or corresponds to Reality, and only when our statements have been translated into the language of their brand of metaphysics will they profess, for philosophical purposes, to understand it. And if we answer them by saying that the connection of the language of practical reasoning with Reality is just that it embodies the conceptual structure on whose terms we can understand the issues of our life as practical agents justly and adequately, and thus provide us with the truth that, in such activities, we require, our answer will be regarded as beside the point. Their concern is with Being as such, or the noumenal realm beyond appearances, or the One in which all practical distinctions ultimately disappear. And if the categories of practical reasoning lose their specific sense in this trans- and super-moral use, and must accordingly be relegated to the lower realm of mere appearance, they regard this as a small price to pay for the illumination finally and esoterically achieved. They, too, must go their way, we ours, though we shall from time to time have occasion to point out the spurious mysteries and made-to-order contradictions in which, in their terms, the work of practical good judgment is inextricably involved. Our purpose is not to make either a metaphysical mystery or meta-ethically certified nonsense of practical understanding, but so to clarify its conceptual structure that we can make sense of it, in its own distinctive terms and about its proper business. And this does, in a quite definite way, set limits to the scope and methods of our inquiry.

Yet there is another sense in which our investigation may properly be described as philosophical. Since the days of Socrates philosophy has often been identified as the love of wisdom, the kind of wisdom that is proper and appropriate to a man who knows his ignorance but is striving, nonetheless, to make the best of his life. And, for Socrates at least, the beginning of such wisdom was for men to know themselves, as moral agents, and to examine and give an account of their actions in terms of a right estimate of goods. This is our purpose, too, and in trying to fulfil it we shall have much to learn from Socrates. And while the speculative adventures of the philosophers of the Unconditioned too often leave us none the wiser, we shall find in such inquiry some truths that, if not the truth about the Ultimate, are nonetheless quite true in the sense that they are truths that we can trust and on which, without cynicism and without illusion, we can rightly build our lives. A wisdom that begins in practical experience cannot wisely stop with the merely human. It must explore the natural and spiritual resources of the wider world, in which, to the full extent of our human powers, we live and move and have our being. Hence our practical inquiry will open out into larger questions and, if we have made a good and sure beginning, we shall find the means to deal with them as we proceed. But it is from this angle, and in this context, that we shall deal with them, for this, in our human situation, is where we are. The understanding we find in it is oddly mixed with ignorance and confusion, and we shall undertake, as we proceed, to suggest some practical and theoretical improvements in its use, but it is more trustworthy than dialectically produced obscurity could be. And if we use it rightly it may take us some appreciable way along the philosophical road toward wisdom.

This, then, is the subject matter, method, and intent of this inquiry. The reader, if he has survived so far and has a mind to undertake the enterprise, is invited to share in it as a responsible participant in our quest for understanding. For now, without further side looks at what we might be doing and are not, we must be about our business. And here, as always, "we" means "you and I."

CHAPTER 2
PRACTICAL REASONS
AS GROUNDS FOR ACTION

WHY SHOULD I DO this rather than that when alternatives for action are presented? What's the good of it? And how is this good so my business and my concern that I ought, in my given situation, so to act to achieve it? These seem *prima facie* to be sensible and serious questions that often in the conduct of our practical affairs, require a rationally cogent answer. The relevant answer to a "why?" is a "because" and to the "why?" of voluntary doing the "because" of grounds for practically rewarding action. You should save your money now because you will need it in your old age and will then have no dependable financial resources but those that present saving can provide. You should help this needy man because he is your father and as his son you have a special obligation for his welfare. As a good American you should oppose all practices of racial segregation in the United States because the continuance of such practices is damaging to the "American image" in other sections of "the free world". These and others like them would normally be understood in specific situations as pertinent responses to the "why?" of practical doing and, if the facts asserted in them are as stated, as proper grounds for action. They might not, in a given case, be adequate or conclusive grounds, for there might be other practically relevant considerations that would properly count against the doing of the act whose "should" *so far* they support. But they are at least the right *kind* of reasons and, in default of better reasons to the contrary, would supply a rationally cogent answer to the question asked. Such questions and answers are familiar factors in our common experience, and our way of dealing with them sometimes makes a difference in the way we live our lives. If this is what we mean by practical reasons it appears, to say the least, far-fetched to deny that we do very often, in our practice, understand them.

Yet the philosophical efforts to make clear what it is that, in this way, we often understand, has proved so far to be a task of profound difficulty and deep obscurity. What *is* the "practical reason" that in this way claims authority for the guidance of our actions? *As rational* it can be cognitively warranted as providing principles of logically valid thinking, and on the basis of empirical evidence, correct information concerning matters of fact about the world and ourselves. *As practical,* it presumes to lay down laws for conduct and, in this capacity to "move" the will or the passions to the doing of one thing rather than another. But as Hume insisted, Reason alone can never influence action and if something other and more than Reason is required to exert this influence this something must be of a non-rational nature. Reason *as such* is not practical and hence action, in principle, falls outside the scope of Reason. On the terms of the categories thus provided there seems to be no place at all for it as something "half wish and half logic," as Charles Stevenson has neatly put it. But what else than something of this sort could "practical reason" be? Hence Hume's dictum that in its practical use reason is and ought only to be the slave of the passions, and Kant's rather desperate appeal, as an alternative, to a causality from beyond the world of sense by which Pure Reason acts timelessly on a noumenally free will to determine moral actions. To say that such a use of "Reason" is "beyond the world of sense" is not an overstatement. But how else *could* Pure Reason be a cause and how, except as such an agency *could* it be "practical" in the determination of action? More recent and analytically cautious attempts to deal with this problem are not on the whole more helpful. For when the problem of practical reason is stated in these terms the categories of practical doing are so twisted that we can no longer use them in the way in which they do make sense of claims on justifiable action. And it is only by reference to this sense and use that we reasonably hope to understand the rational cogency of grounds for action.

The conceptual confusion thus engendered is so deep seated and pervasive in both traditional and current thinking that we shall have to take a closer look at some of its implications if we are not ourselves to be misled by it. The general question: What is Practical Reason? can be subdivided into three apparently more specific sorts of question. (1) What can "Reason" tell us that can relevantly serve us as a ground for action? (2) To what agent or agency are such reasons addressed and how, by their purely rational cogency can such an agent be "moved" to action? (3) Why *should* it be so moved? What is the justification for the authority or normative cogency that is claimed for its "dictates", "directives" or rationally warranted conclusions? We shall consider these questions in this order.

(1) What sort of reasons for doing one thing rather than another can "Reason" give? As logical it can expose self-contradictions and point out formal or syntactical confusion. As factually informative in its fruitful union with experience in "scientific method" it can bring to light matters of fact of which we should, without it, have been unaware. As metaphysical it can (perhaps) disclose to us the nature of true Being. Ultimate

doubts have been raised about its cogency in all these uses, but for our present purposes we need not raise them. Suppose that its authority in these fields is beyond dispute. So what? What rational bearing does this have on what we ought to do? Ultimate Reality is a single, seamless whole and after all is said and done, there is really only One. It may be so but, for practical purposes, what of it? Of contradictory propositions one must be true and the other false. Since this is a logical "must" the proper response is "of course". But which of mutually contradictory propositions is true? And what bearing, if any, does such truth have on the right conduct or our lives? Light travels with a finite velocity and, on a different level of factual information, in Philadelphia nearly everybody reads the *Bulletin*. Though I have no expertise in either field, I take it that there is good factual warrant for these assertions. Now what am I to do with them? Is the fact, if such it be, that in Philadelphia nearly everybody reads the *Bulletin* a reason why I should buy and read it when I am in that vicinity? My own emotive reaction to the dictum happens to be negative and all my sympathies are with the long-nosed man who in the familiar *New Yorker* advertisement stands out in splendid eccentricity against the *Bulletin*-reading crowd. But who are we against so many? Ought we to conform? Why?

The point here is not that further facts are needed to establish the practical relevance of the assertion made. Such facts, if in this way relevant, would certainly be helpful. But with respect to all to them, if understood simply as factually confirmed, and in this sense "rationally" warranted the same question of relevance would arise. Non-conformists lack or lose a sense of "belonging" to the group and, by the current criteria of mental health, are sick, sick, sick. Is that bad? The language of psychological lay preaching is designed to persuade us that it is, while that of "existential" edification points a different moral— "Reminding us of our and Adam's curse, and that, to be healed, our sickness must grow worse." Perhaps the man who does not read the *Bulletin* reads Kierkegaard and T. S. Eliot and understands the "facts" of psychological adjustment in a somewhat different valuational context and perspective.

There is no need to elaborate the obvious, and, in spite of all the dialectical ingenuity that has sometimes been devoted to obscuring it, the implication here is obvious and fundamental. Facts can point a moral or warrant a practical conclusion only for a man for whom a practical communication has a point. This point is something to be done *because* it is in some way worth doing by considerations of worth that he accepts not as information, rationally verified by either logic, science or ontology, but as sufficient grounds for action. A "Reason" limited in its theoretical purity to "the facts" or super-facts as thus "rationally" established would of necessity be practically inconclusive; its pertinence to practice would remain a problem that would not in this way be rationally solved. Hence such a reason could be practical only extrinsically, as hitched to something outside itself that could supply the link still missing between "is" and "ought", or what is the case and what, if anything, should be done about it. This is to say that what are offered in this guise are *so far* not practical reasons at all. And if this is all that "reason" has to offer, we are indeed at a loss to understand not merely how it can influence conduct but what would be the point or function of its doing so. What would rational action be? Surely action done for good and sufficient reasons. But so far we have been unable to discover what good *reasons* for doing would be like.

(2) It is at this point that the question shifts from that of rational justification to that of causal agency. Reason in its logical, scientific, or metaphysical use can at least tell us what we ought to think if we are to think correctly, and such correct

thinking sometimes makes a difference in the way we behave. Evidently it cannot be thus effective simply by itself. But properly hitched to existing wants or passions, or as issuing commands to a reluctant will, it might become a factor in the course of action. If I want financial security in my old age and inquiry convinces me that saving now is the most effective way to get it, I may then want to be thrifty now and this resultant want may be sufficient to produce the behavior required to bring about this end. Especially when we are faced with competing wants, none strong enough as it stands to overcome the opposition of the others and produce effects in conduct, deliberation on the causes and consequences of an action may so beef up one want as against the others that it can then prevail. And if the thinking is factually accurate, and the ensuing behavior satisfies or appeases my existing wants the action may be said to be intelligent. It is in some such way as this that correct thinking is often held to be a guide to conduct and thus practical in its effects. The more we know about the world and ourselves the more enlightened our choice will be, where "choosing" is the doing after deliberation of the action to which the want that has through deliberation become the strongest impels us. In voluntary action we always do what we want to do, but in intelligent action we do what intelligence has caused us to want to do and this is what it is, in practice, to be rational, or intelligent in the satisfaction of our wants.

An account of this sort sounds hard-headed in its down-to-earth adherence to the facts. There is, its proponents like to think, no nonsense about it. In fact, however, if we try in its terms to understand the nature and intent of practical action, there is a discouraging amount of nonsense about it. Thinking that something is the case does often make us want to do something about it, though sometimes it does not. Correct thinking sometimes moves us in this way, and so, unhappily, does incorrect thinking. And the ensuing behavior in the one case as in the other, sometimes leads to the "satisfaction", appeasement or cessation of such wants. It "resolves" our problems of action by relieving the tension or imbalance that, on this account, gave rise to them, i.e., it causes it to disappear. The relevance of thought to human behavior can be considered and described from this point of view and such a description is in its own way enlightening. But what bearing does it have upon the reasonableness of action? Is action caused by a want generated by correct thinking more worth doing that one caused by a want caused by incorrect thinking? How, and by what appeal to "the facts" is this conclusion established? Is it more likely to be successful? Successful *how?* In appeasing the tensions that caused us to start thinking in the first place and thus alleviating the irritation of hesitancy or doubt? Does it in fact reliably do even this? Perhaps it *would* do it in the long run if we kept at it long enough. But why should we concern ourselves about this indefinitely long run when life is short and time is fleeting? There would appear, for many purposes, to be shorter and easier ways of relieving tensions. And is such relief of tensions really what makes life worth living and actions worth doing? Perhaps it is just human nature for us in this way to seek to be intelligent in this satisfaction of our wants. But if the term "human nature" is used descriptively, it is just as much a fact of human nature *not* to be in this way intelligent, to live by myths and faith and "illusions" rather than by facts, especially where basic issues of conduct are concerned. And what right have those who offer this account to use "human nature" in any other than a descriptive sense? No doubt, if rational action is defined in this way then a rational man will be a man who does thus behave. But not much of practical significance can be wrung from this verbal triumph. We do know what we mean, to some degree at least, when we talk of right reason as a guide for conduct, though we are sometimes confused about it, and we are looking for an elucidation that will enable us to grasp *this* meaning better. And considered in this light, the account here under consideration can only lead us further into confusion. For this is not a merely incidental incoherence; it is a categorical mis-handling of the basic concepts of practical thought. Where we ask for grounds for action it gives us practically non-commital information about the causes and consequences of behavior. Where we look for an agent for whom such grounds could have normative or justifying cogency for an action done *because,* it presents us with wants that would not know how to recognize a reason if they saw one, or what to do with it. The satisfaction of a want is its appeasement which may be brought about by any means effective to this end. The satisfaction of a man in his capacity as a responsible self or person is an achievement that can satisfy him as such a person, and as responsibly involved in the normative requirements of the activity in which he is called upon to play his part. For the former a justifying reason simply makes no sense. For the latter it is the heart of the matter. And when we ask why wants, or appetitively unstable organisms seeking equilibrium "should" act intelligently there is no answer to be given but that this is the way they do act—except when they don't. To offer this normatively uninstructive conclusion as a *ground* for liberalism in social action or for any other action is as theoretically unwarranted as it is practically inept. Such a theory has, on principle, no grounds for recommending any sort of practical action, for what it describes as action is behavior which on its terms has no practical sense, no agent, and no justifying end.

Sometimes, and in older-fashioned versions of the causal "why" of practical agency the "moving" force in action is not wants, drives, or impulses and habits but "the will". Of this we shall have much to say at a later stage in our inquiry. The terms "will" and "willing" have an important use in the language of practical action. But of will as an agency which by performing acts of volition, when motives are presented to it, moves our bodies to voluntary action we shall find little that is good to say. It is sufficient, for our present purposes, that such an agent, if there were one, could not do the job here required of it. Theoretically, valid thinking must move the will if reason is to be practical. But is the will itself a rational or irrational agency? If the former, how can there ever be irrational willing? This was Kant's problem, to which he never found a coherent answer. If the latter, what has "reason" to do with "Will" at all? How can an essentially non-rational agent will rationally? And if practical reason means rational willing, what place is there on either alternative for the reasonableness *and* the arbitrariness that we find in the practical affairs of men? It is not Wills, but men, who act, and their actions are reasonable not when they are caused in a peculiar way by a volitional agency uniquely susceptible to the commands of a "Reason" that has in principle no practical commands to give, but rather when they know what in the circumstances they are doing and the point of doing it. The light in which our actions are thus performed is that of practical understanding. Men who walk in this light walk warily and sometimes wisely. They are not merely "moved" by mindless causes; they move or conduct themselves to some purpose, mindful of where they are going and with due regard for both pitfalls and relevant attractions along the way. Yet to walk wisely is not to be caused to walk in some physiologically extraordinary way. It is simply to engage in practically effective walking, a thing that any physiologist of sound mind and body learned to do long before he became an expert in his field of specialized research. It was not from a course in physiological psychology that he learned it, nor will he find in any treatise on this subject the reasons why it is a thing worth doing. But unless he has learned the sense of practical actions of this sort and knows how to act accordingly, he will not get far either as a physiologist or as a human being.

(3) But even if we could find out by logical, scientific, or ontological inquiry that something was worth doing, and explain in causal terms how this information moved us to act in a practically effective way, we should still have an "ultimate" and so far insoluble problem on our hands. Why *should* we act for "worthy" rather than "unworthy" ends or use the "right" means rather than the "wrong" for going after them? This seems to be just our original "why?" of justification over again, and on the terms here offered there seems to be no answer to it that we can practically understand. In one sense it appears to be a foolish question. Surely if we know an action is worth doing we know why we ought to do it. And right methods just *are* the ones that should be used to reach a worthy end. Nobody who understands the practical use of "worth" and "right" could fail to see that point. The trouble is that on the terms here offered we have so far not understood that use, and the emergence of this further problem is a sign not that we have probed beneath the level of practical action to a more mysterious level of "reality" but rather that we have so far simply failed to grasp its sense. The normative cogency, the justifiable authority for action, of the language of practical reasons has escaped us and we must therefore look outside it for the justification that it is its own practical business to supply. To see how this apparent difficulty arises, and how to deal with it, we shall have to examine briefly some current trends in the analysis of practically normative discourse. They may appear at first to lead us rather far afield, but by seeing through them to the situation that, with great ingenuity, they misinterpret, we shall be brought at length to the true center of our subject.

It has recently been customary and, for our purposes, will be convenient, to classify such theories as *cognitivist* or non-*cogniti-*

vist, a *prima facie* logically exhaustive division. The former agree in interpreting the statement that an object is good or an action right as an assertion that it does in cognitively discoverable truth possess some quality, property or capacity to which these terms are properly applied. This may be a "natural" property or capacity discoverable by empirical observation or inquiry—the capacity to produce "value" experiences, for example—or a non-natural quality itself the object of a unique sort of non-empirical or a priori intuition. The epistemological divergences between "naturalists" and "non-naturalists" on this point are emphatic, but for our purposes they are not important. What is important is that for both alike the normatively cogent terms in which we offer justifying reasons for our actions— "This is a better 'X' than that and should as such be chosen," "That is the right thing to do in your situation."—refer to properties of things or actions and, where they are correctly applied, supply us with a kind of normative information concerning them. How we come by this information and what, for practical purposes, we should do with it are further questions, extrinsic to the cognitive status of "good" and "right" as such. This object, or this man, has the property of goodness. How so? Perhaps we just see it with an inner, a priori eye. Perhaps we are acquainted in immediate experience with a "value" quality and in the course of experience learn to make probable predictions concerning the things in the world that will produce it and are valuable accordingly. We will not haggle with the experts on these questionable matters. So the property is (in some sense) really and objectively there and the statement of this fact cognitively certifiable as a truth about the world. So what? Is *this* a reason why I should so act as to secure it? Does such an action have the further property of should-be-doneness and was this what I was looking for when I asked what I should do? As information, why should it move me to perform the action when its other and no less cognitively discoverable properties do not? Actions that have the property of should-be-doneness are should-be-done actions just as objects that have the property of being yellow are yellow objects. And to admit that this action had the property of should-be-doneness and still deny that it is, in this sense, a should-be-done action would be logically irrational. But if a man understood the assertion that he should do this action simply as information that it objectively possessed this rather special property whose acceptance as true left him practically uncommitted with respect to the issue of action, would he be a practically unreasonable man? Why so, on this interpretation? Would he be failing to recognize the further objective truth that this was what he should do? But this, presumably, he already knows since he agrees that it has the property of should-be-doneness. The question here is not as to whether the possession of this information will in fact move him to perform the "right" action, but why it *should* do so. What ground for action has been given him? We should surely say of a man who responded in this way to practical advice that he had so far failed to understand the purport of the communication offered. The assertion was not meant as practically non-committal information, but as establishing a normatively cogent claim upon his conduct, and it was addressed *to him* not as a disinterested inquirer into the "constituents" of a world that is thus shown to contain not only men and triangles and moons and milky ways, and should-be-doneness also, but rather as an agent whose concern and responsibility it is to seek good and to act rightly. An elucidation of its meaning that reduces it to this informational status is in fact a misunderstanding of its function, purport and intent. When such an analysis has done its work the "why?" of practical justification remains, but by stripping it of its normatively cogent import we have systematically deprived ourselves of the means for understanding its practically effective use. We thus have on our hands a *"why?"* that is both practically inescapable and theoretically unanswerable—the time-worn spring board for every sort of philosophical "leap" into the irrational.

The "non-cognitivists" have the considerable merit of seeing that in this analysis something basic to the use of practically normative discourse has been left out. But since they agree with the cognitivists that the resources of reason are exhausted in the discovery of practically non-committal facts, they have tried to supply this something more from "non-cognitive" and hence non-rational sources to which the *why* of practical justification is in principle and in the end inapplicable. The main contenders for "non-cognitive" supremacy are "imperativists" and "emotivists", though assorted blends of the two have proved more popular than either verson taken neat. If statements about "good" and "right" are not to be understood as mere items of cognitive information, how are they to be understood? Perhaps as prescription, directives or somewhat muffled and indirect commands. To tell a man (or to tell oneself) that something is good is (in the last analysis) to tell him to go after it. To tell him (or oneself) that an action is wrong is to order him (or oneself) not to do it. Practical principles are prescriptive rules for action and the moral law an imperative issued by Reason, God, "the group", the Super-Ego or, again, oneself whose authority as a law is referable (in the end) to the natural or supernatural status of its commander. There are endless subtleties and complications in the elaboration of this kind of theory, but we are here concerned not with the gnats that are strained at in its various versions but rather with the camel that, for normative purposes, all alike must swallow. It is a large, unappetizing and unassimilable camel and the attempt to digest it leads to readily predictable results.

Rules, directives and prescriptions have an essential role in human conduct and our learning to respond to them is basic training for the work of practical understanding. But directives are one sort of thing, justifications another, and their practical use is not the same. When a man obeys an order he does as he is told to do. His not to reason why. He needs no "why" for a decision since the decision as to what is to be done is not made by him but by the man in authority who gives the order. In obeying a command I do not choose, and to follow a rule is in many ways like obeying an order. The practical point of the command-obedience relation is to establish and maintain this division of work and of responsibility.

But while in obeying a command I do not choose what is to be done there are occasions when I choose not to obey commands and sometimes for good reasons. Why should I? With what authority is the order given and how is it my obligation or to my advantage to comply with it? In a well-ordered society, and with proper training and discipline these questions do not constantly arise; we learn our place or status in essential shared activities and behave accordingly. But unless they could significantly be asked in a society of self-respecting men, and unless a reasoned answer to them could be given, there would be no way of distinguishing legitimate authority from tyranny and right obedience from subservience to any sort of *de facto* social power. And when they are significantly asked, a command or directive cannot be a valid answer to them. "Do as I say, or as the State or Church or group directs." "Why should I?" "Because I say so, or the State or Church or group says so, and that's an order." The man who in practice offers such a dictate as a justification of his right to give commands is a tyrant, and the man who accepts is as such a moral coward and/or a fool. A directive is not a "because", and to try to make it do the work of one is to strip the command-obedience relation of the justifying sense that is its practical excuse for being. In such a situation might makes right, whether the might be that of God or society or the Super-Ego or the bully on the corner. "Just are the ways of God/And justifiable to man" is one of the grandest of religious affirmations. But it is not by commands that such a justification can be given, or as a dictate merely that its cogency can humanly be understood.

The basic objection to any form of the imperativist account of the normative cogency of this "because" of practical reasons, however generously it may be stated, is that by reducing the language of justification in the end to that of commands and directives, it strips this language of its justifying sense, for a command is not a justification, and deprives us of all rational means of making this distinction.

If the normative force of "this is right" is, after all the qualifying palaver, that of the command "do this—that's an order", then what you have given us when you tell us "This is right" is not a warrant for so acting, but a reiterated command. We heard you the first time. But our question of right remains unanswered and, in the language you provide, can no longer be significantly asked. Yet the need to ask it was never greater than, in our world of ideologically pretentious social pressures, it is today. Here, again, we are in a situation in which the practical need to ask a question to which our theories cannot provide a relevantly cogent answer leads us back to the practically ir- rational, or arbitrary, and, in this case to an irrationality of a peculiarly unsavory sort.

A gentler and in some ways more persuasive variety of "non- cognitivism" is the "emotivist" analysis of the normative sig- nificance of practical discourse. This theory notes correctly the efficacy of the persuasive use of words like "good" and "right" in the influencing of behavior and the maintenance of that agreement in attitude which is essential to the successful conduct of our practical affairs. It then proceeds, with almost beautiful simplicity, to identify the normative significance of such language with its causal efficacy in this use. "Let's dine at the Superior

Restaurant where the élite meet to eat." "Lucky Strike means fine tobacco." "That's what Campbell Soups are—mm, mm good." "Shame on you. It's wrong to hit your little sister." Such locutions are familiar and sometimes effective in arousing those "pro" and "con" responses that in such instances determine what we do. In more complicated cases, it is often effective to "support" such dicta by descriptive statements concerning matters of fact, and such statements are referred to, in this use, as "reasons." But in this use, they are not to be understood *as* reasons, as *valid* grounds for warranted or justifiable action—the question of validity is here, we are told, "of no interest." They are just additional fuel to heat up our appetites or aversions. A false assertion will support this use of "good" as effectively as a true one if it does the causal job required and a true one has no other cogency as a ground for action than its capacity to incite the attitude desired. "Roosevelt was a Jew" is false. "Ribicoff is a Jew" is true. But each can be in this sense a reason for opposing the political aspirations of the man in question. It supports the claim that he is the wrong man for the job, if it lends the word "wrong" the emotive urgency required to produce the aversion wanted. And if we say that both of these are *bad* reasons, and that it is *wrong* to try to win an election by such appeals to "prejudice" we shall on this analysis, be merely expressing our aversion to this sort of "reason" and attempting to persuade others to agree in attitude with us. A mere description, which is all that cognitive inquiry can give us, must be hitched to our "attitudes" if it is to have practical effect. Emotionally charged terms like good and bad supply this linkage by their prejudicial or seductive import and are, in their turn supported by such "facts" as may be useful in specific cases in producing the reaction wanted. This *is* their normative cogency, as contrasted with whatever cognitive warrant they may have as logically or factually true, and this, for the influencing of attitudes, is what matters.

This theory gives no doubt a true account of something. It looks at human action in a certain light—the light that shines on Madison Avenue and in treatises on "motivational research" —and it reports its findings with high, meta-ethical neutrality. But as an elucidation of the sense of practically reasonable action there seems *prima facie* to be something missing in it. And, in spite of the ingenious elaborations and qualifications that have been added to cover its initial nakedness, it is not really difficult to see what this something is. It is precisely the "why" of practical justification and the grounds for action that could supply not merely a persuasive but a rationally cogent answer to it. *Of course* "right" and "good" in their practical use are persuasive words, and the aim of such use is to "influence action." But to influence it *how*, and to what end? For men who know what they are doing these, too, are practical questions. In their justifying use such words have a claim in them and a promise. And unless this claim can be made good and this promise kept in the responsibilities and fulfilments of cooperative action (which is much more than an emotional agreement in attitude) only the silly, the suggestible and the irresponsible will for long be imposed on by their pretentious and portentuous sound. We are most of us careless and suggestible enough to be thus "influenced" in large areas of conduct—the success of the motivational engineering of mass attitudes shows that. But even here the persuasiveness of the "normative" language used is parasitic on the suggestion at least of a practical sense that this analysis would deny it. The "wonder drug" is understood to be somehow *really* wonderful, and the "fact" that it contains GL-7 or MX-231 is supposed to have something beneficent to do with this. And health is really something that we ought to care about. The question of validity is here "of interest" though it is not the advertiser's interest that it be pressed very far. Perhaps the time will come when even this hint of sense can be eliminated and we shall just respond, in well-conditioned mindlessness, to subliminal persuasions of whose influence upon us we are unaware. Whether or not this would be a "good" thing is, of course, a question that cannot, on this analysis, be significantly raised in any other form than to express our own emotional attitudes (pro or con) at the prospect and elicit those of others.

The fuller working out of such a theory may be left to the writers of that brand of "science fiction" which has come in our time, to be too close for comfort to the truth. For our present purposes it is enough to say that at some times and for some purposes most men, ourselves included, still have more sense than this, and that for such men the "why?" of normative justification still has a justifiable use. And the sense we have here is the sense we find in the requirements and the promise of our practical life, understood and used in providing grounds for responsible and rewarding action. It is here that the rationally cogent use of "good" and "right" has an examinable meaning and the validity of the claims that they purport to warrant is indeed "of interest." The basic trouble with the emotivist analysis is that by identifying the normative cogency of practical discourse with its persuasive efficacy in non-rational behavior, it robs us of the right and the capacity to distinguish right from wrong "persuasion" on any but emotive "grounds." Should we, as responsible agents, allow ourselves to be persuaded by a procedure whose rational warrant can be "of no interest" to us? Is the life to which the seductive verbiage of the engineers of our motivations invites us humanly a life worth living? These, today, are questions of some practical importance. In the emotivist's sense of "reason" they can have no valid answer but can serve only as a stimulus to more "persuasive" talk that, for a discerning man, requires and in principle cannot have, a rational warrant for its normative pretensions. This kind of talk can go on indefinitely, and does, and there are those who are persuaded by it. But it is by this time clear, I think, that we shall not find in it a sense of practical reason, or of reasonable practice, that makes practical and moral sense.

Where, then, are we to look for it? Our answer is an obvious but *prima facie* a sensible one. We shall look for it where we might reasonably expect to find it—in that use of reason in which, in the right guidance and appraisal of men's actions, they are understood and used as grounds for justifiable doing. We have already got some notion of what such reasons are and how they work by noting what is lacking in alternative accounts and what must be supplied if we are to make sense of practical understanding in its own terms and about its proper business. It is time now to try to make such first-hand sense of it.

Practical reasons are grounds for action. They answer the question of the "why?" of doing with a "because" that a man who acts responsibly and on his own initiative can understand and use *as* a reason *why*, in his circumstances, he should conduct himself in one way rather than another. And they provide the ground of common understanding on whose terms he can sometimes make sense of the actions of others as thus done and respond to them accordingly. Evidently an action, thus understood, is more than a bodily movement of which a prior happening "in" the mind or body of the agent is the cause. "Why did you fall down the stairs? Did you do it well or badly? And was it in your circumstances a proper thing to do?" The answers "I was drunk," or "I just slipped on the top stair.", or "I was pushed" do not supply this kind of answer, and the point of giving them is frequently to show that none is properly to be expected. Falling down-stairs is not the sort of thing we normally do for reasons and to try to "rationalize" what happens in such cases as an action with an overt or hidden "why" of practical intent would be impertinent and inept. But sometimes this is not the case. "I wanted to attract attention in a dramatic way, and in the circumstances it seemed worth the risk to life and limb involved." In this case the further questions raised are relevant. Some men fall down stairs expertly—they may earn their living as stunt men in the movies by the exercise of this skill. And such a man may be well advised to take such falls intentionally when the rest of us would be fools to do so. Was it a proper thing to do in this situation—at a cocktail party, say, at which the faller was a guest? Would this kind of self-advertising be an abuse of hospitality and an embarassment to his host? Or, rather, perhaps, a welcome contribution to the festivities? Should he have done it? And should I, if the opportunity presents itself, "do so as well"? The considerations that provide a relevant and valid answer to these questions are practical reasons for (or against) the action. And it is only as reasons for or against an action thus performed that they make sense in this use.

It is clear that the essential starting point in any reference to such practical reasons is, as Aristotle long ago asserted, "The thing wanted". This point was made with elegant simplicity by the Cheshire Cat in a well known colloquy with Alice in Wonderland. "Would you tell me, please, which way I ought to go from here?" "That depends a good deal on where you want to go," said the Cat. "I don't much care where" said Alice. "Then it doesn't matter which way you go," said the Cat. And since the "ought to do" of practical reasoning is concerned essentially with what matters, that in the circumstances was the logically correct reply.

Yet, as with so many logical simplicities, there is danger here of oversimplification and consequent sophistry. For Alice did want to get somewhere, as she went on to explain, and the Cat's reply, "Oh, you're sure to do that if you only walk long enough," involves a categorial confusion. To "get somewhere", as Alice meant it, is an expression that belongs to the language of intentional action and achievement, not to the description of physical locomotion. Some of us wander all our lives and never in this sense get anywhere at all, though we cover a good deal of territory. Alice's aim was inadequately expressed, but there was a practical point to her question, nonetheless, that a more responsive mentor than the Cheshire Cat might have grasped. And that point could have been made clearer by a more explicit reference to "the thing wanted", for it is this that gives all action a practical point.

There is, therefore, this much truth at least in the analysis of those who hold that factual information can provide grounds for doing only as it is connected in some way with what we want. That "X" airline provides the cheapest and quickest way of getting from Austin to Chicago is not a reason for patronizing "X" airline if what I want is to go to San Francisco by car. The basic point here is that this is a logical or conceptual, not just a causal connection. What is here said is not that good practical reasons won't *move* us to action or "get a hold on the will" until they are hitched to a want or persuasively incite a "passion". The point is rather that it is only as related to the intentions of practical action that information, no matter how well formally or factually certified, can be a ground for doing anything at all. The question is not "what will make me want to do what it is reasonable in my situation to do?" but rather "what *is* it reasonable for me to do?" It is this latter question that cannot be sensibly asked or answered without a reference to the "thing wanted." It is one thing to say that practical reasons would not be causally effective without the support of non-rational wants. It is another to say that without an intrinsic reference to our wants there could be no practical reasons. Without this connection, the facts would provide no relevant grounds for actions to be done "because". Our acceptance of them as correct information would leave the question "so what?" or "What difference does it make?" unanswered and, if this were all that "reason" could supply, rationally unanswerable. It is for a man with needs and wants to be somehow satisfied and intentions to be rightly fulfilled that reliable information can supply a ground for action. Unless he understood the reasons offered as in this way relevant to action he would not understand them practically at all and would not, as a practical agent, know what to do with them.

There is a complementary truth, however, that must at once be emphasized if this basic but one-sided insight is not to lead us into error. Unless he wanted to achieve or to avoid something a man would never have a reason for doing anything—for him the "why" of action would have no practical sense. But wants as such are not practical reasons, and only in exceptional cases is "because I want to" or "because he wanted to" a proper answer to the "why?" of action. "Why did you do 'X' rather than 'Y'?" The reply "because I wanted to" is indeed, as Nowell-Smith has observed, a "question-stopper" here. But this is not because it is a logically final answer to the question asked. It is an indication rather that the question will not be answered—that, perhaps, there was no "why" of this sort at all, or that, if there was, it is none of the questioner's business and will not on this occasion be disclosed. Such an answer is, in this sense "unresponsive." And if, when I ask seriously *why* I should act in one way rather than another the answer is "because you want to" I shall not, as a rule, be much enlightened. The request for reasons is pertinent precisely where just wanting does *not* answer the question of what is to be done one way or the other. There will, of course, be cases, where a practical question can be answered in this way. I may know what I want to do but be doubtful whether in this case I am entitled to make my want the arbiter of my action. I'm hungry and I want to eat, but should I stop work now to do so when my duties require me to stay on the job? The admonition "if you want to eat, then eat" is understandable advice in such a situation as a warrant for disregarding scruples of this kind and just doing as you want. After all your health comes first and to deny your appetites their "normal" satisfaction gives rise to "repressions" that menace mental health. For some agents in some circumstances it would be good advice, for others bad. In no circumstances would it make sense *as a reason* unless the want was understood and accepted not just as a physiological or psychological occurrence but as a ground for action. This does not mean that we always, or even usually, need a justification for eating when we are hungry. We are fortunately not as "rational" as all that. But it does mean that when the question of a reason does arise, a want is not the proper answer to it unless it is understood not merely *as* a want, but one whose satisfaction, in these circumstances provides a sufficient ground for action.

It must be understood and used as a ground for action. How and by whom can it be so used? Only by an agent who is himself a wanting and purposive being, with concerns to be satisfied and intentions to be fulfilled. Only for such a being can the question, "What should I do?" be practically significant, and it is to this question that the "because" of action is a reasoned answer. It is in the context of his active concerns that this question arises and as a way of dealing with the problems set him by his situation in the world that it has a point for doing. The man who understood "Your home is on fire" as an item of theoretical information, to which "Is that so?" or "Well, I always said the place would burn down some day" would be an adequate response would not *in this way* have understood it. And if we took him to be a sensible man, concerned about the security of his possessions, we should not understand him if this was the sum of his response to it. Surely, given this information there are things a sensible man should do, and things that he should not do to try to deal with the events thus described. The information that the house was burning would provide a ground or reason for such doing for a man concerned about the security of his possessions and the safety of his family. And, of course if he wanted the house to burn down so that he would collect the insurance, for example, it would be a ground for other actions than that of trying to put out the fire. If there were nothing that, in this situation, he was concerned to accomplish or avoid he would have no grounds for doing anything about it.

Yet it is not to our wants, or to ourselves as merely wanting or desiring beings, that grounds for action are practically addressed. They would not know what to do with such a reason if they "saw" one, for they would not see it as a reason. Wants as physiological or psychological occurrents have causes and effects. They do not in this status have and do not need a justifying reason. Does the acceptance as true of the information that my house is on fire cause me to want to act in such a way as to rescue my possessions? It may or it may not. If I am at the moment stupid, lazy, or drunk, it may cause me just to wish to hear no more about the unpleasant subject. Should it do so? It is not of causes and effects as such, but of the actions of sensible men that this question can properly be asked. "You want to save your possessions don't you?" "Yes, of course." "Only prompt and vigorous action on your part now will save them." "Yes, that's true." Therefore you *should* perform such action now. What is the force of this "should"? As was long ago observed, it first emerges in the conclusion and was absent from the premises. Wants as such know no "should" in this sense. Then, given the want, and the factual situation, *why should I?* So far, no ground for action has been given. Well, a *sensible* man would see the point and act accordingly and if you do not you are certainly a fool. What is this but emotive name-calling, effective perhaps in heating up the desire for action to the point at which it is "strong" enough to prevail over my inertia or indifference, but without a shred of rational cogency? Without wants there can be no practical reasons, but even with them there still seems to be something missing.

We are now, I think, in a position to see quite plainly what this is. Any man of ordinary good sense would understand the facts presented as grounds for action and know how not just to behave but to behave himself accordingly. What is it to be a man of good sense? Our appetites are not in this way sensible—how could they be? How would a merely theoretical inquirer whose sole intent was to get the facts, show this kind of sense except in the activity in which facts are got? What would he do with or about his facts when he got them? But we, as practical agents, concerned to satisfy our wants in a way in which we can as selves be satisfied, and to maintain in the process those standards of acceptable and effective performance to which our status as responsible agents commits us, are often sensible men, and it is as thus concerned and competent that grounds for doing make sense for us and have a rationally cogent use. Every communication of practical reason is addressed "to whom it may concern". There is no more sense in offering practical reasons to non-rational attitudes and appetites or to a practically disinterested reason than there would be in making speeches to a lamp post.

When Elizabeth Bennett, in *Pride and Prejudice* asks Mr. Collins to consider her as a rational creature, and speak to her accordingly, she is asking him to speak sensibly in just this way. And we and Jane Austen know what she means, though Mr. Collins, who was "not a sensible man" does not. Their conversation is an amusing failure to reach an understanding, a failure of practical communication.

To become and to act as "rational creatures" is something that we learn, as we learn a language. If we had not some initial capacity for it, we could never learn at all, but given that capacity, which we hopefully impute to "human nature," reasonable action, at the familiar level of good sense, is the reward and fruit of practice and discipline in those activities in which a difference between achievement and failure, between getting things right and getting them wrong can be made out by those with sense enough to make this distinction. The point of such activity is, in a truistic sense, the satisfaction of the man who acts, but it is *his* satisfaction at a level of conduct in which there are not merely appetites to be appeased or attitudes to be emotively expressed but something worth doing to be accomplished. In the context of such action "What do you want?" is answered not by an introspective catalogue of assorted wishes, cravings and inner gnawings of desire but by a statement of practical intent— "This is what I am trying to do." And "Why do you want it?" here means "What's the good of it?" "What purpose does it reliably serve to fulfill?" A causal account of the way in which one came to have such wantings would not be a pertinent answer to such a question. It would rather be an indication that this kind of question should not here be asked. "Why do you want to become President of the United States?" "Because my mother denied me in my infancy the affection that I craved and now I have an urge to be everybody's favorite son." This may account for the occurrence of the urge but it does not justify the action of trying to become President. Has the action any reasonable prospect of success? And even if it did succeed would it be worth doing? Would it satisfy the urge for popular affection by which the man is driven? Presidents are not always or universally beloved. What other satisfaction, including that, perhaps, of personal integrity, would have to be sacrificed to achieve it? Or what sacrifice of others, whose interests the presidential aspirant was in some way obligated to respect would it require? The man who could not see the relevance of these questions to the rightness of his action, of whom there was no more to be said than

"He has this urge; this is how he came by it, and this is what, accordingly, he does," could not be considered as a practically rational creature. His conduct would *in this way* make no sense, though psycho-analysts could doubtless tell us much about his infantile aggressions and repressions. To the extent that we consider all human behavior as in this way "basically" infantile it can make no sense for us. That those who profess this doctrine function also as lay preachers who write books to tell us what we "should" do and give us psychiatric reasons for so doing is one of the minor ironies in the intellectual confusion of our time. They address us practically in a capacity which their theory tells us neither we nor they (since they too, presumably, are the children of their parents) actually possess.

We are all at some times silly, irresponsible and infantile in our conduct. But as we become men we put away childish things, and it is precisely in the process of practical understanding, in the use of cogent grounds for doing as guides to justifiable action that we become men, in this sense, and can act accordingly. This is at once an emotional, a practical and a rational achievement. In it our wants acquire a meaning they do not as such possess and strivings gain that point and direction without which they "lose the name of action" or, more properly, could never have acquired it. Facts are for us no longer merely facts; there is something to be done with and to be done about them, for there is something in the situation which such facts disclose, that for us as men is authentically worth doing. The analyst who has never, in his own person, understood this has not the understanding necessary to make sense of practical reasons. And the man who has it knows, in some concrete instances at least, what it is to have good reasons for doing one thing rather than another. There is much else to be learned before this use of reason is, for philosophical purposes, adequately understood, and careful analysis will sometimes help us in such learning. But this, quite literally, is the beginning of wisdom and if we lack the sense to grasp and build on it we shall go further, whether analytically or practically, only to fare worse.

Finally, it is as thus understood and used that practical reasons can validly do their justifying work, can authentically provide the answers to the "why?" of action. Suppose that "reason" can in some way "prove" an object to be "good" or an action "right". Why *should* I prefer "good" things to bad or do right rather than wrong actions? These questions, we have seen, have an appearance of profundity, and if "this is good" and "that is the right thing to do" were mere aliases for practically non-committal information, or polite commands, or verbal bait for desired attitudes they would be both sensible and cogent. For no such statement thus interpreted could be an answer to the "why?" of action. But we are now prepared to understand these statements in a somewhat different way. To say with normative cogency that a thing is good is to say that it is so far worth choosing, in any situation to which its merits are pertinent as grounds for preferential action, and the thing that is worth choosing simply is, so far the thing that should be chosen. The "so far" must be added because a thing that is in some respect worth choosing, a good rifle for example, for a man concerned to shoot effectively, may be bad in others—it may be too expensive for his present means. What on the whole, and in his present situation is *the* good that warrants practical action is a further question with which we shall later deal at length. But nothing could be *the* good on the whole and in my situation unless it were at least in some way good and so to establish it *as* good is *so far* to provide a ground for preferential action. And so, too, for right. The man who said in a practical situation, "Yes, I see that the thing you recommend is the right one for me to do, but I don't see why I ought to do it," would not be a profound philosopher, probing beyond appearances for a deeper truth. He would simply have failed to understand the normative sense of "right" in this practical use. We do not need to import from outside, from metaphysics, perhaps, or meta-ethics, a normative force to connect the sense of "good" or right with that of grounds for action. "Good" and "right" in practical use are *should* words from the start. If their alleged informational content, or commanding potency, or persuasive efficacy is isolated from this justifying use, we shall then, of course need a further justification to do the work which, as thus mutilated, it cannot perform, and the old "why?" will recur. The undistorted truth, however, is that *in* this use it gives the justification asked for, and when we have it we have got the "why" of practical action. It is only when we refuse to understand a justification as a justification that we need a "higher" justification for it. In practice this would be a silly question, and a theory in which it nonetheless arises with an air of ultimate profundity has something seriously wrong with it as a theory of the practical use of reason.

But while there is no ulterior "why?" of practical justification required to lend its terms a normative cogency that they do not in their own proper use possess, there are "why"s in it that must be rightly answered if this cogency is to be maintained. Of course we should seek good and avoid evil. Any one who practically understands what "good" and "evil" mean knows that. Good *is* what should be sought and evil what should be avoided. The practical problem for a man concerned and competent to use these terms as guides to action is to know what for him and in his situation is in this way good. To call an object good is to claim for it this warranting status as a norm for rational preference. Is this claim sound? Jones is a *good* man for the job and should as such be preferred to other and inferior candidates when a selection is called for. How so? What's good about him? *Why* is he entitled to this preferential status? It is here that practical reasons, in the sense in which we all know how, to some extent at least, to understand and use them, are relevant to the "why?" of conduct. He is well-trained, industrious, cooperative and has the energy and initiative required to get things done. Whether or not these statements are true is something to be found out by inquiry. We look at his record, ask for letters of recommendation from those who have known him and whose judgments we can trust, observe, where possible, his conduct in situations in which these qualifications can reliably be discerned. It is *as* supported in this way by relevant factual considerations that "he is a good man for this job" has in this use the normative cogency for justifiable action that is claimed for it. Are these *relevant* considerations? Any one competently engaged in the business of carrying on a cooperative undertaking and responsibly concerned to get a good man for the job in question has learned that. And it is to such a man that "good" in this use is practically addressed. Are they the only relevant considerations? *Should* his race, color or religion also be considered? This is, in some areas still a "controversial" question, and reasons pro and con are offered with respect to it. But what they, in turn, are reasons for or against is the assignment of a preferential status that, when it has been established, warrants a man's acceptance or rejection for the job to be done. Stripped of the "why?" thus discoverable *in* this use of "good", the "why" of it—"Why should we appoint a 'good' man?"—does indeed become a problem, for without this warrant for its right assignment "good" has itself no warranting validity and cannot do the work required of it which is to justify one action in preference to another. We cannot know that "this is good" without knowing why it is worth having, for it is this *why* rightly answered that shows it to be good, and it is as shown to be in this way good that it provides an answer to the "should" of doing. This status, thus maintained in the cooperative work of practical understanding *is* its normative cogency, and for men who can thus understand each other, and themselves, it has the sense without which no action could be practical and no "good" authentically worth having. The man who is unable thus to understand and use it will never find the answer to a practical "why?" of action because he will not understand the question. It will not then be surprising if he comes up with some other "why" instead, that of causal conditions, for example, or metaphysical "Being" and, when this is shown not to provide the kind of answer asked for, decides that the whole business is either nonsense or else a mystery too deep for human thought to penetrate. The correlate of muddled thinking is a world that is indeed impenetrable to that kind of thought. But to call such thinking "rational" is to dignify it beyond its merits.

In summary, then, the use of practical reasons, for those who know how to understand and use them, is to provide a warrant for the claim that some things are, in our human situation, worth having and some actions worth doing, where their warranted presentation in this status *is* the proper justification for the *should* of doing. In this use they function not as practically non-committal information, nor as commands, nor as instruments of non-rational persuasion for which the question of validity is "of no interest" but as grounds for action. That is what we should expect of them, for that is what they are. In this use they have a clarifying and constructive function in the rational appraisal and self-control of conduct. They are not edifying platitudes—"good should always be preferred to bad" or "it is never right to do wrong" or "an action that has the property of should-be-doneness is a should-be-done action." They are the means by which we find out, where there is any ground for doubt about it, what, in this situation with which we have responsibly to deal is good or right, and should as such be preferred or done. Problems of this kind set the toughest sort of questions that we have to face and any light that ethical theory can shed on the right handling of them would be an authentic contribution to that wisdom that philosophers are supposed to love. One of the saddest facts about our current theories is that by misunderstanding the kind of justification that right action requires they have devoted their considerable abilities to the attempt to prove or show the impossibility of proving, in some higher sense, what anyone for whom such justifying language has a practical point already understands—that we should do what it is right to do—and have ignored as "of no interest", the thing we often tragically fail to understand—the sufficient grounds for accepting one sort of action *as* right, and another wrong, in the complex, changing and demanding world in which we live. Between such a theory and the work of practical understanding there is indeed a "gulf" and, on their terms, an unbridgeable one. But these, as we have come to see, are not the terms of reason in its practical use.

There are, of course, other "shoulds" than that of practical justification in this sense. "Why should I" may mean "What is there in it for me?" and be a hint that some sort of bait or bribe would be in order. For silly and suggestible people the word *may* function merely as a verbal push and for the subservient as a command to behave as Mother, God, the group, or the psychiatrist ordains. And it might be understood as information about the properties of objects. "Look, there is a 'should' inhering in this action. Observe the logical oddity of its epistemologically non-natural behavior. What sort of entity can it be?" Only for men concerned and competent to act as responsible agents in the right conduct of their lives can it have the sense and cogency we have ascribed to it. If there were no such men the language of practical justification would have no use, for nobody would know what to make of it.

Are there such men? Indeed there are and we (you and I) are among them. We are not so always, or at all levels of our response to the world around us. But we are so sometimes and for practical purposes can on some occasions be significantly addressed in this capacity. If we were not there would be, for us, no practical problems, and no question of the justification of actions to be answered. It is sometimes said that a practically justifying answer to the "why?" of justification "begs the question", since all it offers is a justification. The correct logical point here is rather that the question "begs" the answer, for only this kind of answer could be an answer *to it,* and only a questioner concerned and competent to appraise and use the answer as a justification could significantly raise this question. That we and others like us are such men is not an explanatory hypothesis we find it pragmatically useful to adopt or a postulate of "faith" we accept for edifying purposes. We learned to deal with our fellows, and to criticize our own behavior on the terms such understanding sets as we learned to participate as responsible agents in the way of life that is the starting point and basis of our moral world. If this way of thinking were rejected, this way of acting would go with it, for the thinking is the conceptual structure of the action, and the action, practically, makes no sense without it. There can be a society of sorts without this kind of action. Ants and bees appear to have no use for it. And as Ionesco's "Rhinoceros" points out, if we all became rhinoceri we should no longer use it either. To say that in that case something of great worth in man would have been lost is to make an assertion whose cogency no rhinoceros would understand.

It is sufficient, for our present purposes, that *we* understand it and are concerned to defend, preserve and promote the values to which, as responsible sharers in this way of life we are committed. Here for us practical reasons do have a practically reasonable use. Our aim is to make the clearest sense we can of them, to the end that they may be more adequately and justly used by those concerned and competent to do so.

CHAPTER 3

THE JUSTIFYING
USE OF "GOOD"

SO FAR IN THIS inquiry I have used such terms as "good", "worth", and "value" unquestioningly, "without" fear and without research," as though we all knew what was meant by them, in the use to which I put them, and could practically understand each other on the terms they set. I believe that this, within some limits, is in fact the case. But the reader should now be warned, if he does not already know, that both in practice and in theory grave puzzles have arisen about the proper use and meaning of these terms. What are "values" really, and what *is* good? Are they descriptive properties of the objects and persons of which they are predicted? Is value really *in* the object, as its size and weight are there? If so, why is it the case that people who can agree objectively about the size and weight of things disagree endlessly with regard to their worth? Or is our valuing of them rather the expression of a pro-attitude on our part toward them, and is this "in the end" all that we mean when we call them good? Is value "in" the subject rather than the object? In this case, since our attitudes are neither true nor false, how can anything be truly valuable? And if things have no values, what *reason* can we have for valuing them? Does not valuing belong to that noncognitive side of our nature that is essentially impervious to reasons? *De gustibus non disputandum est,* it is said, hence disagreements in our valuations cannot "in the end" be rationally adjudicated. And, finally, if "good" and "value" have, themselves, no rational cogency, how can they validly be used, as we have so far used them, in the justification of action? These appear to be searching questions. They arise when we are faced as we so often are in practice, with disagreements about "good" that are not resolvable, as scientific differences of opinion are supposed to be, by a clear reference to "the facts". Translated into the language of current ethical and meta-ethical theory they provide the springboard for that leap into the irrational in which current intellectual sophistication takes considerable pride. If we cannot deal rationally with them, our confidence in the cogency of practical reason in its own proper use, and in our capacity to use it well, can be seriously undermined. This is one of the ways in which theory, even rather silly theory, makes a difference to practice. It is, in consequence, important that we take these questions as seriously as we can and see what, in relation to our own use of good and worth, can be made of them. This inquiry will serve, I think, not only to eliminate some confusion but to specify more adequately and concretely the sense of terms that will throughout be of crucial significance in our investigation.

We shall not here be concerned with "good" in all its uses, or with what, if anything, is good "in every sense of the word." The term can be employed as a family name, or in an incantation, or to warn, to comfort or command, or to sell cigarettes and soap. The meaning it is our business to articulate is the warranting sense it has in the appraisal and justification of action. The aim of rational action is the accomplishment of something *worth* achieving. Of such an action we can meaningfully ask "what's the *good* of it? What of *value* can be got by doing it?" The supermarkets advertise "Values—Values—Values" and this, if it is to be understood as more than an enticing incantation, presents a promise that it has "goods" to offer that are, for the consumer's purposes, really good and at a price that makes the shopper's trip to buy them *worth* the effort and expenditure it requires. The man who in this sense knows "values" is the man who knows a good thing when he sees one, and cannot be imposed upon by the spurious, the shoddy and the second-rate. A sensible man is one whose preferential conduct is enlightened by this kind of knowledge of the good, and a wise man, as Socrates long ago pointed out, one who can give an account and justification of his life by reference to his choice of goods, which, while by no means limited to those a super-market can supply, have in the wider areas of conduct a comparable justifying status. *Right* action aims at good. It would make no practical sense if it did not. And it is in the light of such a good that the practicality of actions must be appraised if we are in this way to understand them. This is the sense and use of "good" that must make sense if the work of practical reason is to be rightly done. We shall do our best to understand it.

Right action aims at good, and the achievement of such good is the proper answer to the "why" of action. This sounds straightforward enough and if we were analytically unsophisticated we might almost think we understood it as it stands. But when we stop to think about it, there are evidently further questions to be asked. If anything is good then, where excellence in its kind is relevant to the adequate fufillment of our purposes, we have a warrant for the preferential priority we assign to it in action. "Why did you award this picture the first prize in the competition?" "Because it was the best of those exhibited." This answer is in one way normatively conclusive. But in another it is unenlightening. If the questioner was not a fool or a cynic he already understood that the best picture was entitled to the prize. The issue that he meant to raise was, in all likelihood, a different one. "Why do you rate this picture as the best? What are your grounds for attributing such merit to it? Show me that it really is as good as you say it is." The point here is that the warranting status of "good" for action itself involves a claim that must be substantiated if its normative cogency is to be validly maintained. *Of course* if the picture is the best the selection of it for the award is a justified selection. But is it really that good? Can you prove it? How?

It is here that hard questions about the justifying use of good practically arise, and that more light is needed for an adequate answer to them. How *can* we prove that one thing is really better than another? Tastes in art notoriously differ and one man's Picasso is another man's poison. And, apart from what we like, or enjoy, how can anything be good or bad? Is there some unique or justifying property of excellence inherent in the object and discernible to the inner eye of those who have the special gift to "see" it there? Have the empirically observable traits of the picture—its composition, color and the like—anything to do with such excellence and if so, how are we entitled to make the assertion not merely that the picture has these traits but that *because* it has them, it is good? Is there anything *in* the picture at all that justifies this claim to excellence?

Or is the judge, perhaps, in saying that the picture is the best, just expressing his own pro-attitudes toward it and urging (or commanding?) us to share them? Why *should* we do so? He is supposed, of course, to be an expert, but if his expertise with respect to merit is wholly of this emotional and hortatory character, why should his likings and urgings count for more than ours in an estimate of worth? If this were honestly understood, the business of awarding prizes would lose its sense as a recognition and reward of merit, though the emotive talk that such "awards" elicit might still go on and be in its own way "good fun", though in a different sense of "good" than that which we are trying here to understand.

The reader will see at once that these are the same sorts of question that concerned us in the preceding chapter. Following the procedure there exemplified, we shall try to deal with them not in general or a priori, but by reference to specific situations in which we do make the kind of distinctions of excellence that we are here told cannot justifiably be made. The best way to answer the question as to how we *can* walk is to discover how we do walk in the cases where we succeed in doing it. *Solvitur ambulando*. And if a theory continues to assert that we cannot do what in this way we do, we shall know that there is something wrong with the conceptual structure of the theory.

One familiar way in which goods are distinguished for the purposes of rational doing is the practice of grading objects and performances on the grounds of their respective merits. Apples are graded in this way, and restaurants, and Pulitzer Prize plays and a special seal of approval sometimes goes to those who make the grade. An instance which most readers of this book will recognize is that of the grading of examination papers. Some are better than others, and those who write them are rewarded, academically, for their performance. And teachers are sometimes called upon to justify the grades that they have given. The facts to which appeal is made to support the action taken are empirically discoverable and cognitively certifiable facts. You were required to answer six questions and you answered only three. You gave the date of the Battle of Waterloo as 1812 and it was in fact 1815. You confused the ontological with the cosmological proof for the existence of God. There are eight mistakes in your paper—count them—and we grade a paper with so many errors in it no higher than a "C". Any minimally trained hack can check mistakes of this kind, add up the results, and give a grade accordingly. A machine can do it more reliably than most

men, and machines are now often used for this purpose. Within
the limits of its "program" its logical and functional accuracy
are beyond reproach.

But how does the grader know what to look for and how to
"evaluate" what he finds as a measure of the excellence of the
student's performance? Of course if an A paper just means a
paper with less than three mistakes in it (where mistakes are
this identifiable), then that is all that there is to the matter. But
in academic practice this is not the case. We use an "A" grade
as a mark of excellence, as entitling the student to special
consideration for privileges and immunities (he is "on the Dean's
list") and as a ground for the award of fellowships for advanced
study. An "A" student is a *good* student, the sort it is the
business of a university to encourage and reward, and his performance on examinations is supposed to have some decisive
bearing on the right identification of such excellence. "The game
has not only rules, but a point" though in administrative devotion to the "groves of academe" this salutory truth is all too
frequently forgotten.

To grade a student's paper well, and, what is more important,
to set the kind of examination that will bring to light those
qualities of his mind and work that are most relevant to an
estimate of his worth *as* a student, is not an easy business. How
does a man learn to do this job well? At the start, perhaps,
somebody in authority just told him what to do and what he
learns is merely to follow instructions. But if those who give
him the instructions were themselves good teachers, and if he
has the capacity to become one, he gets much more from them
than such instructions. He gets some sense of what good teaching
is *for*, of the way it can elicit and fulfill the capacities for understanding of a growing mind, and of the part examinations play
in this development. In working with his classes he comes to
recognize the dodges lazy students use to avoid the responsibil-

ities of this growing process and the incentives that elicit better effort. He learns to distinguish, on grounds of excellence, between the mindless perfection, which is the flawless reproduction of a well-remembered text, and the promise of a groping, inquiring answer that has got the *sense* of the matter in it, and to value each at its proper worth. And thus, if he has the concern and capacity to teach well, he comes in time to grade his own examinations at first hand, departing in appropriate circumstances from the instructions he once learned and setting his own standards for good work. Only those who in this way know what good work is and are concerned for its achievement, know at first hand how to tell a good examination paper when they see it. In this way the reasons that establish the excellence of such a paper really are reasons of the heart, for only a man whose heart is in his work will make this kind of sense of the papers that he reads.

This does not mean that he must love his students in other ways or be consumed by an over-all passion for their well-being. Such generalized affection may lead to giving everybody "A's", and that is not the function of a good examination. Nor does it mean that he must approach the grading of a particular set of papers with pedagogical enthusiasm. He may, if he is bored or tired, view them with loathing and still do a good job in the trade that he has learned. But what he does in this case makes evaluative sense only in the larger context of this kind of concern and capacity. Others may learn the tricks of the trade and perform acceptably a task whose point they do not understand. Such "graders" are valuers at second hand. They know how to identify a "good" thing when they see it—where "good" is what the authorities, or those who gave them their instructions *call* good—for they have learned to recognize the descriptive properties by which the objects said to be in this way "good" are, according to their rules, identified. What they can never, in this way, understand, is what those who used this term at firsthand, as a term of warranted praise meant by it in this use, or why they picked out just these descriptive properties as grounds for such approval. Hence they cannot tell a *good* thing when *they* see it, but only provide information about the properties of objects that others have found good. Their "valuing" is parasitic on a sense of "value" which in their terms makes no justifying sense. "Why *should* a University place a higher value on good students than on bad?" is a question that answers itself, when we know what good students are and what a university is for. But "why should a university prefer "good" students to "bad", where the "good" and "bad" are those that are so certified in the Registrar's Office by the "marks" they have received in classes is at times a very pertinent question. And it is not by a reiterated reference to grades that it can cogently be answered.

What can we learn from this familiar example that is relevant to our philosophical problem? (1) To see the cogency of the attribution of good in this sense we must understand the point or purpose of the activity in whose right performance this attribution is justifiably made. Without this we can identify what our instructions tell us to label "good" but not what we in our own persons can find to be worth having. The goodness thus identified will not as it stands be a reason for doing anything. So this is a "good" examination paper. So what? For a man who knows the good of giving examinations and how, in its own way, an excellent paper is a fulfilment of this good, this question has a practically cogent answer. He knows what to look for in the paper to find this excellence when it is there, and what to do about it when he finds it. An examination paper may be good in other ways. It may be a fine specimen of penmanship, or an amusing example of verbal inanity and may properly in some circumstances be cherished accordingly. Or it may contain a large number of blank pages which make good scratch paper.

All these in their kind are authentic goods, but they are not the excellence for which a grade is rightly given on examinations by graders who know their pedagogical business.

The goods we have considered are all in this way good for something and for someone, and if there is a good which is good for nothing we cannot expect in this way to find it. This does not mean, however, that they are merely instrumental goods, whose whole worth lies in their capacity to produce or contribute to something else. A really excellent examination paper is good as such and on its own account. To get such papers is one of the rewards of teaching which can be an enduring satisfaction long after the requirements of the course for which they were written have been met. But it could not be *in this way* a source of satisfaction if it were not valued as the achievement of something worth doing for the purposes and within the activity in which teacher and student sometimes work together for a common end. That is what is good about it, and it is as meeting well the understood requirements of this activity that it is, on its own account, in this way good and *as such* worth valuing.

(2) The grounds or reasons for the object being good point, in the first instance, to facts about it that are publicly discoverable. There is no esoteric property of goodness to be intuited here, and it would be of no use for normative purposes if there were. When we ask to be shown that something is good we want to know what *makes* it good, or what is good about it. And it is not, save in a tautologically uninformative sense, its goodness that makes it good. It is good *because* it is accurate and well-organized; its handling of the material shows a genuine mastering of the subject and a capacity to think at first hand and fruitfully about it. The passages in which this capacity is manifest can be cited and will be recognized and approved by others. The more one knows about the discipline in which the examination has been set—and every teachable subject is, its own way, a discipline

—the better. If his judgment is not biased by such irrelevant considerations as that the writer was not *his* student, or is a man he does not like, the examiner can recognize such excellence on the grounds presented. Those who look into their own hearts or pro-attitudes to find the merits of good papers (since value, after all, is "in" the valuer) will not, in general, perform reliably in this capacity.

(3) I have said that the grounds that establish the merits of examination papers are publicly discoverable. If they were not, we should rightly question the cogency of claims based upon them. But the relevant "public" here is not just any kind of public—not that, for example, whose opinions are reported in a Gallup poll. A committee composed of the student's mother, his girl friend, and the president of the local Chamber of Commerce could not be counted on to give a responsible judgment on the merits of the case. The public that has rational authority here is that of the concerned and competent—concerned not just *any* way with the student's welfare or the good of "the community" but for the right attainment of that excellence which is discoverable in the practice in which this specific claim to good makes examinable sense, and competent by training and ability to recognize such excellence when they see it. Only such men will know what facts about the examination paper are relevant here and why they are important. They can understand such facts as grounds for a judgment of worth and make use of them accordingly. Such judgment is not infallible—a more adequate training and a purpose better understood might lead to its warranted revision. But this is the way in which true values are discovered, and the only way to do it better is by doing more adequately and reliably what in this way is done.

A good deal of the nonsense currently written about the "relativity of values" can be traced to failure to grasp this elementary point which, in practice, we quite normally understand. It takes a man who knows horses, and cares about maintaining the standards of the practice in which good horses are distinguishable from bad, to know a good horse when he sees one. And a horse that is good for fox hunting in England may not be one that best meets the normative requirements of an American cowboy. That not everybody likes such horses, or wants to buy them is irrelevant to their worth in this kind, though it is pertinent of course to the question of whether the purchase of such horses would be a *good* investment. Nor are the pro-attitudes of the judger toward the particular horse in question valid grounds for the assessment of such worth. However it may be with an intrinsic quality of goodness which would inhere in horses if they existed quite alone, the worth reliably discoverable *in* them is that which shows itself in such practices as these and for the purposes that give these practices their point. But this "relativity" is by no means a negation of the "objective" validity of the attribution of good, nor to our own pro-attitudes, but to horses. Rather it sets the categorial conditions under which the claim to such goodness can in some instances be objectively, i.e., truly and authentically, established. And this is the kind of objectivity we need if the justifying cogency of such claims in their practical use is to be validly maintained. Nobody, I think, who has heard men who know their business discuss the qualities that make a good horse good, will seriously doubt that they do in this way know what they are talking about and can tell reliably in some instances whether or not what they say is true.

(4) The connection between reasons and value is, in this use, a logically intrinsic connection. We cannot in this way know that a thing is good (except at second-hand and on someone else's say so) without knowing *why* it is good, or what is good about it. The claim to worth presupposes reasons and it is on their credit that it has the warranting or normative cogency that is its practi-

cal significance. So far from "reasons" being irrelevant to "values" in this sense, the truth is rather that it is only on the ground of reasons, understandable and acceptable as such, that the attribution of worth makes normative sense. I may, of course, *like* something for no reason at all—I just *happen* to like it, as we say, and in that sense be attached to it. Such "valuings" as occurences, have no more normative status than a sneeze. They happen, or they don't. But to say that any thing is valuable or has value *because* I like it is a very different matter. And as a generalization it is clearly false. Some things that I like are trash—a certain type of television program for example—but I like them just the same. Whether or how far I ought to indulge my taste for trash is a practical and moral question which mere liking cannot answer. And to affirm that to say that a thing has value is to say that I, or somebody, or most people, like it is practically stultifying. For it robs us of the means of making that distinction between what we like and what is genuinely valuable which it is the practical point of this kind of normative discourse to make. "I value it, or somebody values it or nearly everybody "values" it—i.e., we like it." "Perhaps so. I'll take your word for it." That doesn't mean that it is good. If it did, it would be nonsense to assert that what you, or most people, or I myself "value" in this way is often worthless stuff. And, so far from being nonsense, this is often plainly true. A mistaken liking is as absurd as an invalid sneeze. But with unwarranted claims to worth or excellence we are all familiar. Good in its warranting use *claims* something and as such has a *because* in it. To strip it of this *because* is to rob it of its warranting status and hence of its practically justifying use as a guide and norm for action. It is not surprising that those who have performed this abortion can find little sense in the notion of practical reasons.

It is true, of course, that liking, wants, and non-cognitive "pro-attitudes" in general do come into our estimates of value in another and quite fundamental way. Unless I wanted something nothing could (for me) be good. But it is not as something wanted that it has this status. It must at least be something that will satisfy my want, and satisfy it in a way that is appropriate to the aims and requirements of the practice in which its claim to merit makes examinable sense. And that means that it must satisfy not just my want but *me*, as a being who wants to eat, for example, but not just *any* way, and wants to live, but not at any price. Only for such a being does the distinction between what is valued and what *has* value or is good make normative sense. *For him* to say that anything is good is not to express a pro-attitude or to issue an order. It is to make a claim that must be made good if it is to do the work that is here required of it. And it is by reasons addressed to those concerned and competent to understand and use them rightly that it is in truth made good. A "value" *in this sense*" "irrational" is a vain pretention or an arbitrary claim, and is properly to be appraised as such.

(5) But, in questions of value, do not even experts disagree? There may be no disputing about tastes, but there is endless argument about values. Even "full" professors in the same department do not always agree in grading examination papers. This, of course, is true. But there are disagreements *and* disagreements. There is the mindless conflict of "you shall" and "I won't", and the snobbery of "*we* like this, but *you* (of course) could hardly be expected to." And there is the kind of disagreement that can fruitfully arise between men whose purposes are, at least in part, the same, and who know what they are about in pursuing them. Good fishermen disagree about the best kind of bait for trout, and may learn a good deal from each other in the process. And competent critics may disagree in an enlightening way about the worth of Brahms or Bartok. It is not, as a rule, that either is blind to what the other sees but that they

rate differently the importance of such reasons in an overall estimate of good. Given the diversities of human purposes and appreciation this is to be expected and within limits to be welcomed. Things can be good in many ways and save for special purposes (as in examinations) the urge to rate diverse excellences on a single scale is not a very helpful one. The essential point is that in cases of this kind the disagreements that arise are contained within an underlying agreement, that practical agreement in understanding that gives a normative sense to the disagreement and enables each to understand, though he does not share, the other's estimate of good. Their disagreement is itself a meeting of minds, not a brandishing of verbal weapons, in shared concern for a good which each may learn, perhaps even from the other, more adequately to understand. This is the point of rational disagreement in judgment about values, and this its practical use. Our gravest valuational problems arise when our available supply of practical understanding is not adequate to contain such disagreements, when there is, in fact, no common ground, or not enough of it, on which to stand, to reach a working understanding. In our contemporary world this problem is tragically real, and our best effort will later be devoted to an attempt to deal rationally with it. Beyond the limits of practical understanding the normative cogency of the rational use of good breaks down. This is what on logical grounds we should expect and what, in practical experience, we find. Is this the final word on the subject? Or is it possible that we can grow in understanding and that the resources of human nature for this constructive work have not yet been exhausted? Can we build the kind of world in which the justifying appeal to reasons will for all men make practical sense? There is no other rational ideal for mankind than this. We must see what in practice we can make of it.

Meanwhile, and in the kind of world in which we live today,

on valuational issues "who's to judge?" The answer is that in areas where we are practically concerned and competent, we (you and I) must judge, for it is in this way only that first hand value judgments are ever made. Here we must take the responsibility for judging rightly, for the right conduct of our lives depends on it, and must earn the right to do so by the attainment of the competence required for sound judgment. In other areas, we may follow at second hand the instructions of others who seem to know what they are talking about (though we do not) or indulge our tastes and fancies as we please, so long as we do not claim for them a normative cogency they manifestly do not possess. If you like green toothpaste, go ahead and use it. It would be pretentious and humorless to make a normative issue of this kind of preference. But where normative distinctions are relevant and important, our business is to see that they are rightly made. There is, I think, no ground for doubt that in some cases and for some purposes this can validly be done. In this doing the justifying use of "good" plays a distinctive and essential part.

We are now in a position to look again at the questions that, at the start of this chapter, appeared to cast doubt on the normative cogency of "good" in its practically reasonable use. Is "good" a property of objects? It is so in this sense at least that of some objects, in some circumstances, it can be justifiably affirmed that they are good. I have read some examination papers that were, and many that were not, in this way good. Is this a natural or a non-natural property? In its ordinary applications at least there is nothing supernatural about it. The traits and properties that warrant the assertion of its goodness are empirically discoverable and it is they, when understood and used as a rational man would use them in his practical affairs, that make the object good—that are the grounds for the assertion that it really and authentically has the worth this affirmation claims. Is it a descriptive property? That depends on what you mean by "description." What it affirms is a normative status and while it can truly be said of some objects that they are entitled to this status, i.e., are in this way good, the point of the affirmation is not merely to describe them as having such a property, but to warrant rational preference and the action in which it is fulfilled. Is it an objective property—are values really "in" the object? The goodness of an examination blue book is certainly not in the object in the way in which its pages are in it, or blots are on the pages. Nor have we yet found any way of saying how goodness could be in an object if it existed quite alone. But it is *in* the object in the sense that it is the object itself, and not our feelings about it or our pro-attitude toward it that is found to be in this way good.

Whether or not this claim is warranted is something to be found out by an examination of the object, in the use and for the purposes of the practice in which worth is claimed for it. This finding out is a public process, with its own requirements for accuracy, impartiality and adequacy, and it is by those concerned and competent to meet these requirements that such excellence can be authentically discussed. The claim to objectivity in *this* sense is intrinsic to the warranted predication of good. It is only as thus objectively substantiated by public reasons—and all reasons must be in this way public if they are to be more than appetites in words—that the normative status of the object is validly maintained, and only in this status that *it* is properly called good. "Are the things we value really valuable?" They are if they can in this way show their worth for those concerned and competent to discern and to delight in it. This *is* the "reality" of values, and nobody who has ever known in the firsthand experience the worth of something that fulfilled the promise intrinsic to the claim of "good" has failed at some point to encounter this reality. "Oh taste and see that the Lord is good. Happy is the man who trusteth in him." But to see in this sense is more than to enjoy agreeable gustatory sensations.

If good is really in the object, why cannot everybody find it there as they discover its sensible (empirical?) qualities? Because it is not in this way that values are found. And it does not in the least help here to invent an extrasensory kind of "seeing" to do the job. The finding of authentic values is a co-operative human enterprise in which the things or persons that we put our trust in prove worthy of the confidence that we have placed in them. This is as true, though on a different level, of a good apple as of a good God. That it takes a good man—good, not in general, of course, but in his concern and competence for the right fulfilment of the requirements of the practice in which the claim to good is significantly made—to know at first hand what is good can now be understood for the illuminating truism that it is. One need not be able to lay eggs in order to tell a good egg from a bad one when he tastes or smells it. But for a hen's purposes a bad egg, as we make that distinction, may be better than a good one. It is further along on the way to being hatched. It is for satisfying eating that a "good" egg is good, and no one who did not share our normal tastes in these matters or was unable to see the point of the elementary discrimination required to distinguish those eggs that can be relied on to meet our normative requirements for consummatory goodness in this kind from those that cannot would ever know *why* one egg was in this way better than another. He might then ask *why* "good" eggs are good and never find a convincing answer. Where the valuational problem is more subtle the point seems even plainer. Yet value analysts still sometimes talk as if the fact that a man who wanders through a gallery with no aesthetic interest or competence, and no knowledge of what the artist was about in painting it, can "see" no goodness in a picture when he looks at it, though he can see that it is large and has a lot of red in it, shows somehow that there really is no goodness "in" it. Solemn arguments about the objective validity of value judgments are sometimes based on considerations no more profound than this.

But there are more formidable grounds for the recurring claim that value is not really in the object valued but rather in the feelings, wants, or "pro-attitudes" of the valuer. Certainly, as we have seen, such attitudes have something essential to do with the matter. If a man had no such attitudes he could find nothing valuable, for it is in the right satisfaction of his wants and fulfillment of his purposes that good objects can authentically maintain this status. In a world in which nothing was enjoyed, or wanted, or intended, nothing could be good *for* anything or anyone, and hence "good" in the sense in which we have so far understood it, would have no application and no use. So much is true, and so fundamentally true that we owe a debt of gratitude to those who do not allow us to forget it. This does not mean, however, that once a thing has been found valuable some extra nonrational push is required to make us value it. It means quite radically and basically, that without this rooting in our nature as wanting beings there would be no rationally normative sense in calling one thing rather than another good. Our reasons here, as we have seen, are practical reasons and as such, are addressed "to whom it may concern."

Where the question of the worth of things arises, however, this concern is not merely to get what we want. It is a concern for what is worth seeking and worth having in the light of a good in whose achievement we can be rightly satisfied. Here the question shifts from the nature of the subject to that of the object. Is what I value "really" valuable? A. J. Ayer tells us that the correct answer to this question is: "it is, if you really value it." Of course, you should think about it carefully, considering all aspects of the subject and securing all available information. And then you should look into yourself to see what, after all this thinking, you are really for. That presumably is what, for you, the valuable will be. Think *what* about it? That, for example, it is a book on philosophy, it has been favorably reviewed in *Mind* and has a bright blue cover? That it is 700 pages long and still costs only five dollars—so much for so little? That its author's name begins with "Z"—an unusual and perhaps for you an attractive feature? Well, of course, the considerations thought about must be *relevant* to the "value" of the book if they are to show that *it* is really valuable. Relevant *how*? As causally effective in sustaining or strengthening an antecedent pro-attitude? The information that the book was written by the valuer's wife's brother might—or might not—do that, but it would not normally be considered as good grounds for claiming that it was, or was not, really valuable as—say—a significant contribution to its subject. If Mr. Ayer were reviewing the book he would not, I am sure, give weight to such considerations. When the question of worth is specified, the valuer may think to some purpose and his findings have a valid bearing on the "real" value of the book. Will he then really value it? He may still be drawn to it emotively, or "for" it in some other way, as desiring, for example, that it have a profitable sale, but if he is a competent and responsible judge of good work in philosophy he will not call it really good if it does not discoverably meet the requirements for good work in this field. And one must be a good philosopher to know at first hand what these requirements are. It is not by consulting our pro-attitudes either before or after "thinking" that we find out whether or not the things we value are really valuable, and no man responsibly engaged in a fair appraisal of the worth of things would seek to find it in himself.

But are not things valuable "in the end" because we value them? What is this supposed to mean? If it means that things are valuable *because* we want them to be so, the answer is a plain and emphatic *no*. All of us have sometimes wanted something to be good—our friends' performances in public, for example, or our own—but been regretfully obliged to admit that they were not. Nor are things valuable because we think they are, and in that sense "value" them. If they were, there could be no mistakes in our value judgments, and we could never be deceived in our estimates of worth. But many times we are deceived. And this is just as true if "we" are the "best people" or "the great majority", for these too may be mistaken in their estimates of good and never more clearly so than when what "we" think is that there is no valuational truth beyond our own opinions to be learned. Are things valuable *because* we want or are addicted to them, and in that sense "value" them? By no means. It is true, of course, that if nothing were wanted there could be no reasons for the claim that anything was good. That does not mean, however, that wanting *it* is the reason, or even as it stands, a reason for the thing wanted being good. One of the most stubborn facts which any realistic theory of value must face is that of men's frequent and ardent addiction to trash. Where the question of what is valuable or worth having significantly arises, wanting is not the last word on the subject. It is the raw material not the final arbiter of good. But we have, I think, already dealt sufficiently with this point.

If we now look back over the questions asked, and the answers given, we can discern a common pattern in them. The doubts that threatened to rob our practical use of "good" of its normative cogency arise when we try to analyze or elucidate this use in terms incongruous with its categoreal structure and practical intent. If the warranting of a claim to good were a valuationally neutral description of a practically noncommittal fact, or an expression of the speaker's own pro-attitudes and/or a command to others to share them, how could it ever do its justifying work? The answer is that, as thus understood and used, it could not do it at all. We should then be obliged to look elsewhere, no doubt in the nonnatural or the irrational, for a "missing linkage" that would connect the factual content of our value judgments with their relevance for practice in some other way than by showing them to be the valid grounds for preference that they purport to be. The search for such a missing link can lead to some ingenious and surprising meta-ethical theories, but one thing it cannot give us is the justification that initially we sought. *This* truth is not in it—it was eliminated for methodological purposes by the very terms of the analysis.

How can we prove to those who cannot or will not understand that Mozart's *Don Giovanni* has aesthetic worth, and how refute them if they deny it? Well, in the first place, "he that hath ears to hear, let him hear." But he will need more than good ears for this kind of listening. He must have also a discerning mind and an understanding heart if he is to *find* good where and as it is authentically to be found. It is what is thus found that "refutes" the doubt, though it by no means always silences the doubter. It presents in an authentic instance the worth about which dialecticians argue endlessly, and the man who has found it, whether in music, or examination papers, or super-market "values" or personal relations will know *why* the thing he values is "good" and why, as such it is worth having. And he can share his confidence and delight in it with others who seek excellence in this kind and are competent to know it when they see it. It seems at times as if the theorists who ask us to justify the normative cogency of "good" had never in this way known the worth of anything. For surely, if they had, they would not need to be deductively or inductively "driven" or non-rationally commanded or cajoled into a recognition of its relevance for preferential action. This, however, would be a mistake. They know it, in most instances at least, as well as we do. But their theories will not let them take account of it when they speak professionally on this subject. A trained inattention to the worth of things is a prerequisite for "value theory" as they practice it. And hence, for them, there is indeed an unbridgeable gulf between theoretical and practical reason.

Our inquiry has committed us to a different procedure, and for reasons that, I hope, are now increasingly apparent. The normative status of good in its justifying use is the cogency that *in this use* it discoverably has for those concerned and competent to recognize such excellence when they find it. As a justification of the claim to worth, nothing more is required of it and nothing less or other will suffice. The "why" of good in its justifying use is the answer to no other question than this. But to this question it is the only relevant answer. And for practical purposes—or, indeed, if there are to be practical purposes at all—we cannot do without it.

There are further questions about the normative use of "good" that are both difficult and profound. So far we have considered this term only in a rather wide and general use. We have said nothing specific about moral good, the moral worth of persons, or such super-moral goods as may perhaps be found. To this aspect of the subject we shall now turn. It will lead us further than an examination of super-market values, or of examination papers could ever do. The heights and depths of the spiritual life still lie beyond us. But we have now, at least, some firm ground on which to stand in our investigation of them. The goods we have identified are not all the good there is, but they are nonetheless in their own way authentically good and can be recognized as such by those with the concern and capacity to discern them. The best in this kind are not shadows; they are the substance of things wisely hoped for and a reward for actions rightly done. We can sometimes know them as such when we see them. And if a man cannot find worth in the goods that he has seen how then can we trust him to recognize a good that he has not seen, but has only dialectically and argumentatively identified? We have said that to discern the worth of beings we must see them in a certain light. This light, so far, does not penetrate to the darker areas of our experience. But it may be that, if we use it rightly, we can go forward with it.

CHAPTER 4
RIGHT IN GENERAL AND
MORAL RIGHT IN PARTICULAR

SO FAR WE HAVE chiefly considered what may be called the sunny side of practically rational action, the good it seeks and the fulfilment of our aspirations in which such good is discoverably attained. But anyone who knows the requirements of practical life knows in practice that this is not the whole story, nor even a part of it that can be adequately understood by itself. I have been careful to qualify the characterization of "good" in its normative function as something that must be *rightly* attained in accordance with the rules or requirements of a practice in which we, as practical agents, concerned and competent to meet such requirements, are responsibly engaged. The good is that which can satisfy us *as* such agents, and only so can it be found good in the sense that this term, in its normative use, implies. It is now time for us to take a closer and more critical look at "right" in this use, and its "requirements"—not just as a new aspect of our subject, but as something presupposed from the start in *any* normatively cogent use of practical reason but so far not explicitly nor adequately explored.

The first look here is likely to be disturbing for those who have to this point followed with approval the rather bland "reasonableness" of the theory so far outlined. "Good", in spite of its analytic corruptions, is essentially a reasonable word—it invites us to consider together what we "really" prefer and to act accordingly. But "right" and "requirement" are demanding words, and in their morally admonitory use particularly so. They are associated in our minds with claims, commands, laws, obligations and sanctions and those who use them often speak in a peremptory tone. Duty, "stern daughter of the voice of God," "whispers, 'lo, thou must' " and this is not a "must" with which it seems appropriate to argue. The councils of prudence have an "if" in them—"if you want this, do that"—but the moral law is presented as an unconditional command or categorical imperative which leaves us with no moral ground on which to ask "why should I?" Its dictates are obligations, not incentives, and to be obligated is to be obliged, bound, morally constrained to do not what we should ourselves prefer but what, as thus bound, we *must*. Since this moral "must" or "necessity" is not always, or perhaps even often, sufficient to "move" us to compliance, morality, which enjoins such compliance, has its sanctions in those extrinsic rewards and punishments by which recalcitrant human nature is pushed or cajoled into the acceptance, with such grace as it can muster, of the burdens thus imposed upon it. Such sanctions—threats of Hell and hopes of Paradise or more mundane considerations or social penalties or pressure or prestige—show why it is to the individual's advantage to, or disadvantage not to, conform his conduct to what God, Society, the Super-Ego or the State police require of him. But the obligations of morality have, as such, no reasons *in* them. They are not themselves grounds for action but prescriptions made acceptable by "incentives" or by threats. The "justification" of morality, sometimes regarded as the distinctive function of moral philosophy, then becomes a matter of finding non-moral reasons why it is to a man's interest to do what morality requires him to do without a reason.

No serious account of the "why" of moral action is quite as crude as this, though there are some that have, when stripped of edifying verbiage, little more to offer. But it will be useful to start our consideration of the right and the reasons for it at this level. For, one-sided as it is, such an approach does at least lay salutary stress on one basic aspect of the practical use of reason. There is something peculiarly demanding about moral claims on conduct. It is not from habit or confusion merely that we speak here of obligations as binding us against our inclinations, though not against our will. And the voice of Duty does enjoin us with a "stringency" of a quite distinctive kind. Morality is not a game we may play or not play as we choose, nor have we any right *as* moral agents, to break or bend its rules for our own personal advantage. It is a predicament we are involved or engaged in (as the existentialists would say) and the yoke of such involvement is not easy, nor the burden light.

This is the way in which the right and its requirements look to us when we do not understand them. A child learns that he "must" take the medicine he does not like. No reason he can understand is offered for the necessity of the disagreeable dose, but if he takes it "like a good boy should," he will get candy afterwards while if he does not his parents will be seriously annoyed, with consequences he has learned to fear. It is natural that Freudians who reduce all human conduct (save that of psychoanalysts and their more cooperative patients) to this infantile model find no more than this, internalized and translated into Latin (id, super-ego and ego) in the cogency of moral claims and the rather feeble struggles of the Ego to come to "rational" terms with their repressive influence. Nothing essential is wanting in this account but moral understanding itself. This, however, as we shall see, is a grievous lack, for without it no action, including that of the psychoanalysts and their more cooperative patients, makes justifying sense. If there is no "why" *in* the right and its requirements, there can be no "why" of them that can warrant the claims that are made, in their demanding terms, upon our conduct. The "right" remains an imposition and there is nothing we can "rationally" do but consult our psychoanalyst as to the "best" way of putting up with it. But while this may be the best the mentally infirm can do, we are not always or at *our* best as sick as this. We ask for a practical "why" that we can understand, a "why" not merely of but in the obligations that bind us to right action, and if none can be given *we* are "frustrated" in a way the psychoanalyst, in his professional capacity, cannot be expected to understand. He does not even see the meaning of the question, for, as translated into his terms, it no longer has a normatively cogent sense.

Our aim will be to clarify the sense of this *why* and to specify the terms on which it can be rightly answered. This, as I shall try to show, is a sense that is *in* right action, a *ground* of obligations that is intrinsic to its practical intent, not an extrinsic sanction called in to make us want to do, or fear not to do, what is "demanded" of us. Where such grounds can validly be given, no other *moral* justification for action is required, though in its light a good many morally pretentious claims can be seen to require a justification that those who claim a moral warrant for *their* demands upon us cannot give. The requirements of the right, where they make a valid claim on conduct and the "dictates" of the moral law, in all that is morally authoritative in them, are justifiable on such grounds. When we see how and in what way this is the case, we shall have a better understanding not only of the reasonableness of right action, but of the requirement of rightness involved in any practical use of reason, including that of "good". There is a root of requiredness in *all* authentic worth, and there is an aim at worth in any action that can rightly be required of us. Thus our inquiry, if it is successful, will not only bring the light we have so far discerned into what are reputed to be dark places. It will also broaden and substantiate a theory that, so far, has been one-sided in its emphasis.

"The remembrance of forbidden fruit is the earliest thing in the memory of each of us, as it is in that of mankind." And it is through man's response to this prohibition that he gains, though in difficult and sometimes devious ways, such knowledge as he has of moral good and evil. Forbidden fruit is appetizing, else it would not need to be forbidden and human nature, even in Eden, being what it is, its being forbidden adds to its attractiveness. Its prohibition stands as a barrier to the satisfaction of a felt want, a limitation on man's "freedom" to eat what and as he pleases.

Yet this is not a wholly external limitation. It is the command of a benevolent being, set as a condition under which other satisfactions can be fully enjoyed, a requirement for living well in an earthly Paradise. And it is a requirement that man can, by his own choice, refuse to meet. The fruit is there to be eaten, if he will. He must accept the prohibition as a rule for his own voluntary action if this first commandment is to be kept. He must learn to behave himself with respect to it. If this were not the point of the story, there would have been no sense in placing the tree and its fatal fruit in the Garden. A benevolent Deity would not gratuitously have put temptation in man's way. Without it Eden would indeed have been a fool's paradise, where moral ignorance was bliss and the knowledge of good and evil, as contrasted with the unimpeded satisfaction of wants, a sheer impertinence. But its inhabitants could never have been the progenitors of the race of man as we know it. Adam and Eve, like all their putative descendants, must earn their right to such good as is possible to man by the choices they make in the face of hard requirements laid upon their conduct. And for this Eden was not the appropriate environment. The Fall was "fortunate" in this sense at least that it brought them out into a world in which the knowledge of good and evil is not the forbidden fruit of willful self-indulgence but a requirement for decent human living. It is *in* the Fall and its consequences that their story becomes ours, and the memory of forbidden fruit a significant starting point for a moral history of mankind.

When we move from Genesis to Exodus, from the Garden of Eden to the Ten Commandments there is a clear advance in moral understanding. The Commandments, promulgated to a sinful people with awe-inspiring sanction of fire and thunder, are mainly negative in form—"Thou shalt have no other Gods before me—Thou shalt not kill. Thou shalt not commit adultery"—and even where the injunction is positive the action enjoined is one that men frequently would not perform if it were not thus required. They have a "must" about them which seems not an incentive to but a restriction on our action.

Yet this, once more, is a peculiar sort of "must". It is not, like the laws of nature, something that we cannot but obey. The Commandments can be broken, and have been many times. Obedience is rather something *owed* to the authority who issues the commands and who, for benefits received, is entitled to obedience. The God of the Ten Commandments is also and essentially the God of the Covenant, who brought the children of Israel out of the house of bondage and promises a land of milk and honey if His law is duly kept. The moral cogency of the Commandments is not in the fire and thunder, as physical portents, but in the Covenant which, as God's chosen people, they are not compelled but obligated to respect, as sharers in an enterprise that has good, and *their* good, as its object.

Commandments, thus understood and thus kept, not in "fear and trembling" merely, but as rules for conduct on whose terms men can stand in a right relation to each other and to any God

whom they can rightly worship, have a moral meaning and a
moral cogency. This understanding is not easily achieved, however. The long history of Jehovah's covenant with Israel shows
that both it and the Land of Promise that on its terms could be
reliably achieved, are hard to come by and to keep. If God's
covenant with man is authentically kept, it is in a different way
than even Moses had forseen. "Blessed are they that do hunger
and thirst after righteousness, for they shall be filled." This
blessedness is *in* the keeping of the Covenant and in the way
of life that on its terms alone is possible for man. It is a long
way from the fire and thunder of Sinai to the quiet words of
Micah: "What doth the Lord require of thee but to seek justice
and love mercy and walk humbly with thy God?" Yet the whole
story of man's growth in moral understanding, as it is grandly
portrayed for us in the Hebrew Scriptures is summed up at once
in the continuity and the contrast between the two.

When we turn from Genesis and Exodus to the *Protagoras*
of Plato, we find ourselves in a very different moral and intellectual environment. The question here is about the nature of
virtue and how and by whom it can be taught. Protagoras'
answer to this question has a great deal of abiding truth in it. He
is speaking here of the civic virtues on whose terms men can live
peaceably together. It was to supply these that Zeus sent Hermes
to men "bearing reverence and justice to be the ordering principles of cities and bonds of friendship and conciliation." Virtue
in this sense is not an optional excellence with which only the
specially privileged or gifted need concern themselves. A decent
minimum of it, at least, is a requirement for all who share in
the life of the city, "for cities cannot exist if a few only share
in the virtues as in the arts." So Zeus said: "Make a law by my
order, that he who has no part in reverence and justice shall be
put to death, for he is a plague of the state." The law is explicit
and drastic, but there is a "for" in it. Justice is no mere council

of perfection. There is a demanding aspect to it, it "calls men to account." And so, too, the teaching of virtue is everybody's business, for "the existence of a state implies that virtue is not any man's private possession." "Mother and nurse and father and tutor are vying with one another as soon as ever he is able to understand what is being said to him: he cannot say or do anything without their setting forth to him that this is just and that is unjust; this is honorable, that is dishonorable; this is holy, that is unholy; do this and abstain from that. And if he obeys, well and good; if not he is straightened by threats and blows, like a piece of warped or bent wood."

"This is just and that is unjust—do this and abstain from that." This is indeed the elementary form of a moral teaching that never wholly loses its peremptory character. But if this were the whole of it, nothing moral would be learned. Unless what a man learns in childhood to call "just" is rightly related to a good that is worth achieving, it will not be truly praise*worthy*, though all the parents, tutors and nursemaids of Athens unite to praise and to command it. And unless "justice" is linked essentially with that wisdom which is knowledge of the good, that relationship cannot be cogently maintained. That is why all the virtues, not as they are taught in Athens, but as praise*worthy* traits of character and conduct, come to one thing: wisdom. Such, I take it, is the point of Socrates' reply to Protagoras, as it is that of all rational morality. The justice and reverence which are the ordering principles of cities are requirements for right moral action. We *ought* to obey commandments rightly based upon them whether we want to do so or not. But as thus understood they are not an alien imposition upon a will that might, without this imposition, attain its own proper good in some other and easier fashion. They are requirements *for* this achievement itself and that is why the actions that they enjoin are so far right. It is when this *why* is accepted as a ground for action, and conduct relevantly appraised and justified on the terms it sets, that the "requirements" of moral action make normative sense in their practical use. Socrates' answer, as we shall see, still leaves us with some hard questions to be dealt with, and the hedonistic version of "good" with which in the *Protagoras* it is linked is inadequate to the moral intent of the Socratic doctrine of the "tending of the soul." But it is, so far as it goes, the right kind of answer and there is much that we can learn from it.

These great examples, drawn from the unforgettable experience of our own moral tradition, will serve, I hope, to give some concrete content to our talk about right action and to guard us against the logical oversimplifications through which, in the interest of "clarity" its hard problems and structural complexities are sometimes analytically evaded. Right action often is a crude, demanding business, and any rationality that we can find in it must be not just consistent with but built upon this practically basic truth. Our task is not to substitute for its morally "loaded" terms (since it is just this "loading" that constitutes their practical cogency) the analytically sterilized vocabulary of a "cognitively" neutral inquiry into logic or "the facts" but rather to understand the justifying sense that is sometimes *in* them, when they are rightly used, and on whose terms alone the aims of the practice in which they have this use can be authentically achieved. In one way we already understand this use, as sons and fathers, as citizens, as believers in a righteous God. If we did not we should have no moral problems. But we need to understand them better if this use is not to be confused and practically frustrated in situations with which our customary moral training has not prepared us adequately to deal. Here, as always, this better understanding is the goal of our inquiry.

A first look at our examples is enough to focus our attention on some central features of our moral situation from which we may profitably take our bearings for a more detailed investigation. In *prima facie* contrast with our previous account of practical reasons, moral reasons have a "must" in them; their point is to *bind* us to a way of action we might not on other grounds prefer. As such they present not optimal inducements but requirements to be met. The man who has not understood this does not know the practical meaning of the "ought" of action.

Yet this, as we have already observed, is a peculiar kind of "must". It is not that of either logical, physical or psychological necessity. We can reject its dictates *if we will*, and that we often will do so is one of the most obvious facts of practical experience. It is a *moral* must; its requirements are those for right and righteous action, and we must decide how far we will accept and act on it. It is a requirement for men's conduct, not insofar as this could not be other than it is, but rather insofar as we make or refuse to make it, of our own volition, what it ought to be. To put the matter paradoxically, it is a necessity that binds us only insofar as we are free.

Indeed, it is only *as* such requirements are thus freely accepted and made, by his own will the rules for his action that the action and the agent are, for the requirements of *this* practice, what they ought to be. A man who pays his taxes only under compulsion has complied externally with the requirements of the law, but he has not acted *as* a responsible citizen should in this situation and if we suspect that this is the sum of his concern for civic duty we shall not trust him to meet adequately the larger responsibilities of his life as a citizen. Until "right" action, as conformity to rules externally imposed, becomes the righteous action of a man concerned to act *as* he ought, because he sees the action to be, in his situation, what he is morally required to do, the demands of morality have not been genuinely met. It is those who hunger and thirst *after righteousness* who shall be filled, for it is only in this action that the promise of the moral enterprise can be authentically fulfilled.

But if the requirements of right action are to be *in this way* met, if they are to "command" the will of a being whose will and actions are his own, they must have a *because* in them, they must be requirements *for* a way of living that he can, in his own person, recognize as *worth* maintaining. It is in this way that the question of justification comes in, and comes in essentially, to the business of moral action. There is room here, as we shall see, for endless misunderstanding. It is fatally easy to oversimplify and to distort this use of reason, to reduce it for example to the prudential *quid pro quo* that self-centered men require as a "ground" for action in conformity with obligations whose moral cogency as reasons they do not or will not understand. We must do our best to avoid, and to correct, such misunderstandings. But the basic truth survives this kind of misinterpretation. The "must" of right action is addressed to men as practically willing beings who can and in some instances should demand a *why* for claims thus made upon their conduct. If no such why can validly be given, the claim has moral pretensions but no moral cogency and men with minds and wills of their own will not in the long run be imposed on by it. Moral reasons are the because that answers to this "why?" and without them the "ought" of right action makes no justifying sense—it does not authentically present a moral requirement for action. This is something men learn slowly and with difficulty as they come to understand the "must" of right action not as a prescription that their parents, church or school teachers gave them long ago and that they would feel guilty not to follow but as the morally inescapable requirement *for* the only kind of life that is in human terms worth living. In many areas of our conduct we have hardly learned it yet. The story of such moral progress as we can discern in human history is the story of this kind of growth in understanding.

So far we have not distinguished "right" in general, in its practical use, from moral right in the more limited sense in which that term is often understood. This distinction is sometimes expressed as that between a "broad" and a "narrow" sense of "moral". *Any* action well and rightly done has an aspect of requiredness about it. Games have rules, and to break the rules is not to play the game—it is "not cricket" as our English friends would say. Large theories of the meaning of moral right have been built on this somewhat tenuous foundation. There is a right and wrong of manners and deportment, and actions that violate such customary usage are not "fitting" or "suitable" to the occasion. The observance of such proprieties is a requirement for "gracious living" and those who fail to accept them as rules of conduct are not acceptable as members of the social groups in which they are conventionally respected. There is a right and wrong of writing examinations. This is not merely a matter of putting down correct answers. That might be done by cheating. In every profession and in every art there are not merely ends to be attained, but right as distinct from wrong ways of attaining them. There are standards of professional conduct which set requirements for worthy or acceptable performance and those who cannot or will not live up to them are disbarred from the profession. And, of course, there are legally imposed requirements for membership in a political society, where gaining wealth, for example, is a respected end of action, but some ways of getting it—by theft, fraud and the like—are prohibited by law. There are goods in all of these activities, but only what is rightly got and worthily enjoyed can qualify in this status. And only a man concerned and competent to understand in this way the requirements of right action and to respect them as grounds for claims upon his conduct is fit to share responsibly in the practices in which such goods can be achieved. It is in this way that there is, as has been said, a root of requiredness in all practically justifiable action. To seek pleasure is "natural" to man, and a good whose achievement was not an enjoyable experience would lack the glow of satisfaction without which our lives would be much darker than they are. But it must be the right sort of pleasure, attained in ways that do not unjustly deprive others of their proper pleasure, too, and enjoyed with decency and consideration for the feelings of our fellows, if it is to qualify as normatively good. The notion that the "maximizing" of pleasure or indiscriminate enjoyment, no matter whose or how obtained or how enjoyed if only it be "more", could make sense as an "ultimate" end of practically approvable action is one that only an advanced ethical theorist could seriously defend. A good divorced from right in this use would not make justifying sense.

Yet we do not ordinarily think of the requirements for such action as moral obligations on our conduct. To speak English intelligibly, I must observe, in a rudimentary way at least, the rules of English grammar. There are right as distinct from wrong ways of using the language. And if I cannot or will not master them I am thereby excluded from the community of those who can in this way communicate intelligibly. But only a reluctant novice experiences such rules as imperatives imposed on him by school teachers, dictionaries and other such "authorities" to whose "dictates" he must conform on penalty of censure or promise of reward. They are rather requirements *for* his right use of a language in whose terms alone (whether it be English or another) he *has* thoughts and purposes to express, and mastery in it is the achievement of a range of sharable experience without which he would not, as a thinking and purposive being, be himself. The requirement that a football player *must* get the ball across the goal line not just any way if a score is to be made, but according to the rules, is a limitation on his "freedom" of physical movement, but it sets the conditions for the interest and acceptability of the activity *as a game,* and it is as such that a good player can excel in it. And while the rules may in particular cases be unduly restrictive, and should be changed accordingly, the point of *having* rules that are a must for acceptable action is plain to any but the dullest mind.

The instances that first occur to us as examples of specifically *moral* obligations are of a different sort than these. They occur in situations where such dictates conflict explicitly with what, on other grounds, or on no grounds at all, we want to do and conformity is exacted at a heavy price. There is a kind of stringency about our commitment to them that the rules of grammar or of football do not have. And they seem to bind us not simply *as* players in a game from which, if we choose, we may legitimately withdraw (whereof one cannot speak one *can* at least be silent) but as *men,* and in this way to be inescapable. Their "must" is therefore categorical, not optional, an existential predicament in which we are inextricably involved, not just a requirement for doing acceptably what, for our own purposes, we desire to do. If we are to do justice to our subject we must take full account of this peculiarity (or distinctiveness) of specifically moral action and at the same time keep clear its connection with the requiredness of "right" as we have so far practically understood it.

There is, in this way, a moral side to any practical activity. To accept a bribe to fix a football score is wrong, not as a violation of the rules, but as a blot upon the character of the man who, in so acting, shows himself to be unworthy of the trust that those who play the game have placed in him. The morality of the requirements of intelligible English is more subtle, but current debasements of its use in television, comic strips and various sorts of propaganda will serve as painful instances of it.

Why do we regard such violations as raising specifically moral issues? It is, I suggest, because here the requirements are so basic that without their acceptance no "game" of this kind could be played at all. They are the minimal but inescapable conditions *for* that mutual confidence and respect on whose terms men can work (or play) together in a way in which a distinction between right and wrong that makes normative sense can be practically maintained. An inept or careless bridge player will not be a welcome partner, but a man who deliberately cheats at cards is excluded from the game, not just because we do not like him, but because he will not honor in his conduct the requirements of fair dealing on whose terms alone the game, as a cooperative enterprise, can be played. It is not too much to ask of a man that he refrain from cheating. The requirement is minimal but fundamental. And a man who will not accept it as a "must" for his conduct, even when it would be profitable to cheat, has no acceptable place in the community of players for whom the right and wrong of bridge playing has a normative sense and use.

Bridge-playing is just one game among many and, for most of us, not a very urgent or important one. The community of bridge-players is one we can enter or withdraw from as we please. But there are some communities with respect to which we have no such option, or have it only to far more limited degree. The chief of these are the family, the State and the Church. We are born into families we did not choose to join, and are stuck with our relatives whether we like them or not. A man may, within limits, choose his wife, but the moral consequences of that choice and commitment once made are binding in a way that even the most liberal divorce laws cannot wholly ignore. We do not choose the nation into which we are born, and while we may, under some circumstances, migrate to a new country, we shall then be bound by obligations that we cannot honorably evade. The Church makes still more drastic claims, for this world and the next, and offers us in return a new world to live in. And while a man, in the United States is legally "free" not to join a church, or to sever his ties with the one in which he was brought up, he does so at considerable moral risk. These, for most men at least, are not optional communities, and their minimal requirements for right action have therefore a peculiarly binding character. So much is this the case that we normally associate the "immoral" with those sexual irregularities or deviations that threaten the structure of the family, or with the disloyalty that is subversive of our American way of life or with a violation of the rules of right conduct that the churches teach us are requirements for a right relationship with God and man, or with all of these together. Here we find the practical equivalent of the philosopher's categorical imperatives, presented with a moral stringency that is of a different order from that of the rules of games or the proprieties of speech. As Cecil B. De Mille's first movie version of *The Ten Commandments* put it: "If you break them, they break you."

Such specifically moral rules are requirements for membership in those inescapable communities whose demands in our human situation and as men we are in no position to evade. That is why they are said to bind us, not as football players, or as artists, or as soldiers, for we need be none of these, but as men, and as common sharers in the human enterprise. As Plato's Protagoras well said, they are everybody's business. Local and traditional in their initial application (since family structure and political loyalties and even divine edicts differ in diverse communities) they are universal in their claim to unrestricted cogency. This tension between the universal and the parochial will become a major theme of our inquiry as we proceed. But there can be little doubt that the claim is there in any serious morality (as distinguished say, from a code of good manners whose adherents often pride themselves on their exclusiveness) and that a major part of the progress of morality is bound up with its more adequate articulation. The moral law must be universal or the same for all within the range of its relevant application. The freedom which as Americans we defend with moral fervor is open in principle to all men of good will, and on theoretically equal terms. "The International Party," we are told "unites the human race." And until the God of the chosen people has become a God that all men who love righteousness can worship, the teachings of the prophets have not been fulfilled.

We are now in a position to understand the difference and the continuity between right in general and moral right in particular. Any normative requirement for practical doing is moral to the extent that it constitutes a minimal or *sine qua non* condition for responsible sharing in a practice in which "right" and "wrong" have a justifying use. The minimal requirements of the communities in which we must participate, not for some special purpose of our own but in virtue of our primary, and for the most part unchosen, involvements as men, are moral *par excellence*. The moral law enjoins obedience to commands thus sanctioned and claims thus supported even, and indeed especially, when they run counter to appetites and purposes which, were it not for such injunctions, we should gladly follow. And the righteous man is he who willingly accepts this law as binding on his conduct not of necessity merely, but of right, and makes it the primary ordering principle of his actions. This, or something very like it, is the picture of right action to which an emphasis on peculiarly *moral* demands on conduct leads us.

It is a sobering and salutary picture but it cannot possibly be the whole truth about practically reasonable action, or even a segment of that truth that makes sense by itself. For there are no merely moral actions, and no action would have a moral point if it did not have some further practical point to which its requirements as moral were intrinsically related. We have, as current analysts are constantly reminding us, a moral obligation to keep promises. But there is no action which is just the keeping of a promise. What we promise is not to keep promises but to love, honor and obey, to return a specific sum of money or to tell the truth, the whole truth and nothing but the truth when we give evidence in a court of law. If these actions were not important to the right achievement of the ends of the activities in which promises are sometimes made and kept there would be no *use* for promising as a requirement of righteous conduct. Men do indeed come to hunger and thirst after righteousness, but if they did not hunger and thirst after other things, food, shelter, security and affection, for example, which can be reliably attained, on humanly liveable terms, only on the condition that they deal righteously with each other in the pursuit and enjoyment of them, righteousness would have no content and its dictates no normative cogency. A disembodied "kingdom of ends" in the Kantian style, in which our whole moral concern was to respect this dignity of others as its "legislating members" is a peculiarly empty moral ideal. For it is only in the right doing of actions *worth* doing, as responsible sharers in a common enterprise in which wants are satisfied and goods achieved, that men *have* a moral dignity that is worthy of respect.

It is true, of course, that we have an obligation to keep promises even in cases where no other good than that of promise-keeping is to be expected from it. Within the "practice" of promising we are not free to weigh the particular case on its non-moral merits. My point is that there would not be *this* good, which we are here obligated to respect, unless the cooperative activity—the practice in which promises rightly made and kept play an indispensable part—were one that was in *other* ways important to us. For there *is* no practice which is just that of keeping promises. There are a variety of practical activities in which promise keeping is a requirement for actions that only men who can in this way understand and trust each other can significantly perform. This moral requirement is no dictate of the moral will; it is a requirement *for* a way of life without which our lives would not be worth living, and the failure to understand it as such robs morality of the justifying sense that is its own excuse for being. As Scheler and Hartmann pointed out, moral values "ride on the back of" situational values whose cogency is not that of a "must" merely, but of a "because". We may well hold that in themselves moral values are the "highest" human values that we know, but we must also recognize that they *could* not have this value *by* themselves or make, as merely moral in the strict or narrow sense, the claim we rightly honor in them.

This is a point of considerable practical importance. When the one-sided moralism of mere morality is set up as an ultimate standard for practical justification it becomes morally self-stultifying, and what we get is no longer a "why" *in* moral action but a morality of imperativism, legalism and external or non-moral sanctions. Its requirements become commands or dictates merely, grounded not in the worth of what is dictated but in the will, the sovereignty and, "in the last analysis," the power of the dictator. Whether the sovereign be God, or that great Leviathan, the state, or just, in "conscience", an echo of our infantile dependence on our parents, the final answer to the moral "why?" is "you must because you must." And this is a "must" for which no reason that is not iself a fiat or command can in principle be given. Such a morality is authoritarian, not in the legitimate and proper sense that it invokes authority, as all practical morality must do, but because it can give no moral grounds for distinguishing the dictates of an arbitrary will from the legitimate demands of an authority that, in our moral situation, ought to be obeyed. For the latter we can rightly ask and give a "why". For the former as a "must" which is not merely unconditional, but on principle unjustifiable, to ask a "why" is both theoretically senseless and practically defiant. God, or the legislature or your father says so, and there the right of the matter ends.

There is, of course, a place for "reasons" within this way of thinking. When commands or dictates are presented in universal terms as "laws" there is a question as to which specific actions fall within the scope of their dictates and prohibitions. If I am ordered to bring all the books in this room and this is one of the books in the room, then "reason" tells me that I am ordered to bring this book. But "this room" may be ambiguous. Perhaps there is an alcove which could be counted either as part of this room or as another room. Does my order cover the books in the alcove, too? Here there is room for casuistry and persuasive redefinition and, when the orders were given long ago by a power that cannot now be directly questioned as to their specific sense, for learned disputes. This is the sphere of legalism in morality. "Remember the Sabbath Day to keep it holy." Does the Sabbath mean Saturday or Sunday or, with sufficient ingenuity and erudition, might we not make it even cover a Wednesday half-holiday? The deeper wisdom that can make us see that the Sabbath with its prohibitions was made *for* man, not man for the Sabbath, has no place in this way of understanding moral rules. Yet this kind of interpretation and application of commands and laws, or making precise little dictates out of vaguer big ones, is what the use of reason comes to in a moralism of this type. But even here the why of rational justification can practically arise. Some men, perhaps most, for most of the time at least, are sufficiently submissive to comply with orders issued in morally demanding terms they have been trained in this way to accept without the need of further sanctions. But some are not, and in the experience of almost all of us there are occasions on which we ask about the practical sense, the good, of what is thus demanded of us as a duty. And since in such morality no "why" *in* our moral situation could here be offered as an answer, we must look for a sub-moral or a super-moral sanction to provide the answer. Some will be inspired by accounts of experiences in which, in mystical or quasi-mystical union with the source of our being, our moral questionings are lost in love. There undoubtedly are such experiences, though their bearing on the issues of right conduct is a further question that, when we return from rapture to the affairs of men, still seems to need an answer. One thing, however, is common to them all. What they offer is not a moral justification, and it is not to men as moral agents, but rather on a sub-or super-moral level, that they are persuasively addressed. The man who does "right" acts by a kind of social automatism, because he has been trained to do them, or because he is afraid not to, or hopes to be well paid for so doing, or because his love for a higher power overflows in blind obedience to what the earthly deputies of this power command, is not acting as a man who in his own person understands the normative difference between right and wrong and of his own will acts accordingly. What is lacking in all these accounts is just morality itself and the men for whom its "dictates" can make moral sense as requirements *for* the shared achievement of a common good. This lack is no mere inadvertence. There is, in these interpretations of morality, no place for such men, and no way in which we could understand the import of their actions, or they could understand themselves. A morality of "finally" groundless imperatives, of laws to be legalistically understood and of sub- or super-moral sanctions is a mutilated fragment of a moral life that, on such terms, makes no moral sense.

To correct this distorted picture all that is required is to understand again as in practice we do often understand, the normative connection of right with good and of moral right in its stringent sense with the wide variety of other "rights" in which human aims can be rightly fulfilled. This is not an extrinsic connection, brought in from outside to "link" externally, by political or supernatural sanctions, the worth of what we do with the pressures that "require" us to do it. It is, as we have seen already in a preliminary way and shall see in more detail as we proceed, a "why" of action that is *in* our obligation, insofar as it has moral cogency at all and can serve in this capacity as grounds for justifiable action. Moral requiredness is *for* the attainment of goods worth having that can only in this way and on these terms be had, and it is thus "binding" only for a moral agent who can understand and accept it as such in the right conduct of his life. Without a right thus respected there could be no moral worth, for it is only ends rightly achieved and satisfactions rightly enjoyed and shared that can significantly count as worthy. Every practice in which the practical quest for good makes sense has, in this way, a right and wrong about it and observance of the one and avoidance or correction of the other is an indispensable prerequisite for its meaningful performance. But equally and no less essentially, this right is a ground of justification for action in which the promise of a life of human excellence is authentically fulfilled. This is a good that can be had on no easier terms than those which moral obligation, rightly understood, lays down. But if it were not a good worth having there would be no practical cogency in its requirements and no reason why we should accept them. There is indeed a covenant in the Commandments and it is in the community in which this covenant is kept that commandments have a moral meaning.

Even in the groups in which moral requiredness has its most demanding application—state, church and family—this truth must surely be apparent. A family that is held together only by an emphasis on duties and commands is a poor sort of family and one that will not, without the continued imposition of sanction, hold together long. It is in the course of doing other things

together, things answering in the first instance to non-moral
human needs, things often gladly done in the companionship
and for the sake of those to whom we are "bound" by the deepest
ties of natural affection and dependence, that we have obligations
as members of a family. Without some moral order the family
could not survive, but if it were a *merely* moral order it would
have no reason for surviving. The state must have legal sovereignty if political security is to be preserved, and without some
principles of moral order, willingly accepted for the most part
as a required condition for the living of a common life, no such
political security can long endure. Force and fear are no sufficient
foundations for a state that can significantly make moral claims
upon its citizens. But we are not merely or even mainly citizens.
If the state does not provide the environment in which other
goods besides its own can be secured, and other sides of man's
nature than those fulfilled in obedience to its commands can be
developed, it becomes a state that on the whole is not *worth*
the loyalty it claims from us. The monolithic state in which every
good is judged by its political significance so that religion, for
example, becomes an instrument for "fighting Communism" and
a liberal education primarily a cold war weapon, is a pathological-
ly one-sided state in which the realities of human freedom,
however much they may be honored in its slogans, are gravely
threatened from within. Political loyalty is a great and essential
good, but if it were the only or the *all* important one, it and the
state which claimed it of us would no longer have the worth
that gives this claim its moral cogency. And a monolithic church
is no less morally suspect. The good it promises is indeed a
final good, but unless this good is the fulfilment of a life in
which other goods, that of rational inquiry, for example, with
their own distinctive right and requirements, have an essential
place, then the God whose authority it invokes is not a being
we can love with all our hearts and with all our minds, and its

authority as an arbiter of moral right can, on moral grounds, be rightly questioned.

When we consider the "right" of more optional communities and practices the point is even clearer. These too, have their requirements as we have seen. For the most part, however, when we know how to do well the thing that is being done and are glad to do it, they are not experienced as limitations or restrictions. The man who knows what it is like to get things *right* in this way does not regard the normative requirements of right action as commands that he must be frightened or bribed to accept. He sometimes rejoices in them as a strong man to run a race, when the observance of the exacting conditions under which the race is won are what can make the winning of it an achievement. There is indeed a dark side to the requiredness of right action, but those who would make it a blind side must never have seen at first hand the point of right action or the reasons that there are for honoring the demands it makes upon us. Our business is to make these reasons clear. That task we shall now explicitly undertake.

CHAPTER 5

MORAL REASONS
AS GROUNDS OF OBLIGATION

THE SUSPICION THAT THERE is something "logically odd" and/or ontologically mysterious about practical reasons comes to a focus when we consider moral obligation. We appeal to obligations to warrant claims on conduct that a good man ought to acknowledge, not just theoretically in his thinking but practically in what, of his own will, he does. That my brother needs my help is a ground for such a claim; it is offered not merely as information in which I may or may not be cognitively interested but as demanding something of me that, whether I like it or not, I am somehow bound to do. We seem to understand this kind of talk in practice and our conduct is sometimes influenced by what we make of it. But when we stop to think about it, puzzles multiply. What, in this use, *is* an obligation? Is it some special kind of fact that we just see and if so, with what special faculty do we see it? It does not seem to be an empirical property like size or weight or shape, nor one a scientist need invoke, for explanatory purposes, in his factual enquiries. Perhaps it is a non-natural property, and a special kind of non-empirical seeing or intuition is required to detect its presence. And even if we do see it, where does it get its "demanding" status for our conduct? Facts in themselves demand nothing; the fact that my home is burning does not require that I should now strive to put out the fire. The factual or truthful side of it must somehow be hitched to a want or a will if its practical function is to be effectively performed. What is the nature of this hitching, and what is the missing link required to accomplish it?

Perhaps the obligation statement is not really a descriptive statement at all but rather a command—"help your brother"—here coupled with information—this man is your brother and in need—that somehow supports it. But how *can* facts "support" a command except by showing it to be an instance of a more inclusive command, and by what facts is this command "supported"? Why not just say "Help your brother, that's an order" and be done with it? Or perhaps the language in which the "imperative" is couched is so emotively persuasive as to make me *want* to help him. Now that you speak of him as my brother and call his want a need, my heart is strangely warmed, and I am moved to act accordingly. Here any fact that, presented in this way, can move me to the action that you want from me, will be a moral reason and may, when such language is persuasive in this use, be called a ground of obligation. In such a use the question of the validity of the connection thus established between reasons and the claims they are supposed to "justify" is naturally "of no interest." This is indeed a peculiar use of "reason", though not an unfamiliar one. It purchases a kind of almost-scientific clarity at the price of stripping the normative use of moral language of its claim to rational cogency. But it does not regard that price as a high one. For of such cogency it can, on its own terms, make no sense at all.

Here, as the reader will by now have recognized, we have the familiar "isms" of meta-ethics at work again—cognitivism, imperativism and emotivism—and in what might well appear to be a peculiarly happy hunting ground for their purposes. For there is something peculiar, or at least distinctive, about "obligation" in its moral use, and one way of trying to understand this distinction would be to analyze it into something else that we already, in a different way, know how to handle. If obligations were just empirical facts we could turn them over to science, including, of course the "science" of linguistics, for investigation. And the non-empirical investigation of the a priori has long had its devotees and prophets. The legalistic interpretation of directives or commands has its own familiar logic, and the enforcement of a moral law, so understood, its discoverable sociological sanctions. And the motivational engineering of our attitudes and actions through persuasive speech goes on all around us. PhD's in this kind, too, are now quite readily procurable. The puzzled doctor who, unable to diagnose his patient's ailment, gave him fits because he knew how to cure fits, has his analogue in a good deal of current high level theorizing in the area of what is still called moral philosophy.

There is, however, another way of understanding obligation statements, a way with which, in our discussion, we are now to some degree familiar. *One* distinctive thing about them is that they are offered as grounds or reasons for the validity of claims that as thus warranted we ought to meet. Here the demanding status of the claim *as warranted* requires, for its justifying cogency, the "support" of reasons that the agent to whom it is significantly addressed can understand, accept and use as such in the right direction of his conduct. It is in this light that a morally responsible man would understand "your brother needs your help", if he were seriously considering whether or not he ought to give the man in question a sum of money, for example, that he cannot easily afford. So understood it is a relevant consideration, it states a reason why he ought to give the money. As it stands it may not settle the question of right one way or the other. There may be further and no less relevant reasons for not doing what is thus proposed. But it is the right kind of reason and, where the issue is a moral one, if there are other considerations that can rightly count against the claim which so far, it warrants, they too will be grounds of obligation in just this sense. If I can only help my brother by denying to my children educational opportunities I should provide for them, then I also have a reason for not helping him and hence, a moral problem. If instead of asking what *are* "obligations" (a query comparable in its discernment to the student's query at the end of a lecture on the English poets: "But Professor, what *are* 'keats'?" we ask; what sense do obligation statements have *in* this warranting or justifying moral use? and what sense can we *thus* make of them? we may reach a more relevant and, for our purposes, rewarding conclusion. Following this procedure, I shall suggest, that obligation statements, when rightly understood and used, are grounds for moral action, and that the distinctive grounds for moral action are what is validly affirmed in statements of obligation. It is, in other words, *as reasons* for morally justifiable doing that "obligations" are properly to be understood. An analysis whose purpose is to recognize and adequately articulate the meaning that we find *in* practical doing, and not to impose upon it a sense that is not *its* sense, can here make sense of much that many ethical theories have found occult, esoteric or logically nonsensical. Such, at least, is our project. Let us see what we can make of it.

In the statement, "your brother needs your help", there is obviously a reference to matters of fact that must be factually certified if the statement is to present a rationally cogent ground for moral action. If the man in question is not my brother but an imposter, or if he does not need help, being in fact better off financially than I am, then no good reason for my helping him has been given. This reference to fact is basic and inescapable.

"Because you promised" is not a good reason why I should attend X's lecture if I never promised to attend it. We need not elaborate the obvious.

But suppose the facts, in this sense, are admitted. He is my brother and he does need help that I, though perhaps at some sacrifice, could give him. As information this is unquestioned. Now what of it? "You ought, on this ground to give him the money." Is that another fact of the same sort, to be added to my store of information on the subject? No, it is supposed to follow from the facts already stated. Follow *how*? Can we deduce it syllogistically from the "premises" already supplied? No, we should need an additional normative premise for the purpose. All cases of helping needy brothers are cases of ought to be done actions. This is a case of helping a needy brother. Therefore this is an ought to be done action. Where did this normative major premise come from and how is its truth certified? Perhaps it is the conclusion of a prior syllogism. All actions that maximize happiness are cases of ought-to-be-done actions. All cases of helping brothers are cases of maximizing happiness. Therefore all cases of helping brothers are cases of ought to be done actions. The logic is impeccable, but we have again a major premise to be empirically or non-empirically (a priori) certified. This sort of thing can go on indefinitely and sometimes does. There seems no way out of it except to say at some point, "don't you *see* that this latest major premise (our "ethical first principle") is cognitively true?" or else to cut out the argument and issue orders, or to observe that, for persuasive purposes, the question of validity is "of no interest." Given this initial statement of the problem, the "isms" are hardly to be blamed for their attempts to cut, in this way, the Gordian knot that they themselves have tied.

There seems indeed to be no rational way out of this unhappy situation. But how did we get into it in the first place? Was this trip really necessary, or even well-advised? We have been looking for some additional premise that would establish the relevance as a ground for action of the information initially given. But it was not *as information* merely that "your brother needs your help" was thus presented and, if it is misunderstood as such, no accumulation of further premises, empirical or *a priori,* will "in the end" supply the cogency that has initially been missed. How shall the man who cannot understand that he has in these circumstances an obligation to the brother whom he has seen and lived with, "see" (in a quite different sense) that brotherhood in general entails the ought-to-be-doneness of helpful acts, or, perhaps, that all happiness maximizing actions have this remarkable property and that brother-helping acts are, in general, happiness-maximizing? A man who knows his duty only in this way does not in practice know what duty means, though he may nonetheless write books about its "meaning".

How *do* we come to understand that we have obligations to our brothers—that a brother's need is genuinely a ground of obligation for morally right action? We learn it, of course, as we share practically in the goods and the requirements of family life, *as* sons and brothers bound together by the ties of mutual concern that make the family a moral unit. This is not always as simple and easy a relationship as the word "brotherhood" suggests. Sibling rivalry has a part in it, and it may be suspected that if all men looked on each other as brothers they would still find much to quarrel about, as brothers do. But, where the family is indeed a moral unity, these quarrels are contained within the limits of an area of shared understanding and responsibility whose requirements of mutual regard and helpfulness are a *must* for right family living and are so understood by those for whom it is in fact a way of life. We *are* to some degree our brothers' keepers, and it was this *moral* truth that made Cain's crime so grave an offense. Hence the term "brother", in the statement of a ground of obligation is not a practically non-committal term. To be a brother is not just to be a male sibling—it is a privilege, a burden and, whether we like it or not, a commitment. The man who understood in this way that his brother needed help would know in that acknowledgement, a reason why he ought to help him. And the man who could not in this way understand *some* obligation statements—whether those of brotherhood or some others—would never know why, on moral grounds, he *should* do anything rather than anything else, though he might see that he was prudentially well-advised to conform to rules that others understood as "obligations".

The reasons thus understood are, as are all practical reasons, reasons of the heart. It is not merely as ethical inquirers but as loving, hating, greedy, sympathetic, sociable and self-assertive beings, bound together in the ties of family life, that we understand such obligations and sometimes act accordingly. That is what it is to *be* a brother and it is as brothers that we are bound in this way to mutual helpfulness. What "brotherhood" would morally imply for a man who had no such emotions and "understood" moral requiredness only as he understood—say—a physical compulsion or the necessity that all triangles must have three sides we need not here inquire. For his sense of obligation would not be ours and ours, though he might accurately describe it sociologically, would have no moral significance for him. It is in this way that there is something peculiar, or distinctive, about moral obligation. If we choose, for analytic purposes, to ignore it, we may talk about something logically neater, epistemologically simpler or metaphysically deeper. But what we shall then be talking about will not be moral obligation, and we should not be surprised to find that it cannot in the end supply the moral relevance it ruled out of its calculations at the start.

"But, when we look at obligation statements in this light, what do we see?" "Don't you know? For there is nothing hidden." The "seeing" that is here required is not an intuition of self-evident (yet, in ethical theory, highly controversial) general principles of ought-to-be-doneness which are advanced, with complicated arguments, as the final grounds of moral right. It is that minimum of practical understanding required for membership in any community in which "right" can have a moral cogency for action, in which the requirements of a man's moral situation are recognized and used as grounds for warrantable claims that he is bound, as a brother, for example, or a citizen, to honor in his conduct. A man who could not in this way understand that "because you promised" was a reason why he ought to do a promised act would not know what it was to make a promise and to "bind" his conduct in this way, though he might be well aware that it was a rule of his society that sanctions of a predictable sort would be brought to bear on those who, having said "I promise", did not perform the action to which this locution was attached and think it prudent to conform his behavior to this rule. A society in which men were bound together by no other ties than this would not be the fellowship of kindred minds that gives its moral meaning to the term "community". To be *morally* bound is in this way to be tied to others in a way of life whose mutual requirements can be understood and accepted as grounds for action. Anyone who has at some time shared responsibility in such a way of life knows what it is to have an obligation and why, on the ground it specifies, there are actions that he ought to do. The "why" of moral obligation is just *this* "why" and it is in this way that it is practically to be understood. For it is thus that practical reason can be, and sometimes is, a guide of life.

It is essential to keep in mind that, as we have already seen, the action for which claims are made is never *merely* a moral action. To keep a promise, for example, is to pay a sum of money, or to keep an appointment or to make a public address when and because one has promised to do so. Stripped of the commitment thus involved and described in morally non-committal terms the "action"—paying X a sum of money—has no moral implications. It might be, in a different context, a foolish waste of money, a form of gratuitous self-advertisement, or the giving of a bribe. To describe it in morally relevant terms is already to give a reason why it ought, or ought not to be done. It is sometimes said that we need no "reason" for keeping promises, but only, in special cases, a justification or excuse for not doing so as, e.g., "I haven't got the money" or "he would only use it for bad purposes," or the like. But this is only a careless way of saying that when we describe an action as the keeping of a promise we have thereby given a moral ground for doing it. As understood and used in moral discourse an action that is the keeping of a promise is so far one that should be performed, because the agent promised. Only better reasons—it would do harm that *ought* not to be done—or excuses that show the agent to be in no position to do what, as a promisor, he ought to do, can counter or qualify the moral implication of "you promised" here. Homicide is not as such an immoral action, unless the 6th Commandment is very broadly interpreted indeed. But murder is unjustifiable homicide and as such to be condemned. The question as to whether killing foreign troops in time of war and according to the rules (such as they are) of "civilized" warfare is "murder" is not a merely verbal question. The whole issue of the justification of war turns upon it.

The description of action in morally relevant terms is thus, from the start, a morally "loaded" description. "You took his money—shame on you" can be interpreted as a statement of morally non-committal fact hitched to an "emotive" expression in such a way as to "influence" action. But "you *stole* the money" gives a reason why you merit blame, for stealing, unless on further grounds it can be justified, *is* taking money wrongly. If the "taking" was not *in this sense* "stealing" then there is so far no ground for the emotive expression to which it is non-rationally hitched. If it was *in this sense* stealing—and that is a claim to be warranted by reasons we can understand and accept as such—then no external hitching is required to make plain its normative significance. It may be that the action can still be justified—he stole from the rich to feed his starving children and this, in his desperate circumstances, was where his primary obligation lay. But such considerations themselves are here understood, *as reasons,* in exactly the same sense as the one first given, and the action, seen in all its relevantly moral aspects is the one he ought—or ought not—on such grounds to do.

It cannot be the case, of course, that he stole the money unless in fact he took it, but stealing is not simply "taking" that we happen to dislike and can persuade others to dislike as well. Nor in its moral use is it "taking" in ways that are forbidden by law, for there are circumstances in which a bad law *should* be disobeyed, and it is not on grounds of legality that we sometimes rightly judge a law to be bad. Where then does the stealing get its "ought not" status—its moral relevance to the understanding and appraisal of our actions? The answer is, I hope, by this time clear. Obligation statements have an ought or ought not to do *in* them in any case in which they have a moral sense. This, as we shall see, is not the dictate of an ironclad directive to be blindly followed without regard to any further morally relevant features of the situation in which the action is done.

It is the "why" of moral action, and it is as thus grounded that moral claims on conduct have a "must" about them for a moral agent. What are morally relevant considerations here? They are those which warrantably function in this way as grounds of obligation. Unless they are so understood and used we have no moral reasons for our actions. In this use they are the kind of reasons that can relevantly answer questions of moral right and wrong. And so far as we have learned in the various communities in which we share, to act, for moral purposes, responsibly and well, we do thus understand and use them.

I have said so far that moral reasons are grounds of obligation. It is time now to develop the complementary and no less basic truth that obligations in this use are reasons and must be used as such if they are to do this justifying work. Feelings of constraint, or guilt, or disgust or benevolence or crusading zeal will not do it. And if "conscience" is a name for this kind of compulsive feeling, then conscience is not a trustworthy guide to morally right action. Such feelings are the raw material with which practical reason works and if we did not have them we should not be moral agents. A man who was never angry at injustice or pitiful of suffering or ashamed of failure to meet his responsibility to family or friends would be for, moral purposes, a half-hearted sort of man. Spinoza's attempt to purge us "rationally", or geometrically, of such feelings was an experiment "noble in purpose" which, like prohibition, was bound to fail, and *ought* to fail. For it is the whole man, not just his "reason", that is moral. There is a right way of being angry or afraid just as there is a right way of paying money, and the discipline of the emotions would be self-defeating if it ended by becoming their negation.

But the right way of being angry is not to be reliably discovered by indulging in an anger that *feels* righteous. Nor are we always genuinely guilty when we feel so. Feelings are personal and private and may be caused in a variety of ways not all of which are pertinent to the merits of a moral issue. Reasons are public essentially; they must be *common* grounds for action if they are warrantably to be grounds at all, and it is in the establishment of such community of understanding that they prove their cogency as reasons. All reasons are in *this* sense universal, that if they are valid grounds for one man's actions they *must* be no less so for any other man whose situation is, in all morally relevant circumstances, the same. It is only when we are willing to consider the justifications that we offer for our conduct in this light that we are considering them *as* reasons at all, and not merely as self-righteous slogans that express our feelings and may be used to inflame or intimidate others. To achieve this objectivity about the grounds we offer for our claims is itself a considerable moral achievement. And the community to which they are addressed as grounds of justification is not easily achieved. For only those who are prepared in this way to be reasonable can thus reach an understanding on issues of right or wrong. A man who will not listen to reasons cannot expect to be convinced by them. And to "listen" to reasons here is not just a matter of keeping silent while others vocalize their appetites and aversions. It requires self-control and understanding and good will, for all these are a part of reason in its practical use. Feelings of obligation, of being bound, or pushed or constrained, that cannot be brought to this level of understanding justify nothing, though they may explain, and perhaps in pathological circumstances excuse the behavior of those who are obsessed by them. He feels so strongly about racial discrimination *because* he is a Jew. I can, in a sense, "understand" this feeling. It is natural in the circumstances and I can sympathize with it. The Irish, too, have suffered from such discrimination. But if he and I are to reach an understanding on the merits of the case that will make moral sense not only for indignant Jews and Irishmen but for all responsibly concerned with "fair employment" practices in America, we shall need another sort of "because" than this to *warrant* action whose rightness is to be a "must" for reasonable men within the community in which it claims a moral cogency. A moral indignation not thus warranted by the requirements of the situation in which we are called on to act responsibly together may be in fact sheer emotional self-indulgence that blocks the work of understanding just where it is needed most.

An inner right needs an outer warrant if its cogency as right is to be rationally maintained. No demand for action is moralized merely by being internalized. The commands a man gives himself and the punishment he inflicts upon himself may be quite as arbitrary and immoral as those that others impose on him. It is the kind of man he is that counts for moral purposes. The responsible moral agent is a man who does not make his inner feelings and compulsions the measure of right action but is prepared to base his claims on reasons that can be common grounds for all who are willing to deal fairly with the basic issues of the way of life in which they are mutually involved. If "moral sense" as an inner persuasion is to *make* sense as providing grounds of obligation for right action, its deliverances must be understood and used *as reasons,* and it is as thus public that they are rationally so used.

Obligations, we have said, are reasons. And it is no less important to be clear that in the solution of our moral problems they are *only* reasons, not directives to perform in all circumstances certain kinds of action that are universally required of us. If I have promised to perform an action then this is, in any circumstances to which the promise would apply, a ground of obligation, a reason why I ought to do the promised act and, in default of stronger moral reasons to the contrary, a sufficient reason. Promises ought to be kept. Anyone who can understand what it is to make a promise knows that and a decent man will, in normal circumstances, act accordingly without pondering or moral struggles. He has a reason why he ought to keep his promise and that is, precisely, that he made the promise. But the action which is the keeping of a promise is never *merely* that. It is, e.g., the keeping of an appointment which may, in the circumstances, be something that, in the situation that has now arisen, he has good reasons not to do. It may be that to keep the appointment he would have to risk the safety not only of himself but of others for whose well-being he is responsible. And that is something that, unless he has good reasons to the contrary, he ought not to do. Which obligation in the circumstances should prevail is an authentic moral problem, and it is not reasonably or rightly settled by invoking the principle that "a promise is a promise". That kind of moral simple-mindedness is on a level with Calvin Coolidge's solution to the problem of the Allied war debts after the First World War: "They hired the money, didn't they?" *Of course,* other things being equal, those who borrow money ought to pay it, but the question that any man of practical good sense must ask here is whether, on *moral* grounds, other things are equal. If moral rules are understood as unconditional commands, we are here in the tragic situation of being faced with conflicting moral imperatives, each of which requires unconditional obedience and is thus a "must" for action. We are damned if we do and damned if we don't, for here neither action can be the right one because each violates a categorical prescription for right conduct. It is not surprising that those who take this line are led to say that the solution of moral problems transcends rational morality.

One way out of this moral dilemma is to say that the rules of ordinary morality are not thus categorical. Exceptions to them are allowable. But there must then be a higher rule, or general prescription, on the ground of which such exceptions are rightly made. Since the moral laws *must* be universal, i.e., unconditionally applicable in all situations, there must be a principle that has this kind of generality, and our ultimate moral problem is to find it. This might be done by including in the law itself all allowable exceptions. Promises are always to be kept unless— with a list of all allowable exceptions. This is the way of legalism, and in the administration of the law it has its uses. But for moral purposes it is both theoretically and practically futile. The complexity of specific situations is such that no list of exceptions, drawn up in advance, will actually cover all morally questionable cases. As Bergson well said, there is no general rule that will spare us the trouble, and the responsibility, of thinking in particular cases. But the more fundamental question is that of how the exceptions, the "unlesses", are got into the rule in the first place. Here somebody must make a judgment on what the exceptions ought to be, even if it is then left for the rest of us to follow them as rules of thumb, and it is not by looking up more general instructions in his moral rule book that he can do this. When *ought* such exceptions to be made? Who's to judge? And, more fundamentally, *how* is he to judge? A reference to rules as directives, however elaborate, will not answer these questions.

The other and more drastic alternative is to discover an imperative to which, on moral grounds, there can be no exception and which is thus, in principle, unqualified. Such a principle, in its intention, was Kant's categorical imperative "Act only according to that maxim by which you can at the same time will that it should become a universal law." Whatever may be said on other grounds of Kant's ethical theory, which we shall later have occasion to consider in detail, it obviously will not help us here. For the categorical imperative in this use is a second-order principle, a rule about the rules that are rationally to be accepted as objective moral principles and on which, accordingly, we can rightly act. The imperative is unqualified but, as it stands, it has no practical content. Unless there are first order maxims that can with practical rationality thus be willed universally, we are as much in the dark as ever as to how, on moral grounds, we are to act. Our difficulty was that we seemed to find no such maxims. For there appeared to be cases in which the unconditional application of any of them would lead to morally wrong action. And if none can rightly be willed universally, then the imperative to follow only those that can seems to leave us with no rule to follow. So far from resolving our difficulty, it serves rather to intensify it. It disqualifies all moral maxims as principles of right conduct by demanding of them, in their moral use, an unconditional generality which their rational cogency does not warrant. Taught and used with practical good sense, "Thou shalt not lie" is an excellent and basic moral maxim. Inflated to the status of an unconditional directive, a "right" entitled to prevail in all circumstances and at all costs, it is questionable on moral grounds. Yet it is only in this inflated status that the categorical imperative allows it any moral standing. The consequences of this way of thinking speak for themselves in Kant's well-known essay "On the Supposed Right to Lie from Altruistic Motives."

But surely, there is one moral principle that has, as such, unqualified validity. "Always do your duty" or "always do morally right actions", is a prescription to which there is no morally allowable exception. Of course, I ought to do my duty, i.e., I ought to do what I ought to do. Who could deny it, or would wish to do so? "Let justice prevail, though the heavens fall." But a justice that would require the falling of the heavens for its consummation would, save in extremely unlikely cases, be a very witless kind of justice. How can we tell what justice *is* in any morally usable sense, until we know what its application would mean in the lives of those who were asked to submit to it? And how are we to weight claims based on justice against others which would, in this catastrophic instance, be highly relevant? An appeal to the letter of the law of "justice" will not answer these questions, and until it is rightly answered we shall not know what is morally right in the specific situation and what therefore, with tautological necessity, we ought to do. My obligation as a judge, or an administrator of justice, is cogent and authentic, but it is not the whole of my duty as a moral agent, and to cling to it as a model of rectitude without regard to such further obligations as may in particular cases be relevant to the action to be done is a kind of righteousness that only the moral fanaticism of the willfully simpleminded can "rationally" approve. *Of course* I ought to do what I ought to do. Anyone who is not a moral moron knows that, though not all act accordingly. But what *is* it that I ought to do? To this the reply "always do your duty", if my duty is to do what I ought to do, is not a helpful answer.

The point here is that "ought" and "morally right" and "duty", as applied to action, are warranting words. They claim a special normative status for the actions to which they are validly applied as binding on the will of moral agents. To characterize an action as my duty is to challenge me to consider it in this light. It indicates the kind of reason that would be pertinent to support its normative pretensions, but it does not itself supply such reasons. As it stands, there is a blank in it to be filled in by a more specific reference to the grounds on which the claim is made. It is your duty to help this man *because* he is your brother and needs help. If this is all that there is to it, well and good. Any man who knows what it is morally to be a brother will understand such a claim. It is *a* reason why he should do the act in question. But there may be other reasons, no less relevant, why he should not. Perhaps he has helped his brother before, and with little good effect, and in this case is entitled to give first consideration to his own interests. Moral obligations are reasons, but they are *only* reasons, not unqualified commands, and to interpret them as such is to dodge the responsibility for finding out what, in a morally complex situation, specifically is right. The self-righteousness of those who, in a dispute on moral issues, in this way hurl at each other the reasons that support their cause as categorical imperatives while refusing to recognize the grounds that others have for characterizing the disputed action in a different way is a familiar case of this kind of obscurantism.

When the warranting status of "ought" and "duty" for action is divorced from the grounds that warrant its pretensions, we reach in the end a morality of unconditional commands. The morally right like any other right has a "because" in it, and when it is made its own "because" it becomes at once empty and unwarrantably pretentious. "You must because you must." Some content must be found for this unconditional directive. If we look for it in some particular obligation what we get is an ironclad directive which is in specific cases morally arbitrary. If we seek it in the form of universal law itself we rob it of all moral content. If we resort to the tautology that right actions are always right we are none the wiser. It is not in this way that the hard, important work of being practically reasonable in the meeting of our obligations is reliably done. The reasons which adequately warrant the doing of an act as a moral duty also and intrinsically specify the conditions in which it is to be done, for it is *in* the light of all these morally relevant conditions that it *is* right and as such that it has a rationally cogent claim upon our will as moral agents. An "unconditional" morality in this sense would be an irrational morality.

And this, in fact, is what it "finally" explicitly becomes. For if there are no grounds *in* morality for the "demanding" status of its "ought", then a different sort of reason must be found outside it to make it give its claims a "hold" upon a will that would not know a moral reason if it saw one. Why should I do "right" actions? If this question is raised in the process of trying to find out what is right and whether what is presented in that status really has the moral authority that is claimed for it, it is answered by the reasons that show the action to be right. When I know *why* the action is right I know why, on moral grounds, I ought to do it, and until I know such grounds for it I do not know that it is right. In *this sense* the "why?" of right and duty is intrinsic to the work of moral justification itself, which would lose all normative cogency without it. To say "yes, I can see that this action is right but why am I obligated to do it?" is absurd, for I could not see it to be right (though I might submissively call it so on someone else's say so) without seeing the moral grounds for doing it. And they, precisely, are the answer to this "why?" It may, of course, take further persuasions to "motivate" me to do the act in question, but these will not be moral grounds and for them no other "why" than that of causal efficacy is required. If, however, the moral ought is cut off from its own *intrinsic* reasons, then as it stands it is normatively and morally incomplete and requires a justification that both must be and cannot be a moral justification. It must be, since without it the moral status of the ought reduces to an unwarrantable pretension and there is no justification *in* morality. It cannot be, since such a theory has no moral grounds to give—its categorical imperatives cannot in this way be at once qualified and supported. We must then appeal to the pressures and persuasions of the sub-moral or the higher edicts of the Super-moral before which, as Bradley said, morality "in the end" must prostrate itself. We cannot expect, on moral grounds, to understand them. In theories of this sort the sub- and super-moral are sometimes hard to distinguish. It is clear at least that the distinction cannot be made on moral grounds.

As against this, we have maintained that if moral obligations are understood and used as reasons we can make practical and justifying sense of claims made, in their terms, on our conduct. This is not, of course, the whole truth of the matter. Even if it is accepted, the hardest problems of moral judgment, which are precisely those of weighing reasons for and against specific actions, still confront us. And *moral* right and wrong are by no means the whole of normatively significant human action. That truth has already been emphasized, but since in this chapter we have been concerned with specifically moral issues, it is perhaps advisable to reiterate it for the benefit of those critics who assume that whatever is not mentioned at some particular stage in a philosophical discussion is thereby ignored or even denied. Morality, in its stringent sense of "ought" and "duty" is but one aspect of practical experience and one that could not possibly exist alone. It draws its resources and its reasons from a wider world and uses them for purposes which are never merely moral. But it is an essential and distinctive aspect and we literally should not be ourselves without it. Right answers to its questions will hardly supply us with a solution to the riddle of the Universe —if there is a riddle. It will be sufficient for our purposes if we can understand what its questions are and what would be a relevant and cogent answer to them. We need such answers in the right conduct of our lives, and a perennial unclarity in moral philosophy is one contributing cause, though by no means the only one, of our failure so far to obtain them.

There is, however, one familiar difficulty that should be dealt with at once, since as it stands it appears to cast serious doubt on the empirical applicability of our account and since, in dealing with it, we shall, I think, be able to lay some ghosts that still haunt current ethical theory. Moral reasons, we have said, are significantly addressed to a moral agent. It is *for* such an agent that they are practical reasons, i.e., reasons for doing something, not merely for thinking or believing that something is the case, and as in this way practical that they have a normative function in our conduct. But does not this involve a confusion between two different sorts of reason? Obligations are, no doubt, *justifying* reasons; they provide the grounds on which we can truthfully affirm an action to be right. But they are not always motivating reasons. They do not *necessarily* provide the push that moves us to action. As Frankena has observed: "We are not so constituted as always to want to do what we recognize as objectively right."[1] "The record of human conduct is not such as to make it obvious that human beings always do have some tendency to do what they regard as their duty."[2] It would indeed be psychologically odd if we were never moved by a recognition of duty, based on justifying reasons, to perform actions which we regard as right, and moral suasion would, in such a case, be practically pointless. But while this is often, or perhaps even usually, the case, "it ain't necessarily so." It is at least logically possible that there should be a psychological gap between seeing one's duty and being moved to act accordingly. In such a case our justifying reasons are not sufficient motivating reasons for action and, if the psychological gap between knowing and doing is to be filled, appeal must be made to motivating reasons of a different sort—such "reasons" presumably as will make us want to do what, on the ground of justifying reasons, we regard as right.

There is indeed some confusion here, though not, I think, where the critic thinks he finds it. What, in this use, is a justifying reason supposed to justify? Apparently, the assertion or belief that an action is objectively right. It offers evidence that what is asserted is in fact the case. And the assumption is that it is at least logically possible for a man to assess such evidence, and, on the ground it offers, to "regard an action as his duty" without having any tendency at all to do the action thus regarded. He *might* in this way regard an action as his duty and be quite indifferent to the doing of it. It would be "psychologically odd" if this were the case, i.e., it is not the sort of thing that usually happens. But since justification is one thing and motivation,

---

1 "Obligation and Motivation," in *Essays in Moral Philosophy*, ed. A. I. Melden (Seattle: University of Washington Press, 1958) p. 79.
2 *Ibid.*

logically, quite another, it *could* happen. And the record of human conduct shows us that it sometimes does. Such is the conceptual framework within which the critic works, and in whose terms he warns us against confusing justifying with motivating reasons.

Obviously, this rendering of the situation is just our old acquaintance, "cognitivism", on the job again, and with expectable results. The motivationally non-commital "regard" with which "I regard an action as my duty" is here supposed to be the same in principle as that with which I regard an object as ten feet tall or electrically charged, when I assert it to possess these properties. It may be pointed out, of course, that being a duty is a peculiar (non-natural?) sort of property. It has "should-be-doneness" built into it. The action in which it inheres might be described as a normatively charged action. What of it? If I happen to want, for some further reason or for no reason at all, to do normatively charged or should-be-done actions, the discovery that it has this property will provide me with a motivating reason for doing it. If not, not. It is logically quite possible to understand and accept the cogency of the justifying reasons that show it to have this property, and thus, with cognitive conviction, to "regard it as my duty", with complete motivational indifference as to the doing or not doing of the action.

But this, as we have seen, is practically absurd. A man thus indifferent to the right and wrong of actions would not know a justifying reason as a ground for action if he saw one. For him, to "regard an action as his duty" would make no moral sense. The point is not that he would have justifying reasons but no motivating reasons but that, so far, he would have no justifying reasons, the kind of reasons needed to show an action to be right. He could "regard an action as a duty" in the sense of recognizing, perhaps with complete practical indifference, that it had the traits by which an action is socially identified as "right".

And, if his inner eye were trained in a priori seeing, he might in some way "see" the property of objective rightness face to face. What he could never in this way "see" is how such rightness bound him as a moral agent to the performance of the action in question, whether on other grounds, or no grounds at all, he happened to want to do it. He could not understand why he ought to do it. For this is the practical understanding of a moral agent and without some concern (or "motivation") to act rightly, he would not be a moral agent.

The cognitivist's talk of justifying reasons, of objective rightness, and of duty, borrows its sense from a context in which as morally (and immorally) motivated beings we are inextricably involved. It is as addressed to beings thus concerned that justifying reasons can make normatively cogent sense. A reason that was not *in this way* a "motivating" reason would not be a morally justifying reason either. There are indeed justifications that do not motivate and motivations that have no concern for justification. But the situation in which justifying reasons make moral sense is one in which the motivation that is practically relevant is a concern for justification and the point of the justification is to guide right action. A moral agent motivationally indifferent to the issues of right and wrong would not be a psychological oddity, for the same sort of reason that a round square is not a geometrical oddity. It is as idle to look to experience to supply specimens of the one as of the other. Only a moral agent *can* (a logical 'can') regard an action as his duty in any morally relevant and practically cogent sense of that term. And such an agent, when he understands an action to be his duty, has a "motivating reason" for its performance.

A man can regard an action as his duty and still be unwilling to do it. Interest (based on motivating reasons that are not morally justifying reasons) may conflict with duty, or be brought in, where it proves insufficient, to provide the further incentive needed to "move" him into action. Of course. We are all familiar with such cases. The question is not whether or not they occur but how we are to understand and to appraise them. And here the plain fact is that if the "cognitivist" were right there could be no such conflict or support. To regard an action as a duty in this motivationally non-committal sense in no way conflicts with a practical refusal to perform it. If I happen to want to perform objectively right acts—if I have an appetite for should-be-done-ness—justifying reasons will be practically relevant as showing me which actions have this property. But they will in just the same way be useful for a man who does not want to do his duty and whose practical concern in identifying should-be-done acts is to avoid them whenever possible. The cognitive recognition of the action as a duty is, on this interpretation, as compatible with the one use as the other. Here, at least, Hume was surely right. Such a cognition by itself moves nothing, and cannot be in conflict with any motive for action whatsoever, for it has no push of its own with which to support or to oppose "the influencing motives of the will." Here the problem is not to understand how it is that justifying reasons sometimes fail as motivating reasons, but rather to make sense of the notion that, as justifying, they could ever motivate at all. For their justifying cogency consists in the evidence they provide that the action has, or does not have, the objective property in question and when that fact is established the motivational question is still, in principle, as open as before. If "regarding an action as a duty" commits us practically to nothing, it can conflict with no other commitment, or concern, or passion we may happen to have. The "calm" passion of wanting to do my duty may conflict with the more violent passions of anger or greed, but as a passion, the one is no more justified or justifiable than the other. And so long as their struggle for motivational supremacy does not lead us to false beliefs as to what is or is not objectively right, there is no way in which even the most violent of them could conflict with that cognitive regarding of an action as a duty which it is, on this interpretation, the business of justifying reasons to support.

The puzzling fact, for those who argue in this way, is that it does so often lead to such beliefs. It is not difficult to understand why a man with an appetite for should-be-doneness should want to know which actions truly have this property. And so, equally, for those who wish to avoid it. Surely neither would wish to be deceived on this (for him) important matter. But about the rightness of our actions we do sometimes want to deceive not only others but ourselves. It is hard for a man who understands the language of moral justification well enough to be concerned at all with justifying reasons to admit that he knows an action to be wrong but proposes nonetheless to do it. It is much easier to try to convince others, and himself, that it is not really wrong, though the conventional, or pious, or those with an idealogical axe to grind may so regard it. Only Satan, in *Paradise Lost*, has the temerity to say "Evil, be thou my good." And he goes on to try to show that this "evil" is *really* good, in the situation in which the fallen angels find themselves. Even "demonic" perversions of moral right borrow their persuasive sense from a language in which "good" is a justifying word. Only an "evil" that is in some way good and a "wrong" that is, in the circumstances, and perhaps in a "higher" sense, "right", can be proposed as a practical end of action. The appetite for should-be-doneness, or at least the appearance of it, seems oddly tenacious, even in Hell. And in the cold war of the current international struggle for power it plays a major part. Our public "image" is hardly less important than our military "posture", and if we are to maintain our status in the "free world", our image must be good.

Evidently both motivating and justifying reasons are here elements in a more complex and subtle structure than the analyst has been able to discern. The hunger and thirst after righteousness that can move a man to seek for justifying reasons for his conduct and offer them as grounds for action is not an appetite for the somewhat esoteric property of should-be-doneness, fighting it out for supremacy with other appetites for the motivational control of conduct. It is bound up with his integrity as a self, or practical agent, and it is as a self that he can have justifying reasons for any action at all. To regard an action as a duty *is*, for such a self, to have a "motivating reason" for doing it, for this "motivation" is already present in the recognition of it as a duty. But "motivation" here is not just a bait for appetites; it is the commitment of a self, for reasons, to actions held to be worth doing and, in the agent's situation, the right ones to perform. That, of course, is why it is so important to us to make our actions *look* right, even if in fact they are not. A man who can significantly talk of morally justifying reasons and of duty can live acceptably with others, and himself, on no other terms than these. This motivation is a categorial requirement for the practical use of the language in which morally "justifying reasons" have a justifying sense, and if justifying reasons as reasons "motivate" at all, it is *for* such a self, and within a way of life thus structured, that they do so.

Yet a man may "see" his duty and still not do it—or do it only when additional, non-moral incentives have been offered. Indeed he may. For the moral self is not the whole man, and no actual man is merely or completely such a self. *In so far as* he has this capacity and concern he has a motive for so acting, but he has other concerns and interests also and these will often make it hard for him to do what he regards as right. And frequently he will not do it. These other concerns, however, do not operate externally upon him as appetitive competitors for motivational control. They must somehow borrow the color of righteousness, or the odor of sanctity, if they are to bear the light of public scrutiny and be recognized as *his* reasons for so acting. Hence, the peculiarly twisted and contorted nature of moral evil. The moral conflict is not between appetites seeking information (including information about should-be-doneness) but between false "goods" and true, where the false must present themselves *as* true if they are to maintain their hold upon the will of men who know what it means to ask for justifying reasons for an action. There is endless room here for deception and for self-deception. But unless this concern for justification were present throughout, there would be no point in the deception and no practical sense in the misuse of justifying reasons. The irrationality of a moral agent—and we are often thus irrational—is not the non-rationality of appetites that need and could in principle have no other "justification" than that of their occurrence or nonoccurrence. It is that of a will that perverts and misuses reasons to "justify" conduct that needs the sanction of a justification if it is to be willingly performed. With this aspect of the self and its agency we shall deal more fully in the next chapter. What is here essential is to see that so far from implying a psychological gap between justifying and motivating reasons, it shows the complex nature of their mutual involvement in moral action. As addressed to men concerned to justify their actions, justifying reasons are *so far* motivating reasons, and it is only in this way that they can, as reasons, have a practical bearing on our conduct. We do not always act on the terms they set, but if we had no tendency so to act, this kind of justification, as a guide to conduct, would have for us no sense. What sense it could then retain as a source of information about the normatively charged properties of actions the reader may be left, by this time, to judge for himself.

Does this mean that the man who is wholly indifferent to obligations *has* no obligations and is not to be held morally responsible for what he does? Yes. This may seem initially a drastic saying but all practical good sense supports it. Such a man would be not a moral agent but a moral idiot—he would have neither the concern nor the competence to act on moral grounds and considerations of moral right and wrong addressed to him or offered in appraisal of his conduct would be as irrelevant as attempts to carry on a conversation with a tree. We do not blame a tree for its taciturnity, though we may wish, or some occasions, that it could be more communicative. The difference of course is that we do not really expect such behavior of trees, while we do expect it of men, not as a prediction, merely, but in the sense in which England expects every man to do his duty. Some measure of such concern and competence is a must for adequate participation in all those human activities in which we trust others and ask for their trust in return, and we are reluctant to believe that in any human being it is wholly absent. Such trust is often misplaced, and there are obvious limits to its reliable application. But if it were always misplaced the activities in which it can sometimes be misplaced would cease to function, for no one would trust anyone else. If there are men, like us in other respects, who wholly lack this capacity they must for practical pusposes be dealt with in other ways. We do not trust an alcoholic to keep his promise of abstinence and it would be morally idle to blame him for his failure to do so. He is not, in his condition, a man who can make a promise, though he may use with fervor the words that are normally appropriate in so doing. He must be "treated" in another way. And if we were all in this respect in the condition of the alcoholic, moral judgments would have no relevance to our conduct. Happily this is not the case. And hence it is to us the moral reasons, as ground of obligation, are significantly addressed. We often do not use them as we ought, but it is in the confidence that our fellows can rightly understand and use them that we can work with them as partners in a way of life that is in fact a moral *modus vivendi*. In this humble sense it is literally true that the just shall live by faith, for without this kind of faith there could be no practice in which "justice" as we understand it, had a moral use.

The practical point of such shared activities, as we have seen, is the attainment of goods that only in such activities are possible to man. Moral requirements make practical sense as requirements *for* the preservation of that level of mutual understanding, helpfulness, and respect which is the normative condition for the attainment of such goods. To understand the cogency of moral reasons, as grounds of obligation, in this light is not to substitute a non-moral "why" for the "why" of moral justification. On the contrary, it is just by being in their own right the justification that, on moral grounds, was sought that moral reasons can perform this practically essential function. Rightly used, they do their own justifying work, and only a man who can understand and accept them in this light can use them rightly. But it does help us to see the importance of being justified, the unique and irreplaceable part it has in any and all activities that make practical sense and can have a normatively significant fulfilment. We could not be ourselves without it.

But what *as* selves, the agents in all practical activity, are we? So far we have said much of the nature and requirements of right action, but not much, save incidentally, of the nature and the worth of the agents who perform them. And our account is accordingly so far inadequate. For practical judgments are appraisals not merely of performances, or of actions, but of persons, as the doers of their deeds. A man's character is at least as important to us as his actions, and one of the most important things about his actions is that they in some way shed light upon his character or nature or person. In one sense moral values are minimal values, for they are those attained in maintaining the conditions in human activity without which other goods would not be possible. But in another sense they are among the highest values that we know. The rightness of actions rightly done bears witness to the worth of agents as persons, and these personal values are not merely conditions for others of a different sort; they constitute a kind of fulfilment that is, as Kant said, "beyond price". Current talk of the "dignity of man" is frequently either empty or misapplied, but its misuse does not obscure the fact that it is a great thing that men do sometimes achieve in their own persons that rectitude of purpose and of conduct which makes them authentically worthy of our respect. Moral virtue cannot be the only reward of right action, since if moral action were not a requirement for the right attainment of other goods, there would be no virtue in it. But its attainment is *a* reward (provided always that it is not sought as such) and one without which our lives would be far emptier than they are. Those who hunger and thirst after righteousness are blessed, and this blessedness is not a private possession merely, but an excellence we all can honor, for it is a fulfilment of the authentic worth of man.

And just as a consideration of the practical and moral self can disclose a priceless worth, so can it reveal depths of frustration and depravity that our discussion so far would hardly have led us to expect. A morally "sick" self is capable of evil that is by no means that of a mere miscalculation of goods. This sort of "sickness" has in recent times become a major preoccupation of our culture. The Freudians diagnose it in one way, the Existentialists in another, but both appear to agree that in our human situation it is rationally incurable. "Irrational man" cannot be saved by "reason"—if indeed he can be saved at all. It is thus within the self that the gravest challenge to the claims of rational morality is at present to be found. And it is there that we are now, I think, prepared to meet it.

CHAPTER 6
THE MORAL SELF
IN SICKNESS AND IN HEALTH

WHAT IS A SELF? Or, more sensibly, what is it for a man to be a self and to act and to be understood as such? We distinguish a man's self from his body—there are movements of his body that are not his actions, since he was in no position to control or direct them. Yet, in the sphere of human relations at least, we find it difficult to imagine the actions of a disembodied self. And there are things that go on in a man that are not his doing. They happen to him as e.g., in delirium or under hypnosis he behaves in ways for which, as a self, he is not accountable. Even in more normal cases we make a similar distinction. "I was not myself when I spoke to you last night. I was too tired, or drunk, or disturbed to know what I was doing." And we ask that our behavior be excused accordingly. The acceptability of such excuses will depend on our notion of what it is for a man to be and to act as a self.

There are interesting metaphysical theories of the "true" nature of the self as a transcendent or transcendental ego, presupposed by our experience but not present in it, or as a bundle of sensations related in the peculiar way that is called being "owned" by a self, though there is, of course, no self to own them, or as a fiction that a misunderstanding of our language has misled us into treating as a fact. The self of such speculation may indeed be a fiction. But the self of responsible action is a practical reality, and no language has yet been invented, or is likely to be, in which we can understand each other morally without recurrent reference to it. It is with this self that we are here concerned. Our aim is not to find a place for it in the ultimate furniture of the Universe, or to analyze it out of ultimate existence, but simply to make the kind of sense of our talk about it that will enable us to understand the import and to appraise the truth of normatively cogent statements in which a reference to it has an indispensible role.

We are already familiar with this reference to the self as the agent in practical doing, the man who does the deeds whose sense as practical and whose worth as right or wrong we are concerned to understand. It is to such an agent that considerations of normative cogency with respect to action are meaningfully addressed and by his action in this role or capacity that his character is relevantly judged. The self thus referred to is not a transcendental ego or a bundle of sensations—how could the latter understand or the former do anything of practical significance? He is John Smith or Henry Robinson, the bodily being that we sometimes see before us, with all his appetites and affections and fears about him; the son of one man and, sometimes, the brother of another, called on to act rightly in a world he never made but can sometimes change for the better in assignable ways if he has the sense and the will to do so. But he is this man acting *in* a certain role and capacity, *as* a responsible agent on whom some demands can reasonably be made and of whom a decent level of response can fairly be expected. It is in this light that he understands himself when he asks honestly what he ought to do, and in this light that we understand him when we appraise his conduct as a self or person. As a first approximation we may say that a man is acting as a self or agent in those areas of his conduct of which the "why" of justification, as we have so far understood it, can relevantly be asked. "Why did you hit that defenseless man?" "I didn't mean to hit him. Somebody pushed my arm and it struck him. It all happened so fast that there was nothing *I* could do about it." It would be proper to say that in this case John Jones struck the man, but it was not as a self but only as a body that he did it. Perhaps he should have taken some precautions against the occurrence of this kind of accident, but these, if a "should" is legitimately attached to them, are not just bodily movements but actions there was a reason for doing and that he could and should have done accordingly. For these, as a self, he is responsible; for the doings for which a man is practically responsible are those which, in this capacity, he does. The judgment of responsibility is simply the assignment of such agency—*he* did it and can reasonably be asked to give an account of himself accordingly. If the circumstances were such that his behavior was not, and could not fairly be expected to be, in this way an action, he is excused for a failure that is not his fault. If, however, it was as a self and "of his own will and volition" that he acted, then the why of justification, of his grounds for acting as he did, significantly arises, and it is in the light of the worth of his action as thus done that his conduct and character as a self are relevantly understood. A man who behaves badly in this role or capacity is not merely ineffectual, unfortunate or inept. He is a person whom we cannot trust to meet his obligations with the practical concern and competence required for membership in a community in which men rightly share the responsibilities and rewards of a common way of life. He is thus defective *as a person,* and this deficiency is imputed to him as a defect of character, since the character he bears in such transactions is what as a self he is. This is not a question of the utility of assigning punishments or rewards that may better help *us* to control his conduct in the future. It is a question of the nature of his action and of his character as a practical and moral agent, of the way that he controls himself, and it is on a valid answer to it that any just claim to reward or retribution must be based. It might, in imaginable circumstances, be socially useful to inflict harm on good men for right actions and "reward" bad men for evil-doing. But a decision on this point could not possibly answer the question as to whether or not the men were good and their actions right. And a society that could not make this distinction, for which the only "practical" issue here was that of the social usefulness of rewards and punishments, would be one in which the moral distinctions between right and wrong no longer had a meaning. There have been nations in our own time which seem to come perilously close to this, but the continued use in them of an ideologically moral language would seem to indicate a residual need for a kind of justification that their actual procedures failed to honor.

It is then, to actions done, or not done, for a reason, and to men whose doing can in this way be relevantly understood and appraised that the categories of practical agency significantly apply. And the self, in practice, is the man *as agent* acting in this role. It is as such that he is practically responsible as the doer of his deeds and can meaningfully be, or fail to be, himself in what he does. Moral agency and responsibility are simply practical agency and responsibility in those aspects of our conduct in which specifically moral requirements provide the relevantly cogent grounds for action. To the extent to which we act in this capacity we are all at some time and to some degree moral agents. We are never *merely* such, for if we were, if our reasons for doing were not rooted in our needs and concerns as wanting, loving and competing human beings, we should have nothing to be practical *about*. We learn to understand and accept the normative requirements of such agency as we learn to share responsibly in the practices in which the distinction between right and wrong doing makes a practical difference in what we do. And it is in this process that we—John Smith and Henry Robinson and you and I—become selves in the sense in which that term is here employed. Such selfhood is not a gift of nature, though the capacity under favorable conditions, to achieve it is. It is an achievement, and none of us ever wholly makes the grade. "Man is not yet a self." But while he is not fully the self he ought to be, it is only for the self that, to some degree, he is, that this "ought" makes sense and can have a normative significance. Only a self can reproach itself for not being such a self. This sounds like existential double talk (or "dialectic") but in the context of our practical activity it makes experiential sense.

It will be at once objected that this account of the practical self is "too rationalistic." It does not take account of the irrational elements in the self and, more particularly, in "the will". If man were all appetite plus reason we might expect that at the level of such selfhood his only problem would be to discover that good in which his nature as a rationally wanting being is appropriately fulfilled and the most practically effective means of going after it. If human nature is thus understood then, as Socrates maintained in the *Protagoras,* "To prefer evil to good is not in human nature; and when a man is compelled to choose one of two evils, no one will choose the greater when he may have the less." If we go wrong in our choices it must be through that ignorance which is a mistaken estimate of goods. Once the good is known the rational man cannot but prefer it, for it is as a greater good or a lesser evil that he prefers one thing to another in so far as he is rational, and it is as rational that, as a practical agent, he is himself. But surely there is something missing here. It is possible for a man to know the better and nonetheless to prefer the worse, and to do it. We find this possibility actualized, if not in the conduct of others, then at least, in some familiar cases, in our own. To know the good is one thing; to do it of one's own will and volition something else. Once the facts (even if they be facts about 'the good') are known, the self as agent must decide whether or not he *will* act accordingly. The will expressed in such decision is as much a factor in the conduct of the self as agent as his reason, and while it is, in one sense, a tautology to say that reason must be rational, to affirm that will must be so seems empirically false. The will is as such non-rational, just because it is will and not reason, and may be anti-rational, irrational and arbitrary in its actual decisions. Hence the stage is set for that internal conflict between "will" and "reason", between thought and action (since it is *as* willing that we act) or between the head and the heart which has seemed to many to reveal the deepest truth about our practical and moral nature. The self is neither merely rational nor irrational. It is a contradictory combination of the two (hence 'dialectical') and desperate remedies must be invoked if this contradiction is to be practically resolved and the sick (internally divided) self made spiritually whole.

A classic example of this sort of criticism is that of Kierkegaard in *The Sickness Unto Death*. It will repay our careful consideration. There is, he holds, a dialectical determinant which the Socratic definition of wrong doing (or as Kierkegaard prefers to call it, "sin") lacks. This determinant is will, defiant will. Ideally the transition from understanding what is good to doing it is, for the rational man, accomplished by necessity—

> In the world of reality, on the other hand, where it is a question of the individual man, there is this little, tiny transition from having understood to doing. . . . In the life of the spirit . . . there is no stopping . . . in case then a man the very second he has known what is right does not do it—well, then, first of all the knowledge stops boiling. And next comes the question how the will likes this thing

that is known. If it does not like it, it does not follow that the will goes ahead and does the opposite of that which the intelligence understood, such strong contrasts doubtless occur rather seldom; but the will lets some time pass, there is an interim that means, 'We'll see about that to-morrow.' All this while the intelligence becomes more and more obscured, and the lower nature triumphs more and more. For, alas, the good must be done at once—at once, the moment it is known (and hence the transition goes so easily in the pure ideality where everything is 'at once') but the strength of the lower nature consists in dragging the thing out. The will has no particular objection to it—so it says with its fingers crossed. And then, when the intelligence has become duly darkened, the intelligence and the will can understand one another better; at last they agree entirely, for the intelligence has gone over to the side of the will and acknowledges that the thing is quite right as it would have it.[1]

Most of us, I think, can recognize the empirical truthfulness of this description.

Socrates says, then, that we do wrong because we are ignorant. Kierkegaard replies that in such matters we are *willfully* ignorant, and that the "sin" lies therefore in the will. "Sin does not consist in the fact that man does not understand what is right, but in the fact that he will not understand it, and in the fact that he will not do it."[2] This sin is original and incurable save as by an act of faith his self relates itself rightly to God and is thereby "grounded transparently in the power that constitutes it." "Whatever is not of faith is sin." And this, of course, must be the Christian faith as Kierkegaard interprets it.

In all of this Kierkegaard is talking about something that we find within ourselves and that must, for our purposes, be taken seriously. The human self can be, and often is, irrational. No

---

1 The Sickness Unto Death, tr. W. Lowrie (Princeton: Princeton University Press, 1941), p. 151f.
2 *Ibid.*, p. 153.

one who has honestly tried to understand the actions of others, or himself, can honestly deny it. And this is not the irrationality of intellectual misinformation or miscalculation—it is that of willful wrong doing. In this sense moral evil is indeed "of the will", and Socrates, in *Protagoras*, was wrong in neglecting this essential aspect of the matter. It is as willing and not merely thinking beings that we are practical agents at all, and an account of the self as agent that neglected this basic truth would be manifestly inadequate.

Our problem, however, is not whether we should neglect it but rather how we are to bring it in and what, in the whole context of our practical doing, we are to make of it. What is "the will" to which this "decisive" role is attributed and in what sense can it be *either* rational *or* irrational? It seems in one sense to be just the self *as* acting, yet it is the self, also, that understands and the conflict between will and understanding is dramatized as a struggle within the self in which our "lower nature" also joins. Is "the will", then, a special faculty that acts on its own account and that could or should have reasons for its action? Since it is, in contrast to "the understanding", a non-rational faculty it is hard to see what these could be, or on what grounds, save those "the understanding" offers, it could act. Or is it perhaps, essentially groundless action to which considerations of justification are as such irrelevant? In that sense it could be "irrational" only as a stone is "dead", and there would be no moral sense in calling this deficiency a "sin". Our nature as willing, deciding beings is a fact. It is, indeed, the fact of practical agency itself, though it is not the whole of it. But "the will" as an agency within the self, performing actions of its own which are volitions, fiats of the will, or "oomphs of decision" required to push the self to doings which as rational it does not will and as willing it does not or will not understand is a mystery indeed. If we are to talk responsibly about "irrational man" we must shed such light as we can on this dark subject. This will be the light of practical understanding that has guided us so far. We shall find, I think, that it will not fail us here.

The irrationality with which we are here concerned is that of human actions and the selves or agents who perform them. And to know what it means to call an action irrational we must know what it would be like if it were rational, for it is as in some way violating the canons or exceeding the limits of such rationality that it is significantly thus denominated. For actions, this of course is practical rationality and we have some notion now as to what such rationality consists in. One easy way of exhibiting much of our action, and sometimes the best of it, as irrational, is to define "rationality" so narrowly that only a knave or a fool would in this way be rational—as the technically efficient use of technical means for purely technological ends, for example, or the prudence of the self-seeking man who sees no reason for doing anything that does not contribute to his own self-centered interests. The man who could find a good worth having in no other activities but these, and who recognized no obligations as grounds for action but those that were requirements for the achievement of such goods would be both morally blameworthy and practically blind. If practical reasons were of this sort only, then the heart would indeed have reasons that "reason" could not comprehend, and often very good ones, too. But to call such reasons or the actions they justified "irrational" would invite a misunderstanding of the nature of practical action that only those who wished deliberately to confuse the issue could find helpful. A reason that is not a reason for doing is not a practical reason at all and a doing whose "rationality" was merely that of the efficient use of means for the attainment of ends that, at the price, are not humanly worth having would be a practically unreasonable doing. The understanding that can rightly be a guide for action is not such stuff as this, yet this is the stuffing of the straw men that devotees of the irrational regularly demolish to show that man is really not a rational creature, as he was once supposed to be.

Nor is the situation described as "the conflict between will and reason" that in which a man simply thinks one thing and does another. If the thinking is that of a disinterested "reason" that carries with it no commitments for action then no doing whatever is rationally inconsistent or practically in conflict with it. I may believe that my food is poisoned and still eat it without in any way challenging the factual accuracy of the assertion that it will probably kill me, or at least make me very ill. This would for practical purposes be a strange thing to do, unless I wanted these results, but theoretical reason, thus defined, has no practical purposes, and wants as such know no reasons. My action would certainly be non-rational as, on such as analysis, all action must be, but it could not be irrational—a rejection or defiance of the demand of reason, for such a reason has no demands to make save that of factual correctness in the estimate of what, with respect to the condition of my food, is actually the case. Between a practically neutral reason and a want which has no practical concern for reasons there can be no conflict. And this is just as true for judgments of "good" and "right" if these are understood as designating external properties of objects and of actions as for any others. "Yes, I see that this is good. What of it? I'm not interested in 'good' just now and this information, therefore, leaves me quite unmoved." There is no more "irrationality" here in rejecting "good" than there would be rationality in accepting it. For such a reason has done its job when it has disclosed the facts and what is done about them is simply none of its business. Only reasons whose understanding and acceptance as grounds for justifiable action involved a practical commitment and concern could practically conflict with other factors in the self which wanted or willed a different action. To see the good in this sense is already to be so far committed to it, and it is where this "knowing" as a practical commitment conflicts with others who do not "willingly" accept its normative conclusions that "will" and reason can be practically at odds. For practical decisions can be against reason only because reason in its practical use is *for* something to be done and because we are for it, so far as we are rational.

Nor, finally, does the problem of "the irrational" and "the will" as willfully rejecting reason arise in the situation in which a man does what he takes to be right and good while we, judging the matter from outside, may properly regard his action as unreasonable. This is the problem of what is sometimes called "subjective" and "objective" rightness and we shall deal with it in due course. But it is not our problem here. If the man has done what he considers right then his practical doing (or his "will") has followed *his* understanding, defective as this may be, and there is no internal conflict in his "self" between what his reason knows and his will decides to do. He has done his best "according to his light." If, as Kierkegaard alleges, the inadequacy of his understanding is always a willful ignorance, the situation is more complex. This does not appear to be always in fact the case. There are honest misunderstandings that are not in this way "sinful" and that a better understanding, to be reached by quite rational procedures, could correct. Where it is the case however, a new "dialectical determinant" is added which is precisely that rejection of a good which, if we let ourselves see it clearly, would genuinely commit us to an action that we do not want to do.

Here we reach that hard core of the "irrational" which remains when all antecedent misunderstandings have been eliminated—the perversity of a self that "wills" (or acts) *against* the practical commitment of the good it somehow knows, even in the effort to remain in ignorance of it. This is the "irrationality" that probing thinkers from St. Paul and St. Augustine to Kierkegaard and Sartre have endlessly explored, and no one who wants (or is willing) to know the basic truth about human nature can afford to ignore it. It is by no means my purpose to deny its actuality. On the contrary I propose to build my case on it. My point is just that only a self that is a rational agent, in the sense in which we have understood this term, can *be* in this way irrational. The irrational here is not an agency outside the work of practical reason that may accept or reject its findings without prejudice to its own non-rational integrity; it is a disorder or, as Kierkegaard would say, a "sickness" in the self as practical or willing agent, and only a being committed *as a self* to the acceptance of the standards it rejects can be in this way sick. It is a post-rational phenomenon that presupposes for its practical significance what, in its doing, it rejects and (to borrow from the fashionable jargon of the Existentialists) is not what it is. That is why specifically *moral* evil, as distinguished from mere animal appetite or "brutality", is so "dialectical" a business. There is, to borrow again from Kierkegaard, a kind of double-mindness about it, and there are those who assume that this can be adequately portrayed only in a kind of double talk in which things (or spiritual beings at least) are described as being what they are not and not being what they are. Sartre's account of self-deception will serve as an almost classic instance. It is not my purpose further to indulge in this kind of double-talk (or dialectic) but rather to direct attention to the facts it darkly describes and to see what can for practical purposes be made of them.

How can the self as a practical agent will, or act, against a good it sees and must see to be *its* good as a self, if it is practically to "see" it *as* good at all and as such to reject it? Surely, as Socrates said, such action is not in human nature. The answer is, of course, that the self is not all there is, by any means, of actual human nature. The practical agent is not the whole of man, though it is the whole man acting in a certain role or capacity. This role is often very difficult to maintain. It requires a kind of self-control and understanding and fair dealing that, for a man who is often tired, or envious or hungry (not for food alone) or frightened or confused makes considerable demands on human nature as we know it. It is very "natural" that we should often not want or not have the stamina to do what *as* such agents we can see we ought. We are just not up to it. "I ought but I shall not" may mean no more than this. Such situations provide the raw material of which the irrational is made, and any man of practical good sense knows how to take account of them. Here the spirit is willing but the flesh is weak, and, in our present life at least, we are all fleshly beings.

The harder cases are those in which the spirit is *not* willing —in which the rejection of good is not a mere weakness of the flesh but a spiritual defiance of a "should" that we *will* not accept. Here the "tension" is not between the demands of self-hood and natural wants that may conflict with them. It is within the self itself, and it is here that "willing" as contrasted with wanting has its distinctive place. For what a man wills is what he does *as* a self, or practical agent. The will is not an internal agency which makes him act, it is just the self *as* thus acting, and a will that is defiant of good is a self that is divided against itself, for it is only as committed to the good that, as practical agent, it can be a self at all. Does this ever really occur? Indeed it does and in a way which, though devious, is not really difficult to understand.

The essential fact to see here is that at this "spiritual" level, it is not good that is rejected but "good"—that which is so-called by the lay or clerical authorities or by convention but which the individual who rejects it will not, in its claim to normative cogency, accept. Nor is his "defiance" merely a rejection.

He rejects it *for* some alternative that he is genuinely concerned to justify as at least *his* good and as such worth achieving. The "rationalization" involved in this process is essential to the *willing* of evil, for it is *as good* that it is willed. The worse must be made to appear the better cause if it is to win the assent of those who are asked willingly to accept it. "Evil be thou my *good*" is the appropriate formula for such action, and where it is to be successfully applied the "evil" must be presented as not really so, for those who count at least, and the "good", for them, authentically good. By this formula the gangster is not really a bad man, though the newspapers call him bad names, he is just an enterprising American applying his own rules to a game in which the law-abiding are certainly no better than they should be and in which rewards worth the risk involved in his un-orthodox procedures can be secured not merely for himself but for his friends. There is much cynicism and deception in this. But there is also self-deception. For there is no one in whose eyes a man is more concerned to stand well than himself. And self-deception would be pointless here if self-justification were not important. He will not see his act as morally it is, because if he did thus see it he would not will to do it. As Kierkegaard says, he is willfully ignorant and that is not because moral knowledge is practically impotent, but because he has reason to fear its potency. "Rationalization" is the homage that the ir-rational pays to reason, for it is only under some form of practical justification that the irrational can be willed. And only a self or practical agent can be in this way irrational.

Where ignorance is willful, this homage is, of course, insincere. If it were not, the justification offered would not be a rationaliza-tion but an honest effort to discover what is right. "Bad faith" is of its essence. The appearance of cogency for its "reason" can be maintained only by the willed exclusion of the considerations that would expose their inadequacy. The bad man loves darkness rather than light because his deeds are evil and it is by darkening understanding, his own as well as that of others, that he achieves the unity of purpose he seeks. There is no crime that cannot be "justified" if we can work ourselves up into that state of anger, pride, self-pity or self-righteousness in which we become effectively blind to those considerations of decency, humanity, and respect for others that would disclose its authentic moral status. It was the "injustice" of the treaty of Versailles that "justified" Hitler in all his subsequent aggressions, and "the International Party unites the human race," though it must make man its immoral tools to do it. It is the essence of moral evil that it apes the justifying cogency of good by denying the conditions under which, and the just claims of the community in which, such cogency could be honestly established. Here indeed evil is "of the will", this is a willful evil. But this is not a will that has nothing intrinsically to do with reason. It is a will that *needs* a justification, even though it must corrupt the understanding to secure it. Thus, in Kierkegaard's example, the will must reach an agreement with the understanding if it is to assure that triumph of our lower nature which constitutes the act as "sinful". Successfully to be bad men, in this "spiritual" sense, we must corrupt our reason in the process. For it is in the light of practical understanding that, for better or for worse, the self as agent acts. And if our light be darkness, how great is that darkness.

But *why* do we will to be ignorant? Kierkegaard, having carried the question of willful wrong-doing one step beyond Socrates, is content to leave the matter there, with a pious reference to the theological mystery of original sin to tie it down. But that, for practical purposes, is to say that we act in this way because we are bad men and that it is our nature as "fallen" beings so to act. It would take a miracle of faith and grace to alter our human condition, and it is to that, of course, that he appeals.

In our practical affairs, however, the situation is not, or need not be, as mysterious as this. Human selfhood, as we know it, in ourselves and others, is a precarious achievement—a synthesis, as Kierkegaard, in language borrowed from Hegel, elsewhere says—of elements that must be held together within the requirements of a moral order if a man, John Smith or Henry Robinson, is to act *as* a self at all. It is in the process of this achievement that we come to have wills of our own, to act as beings who can direct their conduct in the light of good and evil as we see them. This knowledge of good and evil is our heritage from the eating of the fateful fruit—it is what made Adam not merely an obedient and contented animal who could talk with others and with God, but a moral person, though a highly defective one. As Freud has overemphasized, the materials of which such a synthesis is built are in many ways recalcitrant to such ordering and there is room for endless perversion and disorder in the effort to become and rightly to be a self. Yet it is only insofar as a man is to some degree a self that his failure to achieve this synthesis can be judged to be a moral failure, for which *he* is responsible. He *makes* his nature as a moral being, but he does not make it by an unconditional decision, given once for all in an arbitrary act of willing. Such a decision would indeed be dreadful freedom. He makes it under the conditions of growing up into responsible membership in a community which is itself in many ways morally defective and with the materials with which his own organic and social nature as a human being provide him. It is in these conditions that he must become and *be* a moral agent if he is in fact to act as one at all. And it is in so acting that he is a self.

The work may be badly done and the self that emerges a twisted and divided self. Moral evil is the expression of the failure to achieve such integrity of a being who is at once concerned to maintain the status of a self and who asks for our respect, and seeks to sustain his own, accordingly, and at the same time is not prepared to pay the price required to deserve it. He is in this way divided against *himself*; and when this effort, which is internally self destructive, breaks down he is spiritually all to pieces. His "will", which makes no sense save as a practical doing, is at odds with his understanding which, as thus divorced from doing, cannot guide his action. And his "lower nature" which, as a self, he can no longer control, impels him to behavior for which as a moral agent he feels a sense of guilt. This is indeed a sickness of the self and it is only a self that can in this way be spiritually sick. Such sickness has become the most fashionable disease of our time.

This talk about the self "in some degree", and "in this way" and "under these conditions" will no doubt offend the Kierkegaardians and other devotees of "dialectical" thinking. It is only by removing all such qualifications and philosophizing "with equal absoluteness everywhere" that they can generate those rationally irreconcilable contradictions that are the "rational" (or argumentatively established) ground for their own pronouncements about the irrationality of human existence. "In this way" their dialectic is the antithesis of responsible good sense, which quite often has the wit to discern that there is no ontological mystery in a thing both being and not being, if we go on to specify is what, how far, in what respect, or under what conditions. A human being, John Jones or Henry Robinson, both is and is not a self, and there is no logical contradiction in this, though there may well be moral difficulty. He is not the self that *as* a self he ought to be, but it is only as the self he is that this negation has a moral sense for him or can give rise to spiritual difficulties. There are so many real difficulties in our human situation that it seems a willful obscurantism to add to them the pseudo-profundities of ontologically loose (since incompletely specified) talk of Being and non-Being, even when this talk is embellished with overtones and undertones of edification.

If this is in fact the nature of moral evil, as the "sickness" of a divided self that will not in its own person achieve the integrity essential to its proper being as a self, then how are we practically to understand and deal with it? "Sickness" at once suggests the need and possibility of a cure and the diagnosis of the illness is preliminary, unless the case is altogether hopeless, to the proposal of a remedy, though this may not in all cases be effective. For this, however, we need to understand what health in such cases would be like, and not only how it might be attained, but why it would be worth attaining. It is on these points particularly that the most influential current diagnoses "of this kind" of sickness leave us rather painfully in the dark.

The genius of Freud as a pioneer worker in this field cannot be fairly questioned. But the moral implications of his findings are questionable indeed. As everybody knows, he disintegrates the divided self into what are essentially three antagonistic agents— id, ego and super-ego—which must somehow get along together if the human individual is not to be a nervous wreck. Each of these has some of the characteristics of a person, but none has enough of them to act in practically rational terms. Their uneasy union in the human personality generates mental disorders that only a psycho-analyst (of the Freudian persuasion) can cure, and even for him the cure is no more than a mitigation of the disease. The *id* is our libidinal nature, essentially unconscious but the source of drives that the super-ego can only by extreme repressive counter-pressures control and the ego rather feebly channel to its egoistic ends. In Freud's account the id is not merely non-moral, as an unconscious force would naturally be, it is deviously and ingeniously anti-moral. Though it has no wits it can frequently outwit the ego and emerge in consciousness in rationally embarrassing ways. It is *essentially* antagonistic to the requirements of moral order and every account of its activity that he will accept as authentic is, from the standpoint of his exposition, a moral exposé. This has made the Freudian account of the libido more exciting to many readers than one that eschewed such moral terminology could be. The super-ego is the agent for all of morality in the self that Freud will recognize as such. It is an agent of internalized repression, authoritarian in its demands but morally blind with respect to any justification of them, that must somehow know what the unconscious is up to in order to censor its activities (and it is *par excellence* a censor) and thus to prevent them from reaching consciousness in their authentically unmoral form. For the purposes of civilization it appears to be a necessary evil, but an evil nonetheless. And finally there is the ego, the rational self within the self. Freud is on its side—"where id was there ego shall be"—and the bringing to light of the conscious sources of neuroses is undertaken in aid of such health as can in this way be achieved. But what a truncated thing this rationality is! Stripped of its appetitive basis in libido which it cannot trust and of its moral concern, now pre-empted, in a distorted form, by the super-ego, against whose punitive activities it must defend itself, it amounts practically to little more than a cautious self-concern for such pleasures as will not be unduly disturbing to its unstable equilibrium. The self in which these agencies compete for power is intrinsically and essentially a divided self, for there is no ground or basis in it on which it could be made whole. Invalidism is its normal portion and the normalization of such sickness is in fact the practical message this account of it has offered to a whole generation of sick souls.

Philip Reiff has expressed this aspect of the doctrine neatly in his book *Freud, the Moralist.* In the Freudian analysis, he tells us, we are all somewhat hysterical . . . the difference between so-called normality and neurosis is only a matter of degree.[3] . . . In the emergent democracy of the sick, every one can to some extent play doctor to others and none is allowed the temerity to claim that he can definitely cure or be cured. The hospital is succeeding the church and the parliament as the archetypal institution of western culture.[4]

If the reader is inclined to feel that all this is itself somewhat sickening he thereby exposes the nature of his own repressions and shows how much he needs to take the cure.

Aware at last that he is chronically ill, psychological man may nevertheless end the quest of his predecessors for a healing doctrine. His experience with the latest one, Freud's, may finally teach him that every cure must expose him to new illness.[5]

What more could a spiritual hypochondriac desire?

There is much more than this, of course, to Freud's teaching, and an adequate account of his penetrating but twisted inquiries would have to take account of it. We are concerned with it here, and with its influence on contemporary thought, only as an example of that normalization of sickness that in our time has made mental and moral disorder more fashionable than the integrity of health and hence has taught men to seek in that irrationality, which is the practical embodiment of this disorder, the archetype of the "true" nature of the self. There can be little doubt, I think, that Freud's analysis of the self has been a major contribution to this way of thinking.

No less influential in recent years, though considerably more edifying in its tone, is the analysis of Kierkegaard and those "existential" thinkers who have borrowed from him. The self, we are told, is a synthesis of the infinite and the finite, of the temporal and the eternal, of freedom and necessity. The sickness

---

[3] Philip Reiff, *Freud, the Moralist* (New York: The Viking Press, 1959), p. 354.
[4] *Ibid.*, p. 355.
[5] *Ibid.*, p. 357.

of the self is a "disrelationship", a failure to achieve this synthesis which is a refusal to will to achieve it in that right relationship to God in which alone the self can be in health as transparently grounded in the power that constitutes it. This sickness is despair. Any self that exists in this disrelationship is *in* despair whether it is aware of it or not. Indeed the less it is aware of it, the more desperate, from a spiritual point of view, is its condition. And since this refusal is made before God, and in disobedience to a divine command, "despair is sin." Kierkegaard has some discerning things to say about the varieties of such despair in human experience. Once the sickness is thus diagnosed the nature of the cure is obvious. The self, by an act of will, must bring itself into this right relationship to God, which is that of unquestioning and non-rational belief, a belief not grounded in the understanding but in specific opposition to it. For "to believe is precisely to lose one's understanding in order to win God."[6] By such belief, or faith, the self becomes at last "transparently grounded in the power that constituted it." The opposite of being in despair is believing—the opposite of sin is faith. And "whatsoever is not of faith is sin."

The language of Kierkegaard's analysis is often opaque, but the essential doctrine is quite simple—too simple, perhaps, to do justice to the situation it purportedly describes. We find in it the traditional oppositon between will and understanding which is the hallmark of the sickness of the self, and a demand for a kind of synthesis or wholeness that would indeed be health. The remedy is willful belief or a faith secured at the price of losing understanding. The price is high but the reward is great, for in such faith, it is claimed, the self becomes transparently *grounded* in the power that constituted it. What sort of "grounding" is this, and how "transparent"? The first question that a self that

---

[6] *Op. cit.*, p. 58.

had not lost its understanding would ask is that of the truth of
what this faith affirms, not grounds for knowing to be sure,
since in matters of faith that is not to be expected, but grounds
for faith, for adopting this believing attitude in the light of all
we know about the world and ourselves. There is no room for
such questions here. "The doctrine says to each individual Thou
shalt believe, i.e., thou shalt either be offended [which is sin] or
thou shalt believe. Not one word more. 'Now I have spoken,'
says God, 'in eternity we shall speak together again. In the
meantime thou canst do what thou wilt, but the Judgment is to
come.' "[7] This is plainly a command, supported by a threat.
And the man who has lost his understanding will accept it as
such. But to say that in such acceptance his being as a self is
transparently "grounded" in the power that, if his faith is sound,
has constituted him is to speak in a gravely misleading way.
Such a faith may be "grounded" in power in the way in which an
electric wire is "grounded", but power *grounds* nothing in the
way in which a justification is a ground for action, and so far
is it from being *morally* transparent that the acceptance of an
order to *believe* on such "grounds" would rightly be accounted as
an act of moral cowardness. Kierkegaard is quite right in calling
it, from the standpoint of the understanding, an offense.

The word "faith", especially as associated with Christianity, is
a word of praise, and when it is pronounced in hortatory terms
we hesitate to challenge its pretensions. But there is faith *and*
faith and our question is what *kind* of faith this is and how far it
can perform the unifying function for the self that is here
claimed for it. The answer pretty plainly is that this kind of
faith, so far from being a cure for the despair of the self, is
rather a symptom of it, the "faith" of a man who is all to pieces
and can find salvation for a groundless will only in an affirmation

---

[7] *Ibid.*, pp. 200f.

that offends his understanding. The self must indeed be "broken" if it is in this way to be saved. "These fragments I have shored against my ruins." To a self thus "healed" it could not truthfully be said "Go thy way. Thy faith hath made thee whole." (Mark 10:52). And Kierkegaard himself is not made whole. He cannot lose his understanding even by an act of will, but can only engage in an endlessly wordy battle with it (Cf. the *Concluding Unscientific Postscript*) [8] and with those rival varieties of faith,that of the Danish Church in particular, that view the matter with less fervor but more sanity. What his doctrine does in effect is to generalize his predicament as the situation "in existence" of "the individual" and thus persuade those who are similarly all to pieces that they are existing "individuals" indeed. In this way his theory, like that of Freud, is an ontological normalization of spiritual disorder.

The relevant objection to be made to this kind of faith is not that it is not knowledge which, as faith, it could not be but that it is a very insecure and disingenuous kind of faith. The man who believes with his will only, and in defiance of his understanding, only half believes. He must be continually on his guard against the light that might disturb his willful credulity, and which he dare not trust. Such faith, as Sartre has said, is "bad faith", and it belongs among the deceptions of the divided self that we considered earlier in this chapter. It is one of the manifestations of the sickness for which it is here offered as a cure. It uses the language of practical justification under conditions that rob it of its justifying sense. A will that wills against practical understanding is a self-destructive will, for only in a right achievement of the good such understanding offers as *its* good can it find its own fulfillment.

Where then are we to look for the "cure" of this sickness?

---

[8] Cf. The Concluding Unscientific Postscript.

The remedy should by now be clear, though the way of its achievement is often hard. In some measure we all know it insofar as we are selves at all. Moral order in our thinking and our doing is by no means as rare or obscure a phenomenon as psychoanalyzing novelists and existential dramatists appear to suppose. The obscurity is largely of our own making—a willed obscurity that a better understanding could dispel. The first step toward such better understanding is to recognize that both "the intellect" and the "will" as the traditional antagonists in the struggles of the divided self are mythological monsters. It is not the will as an inner agency but the man—John Smith or Henry Robinson—who wills and what he wills is just what as a practical agent he does, insofar as he is not in some way prevented from so doing. And it is only as doing something for a reason (which may, of course, be a very bad one) that he is a practical agent at all. And an intellect that was the practically non-committal supplier of information which might then, without prejudice to its cognitively "rational" cogency, be put to *any* use, or none, so far as the intellect was concerned, would have no practical reasons for "struggling" about anything a man might do. Practical understanding in its proper functioning is a commitment to the right doing of things worth doing, and will, when the self acts rightly as a self, is the fulfillment of this commitment in discerning action. An understanding not thus committed and a doing not thus directed are not in this sense practical at all. When the self is functioning adequately as a self its doing is in this way guided by its understanding, and the claims of such understanding, fulfilled and justified in what it does. This is the health or integrity of the self as practical agent and when it acts well in this capacity it is as a self what it ought to be.

The trouble is that, as selves, we frequently do not so function. Our understanding, which is limited enough in any case, may present the issues of conduct in a narrowly restrictive and one-sided way. Against such "reasons" the heart rebels, i.e., there are capacities for good in our nature that cannot find their fulfillment in the "good" that such a reason can identify. There is endless room and need here for that search for *better* reasons that can correct such needless narrowness, and the heart has its essential place in such a search. The correction of "reason" in the light of a better understanding of the creative possibilities of human nature is an essential part of the work of practical reason. Until it is accomplished there will be "reasons" that are not reasonable enough to meet the requirements of practical doing and the self that tries to act rightly on their terms will be frustrated and confused.

And there is also a different sort of conflict. From even the best authenticated demands of right action some appetites will, in some circumstances, stubbornly dissent. As they stand, they cannot be brought into any livable moral order, and we are strongly tempted to accept them as they stand. We do not want to do what we should do, and sometimes we will not do it. And since, as selves, we are concerned even here to justify our conduct, we look for reasons that will put a better face on the matter. These are reasons of the will in the sense that they are willful reasons which can maintain their apparent cogency only so long as their full import is not understood. And hence we willfully refuse to understand them. Here doing and understanding are indeed at odds, not because they are intrinsically alien to each other but because practical doing must have "reasons" which, in this case, understanding will not warrant, and understanding makes demands on action that such doing cannot satisfy. Each must then try to do, without the other, what only both in concert can achieve. That is why their "disrelationship" is indeed a sickness or disorder in the self. It is not surprising that an analysis that reduces practical agency to the self-defeating struggle of such mutilated agents can give us only the pathology of moral selfhood. It can speak with some authority of neurosis and despair but it does not know the meaning of spiritual health —it has not at its command the categories on whose terms it can be understood.

We, however, have them, and they are drawn from the familiar experiences of our practical life. A man who is concerned and competent to play his part worthily and well in the activities that demand the best he has to bring to them as a self has responsibilities to meet, and he does not ask to be excused from them "on account of mental sickness." He is concerned not merely to follow the demands of reason, since reason practically demands nothing but that a man should *be reasonable* in the satisfaction of his desires and affections and the honoring of claims fairly made on him by other men much like himself. He does not search his inner conscience to find out what is right. He looks to the requirements and opportunities of the situation in which, as a moral agent he finds himself and seeks the best solution that he can of the problems with which, *as* a father or citizen or doctor or the like he is obliged to deal. He cannot afford, in such matters, the willful credulity that is merely the projection of his own internal tensions on the Universe at large. He will need the best understanding of the practical requirements of right action that he can get. And to get this, he will need integrity of will or purpose, a will not to believe whatever faith may dictate but to understand what can be done and is here worth doing, and to act accordingly. It will not be much help in such a situation to offer him the edifying tautology that he should will one thing, the Good, in singleness of mind and purity of heart. Of course he should will the good since, in his situation, he is responsible for its achievement—the good *is* just what, in this situation he ought, of his own will, to seek. To find out what *is* in this way good is a different thing and for this he must sometimes be just and subtle and broadly wise. The single-mindedness which is satisfied to will the Good as such and fish its content from the inner depths of its own "individuality" too easily becomes the simple-mindedness of fanaticism. His "will" or action will follow his understanding, not as something dragged along by the alien dictates of a rival power, but as the fulfillment of his own steady purpose to do well the work that as a self, he is called upon to do. Since he is a man who, like the rest of us, is often tired or confused or greedy or afraid, this is sometimes difficult to do. There are those who never make the grade, and are sick at heart accordingly. But there are those who do achieve it, "with malice toward none, with charity for all, with firmness in the right as God gives *us* to see the right—to finish the work that we are in—", for it is in such work as this that moral selfhood can authentically be achieved.

In this process men become selves in the full or eulogistic sense and such selfhood is a kind of mastery in the art of life that makes justifying sense of all the effort that goes into it. We none of us operate at this level all the time. We are too often not the selves we ought to be but unless we could recognize that this was what we ought to be and sometimes act accordingly we should not be the selves we are, with wills and purposes of our own. Moral health is a norm for conduct, and only a man concerned and competent, at his best, to recognize its normative cogency for action will know what to make of it. And to the extent that he does practically know this he is, to some degree, a self. It is on the selfhood that he has that he, and we, must build, not on his sickness and despair, if this sickness is genuinely, and not merely dialectically, to be cured.

It will be said, of course, that such an account is too optimistic. It ignores the ultimate weakness and irrationality of man. There is no use in telling an alcoholic to pull himself together or to give him good reasons for so doing, or in admonishing a man with a broken leg to arise and walk. He must be "treated" in a different way. There is, as in all persuasively false theories, some truth in this. Men—John Smith and Henry Robinson—can act as selves only when they have to some degree the capacity to do so. If we were all, and always, physical, mental or moral cripples, such advice would always be irrelevant, though just who, in that case, would be competent to supply the "treatment" called for it is difficult to see. The essential presupposition of the practical use of normative discourse is that this is not always and in all respects the case. We shall consider the validity of this presupposition, which is that of human freedom, in our next chapter. Here our purpose has been simply to examine the idea of selfhood in its familiar moral use and to try to understand it. And the thing that we can now say with some confidence is that if, as and where the category or conceptual structure of such selfhood applies, irrationality can never rightly be accepted as the last word on the subject. For the irrational here is not the absence but the distortion of practical reason; it "reasons" endlessly in its own twisted way and is parasitic for its practical status on the very norms whose right use, for its own distorted purposes, it perverts. It is a disorder *in* an aim at order, a disrelationship *in* a drive for synthesis in which alone the self as a practical or willing agent could find fulfillment. That is why it makes authentic sense to call it "sickness". To diagnose such sickness, in its more pathological aspects, is a useful work. But to present this diagnosis as the final truth of human self-hood is to dignify it unduly, and, in the process, to block the road to that better understanding in which the hard problems of our precarious self-hood sometimes can in truth be solved. No man who has even so far risen to the occasion as to do well what as a practical and moral agent he was called upon to do will wholly fail to understand what it is, in this way, to be a self.

CHAPTER 7

THE FREEDOM OF PRACTICAL AGENCY

THE "GRAND QUESTION of the freedom of the will" as Jonathan Edwards called it, is time-hallowed and time-worn. Milton tells us that the fallen angels argued it in Hell, "and found no end, in wandering mazes lost." And it can hardly be said that, on the whole, more mundane disputants have dealt with the issue more effectively. For our purposes, fortunately, it is not necessary to add another chapter to this endlessly inconclusive debate. Our concern with the nature and "reality" of human freedom is a quite specific one. We have been trying to understand the practical import of actions done for a reason, and the nature of the reasons that can justify such actions. These, as we saw in the preceding chapter, are in a certain sense willed actions; they are the actions of the self as agent who is rightly held accountable for what, in this way, he does. When we understand men's conduct in this light, the essential categories employed are those of action as practical, of the self as agent, and of reasons for doing in whose terms we can relevantly understand and appraise the action done as right or wrong and the agent as having acquitted himself well or badly in its performance. The freedom that is essential for such action is the capacity of the self as agent to act effectively in this way as this capacity is actualized in what, in this way, he does. That we ourselves, and those with whom we deal in our practical affairs are sometimes *in this sense* free is not an explanatory hypothesis borrowed from the science of psychology, or a metaphysical postulate introduced to "save the appearances" of an otherwise "ultimately" unintelligible world. It is the practical sense of the way in which we act within the practices in which such action is a way of life. We expect such action of others and often trust them to perform it. When this trust is disappointed we are confronted not with a disconfirming instance of an explanatory theory, but with a practical frustration expressed in a negative judgment, not on the theory, but on their conduct and character as agents. It is in this way also that we judge ourselves and sometimes blame ourselves accordingly. The structure of our personality depends on the right maintenance of such personal relationships. We could not be ourselves without them. And it is when men do act in this way that in this fashion they are free.

But do they ever "really" so act? There is another way of describing our behavior that we all use for some purposes, and which has a strong hold on our imaginations, in which the notions essential to the understanding of an action as in this way free appear to have no place. Here man is thought of not as a responsible agent but as a patient, whose conduct is the effect of causes over which "in the end" he has no control, and the cause of effects that, given such prior conditioning, must be what they will be, not "whatever he may do about them" to be sure, but because whatever he *does* do is itself the effect of a volition determined in advance to just this response. Causes and conditions of behavior such an account can empirically discover —it has a great deal to tell us about such conditioning. But for justifying reasons it appears to have no place at all. And none, therefore, for actions done "because", or for a self that can act responsibly for such reasons. Our voluntary actions are the predictable results of antecedent causes, traditionally called volitions, which in turn are caused by prior events over which of course, as effects, they can have no control. And for a self that "wills" outside this sequence of events but somehow produces effects in it, through loopholes of indetermination, perhaps, or by some higher necessity of its own, there seems but little to be said except that somehow, for moral purposes, it *must* be there, else how could we ever rightly blame any one (or ourselves) for what he (or we) did? Hard-headed thinkers are content to leave such questions to metaphysicians and theologians, while they pursue their empirical inquiries into the behavioral facts with results that those concerned with "the management of men" can put to profitable use. Beyond the self-imposed limitations of their professional interest hard questions remain. If all our "volitions" are determined, how can our wills be free? And without a free will, how can a man be a practical and moral agent at all? There seems to be a great mystery here and those who deal professionally in mysteries have not been slow to make use of this one for their own higher purposes. They, too, have their reward.

For an adequate understanding of the practical sense of human action, however, this outcome is less fortunate. We have talked as if there actually and discoverably were such agents, not in some transcendent realm beyond experience but in the very world of space-time events, of biological organisms and social pressures in which, in the practices of our common life, we are called upon to act responsibly as selves. If such talk is a mere reflection of our conventional upbringing or a verbal device for motivating others, similarly conditioned, to behave as we would wish them to, then it can have no rational cogency, for there simply are no agents concerned and competent to understand and use it as a valid ground for action. Nor, of course, are we ourselves such agents, though those who offer such behavioral accounts and recommend ways of thinking and acting on the ground that they provide seem often to assume, for practical purposes, that they, at least, have this capacity. We may continue to use the language of practical agency for ceremonial or manipulative purposes but, if this is the final truth of the matter, we cannot take it seriously. On what grounds indeed, are we to say that anything is, for practical purposes, *worth* taking seriously at all? Obliged to work at once with these incongruous pictures of human action, the mind is divided against itself in a confusion that not only frustrates the understanding but puzzles the will as well. Practical reason is again at odds with itself. It is in this form that the venerable issue of "the freedom of the will" is, for us, an inescapable problem. We must do our best to deal rationally with it.

It will be helpful at the start to try to see more clearly what kind of problem it is. Sometimes it is presented as a conflict between the facts of deterministic science on the one hand and the demands of morality on the other. But theological determinism is quite as much a problem for defenders of free will as is scientific. St. Augustine, Martin Luther and Jonathan Edwards wrestled mightily with it. There have been deterministic moralists, like Spinoza, and scientists who were happy to find in an "indeterminacy principle" an entering wedge for free will in the behavior of electrons. And while advancing psychology and sociology are often supposed to be accumulating a vast supply of facts that discredit such free will, the interpretations put upon such facts are as diverse as ever. The dispute, in fact, does not seem to be primarily about "the facts" at all, but rather about the way in which we are to understand them. Whatever his religious or speculative over-beliefs may be, almost nobody doubts that, for practical purposes and in his present life, at least, man is a creaturely and conditioned being, or that the conditions under and with respect to which he must act are set for him by a world he did not enter of his own free will and a bodily and mental equipment of quite limited capacities. The more we know of such conditions the better, if we use such knowledge rightly. To ignore or to discount such information as a threat to man's spiritual pretensions is to be willfully ignorant of facts that are of great importance for intelligently practical action. By all means here, as in all our human problems, "let knowledge grow from more to more."

The important and seriously controversial issue is as to whether the truth that can in this way be learned is the whole practically relevant truth about our human nature and situation or whether, as it stands, indeed, it is practically relevant truth at all. There does *seem* to be a "more" here that escapes this kind of description, not just because researchers have not yet been ingenious enough to devise the experiments that would disclose it, but because such a disclosure, even if we had it, would not be the right kind of answer to questions that, as practical agents, we are bound to ask. Suppose our knowledge of the human brain reached such a point that we could, by a safe operation performed on infants at the age of six months, so condition their future behavior that they would thereafter happily obey the "moral" dictates of those who controlled their education. Would this be a good thing to do? Should we do it? Who's to judge, and how and on what basis could such a judgment be made? No amount of additional information as to the expectable consequences of such an operation could answer these questions rightly, save as it was relevant to the question as to what consequences ought to be produced, and of this only a moral agent, concerned and competent to deal with such issues on moral grounds, could rightly judge. Unless we were ourselves to some degree such agents, and free accordingly to act for the right as we saw it, it would have no practical meaning for us.

Almost nobody, I think, really doubts this in practice, in his own case at least. We could not reasonably conduct our practical activities, including those of acquiring and disseminating physiological information, on any other basis. The trouble is that when we try to say what in this way we know in the language of the conditioning of our "volitions" by antecedent causes we find that somehow it has lost its moral sense. The reasons we would give here for our actions and the self, as agent, that would give them, have no place in this picture. It is indeed a picture, imbedded in the conceptual structure of our language, that holds us captive. We are obliged to have recourse to the mysterious or the occult, outside practical agency and action, to find a freedom we cannot in this way discover *in* them. The traditional perplexities of the "free will problem" are perennial not because we have not yet found "the facts" that would resolve them—for here there is nothing hidden—but rather because we cannot make sense of something that we already know quite well with the categories in whose terms we have tried to understand it. Our own job here, as always, is to try to specify the nature of the better understanding that we need.

What is the picture which, if our suggestion is correct, is at the source of our perplexities? It is a representation of "the will", its determination and its mode of actions. Our *actions* are free, it is customarily said, when they are uncoerced and unimpeded, when there are alternatives for doing which we can carry out *if* we will, or please, or so decide. In such instances we are free to do or not to do the action as we choose and since the choice is ours, the responsibility for the doing lies with us. It is obvious that in this way we are sometimes free and sometimes not. A prisoner is not free to leave the prison when he chooses; the visitor who comes to see him is. There are, of course, degrees and qualifications of such freedom, but the principle at least seems clear enough. And those who want to speak of freedom with no nonsense about it have often been inclined to say that this is all they mean by it.

A free action, then, is one we can do if we will. But can we will to do it? Is not our choice or willing itself determined by antecedent motives acting on our character (as biologically and socially, or by Adam's fall, conditioned) and, given these, what could a man will but what he does? And since he is free to act only *if* he chooses, and is not really free to choose, are not his apparent alternatives for action actually reduced to one—the one he is bound to choose and thus "voluntarily" to do? As Schopenhauer put it in a famous passage; "To a given man under given circumstances, are two actions possible, or only one?—The answer of all who think deeply, only one."[1] But if no real alternatives, then really no freedom. This is the problem of the *freedom of the will* in its classic form. How "deep" the thinking that leads us to this answer actually is we shall soon inquire. But its surface plausibility, in the language in which it is propounded, is unquestionable. Very deep thinkers indeed, including Schopenhauer himself, have been driven to incredible expedients to salvage from its apparently relentless implications something they could still in some way describe as "freedom of the will."

Stated in this way the question of the "reality" of human freedom is that of the causation of the acts of will (volitions) which in their turn are the causes of "voluntary" acts. The "determinist" will hold that such volitions are wholly the result of antecedent causes or conditions and that, when these are given, the volition follows with whatever necessity or predictability is supposed to be involved in the nature of such causal connection. The indeterminist denies this, and seeks for some gap or loophole in the causal relation that would leave at least some room for a different sort of action. The libertarian invokes a

---

[1] In his Essay on the Freedom of the Will, tr. K. Kolenda (New York: Liberal Arts Press, 1960), p. 62.

higher power of self-determination by which the self, in independence of external causes, is the cause (in a higher sense) of its own volitions. Each theory can find something in "the facts" to support its case and much to say against its rivals which are, when critically examined, of a highly questionable character. Their disputes are endless, for there are enough defects in each to keep the others endlessly engaged. But since none of them can give a sense to freedom that makes sense of practical agency we are, for practical purposes, none the wiser. Yet the question that they ask seems urgent and how else but in their terms are we to answer it?

Where the answers prove so consistently and perennially unrewarding, the suspicion naturally arises that there was something wrong with the question as thus put. What was the question? It was about the causation of the acts of volition that are the causes of the voluntary actions in whose performance a man can practically be said to be free. Are there any such volitions? This seems initially an odd question to ask, for there surely are willed actions, and how could such an action be performed but as the effect of an act of will—i.e., a volition? Moreover, we seem to be aware of such volitions in experiences of choosing, deciding or "opting" for one alternative for action or another. The model case of such deciding is that in which, where wants conflict and there is something to be said for each of the things we can do if we choose but nothing decisive, so far, to be said for any of them, the will simply decides by a kind of fiat of its own that thus it shall be, and acts accordingly. Where this decision is hard to make, or is made by a special effort and against resistance, the activity of will is thought to be particularly obvious. It was such phenomena that William James described vividly and at length under the caption of "will". We find in them what C. I. Lewis called an "oomph of initiation", and it is this that comes most readily to mind when reference is made to volition as an action or activity of the will.

Such experiences undoubtedly do occur and are of importance for the understanding of willed action. But can this be the "I will" that, as Schopenhauer said, "accompanies all our actions"? Evidently not. For there are many instances of willed action in which it does not discoverably occur at all. A man's will is manifest at least as much in actions that he does quite unhesitatingly and directly, without prior pondering or internal pushing or inner effort, as in those in which this inner drama is enacted. A willfully selfish man does not normally have to push himself into acting selfishly, or a morally good man to *decide*, by an effort of his will, to do what he can recognize as right. On the contrary, it is the man of weak or disorded will who, like Hamlet, is continually confronted by such soul struggles. Nor is choice the essence of the matter. We do not choose actions, as we might choose among apples in a dish. We do them, or refuse to do them, for a reason, and when this reason is manifest, as it often is, the man with a clear commitment may well say that he has no choice. Like Martin Luther, he "can do no other." But this does not mean that his action is not the expression of his own will, for which he is rightly held, and holds himself, accountable. On the contrary, it is an impressive example of willed or (as Luther's critics have held) of willful action. It is as a responsible moral agent, so he holds, that he can *rightly* do no other, and, in defiance of all external authority, he *will* act for the right as he sees it. His action is a clear case of practical self-assertion. There are occasions in which the issues are not clear and in which, after pondering and hesitation, a man must simply "decide" by fiat what he is to do. And such decisions are often accompanied by the felt internal struggles that novelists and dramatists portray. But to take such experiences as providing the interior model for all willed action is like taking a description

of the spray of the waves of a stormy sea as a sufficient basis for
an adequate account of the way in which waves move, in seasons
both of calm and storm. It is not surprising that such accounts
have a "literary" flavor to them, more suitable to discussions in
a college classroom than to the practical affairs of men.

There is evidently much more to willed action than this. And
if "acts of volition" are to be identified as the causes of all
willed action, without whose presence in the chain of causes and
effects that is here said to constitute such action the deed a man
does would not be his voluntary doing, nor he responsible for
it as its doer, we must look further if we are to find it. Where
are we to look? Willed action we know. One man kills another
and a jury holds this killing to be willful murder. But here the
action is the murder itself, done, say, by shooting someone with
intent to kill and in a situation in which such killing can be
neither justified nor excused. What about the prior act of volition
that caused the murderer to do his deed? When and under what
conditions did he (or his will) perform this action? Perhaps he
decided days ago that he would do it and has been planning ever
since how best to perform the deed. But deciding to do something
is not doing it, and unless it is the initial stage in doing something
else, that will in due course serve to bring the murder about—
buying a revolver, for example—it is practically no more than
wishful thinking. I cannot kill a man by an act of volition, and
it is the killing, if it is done in this way and under these conditions, that is condemned as willful murder. Of course I did not
do it blindly. I knew what I was doing and what I meant to do.
I had my reasons for it, reasons that the jury holds in this case
do not justify the deed, and it is as an action done in this way
that my doing is relevantly understood and appraised. If I can
be certified to have been insane or at least so mentally deranged
at the time as not to be responsible for my actions, the verdict is
and ought to be a different one. Under the law, only a practically

rational man can in this way be a murderer. In this transaction, we find a deed discoverably done, the killing, the agent who did it, the man himself—John Jones or Henry Robinson—of whom as a member of the community a certain level of non-violent conduct is required, and the grounds which warrant the verdict that the action was willful murder, not just an accident, or justifiable homicide, or, perhaps, the praiseworthy killing of the minions of a hostile power in time of war. In this context "willful murder" makes good and practical sense, and to call *the killing* as thus done an "act of will", i.e., an action of the man as practical agent, to be understood and appraised accordingly, is something that we all can understand.

But this is not the way in which, in the "free will problem", acts of volition are supposed to function. They are not such actions as these, and, if they are ever done, must be done in a quite different way. A *willed action* is done by the self as practical agent and for reasons that justify, or are inadequate to justify, his performance in this role. An *act of will,* as a prior act of volition, is not done in this way at all. It is something done by "the will" which is the postulated inner cause of what we do and, as a link in the chain of mental and/or bodily occurrences that finally eventuate in willed action, is either itself the effect of prior natural causes (motives) or the temporal manifestation of a timeless self that acts independently of such motives, or an uncaused event that just happens and is therefore "free". Here the categories that apply to practical doing are manifestly inappropriate. The motives that cause "volitions" are not reasons, as we have understood that term. I perceive a juicy looking orange, my mouth waters and I go after it, having first performed an act of volition, caused by these prior happenings which in turn somehow causes my body to behave in this way. Wanting the orange, thus perceived, *moved* my will and my will *moved* my body, by playing somehow on the keyboard of nerves and muscles through whose activity this result is presumably brought about. How "the will" does this is something of a puzzle, but unless it came in *somewhere* the ensuing action would not be a voluntary act or I the responsible doer of it, and it is as such a cause that it here comes in. What it accomplishes, except to transmit to my body the effect of the external influences that act on it, to be a kind of occult intermediary in the series of psychical and physiological pulls and pushes which is, in this version, the true nature of human action, it is hard to see. But if it were not there, we should on this view have no will at all, and what should we do without it? It seems that *in this role* we might quite well do without it. Psychologists, for the most part, have ceased to take it seriously, and we should do well to follow their example.

To free the will of this causal bondage is the laudable aim of indeterminists and libertarians. For surely it is not in this way that we act as practically willing beings, as the responsible doers of our deeds. But if the will is essentially the agency that performs acts of volition, what *is* it as thus "freed"? There is much that is obscure in this noble but misguided venture, but one thing at least is clear. Whatever such an act of free volition may be, *it* is not a responsibly willed action. To free it of its causes is to emancipate it from its motives, to affirm that, in part at least, it is undetermined by the "incentives" that would normally be referred to in giving an account of the action as having a practical point. *Why* then does the will act here as it does? The indeterminist must hold that, in so far as it is truly free, it has no "why", for a "why" would here be a determining cause and in so far as it is determined, it is not free. It just decides quite groundlessly that so and not otherwise it shall be and acts accordingly. In our practical affairs this would indeed be called a "willful" action, but such willfulness, if a man was acting as a responsible agent, would be considered an abuse, and not a proper use of freedom. It is what we mean by an arbitrary action. We could not trust such a man or deal with him in terms of mutual understanding and concern. As a free being he *might* do anything and even if he happened to do what we consider to be right, it would not be because he held it to be right that he did it. It would not be "because" of anything, since the only because here would be a cause and that would make the act unfree. Even if the sciences provided strong, affirmative evidence, as they do not, of such an indeterminacy in human conduct, it is obvious that it would be of no constructive use to us for practical and moral purposes. It would simply enlarge the area of the unintelligible, in which anything and therefore nothing we can rely on is to be expected and would narrow proportionately the sphere of practical action in which a common good can be the practical objective of willed action.

Almost nobody is *merely* an indeterminist. The point of this theory is to discover loopholes and gaps for "volition" in the causal nexus and thus to leave open the possibility of a different sort of action by the will, or by the self as a free agent. But what could such action be? *As free* it would have to be undetermined by motives, which would be a negation of such freedom. As responsible agency it would require a "why" of its own, to be found now outside the nexus of events from which it has been "liberated". Where are we to find it? In its own willing nature as rational? This, of course, was Kant's answer. The free will is, in its noumenal and time-transcending character, a "rational" will and what it wills is just itself as rational. Of the practical nature of such "rationality" we shall have more to say in a later chapter. What concerns us here is the alleged "necessity" of such willing. If the noumenally free will *is* in this way a rational will, how can it even will irrationally? How can there even be an evil will? Yet moral evil seems to be as much a fact of our practical experience as moral rationality. And if we

are thus free by the necessity of our noumenal nature, what
room is left for the choice or decision of which libertarians make
so much? There are, it would appear, two choices. One is the
temporal choice we make in particular situations on the basis of
given motives and character. The other is the choice by which,
as timeless selves, we choose our character and our motives. But
choose them how, and on what grounds? The choice of motive
must here be a motiveless choice; what grounds could we give
for it that would not, as themselves "motives", be a negation of
its freedom? And the choice of a character by a will that so far
has no character would not be the expression of a man's character as a self, and hence not, save arbitrarily, imputable to him
as a practical and moral agent. If necessitated, how could it be
free? And if free, how rational? Kant struggled heroically with
these questions in a self-defeating attempt to give some moral
meaning to his noumenally free will. Schopenhauer went the
whole way, and found the *real* will in a groundless, and thus
essentially non-rational wanting, endlessly and aimlessly "affirming" itself in a world of space-time appearance that is only the
deceptive projection of its own insatiable desires. It is no wonder
that he sought salvation in the denial of such a will, though what
would remain of "reality" if the will which *is* reality thus effaced
itself remained for him, as it must for us, a mystery. Later
accounts of such pure, non-rational willing have embellished this
picture with scientific analogies and literary allusions, but they
add nothing that makes sense of it.

The point in all this that is essential for our purposes is that
the self of practical agency and responsibly willed action dis-
appears quite as hopelessly in the libertarian as in the deterministic account of "the will". Whether it is lost in noumenal
heights of pure and therefore groundless willing or in lower
"drives" or unconscious motivations may make a difference to
feelings of self-importance in the matter. In neither case is it

available to do the work that, in our practical functioning and relations as selves, is required of it. Freedom of "the will" in some "higher" sense there may or may not be, but freedom of the self *in* willed action we have not found, and there is no way, on the terms thus set, of finding it. And that is why the "grand question of the freedom of the will" remains, in spite of the great analytic and speculative ingenuity that has been brought to bear on it, so endlessly unrewarding.

But we have had enough now, surely, of "the will" as an interior agency and the caused or uncaused volitions that are its questionable acts. There is another way of looking at the matter which presents the time-worn issues in a different light, the light of practical understanding. In our practical relations with our fellows we do not find "the will" but we do find willed, and sometimes willful, actions. These are often quite familiar actions, like asking a man a question because we need an answer that he is in a position to give, or keeping on asking when it is clear that he does not know or will not give the answer, and we wish merely to annoy or to embarrass him. The agent in such actions is not "the will" as such; it is the man, John Smith or Henry Robinson, who has wants to be satisfied and responsibilities to be met to which the asking of this question is in some way pertinent. To ask a question sometimes in this way makes sense; in others it is merely pointless. There is a right and a wrong way of asking questions, as the procedure of Congressional Investigating Committees has made apparent. There are questions an investigator has no right to ask, and others that no citizen can rightly refuse to answer. To ask *why* did he ask the question? or why should I? is not to ask for an account of his (or my) mental history or a psychological hypothesis as to the hidden causes of the action. It is to ask for, and sometimes get, a reason for the doing of the deed (in this case, the questioning) that will show its practical intent and, if it has one, its warrant as an action.

A man who *in this way* asks questions is acting as a self or agent and his character in this role or capacity is shown by the way in which he asks them. He may do so stupidly, or irresponsibly, or with undue importunity, or sensibly, fairly and with good effect. His wantings do not *make* him ask the question, though if he wanted nothing there would be no point in asking it. Nor, if he knows what he is doing, does his "will" groundlessly irrupt into such an action. He does it intentionally and with a purpose. *He* acts, with all his drives and appetites, emotions and intelligence, but, in this instance, as a self. The capacity so to act as it is actualized in what in this way he does is his freedom as a practical or willing agent. A man who in the whole network of his practical commitments acts well in this capacity, is a man of good will and the excellence of character thus embodied in respect for others and in self-respect is indeed beyond price. But this is not an excellence stored up in a noumenal realm of disembodied selfhood, where neither time nor motive doth corrupt. It is a good we can sometimes discover in quite mundane business of our lives. The "values" of the way of life we call democracy would make no moral sense without it. In this way we are indeed committed to the defense of freedom not as an ideological slogan or a metaphysical abstraction but *as* a way of life maintained, at its best, on this level and hence free from the repressions and injustices that would impede the development and thwart the capacities of men *in this way* free. We do not, in our political behavior, always live up to this commitment but we should not be the people that we are without it.

Of course such freedom is achieved and achievable only under conditions. A man is not in this way born a self. He to some degree becomes one by discipline and training in an environment his free will did not create. He may be, or become, so crippled in body and mind that he never does achieve such selfhood. And, even in the best of circumstances, there will be times when he is not, in this way, himself. We all understand enough of human nature to recognize such situations and to make allowance for them. But when and insofar as he does achieve such selfhood he is *in this way* free. The environmental and bodily conditions for such agency and action are conditions *for* the exercise of freedom, not a negation of it. If we knew more of such conditions we could do more to make men free but, insofar as they were made free, and in fact prepared to act in this capacity we could not *make* them do anything we pleased, but, to enlist their "wills" in our behalf, should have to give them grounds for so acting that they could understand and accept as such. This is one of the risks of "liberation" of which liberators do not always take account.

Of course a man who acts in this way has desires and passions and drives of which, even with the assistance of psychoanalysts, he may be but dimly conscious. These are the stuff of our practical life and it would not be a going concern without them. But it is only as they are understood not as causal pushes merely but as providing grounds for action that they are the subject-matter of willed actions. A practical reason that was not, in Hume's equiv-ocal phrase, "the slave of the passions" in the sense that it was not the answer to a question set by human needs and fears and hopes would not be a reason for doing anything, i.e., it would not be a practical reason. But a man who was the slave of his passions would not be a free man in the sense required for practical agency at all. It is in the rational control and guidance of his passions, in actions done not just because he wants to but for ends that *as a self* he can recognize as good, that such freedom is achieved. A "volition" that did no more than "will" and pass on to the body the causal influence on it of antecedent appetites, would not be the action of such a self and not, therefore, a willed action. We choose an action by doing it for a reason, and we choose our reasons by acting in this way. It is only as thus done that the doing is, for practical purposes, an action at all, whose significance as an action of the self, can properly be assessed. "He gave the old man money." *So far,* this does not establish the action as either right or wrong, or shed light on the nature of the giver's will in so acting. Perhaps he gave the money in payment of a debt, or because the man was his father, or just because he likes to give money away and this was an opportunity to do so. Or perhaps it was the payment of a bribe, or blackmail. When we know *why* he acted as he did we know what *as practical* the action was, and can get some notion accordingly of the "will" and character of its doer. Motives *as reasons* are intrinsic to the sense and import of willed actions, and to "free" an action from *such* motives would be to free it of its practical significance. But to consider such reasons simply as antecedent causal pushes or solicitations struggling with each other for the power to "move" a will—a battle in which, tautologously, the "strongest" (i.e., the winner) always wins—is to ignore the agency of the self in practical doing altogether. It is in what he does *as a self* that the man—John Smith or Henry Robinson—*has* a will of his own. He may perform well or badly in this capacity but if he has not this capacity he cannot in this way perform at all. Where there is no will, there is, of course, no freedom of the will.

And, finally, *of course* a man's character as a self is a factor in determining the nature of his action. His willed actions are self-determined, not in the esoteric sense that they are the effects of "volitions" which are causes of themselves, or have no cause or as the temporal manifestation of a character "the will" has chosen for itself outside space and time, but in the prosaic sense that they are the actions a man does *as* a self. *He* does them, and it is as *his* actions that they are practically to be understood. And it is in what in this way he does, not in a single instance only, but in the whole network of his relations to others as a self that we discover what, as a practical agent, he is. A man who *thus* acts reasonably is a practically reasonable man. But this does not mean that there is something timeless, his rationality, *that necessitates* his rational action and so leaves him no alternative but to behave as he does. It is timelessly, and tautologously necessary that a "rational man" be rational; if he were not, he would not be a rational man. But that John Smith be reasonable in his conduct is not thus a necessity of his nature. It is an achievement of a human organism in a natural and socially conditioning environment. The self that, if he is a self at all, he can recognize he ought to be, is always to some degree an ideal. The "choice" to be this self, or to live up to this ideal, in his conduct is not one made once for all in a super-temporal world and irrevocable thereafter. It must be made continually, in quite mundane circumstances, in the way that he responds to the requirements and opportunities of his situation as a self or agent. For, once more, it is in so acting that he is a self, and has a character that can significantly be called good or bad. *In this sense* it is true that morally "existence precedes essence," for we exist as human beings before we have a moral character and, to some degree, we make ourselves, by our action, what in this character, or as selves, we are. As previously observed, however, we do not make ourselves out of whole cloth. The consequences of past decisions limit or extend the possibilities of present choice. There are men in whom the capacity for responsible action is so meager, or has been so far corrupted, that in many circumstances it would be mere wishful thinking to expect such action of them. It is because we are not all, or in all circumstances, such men, that the language of selfhood and of freedom has for us a practical significance.

The nightmare of a timelessly fixed character meeting antecedently determined motives in a "volition" that can no more than register their joint effect and pass it on to bodily movements which are then called voluntary actions (Schopenhauer's version of "a given man under given circumstances") is therefore just a nightmare. For such a man, indeed, only one action would be possible, but it would not practically be an action at all, nor the man its agent. It is precisely where such circumstances (motives) are not merely given as stimuli but understood and *taken* by the self as agent in their practical significance as grounds for what he as an agent will do, and, in doing *be,* that there is a place for freedom in our actions. What he makes of them, and of himself, in what he does with them, is exercise of his freedom and the measure of his moral worth. This is the burden of our responsibility, and this the greatness of our opportunity as practical and moral agents. That a man who does not understand it finds no place in his philosophy for human freedom, or must make a mystery of it, is precisely what we should expect. For it is in this understanding, and the actions based upon it, that the "reality" of our freedom is authentically to be found.

The issue about freedom here is not about two worlds, one of necessity and the other of freedom, and their ontological connection, nor about how "volitions" are to be inserted into and at the same time kept out of the sequence of conditioning events that issues in behavior. It is about two ways of understanding such behavior and the conceptual structure of the language appropriate to each. Each is, for some purposes, not merely legitimate but indispensable. Man in his present human situation is a conditioned being and the more that we can learn of the nature of such conditioning the wiser—so far—we can be in what we do about it. But this conditioned being is no less an agent, the doer of his deeds, and it is on this basis that we must deal with him if we are to understand him as a self. The Greek notion of the soul as that which moves itself is true in this sense at least, that man in his deeds is not merely "moved", but mover, and is accountable accordingly for what he does. The categories of such agency are not those of natural causation, though there is nothing natural causation has to tell us that is incompatible with what, by their use, we know of man as agent. The appearance of such incompatibility arises only when we try to understand the concepts of practical agency as links in a causal chain of conditioning events. "Will" is pre-eminently such a concept. As a causal agency it makes no justifiable sense, either as "determined" or as "free". We cannot understand moral action as the effect of a "free will" thus dubiously identified, but we can understand it as the action of a practical agent whose freedom *is* his capacity to act or to refuse to act, in the light of options for conduct, for a reason. In this sense the "I will" is not merely something that accompanies all our actions; it is intrinsic to their nature *as* practical, for unless thus done they are not, for purposes of practical understanding and appraisal, actions at all. "Will" is a category of practical reason, not of psychological and physiological description, and that is why psychologists (of the scientific persuasion at least) and physiologists get on so well without it. They have no use in their investigations for this "hypothesis". But as practically responsible men neither we nor they can get along without it. Here we all have a use for it, not as an hypothesis about the psychic causation of bodily movements but as the manifest import of our actions as moral agents. The physiological and psychological conditions in which we thus act as agents are conditions *for* free action, and it is in such action that we have wills of our own. If a theorist were so infatuated with his theory as to maintain that such action never does take place, he would be refuted by the occurrence of his own theorizing, if this is indeed a serious activity, responsibly carried on, and subject to practically normative standards for its right performance.

An adequate appraisal of the resources of human nature must take account of man both as thus conditioned and as free. A freedom divorced from such conditions would be the empty freedom of a will that had no content but itself, and a conditioning divorced from the right use of man's freedom would be practically blind. We hear much today of the ways in which behavior can be conditioned, but to decide how it ought to be conditioned, save perhaps to serve the unexamined purposes of those who have the means to hire such conditioners to do a job for them, would require an exercise of responsible judgment for which the techniques of conditioning appear to leave no place. Nor are the two accounts to be merely juxtaposed. We must take practical account of all that reliable information can tell us about the conditions under which, and the bodily and mental constitution with which, we act. And we must take theoretical account of what our practical understanding and doing show us to be true of man as agent. A theory that took the conditioner's account to be the whole truth of human conduct would be gravely inadequate as theory, though for more limited purposes such professional narrowmindedness clearly has its uses. The two accounts belong together and neither can rightly do its work without the light the other can supply. But they can be fruitfully together—like man and wife—only because each is, in essential respects, different from the other and has its own irreplacable contribution to make to their "togetherness". Nothing but confusion is gained by treating either as if it were, or somehow ought to be, the other, and much of great value may be lost. To be not a disembodied spirit nor a well-behaved animal but a human self is man's predicament, and also his distinction. We cannot argue our way out of it by categorial confusions but, if we recognize it for what it is, we can learn much from it that will help us rightly to achieve in our human situation the great good that is possible for man but of which too frequently, in the limitations of his understanding and the triviality of his aims, he tragically falls short.

There are here, we have said, two ways of understanding human nature, each with the conceptual or categorial structure appropriate to the meaningful assertion of something that is true about it. But these are not alternative ways of understanding practical agency. For if we try to understand such agency in the language of conditioning what we get is something that is not an action at all, nor its doer a responsible self or person. Such a description is an intelligible and sometimes adequate account of the way in which a man behaves when as a practical agent he is *not* himself. It can account for slips of the tongue and of the pen, for (in some cases) the content of our dreams, and for the manipulable suggestibility of the buyer in a super-market who is "deeply" drawn by the color of its package to a worthless product. The essential passivity of the "subject" in such occurrences comes out clearly in the language of motivational engineering now often favoured in the descriptions that educated men give of their own conduct. "Why did you ask that question?" To this a man's answer nowadays is often not "because I was trying to find out . . . , and this was a proper and effective way to do it," but rather "my questioning was motivated by a desire to—" which shifts attention from the practical justification of the action, and of the agent in thus acting, to the causation of the desires that moved him into his behavior which can lead back, as we all know, to the anal preoccupations of his early childhood, or to more recent "conditioning" by the Madison Avenue engineers of his goal-seeking behavior. This is the way a man "acts" when he does not act, but is merely the patient in a transaction he is now in no position to control. Such an account can provide us with no justifications for our actions, but at best with excuses. The advertiser beguiled me, or my parents "rejected" me, and I did buy. It is sometimes said that *in this way* to understand everything is to forgive everything. The truth is rather that if all our conduct were thus "understood" there would be nothing to forgive, and no meaning in the notion of forgiveness. One does not, if he is "intelligent" forgive a door for being warped. In such a world, as judged by moral standards, we are all "patients" to be "treated" accordingly, or "subjects" to be used by motivational engineers for the fulfilment of their purposes, since we have neither the wit nor stamina to maintain as rational creatures any of our own.

But who "motivates" the motivators, or "treats" the psychiatrist, and to what end? If the same account of human conduct applies adequately to their "choices" and their "reasons", it would seem to be a case of the blind leading the blind. The fact is, of course, that practically, when we are not asking as "patients" to be excused from the responsibilities of action but are prepared to act in our own persons and for good reasons, we always exclude ourselves and those whom we respect enough to give them reasons for our action, from this description. And we must do so, if we are to act as selves. The only way to exclude the relevance of the categories of practical agency from our conduct is to eliminate such agency itself, and it sometimes seems as if the manipulative devices of the conditioners were designed to do just that. We have not reached that level yet, though in the conduct of political campaigns we seem sometimes to be approaching it. And if we rightly understand and value the freedom that is not just a slogan but at once the practical presupposition and reward of a way of life in which men respect each other as persons and sometimes act accordingly, we shall not allow ourselves to be reduced to it. A sound understanding of the freedom of the self as practical agent is here, in consequence, a matter of practical, not merely linguistic or philosophical importance.

CHAPTER 8
REASONS, RULES, AND "THE COMMUNITY"

THERE IS A PERSISTENT misunderstanding to which a theory of the sort so far outlined is open and which, if not explicitly corrected, will lead to a distorted picture of the nature and the work of practical reason. Right actions, we have said, are warrantable by reasons. It is only as thus warrantable that the characterization of an action as right has a normative force or cogency that makes practically justifying sense. And in answer to the questions: where do we get such reasons? and how can we understand and use them in this way? we have replied that we learn their use and cogency as we become responsibly participating members in the communities in which, in practice, the distinction between right and wrong ways of acting functions as a guide to justifiable conduct. Here training must precede questioning and argument. The man who in such training has learned the difference between right and wrong understands, in some instances at least, what it is to act justifiably or for good reasons, and the man who does not know this cannot significantly ask for the reason for an action for which a practically justifying "because" would provide a relevant answer. He would not have the understanding—the mastery of the conceptual structure of the practice—required to make practical sense of such a reason if he saw one. So much, I have maintained, is true and of fundamental importance for our subject. But it is at just this point that the misunderstanding referred to above may arise, and too often does. For when we look for the content of the reasons that in this way and initially we learn, we find it in the accepted rules and approvals of the social groups in which such training actually is given. And if to act justifiably is simply to conform our actions to such rules, then the work of practical reason seems to be "in the end" just that of following learned instructions. In its beginning is its end, so far as being reasonable is concerned. C. S. Peirce expressed and embraced this implication, for moral reasoning at least, with characteristic explicitness.

> We all know what morality is: it is behaving as you were brought up to behave; that is, to think you ought to be punished for not behaving. But to believe in thinking as you were brought up to think defines *conservatism*. It needs no reasoning to perceive that morality is conservatism. But conservatism again means, as you will surely agree, not trusting to one's reasoning powers. To be a moral man is to obey the traditional maxims of your community without hesitation or discussion. Hence, ethics, which is reasoning out an explanation of morality, is—I will not say immoral [for] that would be going too far—composed of the very substance of immorality.[1]

Not many philosophers are as forthright as Peirce or as ready to carry a wrong-headed argument to its logical conclusion. But, as we shall see, there are some contemporary accounts of moral reasons that appear, though more equivocally, to lead us in the same direction. And these accounts have, in some respects, a disturbing similarity to our own. They, too, stress practices and

---

[1] *Collected Papers of Charles Sanders Peirce*, eds. Charles Hartshorne and Paul Weiss (Cambridge: Harvard University Press, 1931), I, Paragraph 666.

learning and community. And some of them have learned from Wittgenstein to describe practically justifiable behavior as the mastery of a technique in which games are played and rules followed according to learned instructions. It may even be suspected that this is what we also ought to say. For, if we bring the learning of moral reasons back to training *of this sort,* what more can be learned from it than to behave as you were brought up to behave? If this is all there is to learning moral reasons in the beginning, what more than this can there be to a "rational" use of them in the end? And if there were a "more", of what nature could it be?

The answer is, of course, that this is not all there is to moral training (or to any other in which it is *reasons* that are to be understood and used) in the beginning. An account that so represents the matter is wrong not merely incidentally or on minor issues but fundamentally. It does not have the root of the matter in it. This should be plain from what has already been said, especially in Chapter V. But since there are strong temptations, both analytical and practical, not to understand it, we shall perhaps be well-advised to say it again, as explicitly as possible and in specific contrast to those theories that sound, in some respects, like our own but whose sense is by no means the same. Such a statement will enable us to bring together and get clearly into focus considerations so far discussed piecemeal and in this way to sum up what we have to say about the reasonableness of practical, and especially of moral, reasons in their proper and distinctive use.

"Morality is behaving as you were brought up to behave; that is, to think you ought to be punished for not behaving." The "that is" in this sentence suggests that the clause that follows it says nothing more than was asserted in the one by which it is preceded. It takes but little reasoning, however, to show that this is not the case. To behave as you were brought up to behave is, so far, not to "behave" morally at all. Dogs and other dumb creatures are trained to behave in this way as well as men and whether or not such behavior is moral is not the question as to whether or not the training has been successful. The expectation of punishment may play a part in such training, but it does not always do so. "Position re-enforcement" is more basic than negative and may do the job by itself. But to think one ought to be punished for not behaving is thinking of a different kind than this. The action that ought to be punished is one that deserves or merits punishment. And to think of one's own actions in this way is to view them in a certain light, *as* right or wrong, and of oneself as rightly held responsible for them, as justified or un-justified in their performance.

The categories in whose terms such thinking is done and the language in which they have a practically significant use are not those of behavioral conditioning but of moral understanding, of practical action, agent and justifying or normatively cogent rea-sons. Until we have learned to view our own conduct and that of others in this light nothing moral has been learned and the training given is not moral training. A man whose behavior was appropriately conditioned might behave all his life as he had been brought up to behave and still be a moral moron. How far this is the case with what Peirce calls "conservatism" the reader, from his own political experience, may judge.

What, then, is *moral* training? The account in Plato's *Prota-goras*, which we considered in Chapter IV, will again be useful here. The formula for such instruction, it will be recalled, is not just "do this" under specified conditions, but "this is right: do this." If this "right" were understood merely as a reiterated command, from those we are afraid of, or as verbal bait for the performance ordered, like fish for trained seals, such instruction would reduce without remainder to the "conditioning" we have just considered. We have seen that such reductions have been attempted and that, and why, they make no moral sense. No doubt what passes for "moral" training is often given and understood in just this way. But this is not the way in which a man learns to become, and to conduct himself as, a moral agent. Those who learned no more than this would rightly be regarded not as men we could respect as persons but, morally, as cases of arrested development. Peirce is quite right in saying that in such "morality" there is no place for reasoning. Indeed, he understates the case. For men thus trained what would be the sense or use of justifying reasons? They would need only to remember their instructions and in fear and trembling or with a glow of conformist satisfaction or just as a matter of course, of social habit and routine, to do as they had long ago been told. They would "obey the traditional maxims of their community without hesitation or discussion." What, with respect to the morality of the action, would there be to discuss? But he is wrong in describing this as "thinking as you were brought up to think." It is rather a way of behaving as you were brought up to behave in situations in which you were brought up *not* to think. To suppose that it is in such "bringing up" as this that we learn the meaning and the use of moral reasons would be patently absurd.

But what other use than this *could* there be for the "right" that is a distinctive factor in moral instruction? We saw in Chapter V that there is one at least. Here "right" functions as an admonition to the learner to look at his action in a distinctive way, to consider it not merely as something he is told to do or not to do but as something that he, of his own will, ought or ought not to do "because"—where the ground for so doing is specified in the reasons that show the action to be in this way right or wrong. "Wrong", *thus understood,* is not the name of a class of not-to-be-done acts any more than "poisonous" is the name of a class of not-to-be-eaten foods. A poison is a not-to-be-eaten thing not just because our instructors tell us to avoid it but because it is lethal and should as such be shunned by a man concerned to preserve his life even when no one in authority has ordered him to shun it. A man who has not learned that has not learned how to deal rationally with poisons. No matter how docile he might be in following instructions, he would be quite helpless in a situation that they did not cover or where they had been wrongly given. His not to reason why; his but to eat and die. For he would so far have nothing to reason with, or about. His training would not have taught him to think and act as a practical agent.

So for "right". "This is right", where it makes rational sense at all, is a "move" in a different game from that of the conditioning of behavior by peremptory and/or persuasive speech. The action is something to be done or not done for a reason, and "right" in its moral use is an indicator of the kind of reason that would here be relevant to warrant action. "Look at it this way." To characterize an action as honorable or as dishonorable, or in any other moral terms, is to place it in this practical context, to give a reason why it should or should not be done. Unless the "done thing" is *in this way* understood as the ought to be done thing it has no moral warrant and in the teaching of it nothing moral has been taught.

Such admonitions are addressed to men *as* moral agents, and it is in this capacity that they can practically respond to them as such. Moral training is the training of actual human beings to become and act as such agents—men who, in their own persons can distinguish between right and wrong and will sometimes, of their own will, act accordingly. For the right is, as we have seen, a necessity by which men are bound only in so far as they are free. This must be a training of a different sort than that used for trained dogs or seals. For it is training in the development and right exercise of *this* capacity. Here the appeal to justifying reasons has a distinctive and essential place. A "right" thus understood has a "because" in it and until this "because" has been given, the "normative force" of right has not been established for a responsible moral agent. To learn what moral reasons are is to learn what considerations are in this way grounds for right action, to learn their justifying use and cogency in *this* "game". A training that does not teach this is not moral training and the use in it of terms that claim a moral cogency is analytically a categorial confusion and practically a fraud.

Our first and primary answer, then, to those who in this way "analyze" morality and moral training is that they have here confused their "games". They are trying to get a language of justifying reasons out of procedures of social conditioning in which this kind of justification, with the reasons that support it, has no place. It is not surprising to discover that in such "training" nothing normatively cogent can be learned, and that moral reasons, thus understood, can have no practically rational use. It is, on the contrary, exactly what, by this time, we should expect.

What, then, *is* moral training? Before the use of justifying reasons can be taught, there must *be* such a use. The "game" in which they have a normative cogency must be played. A society that offers effective training in such use must practice what it preaches, for it is in this practice that the preaching makes practical sense. And if the training is to be moral, this practice must be that of a community in which a going concern for right action is an effective factor in the way of life in which the learner is called upon responsibly to share. It is in such sharing that a child can learn what it is to have good reasons for what he does, and to do an action for such reasons. Admonitory speech has a useful part in such training, and rewards and punishments may support it, but unless the practice itself supports it in a different way, by example and not by punishment and precept merely, only the timid or the gullible will in the long run be imposed on by it. Here as elsewhere we learn to do by doing, under the practical guidance of those who do well the thing that we are learning how to do. And what, in this case we are learning how to do is to act as moral agents. At what point in a child's development he can be reached by considerations of this sort is a question "child psychologists" must answer, where that term refers to their subject-matter and not to the conceptual discernment of their treatment of it. Obviously the child's behavior must be "conditioned" in other ways before he is able so to act. But this, when and as it becomes possible, is what moral training is, and without it no amount of conditioning will be the training of a moral agent.

Of course, the content of such training, as formulated in familiar maxims, will be the accepted moral precepts of the group in which the training is given. It is only on the basis of an agreed or understood consensus that there can be common grounds for action, and a ground that is not in its intention "common" is not a practical reason. If everything in a moral situation were arguable or questionable at once there could be no significant questioning or argument. And until the learner has acquired this working basis of understanding, until he knows in some cases what good reasons are, he will have nothing to reason with or about when he is called on in his own person to distinguish between actions that are right and wrong. *Of course* his having promised is a reason why he ought to do a promised act; a man who could not understand this, or other reasons of a similarly rudimentary nature, would be one with whom we could never hope to reach a moral understanding on the issues of our common life. But while this is the beginning of moral wisdom it cannot in principle, or in hard cases, be the end. For such reasons are not reasons for themselves, self-evident bits of final moral truth, to be cognitively cherished on their own account. They are grounds *for* actions to be done and whether in specific cases they are sufficient grounds, is a question that cannot be answered by an appeal to their initial unquestioning acceptance as reasons. And this question is inherent in their right use *as reasons* from the start, though, fortunately, in many instances, it need not be raised. In moral training, as in any other, we must begin with the rudiments. There cannot be exceptions to rules unless there are rules and the rule, as a moral maxim, is the norm for normal cases. But the rudiments must have the root of the matter in them, else the seed thus planted could not grow up to bear the fruit which is moral agency and moral judgment. And this root is precisely the understanding and use of the reasons taught *as reasons* as grounds for action to be done not because that is the way we learned it, or because it is the done thing but because, for good and sufficient reasons, it is right. The learner thus equipped is launched on a voyage of discovery that can carry him a long way from his starting point. For the process of the use of reasons is a self-correcting process. The customary acceptances with which it begins are the grounds for action each of us has learned to respect in the local communities in which he was brought up to play his part well as a son, a team mate or a citizen. In many situations they are good enough. If they were not the group that taught him what it is to be a responsible agent would not be itself a moral community. But in changing conditions and in the larger situations with which he and his group, since it is never morally isolated, have to deal, they are sometimes not good enough. There are issues that cannot on their local and parochial terms be adequately met and other people's reasons to be weighed that are not those he learned in childhood to respect. And if he has not merely been "brought up" but has grown up he must come to understand and use the better reasons here required—better in the same way in which these are good, as requirements for a moral *modus vivendi*—but adequate, as those that he initially learned are not, to serve here as foundations for a good society. Moral learning is not for children merely; we must go on learning all our lives if the requirements of our moral situation are rightly to be met. The point of moral training is to supply a starting point and to develop the concern and capacity with which we can thus go on. It is a teaching that prepares us to go beyond our instructions and to solve a problem for ourselves. And it is in just this way that it is a training in the practical use of reason.

Do we ever get this kind of training? Indeed we do—not in admonitory verbal slaps and sweetmeats, though for the very young and for those who never do grow up such admonitions have a social use, but in living and working with those who in their own persons embody this kind of excellence and, by precept and example, can bring out the best in us. It is in this way and in the light of their achievement that we come to understand what makes good reasons "good" and how, in their terms, to distinguish between right and wrong as we share with them in the concerns and responsibilities of a way of life in which such goodness has a practical sense and use. And if we have learned to understand their reasons, not just to mimic their behavior, we can go on to do for ourselves what in our own situation, which may not be theirs, it is our business to do. This capacity to go on is the authentic mark of the mastery of the technique of this practice and it is in the right use of it that all that is moral in "moral training" is fulfilled. That much of what is offered as moral falls far short of this we must not merely admit but emphasize. There are those who believe that men are made morally good by the kind of conditioning that would train a monkey or a seal, and that compulsory indoctrination in "our ideology" will somehow "make man free". But moral persons are not made; they grow. And it is in the exercise of freedom that we become free men. The training that can fruitfully foster this growth is indeed a special kind of training. For to become such a person is a special kind of achievement. That achievement and nothing less is the point of moral training.

A subtler form of the same misconception is embedded in what is currently known as the "rules" or "practice" conception of obligation and of duty. Here the language of justifying reasons is employed and it is recognized that the "why" required to make sense of it is that of moral justification. It turns out, however, on this analysis, that there are really two different "whys" here—each the answer to a quite distinct problem and applicable in a special area of conduct. The area of duty and obligation is that of actions covered by the rules of a practice in which the individual has a definitely assignable role, the area, roughly, of "my station and its duties". Here, it is alleged, to justify an action is just to show that there is a rule that governs it and is thus binding on the individual in his role or "office" within the practice. That the rule exists is a social fact, the fact that it is accepted as a justifying norm for action. Within the practice, references to the rule, as thus accepted, are reasons that justify doing, or refusing to do, a particular action, and they owe their "moral force" to this reference. As H. L. A. Hart puts it, "The morality of duty and obligation is that of principles which would lose their moral force unless they were widely accepted in a particular group."[2] For they are the principles or rules of this specific practice, and it is as they are thus accepted that there *is* this practice. This game is played.

The "why" of obligation is answered by reference to the rules as thus existing. It's three strikes and you're out in the old ball game, for that is the way this game is played. If there is any doubt on this point, we need only refer to the official rule book

---

[2] In "Legal and Moral Obligation," in *Essays in Moral Philosophy*, ed. A. I. Melden (Seattle: University of Washington Press, 1958), p. 101.

to confirm it. And it is the duty of the umpire to enforce this rule, not because he wants to, or thinks on other grounds that it is a good idea, but because as an umpire it is his office to do so. This is the "why" inside the game, and, in its own domain, it is quite final.

For the rules themselves, however, there is no "why" of this sort at all. They simply are the structure of the way this game is played and unless we act in accordance with them it is not this game that we are playing. Their correct observance is a conceptual *must* of the practice that, as a social fact, exists. In this way promising is one of the practices of our society. As Toulmin puts it, " 'It is wrong to keep this book because it is wrong to break a promise' is accepted in our society because making and keeping promises is one of the things we do; 'the promise' is one of our institutions."[3] Given this acceptance the "obligation" is clear. Rawls states it succinctly: "The promisor is bound because he promised. Weighing the merits of the case is not open to him."[4]

The analysts of this persuasion are emphatic in affirming that this "why" of rule bound behavior does not cover the whole area of moral action. On the contrary, they insist, there is another sphere of morality, beyond obligation and duty, in which we are not thus bound at all. The wrong of inflicting gratuitous suffering, Hart tells us, does not depend on its actual acceptance by the social group but is something by which we may judge the morality of social groups. Here what we ask for is the "why" of the rules themselves and it is obviously not by reference to the rules as socially existing that we can get an answer to this question. How, then, are we to get it? By reference to the good or interests of the society to whose welfare the observance of

---

[3] *The Place of Reason in Ethics* (Cambridge: Cambridge University Press, 1950), p. 170.

[4] "Two Concepts of Rules," *The Philosophical Review*, January, 1955, p. 16.

the rules, and of the practice they define, contributes. The question that we cannot raise within the practice can and should be asked about it and about the good of it. Of the nature of this good the analysts have so far not had much to say. Their remarks concerning it are utilitarian in a large, loose way; it is to be estimated somehow in terms of consequences and of welfare for "society". But they are careful to leave the door open for it and to point out that the rule-bound morality of duty and obligation, or of "practices" with which they chiefly deal, is morally incomplete without it.

This is a plausible and ingenious theory. But it seems to me, as it stands, to be seriously misleading. For it cuts the "why" of moral justification up into two quite different "whys", neither of which makes moral sense by itself nor, as thus analyzed, in combination with the other. The "why" of obligation, as thus elucidated, is something less than moral and the "why" of the good unbound by obligation is morally equivocal. From their juxtaposition we get an analytically distorted picture of the authentic cogency of moral reasons. And since the language of the analysis is, in some respects, much like our own, it is important that we see how and why this is the case.

Consider first the why of action for which a reference to the socially accepted rules of a practice is supposed to supply not only a sufficient but the only logically possible justification. Why did you—or why should I—pay this man this sum of money? Because I or you promised to do so, and that one keeps a promise is a rule of a practice which is one of our institutions. This rule defines the status of the promisor within the practice and specifies what, in a particular case, it is his office, or his obligation, to do. A man who did not understand this would not know what it was to make a promise, just as one who thought that he could steal a base in baseball by picking up the bag and walking away with it would not know what it was, in that game or practice, to steal a base. If he asked *why* he could not steal it that way, an elucidation of the rules would provide a logically conclusive answer. For it is only on the terms set by the rules that stealing a base counts as a move in this game at all, and the rules do not permit this move. This does not mean, of course, that a man might not in fact pick up the bag and make off with it but that if he did he would not be playing baseball. His action would count as "stealing" not in the official boxscore of the game but rather, perhaps, in a police court. So equally for promising, and, on this account, for all behavior that is in this way "covered by rules."

Now there is evidently a stage—normally an early one—in learning to play baseball at which this kind of misunderstanding might arise, and it is by this sort of instruction that it would properly be corrected. Here, as Rawls well says, one does not so much justify a particular action as explain it. "When a particular action is specified by a practice there is no justification possible of the particular action of a particular person save by reference to the practice."[5] And if it is this kind of "justification" that is wanted, this surely is the way to give it.

But is it what is wanted when a man asks for—or offers—moral grounds for action? The question here is not, save incidentally or in special cases, as to what the rules are but rather as to the account he ought to take of them in his conduct. So this is the way baseball or "the institution of the promise" is played. So what? If the explanation given is understood merely *as* an explanation or elucidation it leaves the man who accepts it as practically uncommitted as before. "If the game is not thus played it will not be baseball as the rules define it." "Of course not. Should it be? Why so?" "Baseball is one of our institutions. This game is played." "I accept this as sociological information

---

[5] *Loc. cit.*, p. 32.

but I do not see how I am morally bound by it. Why should I do the done thing?" "It has been empirically established that the playing of baseball by these rules contributes to the interests of society." "Perhaps so. If I had a clearer notion what you took to be the interest of society I might be able to agree or disagree with that assertion. But, in any case, why should I so act as to contribute in this way to the interests of society? So far you have given me a logical elucidation, some sociological information, and a very loose generalization about the interests of society. But you have given me no moral grounds for doing anything at all. And it was for such grounds that I asked."

Obviously the man who plays his part well and fairly in the game of baseball or any other does not in this way understand the rules, or his own role or office with respect to them. He is "bound" by them not logically or sociologically but morally. To respect and follow them is a requirement for the right playing of this game in which he is involved as a responsible participant, and as such an obligation which he ought to meet. Only as thus understood can a reference to the rules, however analytically precise, provide a moral ground for action. The "practice" analysts have not reduced the justifying sense of obligation to the explanatory sense of a conceptual elucidation of socially accepted rules. On the contrary, it is only when what is thus elucidated is understood *as* a ground of obligation that it has any relevance to moral problems, or can be *in this way*, a justifying reason. We often have an obligation to follow socially accepted rules—though we sometimes also have an obligation to break them. But the moral sense of the rule is in the obligation and it is only by bringing back into the picture what their analysis cuts out of it that we can make such sense of what the analysts tell us about rules.

At this point we shall be told, perhaps, that we have misunderstood the theory. Its aim is not at all to eliminate the "why" of obligation, in its use as a moral reason, but rather to show more clearly in what this consists and how, for analytic or "linguistic" purposes, it is to be understood. Its purpose is to clarify *this* use—not to substitute another for it. Perhaps, but in that case our objection must be that this is precisely what it fails to do. For what it tells us is that where obligation is in question the only justifying "why" for action is an explanation or elucidation of the rules themselves. And when we ask how this elucidation provides a ground for action it tells us that, within the practice itself, there is no more to be said than that as socially accepted the rules thus elucidated have "moral force", i.e., that their acceptance as thus cogent is a social fact. And neither of these considerations, nor both together, are the reasons that, for the moral grounding of our actions, we need. If they were so understood, they would be the wrong kind of reasons. It is true, of course, that if the rules were not socially accepted in this way they would have no "moral force", for then *this* game would not be played and it is within this game, and as responsible participants, that we have an obligation to respect them. If baseball were not played, no one would have an obligation, as a baseball player, to abide by its rules. But the moral force—i.e., the normative cogency—of the obligation does not consist in its social acceptance. That the rules are so accepted is not a sufficient answer to the "why" of duty. If it were, social conformity, or doing the done thing, would be the final *ground* of moral obligation. When the analysts so far forget themselves as to import a moral significance into their elucidations, the words are those of the (informal) logician, but the voice is that of the games master, or football coach exhorting us to "play up and play the game" or "pull, pull together." It is not surprising that those who have thus understood them have interpreted what they have to say as an expression of the ideology of socially respectable conservatism.

We are assured that this is a misunderstanding—that in fact what is offered is *only* an analysis and elucidation which has as such no moral import. What we do—or ought to do—with the rules thus elucidated and moored to their appropriate social context is another question altogether. But if this is so, then what was offered was not an account of moral reasons in their morally justifying or normatively cogent use—i.e., it was not an account of the "why" of obligation and of duty. It was *this* "why", in the whole area of obligation and of duty, that the analyst was supposed to elucidate, and if this in his terms is all that justification comes to, then so far we have not got a moral reason. The irony of the situation is that we *must* "misunderstand" what is thus offered *as* a moral reason if we are to understand it in a moral sense at all. For this is the sense of "justification" as a ground for morally right action.

Here, however, we shall be reminded that we have so far left out half the theory. The game has not only rules but a point, and the question of why the rules should be followed, which cannot be raised within the game itself, since here a reference to the rules as socially accepted is all the justification that there logically can be, can be raised about it. Is such rule-bound behavior conducive to the general welfare or to the interests of society? Should this game be played? Here we do not accept the rules as the final norm of justification but demand that they be justified in their turn. This is the other side of moral reasoning, not bound by rules or obligations at all but free to examine all our social practices from an obligation-free standpoint and hold fast only those that are good. If the rule-bound side of moral justification seemed to imply conservatism, this one is "liberal" indeed.

For what is this "good" and why should the rightness of our practices be measured in its terms? "Good" in general, as we have seen, is tautologously what we ought to seek and a "larger" good in preference to a lesser one. But whose good, how achieved, and on what terms shared by those for whom an *obligation* to seek it has a moral sense? The answers given here are vaguely utilitarian in tone. It is the good of all concerned, or most of them at least, and if it is not pleasure—the modern Utilitarian is usually too cautious to say that—it is welfare, or the satisfaction of interests or the like. How it is to be achieved is a problem for the social planners—the Sidney and Beatrice Webbs of the future, perhaps. With such questions the linguistic analyst of moral language is not professionally concerned. His job is simply to point out what kind of questions they are and what, in principle, would be an answer to them.

Our objection must be that he has done this job badly and that, given his account of obligation and duty, he was bound to do so. For just as there is no obligation that makes moral sense without good, so there is no normatively cogent good that does not have its roots in obligation, understood not as rule-bound conformity to the formal requirements of a game, but as obligation-bound acceptance of the moral requirements of a way of life. Utilitarianism is by no means a no-obligation theory. Rather it is a doctrine that sets up one obligation—to maximize "happiness" no matter whose, or of what sort, or how attained if only in the total felicific balance it be "more"—as unconditionally binding, and treats all others as empirical maxims concerning ways in which this "more" is normally to be achieved. That an action is in this way happiness-producing is the final, and finally the only reason why, on moral grounds, we ought to do it. Other rules have exceptions, but it allows none and is as inflexible as the strictest Puritan could ask. In invoking this philosophy, therefore, we have not reached an obligation-free standpoint. For in our estimate of the good that ought to be produced we are still bound by an obligation and a very rigid one. And we cannot appraise the moral cogency of this rule from the outside, for it is only on the terms it sets that "good" has normative significance for action. If "rule-bound" means obligation-bound action then in Utilitarianism there is no moral action that is not "rule-bound".

This, however, is not what the analysts have in mind when they talk of rules and obligations. They would limit the application of such terms to principles socially accepted in *particular* groups, which would lose their moral force without such acceptance. Where right and wrong are not thus localized but would hold (as socially accepted?) in any society, they are not in this way grounds of obligation. Thus Hart tells us, "It is absurd to speak of a moral *duty* not to kill another human being, or an *obligation* not to torture a child."[6] The "right" of happiness-maximizing actions is presumably of this practice-transcending character and can therefore be used as a standard by which the morality of accepted practices can be judged. It was in this way, certainly, that Bentham tried to use it.

Is this narrowing of the sense of duty and of obligation helpful here? I should have thought that it at least made sense in our society to say that the observance of the Sixth Commandment was a moral duty. At Oxford it may not be so. But linguistic proprieties of this sort are not the major issue here. The question rather is about the meaning of a right and wrong from which the content of particular obligations, within a morally structured community, has been eliminated as mere rule-bound conformity to the requirements of a socially accepted practice. "Torture", or the infliction of gratuitous suffering is universally disapproved. But that is because "torture", in this use, is itself a condemnatory term and any action to which it is properly applied is so far condemned. If moral language is to have a coherent use at all, this much must be true. But when is it properly applied? What

---

[6] *Loc. cit.*, p. 82.

infliction of suffering on children is "gratuitous"? Is corporal
punishment "torture"? Or allowing a child to be hurt by the
consequences of his own willful act? Or requiring him to be quiet
when he wants to make a noise? Here a Spartan parent may
judge the rightness of an action differently than would a devotee
of progressive education. These differences are not extrinsic to
the moral significance of the action. They are bound up with
conceptions of what it is to be a child and to become a man—
of what is essential and what is admirable in the preservation
of a moral order. And the same, of course, is true of "welfare"
and of "happiness". Whatever merits these eulogistic designations
is thereby established as a worthy end of action. It is the
function of such words of praise to present it in this status. But
what kind of living can rightly be thus characterized, and on
what terms can such a life be rightly lived? Is welfare to be
identified with a multiplication of creature comforts on equalitarian terms? Or happiness with a sum of pleasures distinguished
from all lesser "goods" only by the fact that somehow it is more?
And what does the achievement of such a good require of men
who would *justly* share it? These are questions that a reference
to universal moral platitudes does not answer. Yet an answer to
them is presupposed in any appeal to happiness or welfare as a
worthy end of action that makes practical sense and can thus
serve as a normative guide to action. The "felicity" for whose
attainment Bentham laid down legislative rules was not that
of the whole sentient creation, calculated from the point of view
of the Universe, but that of respectable, sensibly self-interested,
law-abiding Englishmen, calculated from the point of view of a
reformer who for the most part shared the business-like values
of the community to which his "moral arithmetic" was addressed
and was concerned to bring its penal procedures, for example,
into line with such a reasonably calculable good. In this context
his appeal to utility makes good moral sense. Divorced from

it, and set up as a "principle" about good in general, it becomes morally indeterminate and hence equivocal in its practical implications. Whose pleasure, how secured and how enjoyed? To say that "in the end" these considerations matter only instrumentally as means to the attainment of more pleasure "on the whole" is morally preposterous. Yet if happiness, now identified as pleasure, is *the* good, and right action that which maximizes it, what else is there to say? In the making of responsible moral judgments we must have grounds more relative than this. And these grounds are just the obligations of a morally structured community whose practices have a justifying "why" in them and whose good is the fulfillment of their own intent. There is no morally acceptable good without obligations and there are no obligations whose "why" is not a requirement for the attainment of such good.

When we try to combine the "why" of rule-bound action with the obligation-free good of generalized welfare or social interest what, more specifically, do we get? *Within* the practice, as we have seen, the question of good cannot be raised. As Rawls says: "The promisor is bound because he promised. Weighing the case on its general merits is not open to him."[7] Outside the practice, however, the question of general merits is the only one that counts. Thus we may ask whether the practice of keeping promises is in general beneficial to society. If it is, then this game should be played, and if it is played it must be played in this way; the promisor must abide by the rule and is "bound" accordingly. What such general merits would be and how they could be ascertained in abstraction from the requirements of a way of life in which "merit" already had a moral meaning it is difficult to see. But let us suppose that these questions could be cogently answered and that, in terms of such an answer, it could

---

[7] *Loc. cit.*

be established that the playing of the promise-keeping game was in general, in its consequences, beneficial to such social interests. This would still not take us far toward the solution of any moral questions about the right of keeping a specific promise. Almost nobody would deny that *in general* promises should be kept. The serious question is that of whether *this* action, which would be the keeping of a promise, should be done when it would also be, e.g., giving aid and comfort to enemies of my country and this, in general, is something that I ought *not* to do. Here the "practice" that we are morally involved in is not just that of promise keeping. There are no *merely* moral practices. It involves the whole network of relations in which a man is involved as a promisor, of course, but also as a citizen and much more besides, and the merits of the case as specified by *all* these obligations are profoundly relevant to what in this case and in his "office" as a moral agent, he ought or ought not to do. It is not only open to him here to take account of such merits; it is his duty as a responsible moral agent to do so. To say "It is good in general or on the whole that the game of promise-keeping should be played and therefore, as a promisor, I am bound to keep my promise without regard for any other obligation than that which the rule for promise-keeping defines" would be, in practice, a highly *un*reasonable procedure. That is not the way in which *this* game— the game of rational justification—is played by those who understand the meaning and the use of moral reasons.

Almost no one who is not infatuated by a theory would suppose it was. The rules of such a practice must be in some way "defeasible"—exception must be made for cases in which it would be morally unreasonable to follow a "rule" thus simple-mindedly understood and "defenses" allowed for those who, in the interests of good sense and fairness, refuse, in such instances, to conform to it. The question is as to how this defeasibility and these exceptions are to be understood. One way is that of legalism. We must somehow get the "defenses" into the rule itself. If the rule has all allowable exceptions in it, it can, as thus qualified, be followed without exception, and a reference to it will be sufficient in particular cases to tell us what it is our "obligation" to do. It is, as Hart has observed,[8] where obligations are "legally colored" that this version of the matter is most plausible. We may, indeed, suspect that it is just to the legal coloring that it plausibly applies. In the administration of the law this kind of legalism has its plain and proper place, though even here considerations of "general merit" sometimes rightly guide the decisions of judges. But where the issue is moral there is little to be said for it. For here we are not just giving previously promulgated laws to ourselves but judging a particular moral issue on its merits. To suppose that all that is relevant to such an estimate is embalmed in "exceptions" designed to deal with past cases and duly canonized in our rule book is moral superstition. It is not merely that old rules will not adequately "cover" new cases. The question, as we have seen, is that of how, and on what grounds, the exceptions got into the rule in the first place. Those who put them there did not have antecedent rules for so doing. *They* must have made a judgment on the merits of the case. And to suppose that we, in the complex, novel and demanding world that now confronts us, are called on to do less is dangerously simple-minded.

The other way is that of moral judgment and the reasons that support it. Here moral rules are understood as maxims that rightly claim our allegiance and respect. But to respect them *as reasons* is not to set them up as the logical requirements of games that, in the general interest, it is good to play. Their defeasibility is not that of laws with built-in loopholes (exceptions) in them. It is rather that of grounds for action which,

---

[8] *Loc. cit.*

though good as *so far* cogent, may be insufficient for the resolution of concrete problems on their specific merits. Here an obligation, as a ground for action, is in one way less, and in another more, than the "rules" conception would make of it. It is less in the sense that it is never, simply as it stands, a final justification for moral action. In normal circumstances, it is a sufficient reason for an action to be done. And if circumstances were not usually normal, the "rule" as a maxim would have no moral standing. But in some circumstances it may not be, and where *on moral grounds* the question of its adequacy can be fairly raised, a reference to the rule as final will not meet the issue, for it is precisely its *moral* finality in this instance, not its justification in general that is here in question. But, in another sense, it is more. For, as it stands, it is a moral reason and as such a ground for action, as no elucidation of *de facto* rules could ever be. It is a good reason, the right *kind* of reason, and if in specific cases it is not good enough, the better reasons that can justify a different action than the one which, by itself, it warrants, will themselves be obligations, understood as requirements for the achievement of a moral order which it genuinely, but so far incompletely, serves to specify. The right that can carry us beyond our customarily accepted maxims is an ought that is *in* them, as grounds for justifiable action, and it is the right playing of this game that their intent in this use is adequately fulfilled. Unless the new commandments were the fulfillment of the old, we could not morally understand them. But when we do thus understand them we are launched on a voyage of discovery that no rule book yet devised can adequately chart.

Why is it that a theory with so much truth in it should with such ingenuity in this way go wrong? The answer is, I think, two-fold. There is a deeply ingrained notion in "linguistic analysis" that an account of moral justification in moral terms has not really done its job. We *begin* with "obligation" and "duty", understood in a specifically moral sense, but if we are *really* to clarify them, we must end with something else—with a logical elucidation of rules, or a social fact or something like a legal system. And perhaps even these are not really basic. It may be that on metaphysical analysis assertions of these kinds "unfold into facts" of a still more basic and rudimentory sort. If this should prove to be the case, how simple (ultimately) everything would be. This kind of analysis does, indeed, have its attractions.

There is a practical persuasiveness about it, too. If we could just bring moral reasons (at least those of obligation) back to logical truths and sociological, legal and/or linguistic facts, we could "finally" reach a point at which we were relieved of the responsibility of making moral judgments. The question of meaning could be handed over to the (informal) logician and that of fact to the scientists or near-scientists of the areas in question. As analysts we should not be required to accept the moral implications of the considerations we identified as justifying reasons for as thus processed, they would have no moral implications. And if any area of moral justification—that of "good", for example—remained uncovered by such an analysis, we could safely leave it in that realm of edifying generalities in which traditional "liberal" ethical theorizing—Utilitarianism for example—has enshrined it. All this seems modest, circumspect and in harmony with approved academic procedure.

The one major difficulty with it, as we have seen, is that under such analysis "moral reasons" lost their moral sense and use. This loss is a high price to pay for an observance of academic proprieties—too high if our purpose is so to understand the "language" of morality that we can use it reasonably for practical ends. Hence, while we may respect the good intentions and admire the skill of the analysts of this persuasion we cannot follow their example nor expect to find in their description of morality the substance of the thing we seek. They have, for their own purposes, changed the subject.

Just as the moral use of "reasons" and "rules" may, in our current climate of opinion, be analytically misunderstood, so, too, may that of "community", and with comparable results. We have held that the requirements of morality are those for the maintenance of a moral order, or *modus vivendi* in the communities to which men belong as moral agents, and that it is to such agents that moral claims on conduct are significantly addressed. Experience has shown that there are those who will suppose at once that they understand us here, and will agree with what they take to be our main conclusion, though they will be unhappy about the unduly moralistic terms in which it is presented. For "community" they will substitute "society", for the moral agent the socialized "self" or "me" of the will-conditioned organism, and for "obligations" the pressures of "the group" as these are "internalized" and generalized in individual behavior as goals and guides for socially normalized behavior. Such a substitution appears to put the discussion on a sound factual basis and to bring it into fruitful connection with the advancing sciences of sociology and social psychology. Nothing is lost save a scientifically outmoded terminology and, on the level of the engineering of human attitudes, there is a world to win. If only philosophers would say plainly that this is what they mean, what profitable interdisciplinary and crossfertilizing research projects might be organized with at least one philosopher on every team.

This, of course, is not what we mean. And, if taken as an account of the moral meaning of "community" it is not only theoretically incorrect but morally indefensible. The reader who has followed our account so far will hardly need to be told that and why this is the case. But since the urge to such misunderstanding is strong and the terminology for its articulation academically well established, it will perhaps be wise to sum the matter up as explicitly as possible.

What such a theory—sometimes called "social behaviorism"—tells us is that what we call moral obligations are the pressures of society upon its members, generalized as rules of good behavior and internalized through social training as the "self" or "me" of the behaving organism. Moral principles are the directives of such generally sanctioned behavior as these are accepted and acted on voluntarily by the socially adjusted individual. The voice of the generalized other is the voice of conscience and to be a self is to respond in this way—taking the role of the other—to one's own organic responses and "behaving oneself" accordingly. Since such theories claim to be factually descriptive in the best scientific manner, there can be no question here of whether conduct thus controlled is "really" right. Within the group in which such conditioning effectively functions it will be what is called right and as such a norm for the normalized individual. And those who conform to it will be acting rightly in the only sense of that term which here makes sociological sense.

The "facts" stressed by such theories, so far as they are factually confirmed, are instructive. And since the moral process is at least a social process, they are clearly relevant to our subject. But as an account of moral action they are theoretically incongruous and practically misleading. An obligation, as a ground for action, is not a social pressure. A moral self is not a mechanism of social control built into the individual by the appropriate conditioning of his responses. And a community that can rightly claim the loyalty of its members is not a pressure group thus organized. Something has been left out here that makes all the difference between a social tool, however well processed, and a moral person. And it is not really difficult to see what this something is. For it is just morality itself.

Why should I conform to the pressures of society? For the "social self" this could not be a moral question, for these pressures themselves, as generalized and internalized in "conscience", are the only moral "should" he knows. But there is often urgent need for us to ask them, if we are to live as free men in the socially engineered world that now confronts us. And what kind of answer can "society" give to such a question? Because it is the done thing? But sometimes it is not done. That is why pressures are required to bring "deviant" conduct into conformity with it. It is not as the done thing merely but as the ought-to-be-done thing that it is supposed to influence my conduct. What gives it this status? Is it because this is what society requires of me and I am a social being? But the voice of "society" may here be anything from the shouts of a lynching mob to the dictates of Mrs. Emily Post. Gangsters, pickpockets and prostitutes are no less social in their fashion than are men and women of distinction. Is it what the best people do, or at least approve of others doing? Who, then, are the best? Those whose social status establishes them as the elite of the society in question? If the wife of the President of General Motors approves of Gladiola Cake Mix or contributes to the United Fund is there not a clear social mandate for Mrs. Jones and Mrs. Robinson to "do so as well"? Or is it simply those who by one sort of "conditioning" or another have the power to exert this kind of influence on my thought and conduct? Here "might" (if we include all forms of social power and not mere physical force) does indeed, and tautologically, make "right". For "right" in this use, is just "internalized" conformity to this sort of might. Other societies with a different sort of power structure will, of course, have different "rights" and, where these practically conflict only might (including that of propaganda) can decide which "right" is to prevail. If it really does prevail a future generation, if not ours, will be trained as "social selves" to accept its dictates as their "moral" principles. Their "consciences" will have been conditioned to this end.

Just as the "right" thus established is not moral right, so the self that thus responds to it is not a moral agent. He is the adjustable man and one of the ways in which he can be thus adjusted is by the use of generalized directives whose dictates he is trained, by moral engineering, to impose upon "himself". The voice of the generalized other speaks in him; it is for moral purposes, the only voice he has. The language of traditional morality is often effectively employed in the processing of such dictates for generalized consumption. In such a use they lose nothing but their rationally justifying sense. For beings thus conditioned, however, this loss would not appear as a defect. For they would not know what to make of such a justification if they had it. Their "responses" to "moral" issues are conditioned in a different way and, if they have been well conditioned, "society" will do their thinking for them. "Oh brave new world, that has such people in it."

A society thus organized would have great power at its command. But there is one sort of "force" that cannot be thus commanded. That is the moral force or cogency of a valid claim on the loyalty of men as moral agents. The words in which such claims have traditionally been made are still available to it—"Community", "right", "freedom" and the like—but their use will be a different one and their sense will alter with that use. They may excite or intimidate or soothe those trained in this way to respond to them, but they can justify nothing for the grounds of obligation that would warrant their cogency in such a use will no longer have a rationally examinable meaning, nor would those to whom they were addressed be morally or rationally in a position to examine them. To such individuals anything could be "justified"—i.e., made socially acceptable—by those who had the power to control the instruments of conscience-making.

But nothing could be justified by being shown to be right. For a social pressure, thus imposed, is not a moral reason. And whether any given "pressurizing" was itself justifiable could be answered only by more justification (pressurizing) which would establish "right" to the degree that it was socially effective. To say that this is not what we meant when we spoke of moral reasons as addressed to men as members of communities is not an overstatement.

To see precisely where the difference lies between the two accounts, we need only take a closer look at "community". This is a word of many uses and I do not claim that the one here followed is its only proper use. It is, however, a common and distinctive one, and I have tried to adhere consistently to it throughout. In this use, a "community" is not just any group that influences the behavior of its members. It is a group whose members are related in a quite distinctive way, the way of moral understanding, and the group is a community only insofar as they are thus related. The categories that make sense of this relationship are those of practical reason: of action, agent, public right and common good. And they make this kind of sense only in their normatively cogent or justifying use. That an action will further the "interests" of the community is a reason why I ought to do it. How so? What is the community to me, or I to it, that I should work for it? Why should its interests have precedence over mine, when these are *prima facie* different? If the interests of the community define a good that is somehow my good, too—a common good to whose achievement I am morally committed and in which I can rightly share, these questions can have a reasonable answer. But the "I" that can *thus* share in a good that can in truth be common to all who will rightly meet the requirements of its shared achievement is a free moral agent, not the manipulable end product of whatever processes of social conditioning have successfully been brought to bear on him. Such an "I" needs reasons for his action that the persuasive reiteration of the word "community" cannot supply. Is the pressure group that makes demands on me in fact such a community? Is the "good" in whose name it speaks in truth a common good or rather a false front for interests whose pretentions and claims will not bear rational inspection? It is not in internalized conformity to generalized directives that such questions can be significantly asked or rightly answered. For the answers may well lead to a rejection of demands thus made and to a counter-demand that the social directives of "the group" be altered for the better achievement of the common good whose interests it claims to represent. Considered in their normative cogency its pretensions are examinable by those who have the concern and capacity to act on them as reasons, i.e., by moral agents, and it is only for such agents that they can have a rationally justifying sense.

What "social behaviorism" does in practice is to strip the concept of community of this justifying use and sense and at the same time to trade on its persuasive or "engineering" potency as propaganda. We are still urged to serve "the community", for "community" is a "good" word for manipulative purposes. And "togetherness" has recently been a very good word indeed, in this use, though it appears now to be losing something of its glamour. That there are ways in which men can be "together" where, for the good of their soul, they had much better be apart, and that well-fed gregariousness is not as such the moral equivalent of virtue are here considerations "of no interest"—who, in such a "community" would be concerned or competent to make such a judgment? There is in this use a kind of sentimental cynicism, a combination of tongue in the cheek and tear in the eye that sometimes leaves even the engineer of our attitudes deeply moved. For he, too, is the product of his social environment and is playing out his "role" as senselessly as are the rest of us. That this is not the role of a moral agent is not surprising. In the world of social behaviorism there is no place for such a role.

It is not, then, by inadvertance, or as a concession to philosophically customary ways of speaking, that we have described the community that makes sense of moral action in morally loaded rather than in sociologically neutral terms. For it is precisely this moral loading which is its normatively relevant and cogent import and it is as considered in this light that the interests of "the community" make sense as grounds for moral action. The attempt to "clarify" this sense, or to evade its normatively rational commitments by reducing moral obligation to social pressures is based on a categorial confusion—the confusion it has been our aim throughout to eliminate. We must respectfully refuse to play on the social scientist's team, for it is not his game that we are playing. But ours though moralistic and, by current research standards, old fashioned is a game that all of us are obliged to play, not as professional researchers merely, but as men. It is of some importance therefore that its normative requirements be adequately understood.

There is one further source of misunderstanding that should be noted here. Even if we are careful to distinguish the normative claims of community as moral from the *de facto* pressures of existing social groups, does not a theory that holds that it is only for men as responsible participants in such communities that moral reasons have a moral use require us to conclude that a right action simply *is* one that serves the community of which one is a member? Does not this mean that our duty "in the end" is just to "serve and preserve the community"? And what is this but the identification of moral right with the "service" of existing institutions on the terms that their existing structure sets? In his very enlightening discussion in *Rights and Right Conduct* Melden tells us that "It is self-evident—analytic—that it is right that one maintain the moral community of which one is a member. There is no further feature over and above this one that is the rightness and that needs to be connected with it."[9] I do not think that, in its context, this assertion need or should be interpreted as a kind of analytic Hegelianism, a reduction of moral rightness to the maintenance of "my station and its duties." But since it has been so interpreted we had best point out, even at the cost of some repetition, that no such implication follows from a theory of the sort here presented. On the contrary, such a theory provides the grounds on which it can, and should, be decisively rejected.

The first thing to be noted is that it is the *moral* community of which Melden speaks, and no existing social institution is *as such,* or as "socially existing" a community in this sense. It is entitled to this status and can, accordingly, make valid claims of right upon our conduct, only in so far as it can show itself to be, in rationally warrantable terms, a moral order. *Of course,* insofar as the families, or "teams" or nations or churches of which we are *de facto* members are in this way moral communities it is right that we serve and preserve them, for in so doing we are serving and preserving moral right. No *further* feature needs to be connected with this to establish rightness, for this connection is already made when "the community" is characterized as in this way moral. But so to characterize existing institutions is to make a claim that sometimes needs very careful scrutiny indeed. That right actions are those that serve a *moral* community is indeed analytic, for in this context, it is a tautology. It tells us that it is right to preserve existing institutions insofar as they are genuinely the embodiment of a moral right which it is our duty to maintain, i.e., that it is right to do right actions. It is illuminating in so far as it refers us to the context in which

---

[9] A. I. Melden, *Rights and Right Conduct* (Oxford: Basil Blackwell, 1959), p. 71.

"right" can have a moral use and meaning. But as it stands it justifies the *de facto* demands of no existing social institution. It only indicates the light—which is that of moral reason itself —in which we must consider such demands if we are to judge their moral cogency.

Putting the issue in this light enables us to see quite clearly what is wrong with the morality of "my station and its duties." For moral relations are essentially and inescapably relations between persons. My duty is not to "the family" or "the state" or "the community" as such. It is to other men united with me in activities whose normatively practical requirements, as mutually acknowledged, can give our common life a moral meaning. My *moral* station in any community is that of such a person, and its duties are not the grooved conformities of the "organization man" but the responsibilities of one who acts in his own person for a right that makes a valid claim upon his conduct. It is only *in* a social context that he has such duties. But it is only *as* a moral agent that he has them, and what they are is something he, and not the institution must judge. For institutions have no minds of their own, and only men with minds and wills of their own can constitute a free society. What constitutes a state, in the sense in which the state is a community that rightly claims the loyalty of its citizens? In the words of a poem quoted by Thomas Jefferson, it is not battlements and towers—nor guided missiles, we might add, though these have their uses—but men: "High-minded men—men who their duties know but know their rights and, knowing, dare maintain. These constitute a State."[10] This, too, when the state is thought of as a moral community, is an analytic truth. But, for our times particularly, it is an enlightening one.

---

[10] In a letter to John Taylor, dated May 28, 1816. The letter is printed in *The Life and Selected Writings of Thomas Jefferson* (New York: The Modern Library, 1944), pp. 668-673.

Moreover, when we understand the concept of community in this sense—and it is in this sense only that we have used it as a moral notion—we can see that our duty is not merely to serve and preserve but to create "the community". *What* community? The groups in which we have our moral roots are to some degree communities in this sense. If they were not, we could not have learned in them, as we have, how obligations can be moral reasons. But they are incomplete, onesided and in many ways parochial in the range and level of their moral understanding. The good reasons we have learned in them are sometimes not good enough for the achievement of an effective moral order in our actual social relations. The communities in which their moral intent could be adequately fulfilled has still in large measure, and under great difficulties, to be built. To treat the limits of existing social acceptances or institutional organization as the ultimate boundaries of such understanding whose "preservation" is our final duty would be a betrayal of the continuing work to which, in the use of moral reasons, we are rationally and morally committed. Those who have not seen this still do not adequately understand the sense and use of moral reasons.

The main conceptual outlines of our theory of practical reasons have now been drawn. We have said, and tried to show, that in their appropriate use its categories make rational sense and that this sense is practically relevant to our conduct. So far this relevance has been indicated only in a rather general way. But it is not the business of moral philosophy to end in generalities. The cogency of such a theory is to be found not in its own inner luminosity but in what, in its light, we can understand about the right solutions of our moral problems. Part II offers some examples of the way such understanding works and in this way tries to show how, and within what limits, a theory of this sort can itself be practical.

CHAPTER 9
MORAL PROBLEMS
AND QUESTIONS OF ETHICS

IN PART I, I have tried to present plainly a clear account of the categorial conditions and conceptual structure of the situation in which moral problems arise and can rationally be resolved. The primary reference here has been to such situations *as we find them,* and to truths a man need only open his eyes to see, if he is prepared to see it candidly and for what it is. Experience has shown, however, that some, at least, who try quite seriously in this way to understand it will find this account very puzzling indeed. They do not see what we are trying to make of it, or what ethical conclusions it is supposed to warrant. And this in the circumstances is not surprising. Hardly anyone will read this book who has not already had at least an introductory course in college ethics. Such a reader knows by this time what the questions of ethics are and will naturally expect what is here offered to provide its own version of an answer to them. It is presented as a contribution to moral philosophy, is it not, and what else but this can moral philosophy be? Looked at in this light, however, what we have to offer is indeed perplexing. Where are our first principles and our last analyses, where the ultimate goals or unqualified imperatives on which an ultimate analysis, in the end, must surely rest? Kant would have given them to us, or Sidgwick, and if we now have none of our own to offer we might at least have given one more dialectical twist to the restatement of the perennial problems from which it seems that we are never to escape. Instead we seem to have talked all around the subject and to have lingered dubiously in its neighborhood without ever getting precisely to the point. All those examples—what do they really *prove*? What conclusions can be deduced from them that will warrant an unqualified and incorrigible conclusion? Blanshard well expresses this state of mind in his comment on "linguistic moralists."

> They are obviously an able group. But for that reason perhaps we may be permitted a gesture of protest against what we conceive Wittgenstein to have done to their generation. In reading such men as Sidgwick, Moore, and Ross, we might and often did disagree with them, but we knew where they stood on fundamentals. They had an eye for the essential points, and argued from them with a force and lucidity that left us with an exhilarated feeling of getting clear on major issues. In reading the linguistic analysts, one has a feeling of being led over interminable feats to no firm conclusion and in no fixed direction. It is as if the very idea that there were any fundamental issues or crucial points had been repudiated.[1]

The earnest reader may at this point, find himself in substantial sympathy with Blanshard's comment. He has not found what he was looking for. What then was he looking for and what, of moral relevance, did he expect to learn from it? At this point, obviously, the issue is deeper than at first appearance. He feels that we have not answered his ethical questions, and in this he is quite correct. But where did he get those questions and how would a final answer to them be pertinent to the right solution of concrete moral problems? The answer is, of course, that they come from the great "systems of ethics," which, in

---

[1] *Reason and Goodness* (New York: The Macmillan Company, 1961), p. 262.

his previous training, he has, like Blanshard, learned to accept as models in his field. An illuminative title for most courses that purport to supply an introduction to moral philosophy is "types of ethical theory." It is these theories whose conflicting claims are presented as the possible alternatives for rational thinking in this field, and the student is asked "in the end" to choose between them or, if he finds this impossible, at least to remember what is said in them as deep insights into what must perhaps remain for us as perennial problems. Sidgwick's *Methods of Ethics* may well serve as a paradigm for this sort of discussion. Blanshard tells us that he agrees with Broad in holding that that work is "on the whole the best treatise on moral theory that has ever been written."[2] For the last century, Sidgwick's questions have been considered, in England and America at least, as *the* questions of ethics, and the "rational" way he deals with them a model for objective thinking. It will pay us now, I think, to take a closer look at this model. Our aim will not be to give reasons why at some points we feel obliged to depart from it, but rather to try to show that it is wrong from beginning to end—a source of endlessly argumentative disagreement, no doubt, but as a way of dealing with our moral problems "in the end" as in the beginning, incompetent, irrelevant, and immaterial. It set us looking for the unattainable answers to questions which are such only when and if the specific nature and use of moral reasons have initially been misunderstood. On this misunderstanding, it builds a theoretic structure that is, in its own way, impressive, but of which no reliable use can be made in further and constructive inquiry. This, in the current state of philosophical opinion, is something that will obviously take some showing. The only way that we can hope to do it is by a con-

---

[2] *Ibid.*, p. 90. See C. D. Broad, *Five Types of Ethical Theory* (London: Routledge and Kegan Paul Ltd., 1930), p. 143.

frontation of the theories offered with the actual work of being practically reasonable as men, who are not ethical theorists, are responsibly engaged in it. The materials for this confrontation have been substantially presented in Part I. Our task now is to carry through, in more detailed analysis, the comparison required. If our puzzled reader is in any way to be persuaded to remove from his nose the theoretical spectacles that blur his vision and still prevent him from seeing moral facts as they are, it is in this way that it must be done. And this, and nothing less, is what in this book is asked of him. It will not be easy, but there is at least some ground for hope that it may prove rewarding. The ensuing chapters of Part II will be devoted to this effort.

Sidgwick's "scientific ethics" takes off in its speculative pursuit, as all such theories must, from the common ground of our moral experience. He proposes to analyze the methods of ethics which, he tells us, are methods of procedure "by which we determine what individual human beings 'ought'—or what it is 'right' for them—to do or seek to realize by voluntary action."[3] The emphasis, as always in Sidgwick, is on "rational". For those who are not content to claim that they can simply "see" in individual cases the right and wrong of action (and this claim is soon rationally undermined), the prominant reference is to rules that claim at least a general cogency for all relevantly similar instances that fall under them. This feature of generality is of their essence as reasons and respect for it is the first requirement for their rational use. Sidgwick's laboriously careful inspection of the "rules" of common sense morality warrants the conclusion that they do not rationally meet this requirement. They are not sufficiently precise and general to cover unequivocally all cases to which they proximately apply. If it is sometimes right to lie, then the rational prohibition against lying cannot be an un-

---

[3] The Methods of Ethics (5th ed., London: Macmillan Co., 1893), p. 1.

conditional, and hence not a truly general, dictate of our reason. Hence the quest for truly universal first principles—universal and absolute rules of duty that are self-evidently true.[4] These will be real ethical axioms—intuitive propositions of "real clearness and certainty" and they will be not only certain in themselves but such that, by their "scientific application," "the common moral thought of mankind may be at once systematized and corrected."[5] As such, they would be the *first* principles of scientific morality.

Sidgwick never doubts that we must find such principles if we are to ground our ethics in rationally cognitive truth. The familiar fact that our common sense rules conflict is enough to prove it. Somehow the actions they *prima facie* endorse must be rationally compared and weighed if their bearing on *ultimate* right and good is to be objectively established. We must have a final criterion of comparative value. Sidgwick finds such a standard by affirming Universal Happiness to be their common end (Universalist Hedonism) and measuring the rightness of all actions by their capacity to maximize such happiness, no matter whose, or how, or when, or by what means achieved, if only from the standpoint of the Universe, it is "more." And, he inquires, "If we are not to systematize human action by taking Universal Happiness as their common end, on what other principle are we to systematize them?"[6] Surely none which does not impose the claims of Universal Happiness will be adequate for the purpose. Some *final* end we must have "in the end," and some one big obligation, in this case the duty to contribute impartially to it, as our final principle of decision in the adjudication of conflicting claims. How else are we ultimately to be rational at all? It is to this end and this principle (plus those of impartiality and,

---

[4] *Ibid.*, p. 354.
[5] *Ibid.*, p. 373f.
[6] *Ibid.*, p. 406.

somewhat dubiously linked with it, of prudence) to which Sidgwick's *Methods* brings us in the end. Only in strict subordination to this, or as means to what is good *per se,* have our more familiar reasons any rational warrant. On it they depend for the final justification of their use in specific cases, and until its cogency is settled, all else must, in the end, remain in doubt.

Divergence as to "ultimates" accounts for characteristic differences in the methods of ethics employed to analyze moral action. "For if a man accepts any end as ultimate and paramount, he accepts implicitly as his 'method of ethics' whatever process of reasoning enables us to determine the conduct most conducive to this end."[7] For himself, he has been able to discover only two such ends, Happiness and Perfection, and it is between them as he sees it, that the decision ultimately must be made. By happiness he intends, ultimately, pleasure; and this he defines as "feeling which the sentient individual . . . apprehends to be desirable; desirable, that is, when considered merely as feeling, and not in respect of its objective conditions or consequences."[8] It is only as thus considered that it presents itself to impartial reason as desirable *per se* and only in this status that it can be ultimately good. All else must in the end be estimated, in its moral worth, as a contribution to the production of such feeling. Whose pleasure? From the point of the Universe, this question is impertinent. And it is evident that "as a rational being I am bound to seek good generally," and since from the point of view of the Universe it is self-evident that the good of one individual is no more important than the good of another, it follows that "each one is bound to regard the good of any other individual as much as his own, except in so far as he judges it to be less, when impartially viewed, or less certainly knowable or attainable by

---

[7] *Ibid.,* p. 8.
[8] *Ibid.,* p. 132.

him."[9] To the rationality of this only an Egoistic Hedonist could dissent, but while Sidgwick cannot refute the Egotist who prudently takes his own good as his final end—thus leaving an alarming duality of practical reason for which, as Sidgwick sees it, only a theological reconciliation is possible—he leaves no doubt of the benevolent universality of his own commitment. And this, of course, is Universalistic Hedonism and, like the poor, in one form or another it is always with us. It is on this high ground that Sidgwick asks us to understand and to solve the true or basic problems of ethics. In the beginning, we were concerned with the complexities of specific actions, for which conflicting claims are made, but "in the end it all comes back to this. What are your ultimates and how are they authenticated?" How, as F. H. Bradley was never weary of inquiring, can Reason give an end? And can it be this end only as desirable *per se* that alone justifies all moral means that contribute, in whatever way, to its attainment? And what further intuitions of reason, if any, are required to make good its universalistic claim? Sidgwick held that it was self-evident that when our desire for a particular good conflicts with that for our whole good it is self-evident that we ought to be moved by our desire of, that is to aim at, the latter rather than the former. To which Prichard responds, "On this part of the argument the only comment that is needed is that it is self-evident that there is no such duty."[10]

Between these rival intuitions of self-evidence, who is to judge? What ground, indeed, is there for judging anything? In such a final confrontation of ultimate assurances, there seems nothing to be done except choose sides and come out arguing. Or again, what of ultimate good itself? And indeed, what of it? While there have been many later thinkers who would agree with

9 *Ibid.*, p. 382.
10 *Moral Obligation* (Oxford: The Clarendon Press, 1949), p. 139.

Sidgwick that there must be good *per se,* few would accept his conclusion that it must be pleasure. For it is pleasure, par excellence, that seems to require normative qualification before it can be admitted to the status of even a constituent in final good. What then can it be? Just "good" itself, as a simple, indefinable quality that can belong to some things in their existence "quite alone"? And what if we cannot see this? At least we are launched on a whole sea of problems which only a meta-ethicist could resolve. But this is a question we have already considered, in its place. And finally, if such a good could be identified, what of it? What bearing would it have on the solution of our *de facto* moral problems? Sidgwick relies heavily on the middle axioms of Utilitarianism, as warranted by our accumulated moral experience. But what right has he to this reliance? No doubt, for men situated as we are, and within our familiar network of bourgeois values, they have worked well enough. But from the point of view of the Universe, that includes impartially all present, past and future, and weighs with impartial benevolence the pains and the pleasure of all sentient creatures, who knows? And how are we to know? Doubtless the consumption of Christians by lions in the Roman arena was very painful to the Christians. But there is the large audience to consider, and the lions. And whether, in the long run of recorded history, such spectacles cause more pleasure than pain. At least they fortify the moral stamina of the sufferers. Again, who knows? And who's to judge? Yet, on Sidgwick's view, unless we can know this, the right of the particular action must *in principle* remain in doubt. Our more proximate principles have not in principle any final moral cogency. As such they are merely empirical generalizations as to means. Until their contribution to "the end" has been determined, their own validity as rules will "in the end" remain in doubt. For in the end it is the end only and the one big end that we maximized, that can count as reasons. We, perhaps fortunately, are in no moral position to take the point of view of the Universe in such matters. We have quite special duties and commitments where we are, and cannot surrender them to a maxim of universal benevolence whose bearing in our own responsibilities remains morally equivocal. *We* must have grounds more relative than this. And Sidgwick has by no means shown us where to find them. On the contrary, the whole animus of this procedure is to send him, and those who follow him, looking in a wrong direction for a reason *for* our reasons that, if we take it seriously, makes equivocal and insecure their right use *as reasons* in just the cases where we need them most. I now propose to show, in more detail, the consequences, for ethical theorizing *and* for moral practice, of the "rational" disorientation thus brought about.

To make our own standpoint clear, however, we must first state what, as we can understand them, moral problems—those in which a right use of practical reasons could be relevant and effective in reaching a solution—are, and what specifically the achievement of this solution demands of us as rational inquirers. In such a situation there must be ground for doubt, else there would be no occasion for inquiry or reflection. But equally, in such a situation, not everything is doubtful. Unless there were discoverable in it some factors that, as they stand, and without question, we could recognize as grounds of obligation, as reasons for or against the doing of an action, there would be nothing, morally, to be in doubt about, and no question as to the right or wrong of doing could significantly arise. And unless such factors were discoverably relevant to the specific point at issue, there could be no such doubt concerning it. A deed that we have no reason for either doing or not doing would be morally indifferent; we should be "free" to deal with it as we pleased—if we had any pleasure in the matter. The "why?" of justification would be impertinent.

Our actual problems of right action, as we know, are not at all like this. In them, from the start, the true issue is a moral one precisely because we do have reasons for or against its voluntary doing. To say that an action would be the giving of a sum of money is so far to leave the issue open as to whether or not it should be done. To specify it as a bribe is already to give a reason against its performance—to say why, unless there are better reasons to the contrary, it should not be done. We are not called upon to invent such reasons for themselves or to read into them by inference from "higher" truths a moral implication that they do not carry on their face. We learned their use and cogency in the process in which we became moral agents, and it is only as such agents that we have problems of this sort to solve. And the reasons that we have thus learned are normally sufficient to specify the moral merit of specific actions without pondering or doubt. They provide the working basis of the understanding on whose terms the distinction between right and wrong makes practical sense. Without such an agreement there would be no "game" in which its principles could be invoked as "rules" that in specific cases should be followed, and in the *why* which is the right use of such rules no normative significance or cogency could be discovered. This game would not be played; and it is inside this game and subject to its categorial requirements that we have moral problems.

When such reasons clearly apply, and where no counter reasons relevantly appear, a good man will see and do his duty without argument or question. The doubter who, in this situation, still demands a reason why he ought to do what will push him into action, is no longer asking what he ought to do, but demanding some extrinsic and additional inducement to perform it. And it is in this way that we should normally understand him. His is not a moral problem, and it is not on moral grounds that we can deal with him. But there are situations where our obvious and familiar reasons do not unequivocally apply—not because they have no moral cogency in such cases, but because they are not here sufficient as they stand to specify the moral merits of specific cases. The act that is the giving of a bribe is never *merely* that. It may also be a way of getting needed help from those whom only bribes can "persuade" to supply it. And if the cause for which the help is needed is a good one, which it is our responsibility to further where we can, there is so far a reason why the payment should be made. And these reasons as they stand conflict, not in the abstract or in principle—we ought in general both to support good causes *and* to refuse to pay bribes—but in the judgment on specific action that each, taken by itself, would warrant.

This is indeed a moral problem. And it arises not where we have no reasons, but are faced with a merely blank or groundless doubt, but where *prima facie* we have too many and no "principle" as yet, for their right combination. Either and neither of the alternatives presented can be justified "by reason" as the right one. We are damned if we do, and damned if we don't. And this is a situation in which we cannot rationally acquiesce. But how are we to deal with it?

One way of dealing with it is, of course, to insist on the unqualified finality of some such reason, to the exclusion of all others, and hence to exclude those who would base conflicting claims upon the latter from the area of rational consideration. If political dishonesty is always wrong, then no apparent "reasons" to the contrary *can* count against it in the end. The "considerations" adduced by those who would excuse themselves for a failure to respect it are only "double-mindedness"—a way of trying to see all sides of a subject when only one side can be the right one. "Right is right though the heavens fall" and those who counsel us to take this probable collapse into account when we decide a moral issue, are no better than they should be. They are subtle and devious minds who, if we listened to them, would confuse our judgment on the simple right and wrong of things. This attitude, if it has firm indoctrination and strong will power to support it, can be maintained in self-righteous confidence over long periods of time and in magnificent disregard of all that does not fit its ironclad preconceptions, and there can be no doubt that it does in one way "solve" our problems. Whether or not this is a right solution is a question to which it already knew the answer without troubling to think about it, and it can therefore see no moral sense, but only moral willfulness, in raising it. "Purity of heart is to will one thing—the good"—and what this good is the good man, in his heart, has always known. There is no room for moral inquiry for, on the basic issue, there is nothing of moral relevance still to be discovered. All that is required is the unconditional submission of our wills to "right" as thus determined. For the morally single-minded man the decision is, in the end, as simple as that. And all men of good will know how to make it.

Where there are strong apparent grounds for doubt, however, not of the initial relevance but of the over-all moral adequacy of our initial self-assurances, this self-righteous dogmatism will, in practice, engender more problems than it solves. And it becomes increasingly difficult, in the moral complexities of the world we live in, to deny that these are moral problems. If we are to be reasonable about them, we must at least be willing to consider them as reasons, not as mere blind appetites or willful passions, and to try to understand what, in this guise, can be made of them. This process, once it has begun, is hard to stop until *its* questions have been fairly answered. We begin, in its terms, to see the issue in a new light, and those who would put out this light must ask us for increasingly drastic "prostrations" of intelligence to do it. In this way what began as unqualified adherence to a single reason becomes an enemy of *all* reasons, in their rational or justifying use, and the sheer groundless re-affirmation of the finality of a "truth" whose pretensions in this status will not bear examination. This, as we have seen, is what is called in some circles "the primacy of the will." And it is, *in practice,* precisely what we mean by being arbitrary, or un-reasonable, in our moral judgments.

Here, surely, something has gone badly wrong. For it was not as self-sufficient fragments of incorrigible truth, but as a ground for reasonable action that the "right" to which the dogmatism still clings, had its initial normative cogency for action. Its "ground" was not just in itself but in its justifying use, and where in this use it functions as a ground for action in which all concerned can share on terms of mutual respect and under-standing, it shows its adequacy in this use. In this situation, however, it has failed to do so. For there are considerations, that others who are trying also to be reasonable, and to justify their claims on grounds of common understanding, relevantly bring against it, that *raise* doubt as to the self-sufficiency of its claim upon us. These are the doubts that call for rational resolu-tion, and to meet them by a blank refusal to entertain such questions, and a condemnation of those who raise them as evil men, is precisely not to be rational about them. And without the validation that only its reasonable use could warrant, their initial reason loses its own significance and function *as* a reason; it would be a mistake any longer to so interpret or appraise it. Its status now is merely that of willful self-affirmation. It is not surprising therefore that those who, like Kierkegaard, have thought this problem through to its plain conclusion, have no use for practical reason. They ask us rather to accept the absurd, and to do it by a groundless act of will. There is no place here for such "filthy rugs of righteousness."

But how, here, *could* we rationally proceed? If our initial reasons were the rational finalities that they are claimed to be, and in this way ultimate, there could be no intelligible answer to this question. It is precisely by considering them as in this way *not* ultimate, as finding their warrant as reasons not in themselves, but in what they can contribute to the work of the understanding that their reasonable use makes possible, that we can make sense of it. For our problem here is not what any taken by itself would justify, but rather where and in what way the "right" they claim can be preserved in the light of other morally relevant considerations. And that in some situations, there are other morally relevant considerations is beyond reasonable doubt. That an action would give needed help to a deserving cause *is*, so far, a reason for performing it. Those who honestly ground their action on respect for it are not merely willful or opinionated men. How far, in this situation, it should count against the obvious "wrong" of bribery is a further question. The end does not always justify the means. But it could not be a moral question at all unless each of the considerations offered was, in its own way, a reason and, *so far,* entitled to a hearing. Unless we are willing to consider it in this light we could not even begin to think rationally and objectively about the merits of a moral issue. The reasonable solution of a moral problem has significance only for those who in this way are trying to be reasonable, and are prepared to think and act accordingly. This point is rudimentary, but there are still those who, when their own self-assured finalities are in question, find it difficult to accept.

If however we are not prepared to accept this impasse of competing ultimates as final, if we recognize an obligation to go on, how are we rationally to proceed and in what direction to look for a solution? The problem, let us say, concerns a rise in wages for the members of the Teamster's Union which we, as citizens, are invited to approve. Some grounds will normally be offered to support the claim to such a rise, and these will not be merely arbitrary or idle. The salary hike would enable the union to increase its security funds, and this in turn would contribute to the health and welfare of its members in their declining years. Taken by itself, this is a reason, and a good one, for the action proposed. And those who make it on this ground are entitled, as our fellow citizens trying in this characteristically American way to raise their living standard, to a fair and friendly hearing. And if we concentrate our attention, as do its advocates, exclusively upon the strength of this consideration taken simply by itself, the cogency of claims based upon it can be made to seem almost self-evident. It is thus that the issue is normally presented in the Union Halls where it originates.

But, as we all know, there is more *to* the problem than this. If the proposed advance in wages is likely to initiate an inflationary spiral and thus bring increased financial burdens to others in the community already in a comparatively unfavorable position and less able than the Teamsters to bear the cost of the expected price increase—widows, orphans, and college professors, for example—then there is a reason why it should not be approved and it too, as it stands, is a good one. And it can plausibly be so presented as to appear to be the only reason that ought to count in the present case. We can be sure, in fact, that there are those who will so present it. Between the relative merits of such competing reasons, how are we to judge? What ground, indeed, is there on which an impartial judgment can objectively be made? So far there seems to be none. Each party to the controversy has his own "right", and if he is prepared to stand intransigently upon it, will never lack for arguments with which to justify his cause. All he has to do is maintain in his supporters that state of mind in which it is morally self-evident that the counter-claims of others do not count. They represent instead the ruthless push for power of unscrupulous men whose conduct, as Congressional Investigations of Communists have shown, is by no means above reproach. *Or* they echo the special pleading of those vested interests that have always blocked the path of Industrial Democracy, the kind that advancing labor has had to fight in the past in battles in which its present leaders played a courageous part, and is prepared to fight again if need be, to advance its legitimate interests in our society. The reader will have no difficulty in recognizing this sort of argument; we have heard it all before and shall do so again, with dark references to the subversive and/or reactionary forces of the extreme left or right that are alleged to lurk behind it. And in all of this debate each side will exhort the other, and above all, the public, to be reasonable. But what, in such a case, would it be *like* to be reasonable?

If the competing claims existed quite alone, and in this naked conflict, there could in principle be no answer to this question. We should simply have to "see" that the one claim, with its supporting reason, was "stronger" than the other, and to judge its worth accordingly. Fortunately, in more normal instances, this is not the case. These claims do not exist, and cannot be supported, quite alone. They are made within a social situation in which *other* claims and interests than theirs are no less entitled to consideration, and in which the claims of all contenders must be contained within the structure of a moral order in which all alike can justly share. Only in this context and as grounds for a justification that can have equal cogency for all do their own proffered reasons make such moral sense as in fact they have. And this is true not merely in theory, where we like to talk about the common good, but in practice also. If the Teamsters' claim can be enforced on reluctant employers only by the use of unfair practices then it ought to be opposed at any cost. There are limits to the methods by which "advancing labor" can legitimately advance its cause, and "in the end," these are moral limits. When we have reached them there can be no compromise with evil, and any demands that can be shown to exceed them are thereby condemned. The trouble is that these limits, in particular cases, are sometimes hard to draw. But it is just *in* particular cases that we often have good grounds for drawing it. There are, in the first place, relevant factual questions to be asked. How much, specifically, would the proposal cost, not just in money, but in sacrifice from those adversely affected by it? On whom would this cost chiefly bear, and is it one that, in their present situation, they can be rightly asked to bear? Could the harm that would result from it be compensated for elsewhere, and the burden shifted to those in a better position to bear it? Is the proposal here made for the Teamsters' Union one we could accept not in their case only but in that of other unions also which, we may be sure, would be prompt to advance a comparable claim? Would concessions now made be just an incentive to more drastic demands to follow? What bearing on the efficiency of our national economy and, above all, on our relative power position in the world could it be expected to have? These, in their turn, are not easy questions, but they are often not beyond our power to answer reasonably, *if* we will inquire honestly about them, and a right answer there would clearly have some bearing on the merits of the specific case at issue. For they are all morally relevant considerations, and in their light we should be able to judge better what we ought to do. This better judgment, and the reasons that can adequately support it, are the goal of rational inquiry on moral issues.

What such inquiry can give us, if it is fairly carried through, is not just new information but, if we are prepared to see and weigh its moral relevance, a new light in which to understand the merits of the issue whose appraisal is here called for. For in our reasonable use of it we are acting not merely as partisans of one side or the other, whose case is to be defended at all costs, but as spokesmen for a good which, by a right combination of competing interests, can be practically the good of all. And this, if we are serious in our language, is what we mean by the common good which is normatively entitled, in such situations, to take precedence over that of any competing or divisive interest. The standpoint from which judgments of common good are made is in this sense that of the community—not an ideal or abstract community but that of the actual moral order in which diverse interests may pursue their several goods in common. This is not merely nor primarily a "larger" good in which everybody gets as big a cut as possible of what he wants. It may, in hard cases, be one in which the many are asked to sacrifice their special interests for the preservation and protection of a numerically smaller group whose minimal requirements for decent living must at all costs be met. Nor, in consequence, is it one on which all appetites will be equally appeased. There will inevitably be those who do not like it, and will go on pressing their more special claims. And so long as these pressures respect the limits of due process in a public argument, they will be entitled to a hearing. But it will constitute, if it is reasonable in fact and not merely in its pretensions, a working basis or *modus vivendi* in which all concerned can fairly be asked to go on together, and it must find its warrant in the answering judgment of those who are willing *in this way* to go on and on these terms to live and work together. It is in this way that just government, and the claims of all authority that claims normative cogency, rest on and are confirmed in the consent of the governed. Nothing more than this is needed for a right solution of all moral problems; nothing less will suffice. The preservation and development of that community of *understanding* in which it is reliably achieved is the point of responsible moral inquiry.

There will, of course, be cases where not all relevant questions can be conclusively answered, and where a judgment must be based on inconclusive grounds. Here we proceed at considerable moral risk and must be prepared to take the consequences. We may find out that a judgment confidently made was wrong and that in fact our verdict will not stand up under the demands of actual living. This is a wise and humbling reflection and may well lead us, where no judgment on our part is practically called for, to follow the biblical admonition: "Judge not." But there are situations in which we *are* called on to judge in our own persons between right and wrong and to act accordingly. As responsible moral agents we cannot avoid the responsibilities of such judgments. What are these responsibilities? Infallibility is not reasonably expected of us. But it is required of us that we do our best to reach a just decision. And until all discoverably relevant considerations in the situation have been weighed, in an appraised judgment on the merits of this specific case, we have not done our best. Nor have we done it if, once a verdict has been given, we close our eyes to further light on the subject. The "game" in which "decisions" are responsibly made does not end with the making of decisions. We must go on, in action shared with others, to live in the moral world whose structure they have gone some way to determine. The process of being reasonable is a continuing and a self-correcting process, and the capacity to change our minds in the light of what it has to teach us, is essential to its proper use. But to profit by our past mistakes we must be able to recognize these *as mistakes,* and it is only in the light of a better understanding, in this way achieved, that it can responsibly be done. This is what it is, in practice, to be morally reasonable in our conduct, and it is in the right exercise of this capacity that we can rightly live and learn together.

It is at this point, of course, that the hankering for some one big final reason, or some good so ultimate that in relation to its achievement all others have but the borrowed cogency of means, reasserts itself. To balance *prima facie* "rights" against each other and achieve a working balance between them is a complex and endlessly demanding business. The judgment that it calls for is not Q.E.D., one that follows necessarily from a minor pre-miss of mere fact, and a normative major so all-inclusive and unqualified in its scope that only fools or knaves, or the wrong-headed defenders of a rival theory, would question its universal cogency. It calls rather for that spirit of finesse that is required in instances in which the many-sidedness of a complex issue is just what sets the problem for a right decision and in which imponderables must somehow be weighed in the attempt to understand it as it is. It is not surprising that we sometimes make mistakes in such judgment. The wonder rather is that we do sometimes get things straight and can reach a verdict that will stand the test of subsequent experience and inquiry. Yet the plain fact is that we do; the whole history of the achieved wisdom embodied in our present moral order is there to prove it. And we ourselves have sometimes made such judgments and are prepared, even now, to take our stand on them. And it was not by chance or by a lucky guess, but with the best intelligence that we could bring to bear on the specific problem that we made them.

But still, if we just knew that there were some *final* principle of judgment here, even if we found its application hard to make in individual cases, how much simpler, in principle, everything would be. *Must* there not, in the end at least, if not for ordinary use, *be* such a principle? Without it how can we have any final guarantee of any moral truth at all? And how, without such a guarantee, can we properly go on? These questions open the door for the higher simple-mindedness of ethical theory, as we have already had a sample of it in the work of Sidgwick. The problems they set us are of a *prima facie* different sort from those with which, in the last few pages, we have been concerned. What can such ultimate good, considered merely as a good *per se,* be found to be, and how can we infallibly "know" it as such when we see it? By what processes of reasoning (or methods of ethics) can it be shown that what all our obligations come to in the end is just the one, big, final obligation to produce as much of it as possible, no matter whose, or why, or how, if only in the total felicific balance of the Universe, it is "more"? And what would this higher information tell us that could practically and unequivocally contribute to the resolution of *our* problems, which must find their adequate solution, if they have one, not from the "impartial" standpoint of the Universe, but from that of the practical commitments in which as limited and responsible moral agents we are here and now involved? These are par excellence the problems of ethics, and they are those to which a moral philosophy that knows its business is supposed to provide us with a reasonable answer. In the three chapters that follow, we shall follow them through some of their familiar applications. Here it will perhaps be sufficient to observe that their relevance to our problems, where we are trying to be practically reasonable, has yet to be established. They arise not when we are actually using moral reasons but rather when we try to devise a language in which misuse can itself be justified in terms of an incorrigible "ultimacy" or finality that are not its own. As such they are endlessly arguable, but grounds sufficient to warrant the pretensions of their all-inclusive mandates do not yet appear. Perhaps, in our continuing question, we shall yet find them— perhaps not. Meanwhile we must be about our present business which, though still lacking their impressive sanction, must be carried forward, in humility always, but with firm determination, on a different level of discourse.

We shall be told, of course, that what we are here saying is mere pragmatism, and if this word had any clear sense or precise application we should not quarrel about the use of this term to describe it. In this case, however, it unhappily does not. The general "movement of thought" which is commonly identified by this title, and with which the names of James, Peirce, Dewey and Mead are chiefly associated, profoundly influenced American thought in the first half of the 20th century. I was myself brought up in it and, in my earlier days especially, shared all its liberal enthusiasms. It would be surprising if my present thinking did not reflect some measure of such allegiance. But I know of no systematic statement of what pragmatism is that is either theoretically coherent or practically defensible. The identification of the truth of a belief with the "good" consequences of believing it was a basic error, far-reaching in its implications. And while the consequences of an *action* are often relevant to an estimate of its rightness, they have this status not as external rewards or penalties for performing it but rather as showing what, in morally relevant respects, the action is. An action that helps no one is not a helpful act and, when we come thus to understand it, is not approvable as such, however generous the intentions of its doer. And it is in its consequences that we *find out* who or what it helps. The truth of reliable moral judgment, *in this use,* is one thing; the usefulness of this truth for any further or ulterior purpose is something else. To confuse "use" here with utility is not an aid to that clarification of ideas which pragmatism seeks. Yet it is from just this confusion that much that has seemed most novel and iconoclastic in pragmatic doctrine draws its plausibility.

There has always been, moreover, a notable reluctance among the pragmatists to discuss moral issues in specifically moral terms. In their zeal to absorb the moral into the practical and the practical into its evolutionary progress or sociological conditioning, or resolve them into a "thirdness" that pervades the universe, they have rarely shown much respect for its own distinctive structure and content, and for the specificity of the demands it makes upon us. This becomes particularly apparent in those second generation pragmatists whose enthusiasm for advancing science sometimes tempts them to regard any serious reference to righteousness or moral evil as socially reactionary. We shall explore some of the consequences of this attitude in Chapter X. Since our aim, on the contrary, is to make just these notions central in our own analysis of conduct, it is evident that we must proceed in our own way and on our own terms in these matters. If there are pragmatists who will agree with us, we shall be glad to greet them as co-workers in a common cause. But, as experience has amply shown, we cannot in general count on such agreement.

The goal of rational inquiry, we have said, is to enable men to reach a working understanding of the over-all right and wrong of actions on whose terms competing claims can properly be weighed against each other. This understanding would be itself a kind of agreement—an agreement, as Wittgenstein has observed, "not in opinion but in form of life,"[11] in the whole body of acceptances and forbearances that constitute a social group as a community.

"So now we know. It is 'agreement' that is your 'final' good, and rational inquiry is just a means to the achievement of this end, no matter how or on what terms, if only everybody will agree to them? Is this not what you really mean?" Of course not. In any actual society, and it is in such only that we are called on to make moral judgments, there are moral limits to any rationally acceptable agreement. When these limits have been reached, we must simply take a stand, however potent be the powers that disagree, and defend the right as we see it. There can never rightly be a compromise with evil. But before we take a stand on the right as thus uncompromisingly affirmed, we ought to find out what, in the particular case, it is. What is thus specifically right can be maintained at all costs because the cost of thus maintaining our position has already been estimated *in* the

---

[11] *Philosophical Investigations* (Oxford: Basil Blackwell, 1953), p. 88e.

determination of what *here* is right. A "right" pronounced on the basis of our antecedent preconceptions only and in disregard of the cost, not just for our enemies but for ourselves and our civilization, would have no right to normative authority in practical decision. Responsible men know this, and will speak and act accordingly.

But when all calculations and qualifications have been made, there will still be cases where we find in the wills of intransigent and ambitious men a barrier that no moral understanding we can offer can surmount. Here, when the worst comes to the worst, there is nothing for us to do but defend the goods *we* know to be good and ask all who share our faith in freedom to unite with us in a common cause. And it is an essential part of our political policy to guarantee that if this time comes this defense will be effective and decisive. Meanwhile, however, it is our business to see to it if we can that the worst does not come to the worst. This is the point where rational inquiry can be of constructive use to us, and it is this use that we have here described. The agreement that it seeks is not that which everyone can share at any price. It is rather, as we have now perhaps too often said, that which is attainable by those who are willing to be reasonable, who *seek* an understanding in which all can honorably live together. That this aspiration exists to some degree in all men is so far a faith not adequately verified in experience. But such prospects as we have of a world of human decency are based upon it, and we shall not have done our best until we have done what we can to make the most of them.

The hard and interesting question is precisely that of *how far*, in particular cases, accommodations that require a qualification of what once passed for categorical imperatives can safely be accepted, and this, when adequately specified, is not beyond our powers of calculations. Here the conservative has always, *prima facie*, the stronger moral argument in his favor. He speaks for the unqualified finality of the only moral order that we really know, the one in which, through discipline and training, we have come to be what we are as moral agents. And he rightly warns us that any departure from a strict adherence to rules thus laid down is made at considerable moral risk. In this capacity he deserves at all times a respectful hearing. But, if he is an intelligent conservative, he knows as well as we that this position cannot be inflexibly maintained. The world does change, and old principles, however nobly stated, become equivocal in their application to hard cases that the wise men who formulated them could not have anticipated. *Some* reinterpretation is in any case called for, and the question is again, how far, in any given case, this process shall be carried. There will surely never be a time when "bribery" is generally condoned in our society. But whether promises of political favors to strongly organized pressure groups whose vote is wanted in an election is bribery or not, is a still disputed question. It may be that the moral fiber of our society has been weakened by this commonly accepted practice—the point is arguable at least. But, taken in the context of the general upsurge of the underprivileged and the consequences for democracy of their new controlling voice in our society, it seems not beyond the limits of rational appraisal. And there is good ground for hope that in one form or another we can find an answer to it that we can live with as members of a free society.

We depart from the firm ground of antecedently fixed rules at considerable risk. But there are times when the risk must be taken. For while moral inquiry begins and ends in understanding, it does not always end in the understanding in which it began. It must go on, in hard cases, through the constructive use of its own cooperative methods, to help build the better understanding in which its own aims can be adequately fulfilled. It is in this way, as has been said, that we can grow in understanding, and we must grow if what we value most in our own moral order is to survive. This is the plain truth of our own moral situations, and this the work that practical reason has to do in it.

In subsequent chapters we shall trace out in more detail the nature of this process. In so doing, we shall at all points keep in mind the contrast between problems thus encountered and thus resoluble and those questions of ethics with which philosophers have more traditionally been concerned. Our aim in this is at once critical and constructive. It is because this latter sort of question sends us looking in the wrong direction for the practical wisdom that we need, that it seems today worth criticizing. If it did not have this practical bearing, we might more appropriately leave it to the dialectical ministrations of those who, as Broad puts it, "enjoy that sort of thing." The way to correct this misapprehension seems to be just to turn our attention back to the structure, requirements and opportunities of the situation in which, as moral agents, we are involved. It is in this light that all we shall have to say is properly to be understood.

CHAPTER **10** FACTS AND VALUES

WHY SHOULD THERE BE a problem about the relation in general between facts and values or, as Josiah Royce put it, between the "world of description" and the "world of appreciation"? Scientists, theologians and philosophers have written formidable books about this problem and nearly all agree on its importance, though they frequently agree on little else. Where there is so much smoke we naturally look for fire. And since this fire, if there is one, threatens the work of practical reason at a crucial point, prudence would suggest that we find out what sort and how much of a fire it is and what, if anything, we should do about it.

Prima facie, nothing appears more obvious than the basic role of factually accurate information in the validation of judgments of value, of the worth of things and persons. The reasons offered to support such judgments affirm that something is the case, and unless this affirmation is true they cannot validly support them. This is a good knife because (for one thing) it has a sharp blade. This is a good man because he contributes largely to civic causes. This is a wrong action because it is the telling of a lie. There is much more to the matter than this, as we have seen, but this is fundamental. If the knife has not a sharp blade, if the man's contributions have in fact been meager, or the statement not a lie, then so far no good reasons have been given. And whether or not the knife is sharp, the contribution large or the statement false is something to be found out by strictly factual investigation.

Nor need the facts be of any special kind, or drawn from any privileged area of experience. If astrologers can in fact read a man's future from his horoscope, then their services have a value they would not otherwise possess. Whether they can or not is a matter for factual inquiry as to the dependable information they can in this way supply that would not otherwise be available to us. If X brand tablets do in fact relieve the miseries of cold distress in cases where other remedies fail, and without producing harmful effects, that would make their use unwise, then X brand tablets are for many sufferers worth buying. One of the essential questions we reasonably ask in estimating the worth of anything is: *what are the relevant facts about it?* And, *other things being equal,* the wider and more accurate our knowledge of such facts, the sounder our appraisal of its worth will be. A "value" that has not this kind of factual support is simply an expression of the predilections and pro-attitudes of the valuer. What he values in this way may mean the world to him, and his having such predilections is itself a fact of which others would be wise, for many purposes, to take account. In this status "value" makes no claim to normative cogency. If such a claim is made for it, however, the valuer must show that the object of his affections is in some way worth valuing. To do this he will have to tell us things about it that show it to be good. And unless what he tells us is in fact the case, it cannot do this job. A "world of values" not *thus* grounded in a "world of facts" would be a world in which a minimum requirement for the validation of value claims could not truthfully be met. In the interest of sanity and responsible good sense in all high talk about values it is important that this rudimentary but quite basic truth be firmly set upon the record.

But this, of course, is only the beginning of the matter. So far we have been using "fact" in the wide and catholic sense in which a fact is what is asserted in a true proposition, and truth is established by whatever methods are appropriate to the investigation or inquiry in which a distinction between what is and what is not the case can reliably be made out. In this sense it is quite proper to speak of moral truths, and of the facts of our moral lives, though, as we have seen, there could be no truths of this sort if truths of other sorts (of what will happen if—, for example) could not be established. But there is also a narrower use of "fact" in which the only *real* or really authentic facts are those discovered and authenticated by the sciences, or by what is called "the scientific method". As to what, in general, this method is, experts disagree, and their disagreement does not seem to be of a sort resolvable by "the scientific method". But clearly there are sciences like physics, chemistry and biology whose procedures are a model of this kind, and other more marginal inquiries, the "social sciences", for example, whose practitioners frequently aspire to methods of a comparable rigor and precision. And mathematics and logic have a different sort of rigor of their own. If a "world of facts" is the world as these disciplines describe it, then there does indeed appear to be no place in it for the validation of normative claims, for it is not by their methods that such claims are validated. In such a world there can be no place for "values" in our sense at all, though of course the *occurrence* of valuings and value claims will be duly recorded and "explained" by the psychologists and sociologists who deal professionally with such matters. It is in this area that the smoke we previously noted rises, in such volume as considerably to obscure the landscape. We must do our best to try to see, and understand, what lies behind it.

On closer inspection, the difficulty that sets the problem about "facts" and "values" seems to be this. We appeal to facts to validate our value judgments and must do so if these, in their turn, are to make an examinable claim to truth. But there is nothing in "the facts" as scientifically processed and certified to warrant any value judgments. How could there be? Scientific inquiry, in its strictly objective and factual investigations, tells us what is the case, not what ought to be. And "you can't get an *ought* out of an *is.*" Practical reasons are bound up essentially with our likings, with our wants and fears and aspirations. But factual inquiry has no use for such wishful thinking; its business is to tell us what, whether we like it or not, things *are* and how on their own terms, not ours, they operate. With "moral implications" it has professionally no concern. Yet it was just such implications in which, for practical purposes, we are interested. *Given* "the facts" what can we reasonably do? What should we do? What is worth doing? Why? These seem to be questions of a different order. If science as factual inquiry in its pure form is the only rational method of inquiry that we have, there would seem to be no rational way of answering these questions. At this point the "problem" of facts and values does indeed appear to threaten the work of practical reason, as we have tried to understand it, at a crucial point. For in a world as thus described there seems to be no cognitively respectable room or ground for it. What, then, are we to do? We may dismiss such talk of normatively cogent justification to the limbo of the irrational, while recognizing that the manipulation of likings for such ends as the manipulator, as a matter of fact, may himself happen to favor, is a fruitful subject for further scientific inquiry. Or we may, by postulates and faith, build a super-scientific world of norms in which, with divided minds, we can raise altars to the ideal and, if we bring in metaphysics to support them, to the ultimately real. Or we may, as scientific humanists, read moralistic imperatives into the procedures of impartial inquiry itself, though these will now be mere imperatives to discover impartially as many facts as possible and to "respect" them. What we cannot any longer reasonably do is to use the procedures of rational justification that we already have to support our value judgments by reference to the facts (how could such facts support them?) and in this way to use the facts as guides to practically justifiable action (what, in factual terms, would such a "justification" be?).

The problem was stated in its classic form by Hume and his version of it, though familiar, will bear repeating here. For, as usual, his questions go to the heart of the matter, though his answers are peculiarly unenlightening.

I cannot forbear adding to these reasonings an observation which may, perhaps, be found of some importance. In every system of morality which I have hitherto dealt with, I have always remarked that the author proceeds for some time in the ordinary way of reasoning, and establishes the being of a God, or makes observations concerning human affairs; when of a sudden I am surprised to find that instead of the usual copulation of propositions, *is* and *is not*, I meet with no proposition that is not connected with an *ought* or *ought not*. The change is imperceptible: but is, however, of the last consequence. For as this ought or ought not expresses some new relation in affirmation, it is necessary that it should be observed and explained; and that at the same time a reason should be given for what seems altogether inconceivable, how this new relation can be a deduction from others, which are entirely different from it. But as authors do not commonly use this precaution, I shall presume to recommend it to the readers; and am persuaded that this small attention would subvert all the vulgar systems of morality and let us see that the distinction of vice and virtue is not founded merely on the relations of objects, nor is derived from reason.[1]

Or, in the form in which the issue is now familiar to any college sophomore, "You can't get an *ought* out of an *is*." Yet the attempt to do so, to ground moral judgments on reasonings concerning matters of fact and real existence, which should really not have "surprised" Hume, since in practice he was sufficiently familiar with it, seems to be a basic step in moral reasoning. If this step is rationally illegitimate, then not only the "vulgar systems of morality" but the whole structure of practical reasoning is subverted and we are driven straight to Hume's conclusion that moral distinctions have no rational warrant or foundation. This is the fire behind the smoke of current controversy and given the "cognitive" fuel on which it feeds, it is of formidable proportions.

In the centuries since Hume's *Treatise* first appeared there have been heroic attempts to deal with it. Where these are made by the defenders of absolute values and categorical imperatives beyond the reach of mundane facts and hence requiring no support from them, they are themselves open to the imputation of wishful thinking, and sometimes gladly accept it. Where fact-bound understanding fails them, they appeal to Reason and, when a disembodied Reason proves too meager and abstract to do the job, to a faith whose willfully groundless affirmations require no justification, either factual or rational or, in our sense, moral. These are desperate remedies and if no other recourse were open to us, we might as a last resort find it necessary to make this leap, carrying with us such of our cherished valuables as could in this way be salvaged from the conflagration. Until it has been shown, however, that our values are indeed in peril

[1] David Hume, *A Treatise of Human Nature,* Selby-Bigge Edition, Part I, sec. 1, pp. 460f.

such desperate measures seem at least premature, if not a little silly. Has this been shown? There is certainly something wrong here somewhere, but the trouble so far seems to occur mainly in the study, the classroom and the library. In our practical affairs we go on justifying value claims in spite of it and seem sometimes and for some purposes to understand each other in the process. Perhaps if we paid more attention to such practice and its reasonableness, instead of trying to remodel it to fit the terms of the preconceptions of our own, or Hume's, epistemology, we should ourselves be able to find some solid sense in it. It seems, at least, a possibility worth exploring. For where we can walk in the light a leap into the dark is indeed irrational.

More interesting, for our purposes, is the attempt to bridge the gap between facts and values by a further use of the "scientific method" itself. It is easy to understand why such attempts are continually made. For scientific inquiry, as a continuing, co-operative enterprise, is itself a practical activity of a high order. It has its own rules for legitimate procedure, and at least a minimal observance of these rules must be accepted by those who engage in the activity as an obligation for right action if its work is practically to be done. And, as a human practice, the "game" has not only rules but a point. It does not end with the accumulation of reliable information or the production of theories as to how things—or human beings—work. There is an essential place for the satisfaction of "idle curiosity" in it but, as those who praise it on this ground go on to say, it is just such idle curiosity that has frequently led to discoveries of the greatest value. Value for whom and for what? Not just for those who thus enjoy it, but for all whose lives are "enriched" by the uses to which its findings can be put. Scientific knowledge—in personal, disinterested, factual knowledge—gives us power to control and direct the course of events for human purposes. It thus enlarges the area of our practical freedom and makes possible the actualization of values that, without its guidance, we should never have achieved. So far from menacing our values, it "implements" them by supplying us with instruments we never had before, for getting what we want. And, as the social sciences develop, it extends our mastery not only over nature, but over man as well. There is almost nothing that our hearts desire that seems to be beyond the reach of scientific planning, if only we will let it carry forward freely its beneficent work.

Not all scientists speak in this way, and some, amid the preoccupations of their laboratories, are allergic to this kind of talk. For them, so long as someone can be found to subsidize their research, the facts as facts are enough. But this clearly is the animus of those scientific humanists who ask us to accept the scientific method as the guide of life. And there is something in the scientific enterprise itself that seems to need this kind of warrant. For of this, as of any other human activity, we can significantly ask: what's the *good* of it? And if this good is restricted to the mutual satisfaction of scientists in the accuracy of their own findings, the practical sense of their activity is trivialized out of all proportion to its actual importance in human life. The activity of science finds its own justification in values, both those that are actualized in its own truth-seeking inquiry and those to whose actualization it contributes by supplying us that knowledge of conditions and consequences essential to their secure attainments.

The reference to scientific inquiry seems constructive, since it brings "values" and their "implementation" into the picture not as facts merely but as norms for justifiable action. But it leaves our basic question still unanswered. What "values" should we "implement" and why? If by "value" we mean *good*, in its warranting use and as supported by the reasons that show what is valued to be in this way worth "implementing", the question has a practical sense and may have a reasonable answer, for this good has the warrant of an ought in it. But it is just that use of "good" for which the procedures of scientific fact-finding seem to have no use, and such fact-finding, we have been told, is all the "reason" an enlightened mind can recognize or accept. Without it, the implementation of "values", as *de facto* wants and likings, through the use of tools that scientific inquiry, in its "engineering" applications can provide, becomes a morally equivocal and sometimes a practically disastrous business. The tools themselves, and the knowledge that produced them, are normatively noncommittal with respect to should and should not, right and wrong. Such knowledge may be put to any use we, or those whose wants conflict with ours, happen to want to make of it without prejudice to its own cognitive correctness. In this way, such knowledge is, or may be, power. But, as Socrates showed long ago, power not limited and enlightened by a knowledge of good, works havoc in the souls of men. Never was such knowledge more needed than it is today. But where, if normatively neutral information is all the knowledge we can have, could we conceivably expect to find it?

Evidently a further step must here be taken if the appeal to the practical worth of factual inquiry is to make any kind of moral sense. It must be held that "the scientific method" can itself supply the knowledge of the good we seek, that it can have a normative or regulative use in the right direction of our conduct, that in this way it does have an ought in it and that this ought is all we need for valid moral judgment. John Dewey saw this implication clearly, though he did not clearly see much else about the problem, and his moral philosophy constitutes the most sustained and thorough-going effort that has yet been made to deal with it on strictly scientific terms. As such, it will repay our careful scrutiny.

That it is by "the scientific method" and by it alone that we can rightly solve our moral problems Dewey never doubts. Our present difficulties in this field arise from the fact that we have so far not been scientific enough. In physics and biology we now use it without question and with unquestionable success, but in our dealings with each other we are still addicted to moralistic preconceptions that are of pre-scientific origin and anti-scientific import. This is particularly true where the issues of social policy are in question.

One of the many obstructions in the way of satisfying the logical conditions of scientific method should receive special attention. Serious social issues tend to be interpreted in *moral* terms. That the situations themselves are profoundly moral in their causes and consequences, in the genuine sense of moral, need not be denied. But conversion of the situations investigated into definite problems that can be intelligently dealt with, demands objective *intellectual* formulation of conditions; and such a formulation demands in turn complete abstraction from the qualities of sin and righteousness, of vicious and virtuous motives, that are so readily attributed to individuals, groups, classes, nations. . . . Spinoza's contention that the occurrence of moral evils should be treated on the same basis and plane as the occurrence of thunderstorms is justifiable on the ground of the requirements of scientific method, independently of its context in his own philosophical system. For such procedure is the only way in which they can be formulated objectively or in terms of selected and ordered conditions. And such formulation is the sole mode of approach through which plans of remedial procedure can be projected in objective terms. Approach to human problems in terms of moral blame and moral approbation, of wickedness or righteousness, is probably the greatest single obstacle now existing to the development of competent method in the field of social subject matter.[2]

This appears to mean that the only way in which we can deal with moral problems scientifically is by treating them as if they were not moral problems at all—"in complete abstraction from

---

2 John Dewey, *The Theory of Inquiry* (New York: Henry Holt and Co., 1938), 494f.

the qualities of sin and righteousness, of virtuous and vicious motives"—as if moral "evils" were "occurrences"—"on the same basis and plane as the occurrence of thunderstorms"—and those involved in them to be treated accordingly. "Objectivity" here *is* "logically" just this abstraction, whose function is to shift our inquiry from the justifiability of the action done to causes and consequences of its occurrences. Only thus, we are told, can plans of remedial procedure be projected in objective terms, though why, if we do not know that an action *is* evil, we *should* try to remedy it remains, at this stage, unclear. How, in the "genuine" sense of "moral", such *situations* are "profoundly moral" *in their causes and consequences,* we have still to learn. But it is worth noting that, for Dewey, it is in respect of their scientifically ascertainable causes and consequences that they are so.

That, from such a starting point, Dewey should have found it possible to develop, not just a moral, but a moralistic and moralizing philosophy of liberal reform is indeed remarkable. Men do not often gather grapes from thorns, or "oughts" from their thunderstorms, in quite this way. But the experiment, as Herbert Hoover said of Prohibition, is noble in purpose, and we must do our best to understand it.

What place is there for moral judgments or any sort of "value" judgments on a problem thus "objectively" formulated? In Dewey's book, *The Quest for Certainty,* his answer is explicit, if not clear. "Judgments about values are judgments about the conditions and result of experienced objects; judgments about what should regulate the formation of our desires, affections and enjoyments."[3] What is it that we thus judge about experienced objects? That in fact, or in probability, they have just these

---

[3] John Dewey, *The Quest for Certainty* (New York: Minton, Balch and Co., 1929), p. 265.

conditions and results? This is something that is, in principle, scientifically discoverable, if it is discoverable at all; and as we have seen, it is often highly relevant to the question of what we ought to do. But so far, it is not itself a value judgment at all; it is a factual assertion whose relevance to what we ought to do, or what is worth doing, has still to be determined. Then, after a semi-colon, comes a "should", which appears to tell us that a judgment about the conditions and results of experienced objects *is* a judgment as to what should regulate the formation of our desires, etc. But of course it isn't. What is the case and what we should do about it are two questions, not one, and a judgment on the one is not, *eo ipso*, a judgment on the other. Cigarette smoking sometimes causes lung cancer. So what? You should so regulate the formation of your desires as to stop wanting to smoke cigarettes. Why should I? *Because* cigarette smoking sometimes causes lung cancer. Here the judgment about conditions and results appears not as the content of the value judgment, but as offering a reason to support it. We have no difficulty in understanding it as such a reason. But when we do thus understand it, it is not as fact finders that we accept or reject the judgment it is offered to support. There is no logical incoherence whatever in acknowledging the fact and denying the value judgment (the "should") with which it is here questionably linked. If my life would not be worth living without the satisfaction a cigarette brings, or if I have an obligation to continue smoking —perhaps to demonstrate my loyalty to the tobacco company that employs me—then the risks, which I fully recognize on the evidence presented, may be well worth taking. My value judgment to this effect may be irrational, but, if so, it is not because it is ill-informed and in that sense unintelligent. The why of causal conditioning is one thing; the why of practical justification is another. Each has its own use and point in our thinking and only confusion can result from a "logical" formulation of the one sort of question in "objective" terms appropriate only to the other. It is to just such confusion that Dewey's generalization of "the scientific method" beyond the context and conceptual structure of its scientific use leads us "in the end." That this, for the purposes of practical reason, is a dead end, we have already had occasion to observe.

Where, then, does "scientific humanism" of this sort get its moral animus and tone? The answer is not far to seek. It borrows them from the moral preconceptions of its advocates here not recognized as such but projected on "the facts" themselves as something that the scientific method, in complete abstraction from all considerations of sin and righteousness, virtuous or vicious motives, has somehow discovered in them. If we will only "face the facts" they will tell us what we ought to do, for "remedial procedures" can then be projected in objective terms. But surely what would be a remedy, and not merely a causally induced change, will depend on our estimate of what is good, and at what price it can properly be secured. What are remedial procedures for thunderstorms, save those that will protect us from the harm they do, where such protection is recognized as a good worth having? And what are remedial procedures in social policy save those that will create or preserve the conditions in which we can well and honorably live? In many situations this sort of question need not be explicitly raised, for we are so united in our practical commitments that all we need to inquire about are the causal means by which they can most effectively be "implemented". If a man is sick the right "remedial proce-dure" is to make him well, or at least to mitigate his suffering, and all we need is expert medical advice on how to do it. How could any decent man view the situation, practically, in any other light? And if famine, flood or earthquake has left thousands helpless and homeless in our country, any good citizen knows that we ought to aid the sufferers, though it may take expert knowledge to determine how, with maximum efficiency, this is to be done. If, however, the famine is in Red China the question is more complex. It is as members of a community and as sharing its values and responsibilities that we understand the fact of famine as a ground of obligation, and it is this obligation, understood as sufficient to decide the moral import of the case in question, that established the "ought" of practical doing. How, and on what terms, we can stand in this relation to the citizens of Red China is the hardest sort of moral problem. Of course all men are human and equal amounts of suffering are as painful in Peking as in Peoria. But the humanitarian who uses these considerations to support the conclusion that equal amounts of suffering everywhere have equal claims upon our conduct is speaking not as a mere reporter of the fact of suffering but as the advocate of a quite distinctive moral ideal whose adequacy to the requirements of our present situation may, on rational grounds, be called in question. That the fact of suffering anywhere in the world is a morally relevant consideration, a ground of obligation, and how much it ought to count as against other such considerations (e.g., the support of a political regime that we believe to be a moral evil) are matters that a man who could give an accurate account of the occurrence of the famine and a scientific estimate of its conditions and results might never grasp. The facts can point a moral only for a man for whom a moral communication has a point. And it owes this point not simply to the facts as "objectively" formulated, but to the conceptual structure of the "values" in whose light we estimate their bearing on right conduct.

The irony of the situation is that scientific humanists whose moral commitments are so obvious to them that all they need to inquire about are the next things to be done, or "ends in view" for their fulfilment, come to suppose that their moral judgments involve no specifically moral considerations at all but are based merely on an "objective" estimate of conditions and results. Hence they offer as the findings of scientific inquiry programs of social policy that borrow their moral significance from humanitarian ideals they learned to accept as gospel long ago. This does credit to the goodness of their hearts, but hardly to their powers of critical discernment. It is not a way of being scientifically exact but rather of being practically naive in concrete issues of "remedial" action. So long as such unexamined pieties function only in the local and familiar situations in which their adequacy need not be questioned, such morally uncritical moralizing works well enough. The "scientific method and the democratic faith" (where the democratic faith means the progressivism of the early years of this century projected into the post-war world as a practical ground for liberal social policy) are good enough for us, and since our minds are already morally made up, our only "moral" problems will be those of social engineering. But our world today is not morally as simple as that. And where moral problems do arise, how in abstraction from sin and righteousness, virtuous and vicious motives are we to tell a *rightly* remedial procedure when we see one?

In our time of moral conflict and confusion, those who put their faith in science as a moral guide have given many different answers to this question. For a dedicated behaviorist what could be better than a society that put all power to make decisions into the hands of experts in behavioral conditioning and provides unlimited opportunity for the exercise of their professional skills? B. F. Skinner's *Walden Two* is a frightening example of such a behaviorist's Utopia.[4] The scientifically instructed social welfare worker sees the need and accepts the obligation to do good to the underprivileged. A welfare state is his ideal for the good society, and he has a Ph. D. to support it. Some physicists,

---

[4] B. F. Skinner, *Walden Two* (New York: Macmillan Co., 1948).

shocked by the havoc that scientific instruments of war, for which they feel in part responsible, can now cause, discern a scientific imperative to peace on what might otherwise seem morally questionable terms. Some—now rather old-fashioned—still discern an "upward" movement in the march of biological evolution, or of advancing social trends, and are confident that evolution or the trends themselves can tell us which way, morally, is up. Anthropologists look beyond the facts of racial difference and cultural diversity to find a factual ground for the moral unity of a world society. But this again is a question not alone of what they find but of what they want to find, of what will serve their moral purposes. Even Marxists are scientific, in their fashion, and present the historically "inevitable" triumph of their cause as a reason why we *should* now submit to its requirements. But it is by a patently ideological interpretation of history that they do it.

The point of noting these varieties of scientific moralizing is by no means to disparage science—what should or could we do without it?—but to indicate that the *remedial* formulations of reforming scientists of the issues of social policy are colored by their personal and professional preferences and vocational commitments, and would make no practical sense without them. In this scientists do not differ from the rest of us. The danger of moral confusion arises when such recommendations are presented or understood, not as in this sense practical, but rather as impersonal disclosures of objective fact, with which it would be sheer obscurantism and wishful thinking to disagree. Those who question their moral adequacy are just not facing facts—they are not realistic but "autistic" thinkers and hence not licensed to preach in the field of scientific morality. Thus the preconceptions of such moralizing become "factually" certified categorical imperatives for right—or "remedial"—action, and intelligence marches on, why or whither only the facts (as thus interpreted) and the experts who speak for them can tell us. When such pronouncements are made in the name of a deterministic account of human nature and history, so that what we are advised to do is to assist the inevitable to occur, or to implement the inescapable, a further practical incongruity is apparent. Predictions are supposed to guide our actions, but if these predictions and the "decisions" we will make in response to them are in the same impersonal way predictable, what is there for us to do but follow the script and play our parts accordingly? And what then is the point of exhorting us so to act, save as such exhortation is itself just one of the things that, under assignable conditions, predictably occurs? Such incongruities are none of the scientist's business within the area of his professional specialization. But they are our business and his as practical and moral agents. And it is not on such terms as these that they can be answered in a way that makes practical and moral sense.

The old quarrel, in practical affairs, between the intellectual and the man of action, the thinker and the doer, brings this rather abstract discussion into a more concrete focus. That action without ideas, and ideas without adequate information, are blind is both theoretically and practically apparent. There are things we need to know if we are to act with practical success, if our doing is to be the achievement that it was meant to be, that only those with expert knowledge of the facts can tell us. We ought to welcome such knowledge and make all possible uses of it, but very often we do not. Where it would upset our preconceived opinions or discredit the claims of strongly established interests those who represent such opinions and interests do not hear it gladly, and sometimes take practical steps to see that others do not hear it either. As Bertrand Russell once observed, one reason why we do not more often arrive at truth in social inquiry is because we do not want to reach it. The struggle of the inquiring mind to free its own truth-seeking work from such limitations, and the practical worth of such value-free inquiry where this freedom has been gained are major factors in the development of western civilization. If freedom of inquiry is not respected and maintained, no other freedom that we value will for long be safe. A generation that has seen the rise, and the consequences, of McCarthyism will be blind indeed if it does not learn this lesson.

But there is another side to this question that, in fairness and good sense, must be borne in mind. The idea man is often practically a one-idea man and his expert information specialized and limited to the area of his professional competence. There are relevant considerations for decisions of social policy on which he was not examined when he received his Ph. D., and sound judgment in the weighing of such considerations is not learned in books on the logic of decision-making, or the moral commitments in whose light it should be made in courses on the meta-ethical analysis of ethical sentences. And where the "intellectual" is the man who, thus equipped, sets up in business as a social planner and/or moral prophet, then there are often good grounds for distrusting his judgment. The theory that can be a guide for action is the theory that is normatively relevant to action, and only on the terms that are practically reasonable can such relevance reliably be made out. Those intellectuals who deny the normative validity of such a use of reason should not be surprised when their own enthusiasm for liberal causes is treated practically as a kind of egg-head emotivism by those who do not share their academic predilections, or whose heads are differently shaped. What else, on their own terms, could it be, and how on such terms could any practical issue be rightly settled? "We approve of this; do so as well," is not the basis on which a working community of practical understanding can be maintained, even where the approvers have advanced degrees in economics or educational psychology with which to decorate their approvals. And for this lack of understanding the practical man is not wholly to blame.

And what, by this time, has become of the problem of the relation between facts and values with which we started? In tracing out the nature of that problem and the confusions, theoretical and practical, to which, in its traditional form, it leads, we have found, I think, the grounds for its rational solution. It remains now to state that solution as explicitly and clearly as we can. It will offer no considerations with which the reader is not already familiar, but it may help to show how those considerations make sense of what is otherwise a rather senseless business.

What we have found reasserting itself in every attempt to state the problem of their separation is at once a distinction and a connection between facts and values. And we have further found that it is only as the distinction is kept clear that the connection can be understood. If "fact" is broadly used to cover everything that is discoverably the case, then it is a fact that there are some things we ought, and others we ought not, to do. But whether or not this is the case is not a question of whether we have a pro-attitude toward its being so, or a moral mandate to think and act as if it were. It is something to be found out by the methods appropriate to the discovery of truth in this area of responsible inquiry. Facts are facts, whatever be their value, and a fact is what is asserted in a true proposition. Moral evil is as much a fact as moral good and, here as elsewhere, when it is facts that we are looking for, the only rational procedure is to face the facts.

When "fact" is narrowed, as it normally is in discussions of this sort, to those whose facticity can be established without reference to considerations of good and evil, right and wrong, this is, of course, more obvious. *Of course,* you can't get an "ought" out of an "is" as thus established. For here to *keep* the "ought" out of the "is", to free the inquiry into causes and consequences from preconceptions as to what ought to be, or what we wish were so, is one essential part of the work of accurately finding out what is the case. Thunderstorms occur and the rain falls alike on the just and the unjust. A consideration of the moral character of those who will be helped or harmed by it is therefore of no use in the prediction of where, when and in what circumstances rain will occur. To recognize this fact, and to keep our moral judgments out of predictions and explanations of the weather is one of the things that "advancing science" has most clearly taught us. In this kind of inquiry into causes and consequences the "facts" in the process of inquiry itself, have been so processed as to eliminate just such considerations. You can no more get an *ought* out of such an *is* than you can get juice from a dehydrated prune, and for a somewhat similar reason. In the case of thunderstorms, such information tells us all that, unless we are poets or Whiteheadians, we need to know about them. And if human actions were as impersonal as the behavior of the weather it would tell us all we need to know about them, too. But the plain fact is that they are not.

For one of the things we need to know about human actions is why they are, and why they should be, done. And here the *why* is not that of causal explanation but of practical justification. Here, again, we refer to the facts, but in a different way. We use them to recommend "remedial procedures" or to point a moral, and this makes sense only for a being who is concerned with what is good, and what should be done, and is prepared, in some instances at least, to act accordingly. *In this use* the facts must have practical and moral implications if they are to do the work required of them, for here we do, in some way, base a "should" upon a fact. Unless this can rationally be done, we have no grounds at all for action. And this applies as much to the action of the scientist, as a responsible agent, as to any other.

How *can* a fact, thus processed, have moral implications? The answer is, of course, that it has them when and insofar as it is understood and used, not as a fact merely, though it must be this at least, but as a ground for action. The categories of such understanding, as we have seen, are not those of impersonal description, but of intentional action, personal agency or freedom, and the justifying reasons that make sense of it. An action that has not this kind of why in it—whether adequate or inadequate to justify the action, not merely to explain it causally— is not a moral action and hence not a proper subject for moral judgment. An agent not to some degree concerned and competent to direct his conduct in the light of such a why is not a moral agent but a thing to be treated on the same plane as thunderstorms, as the conditioners are now prepared to treat him. And a fact that is not as thus understood and used as a justifying reason is not a reason for doing anything at all, and hence not a ground for any remedial procedures that make practical sense. It is therefore not surprising that those who refuse, on grounds of scientific method, to think in these terms can make no sense of them.

Hence the embarrassment of "scientific humanists" when they are "moved" as citizens to make practical judgments on the issues of social policy. Their "facts" are a specialized selection from the area of their own professional competence, and the use to which they put them is, on their own terms, an unscientific use. If they are liberals by antecedent training and conviction, they will pour the sugar and water of a humanitarian progressivism over their dehydrated "value judgments" and, warming the mixture in the heat of their own time-honored preferences, offer us a brew that bears about as much resemblance to sound practical judgment as the flavor of prune juice does to that of any self-respecting plum. If they are Marxists, they will twist the facts of history and economics to serve their (academically) revolutionary purposes. And if they are, in their own interests, practical men, they will sell their specialized skills and information to those who, for their own quite different purposes, know how to use them. Why not? There is nothing in "the facts" as thus understood, that could show such a use to be factually incorrect. What they cannot do is to accept the commitments and responsibility that moral judgment requires, if it is to have a rational warrant. For this kind of rationality they are bound, on principle, to refuse to recognize. They have methodologically deprived themselves of the proper means of understanding it. How this attitude can lead to practical as well as theoretical confusion we have already seen.

It is natural that those who see the normatively destructive implications of a "world of facts" thus understood should try to find a refuge from it in a transcendental realm of self-validating values or theologically determined good. It is natural, but for practical purposes, it is unwise. For, however it may be in a Reality beyond space and time, in the world in which we now must act responsibly, we need the reference to facts to validate our value judgments. A "helpful" act that cannot sensibly be expected to help anybody is not, for moral purposes, a helpful act. And to know what acts, in all likelihood, will be helpful, we need at least a knowledge of what the conditions and results of such action will probably be, or what will happen if—. No amount of transcendental argument or searching of old texts for new meanings can be depended on to tell us this as reliably as can information as to what, under discoverable conditions, has happened and does happen in such cases. It does not always take a researcher with a Ph.D. to supply such information, but there are crucial cases where it does. The darkness of a faith that does not seek such information and know how to use it for valuational purposes is a self-induced darkness, a kind of willful blindness. Its self-complete world of values is, in comparison with the world of claims and counter-claims of which we are morally obliged to make the best we can, a half-world in which we gain peace of mind by using only that piece or fragment of our own mind that can, in this rarified environment, sustain itself. And, for enlightened action, that is not enough.

We have not found for such action two worlds, of "description" and "appreciation", but we have found why profound thinkers should have thought it necessary to postulate them. For we have found two ways of understanding "facts", each with its own distinctive categorial structure and its own proper use. In the one, facts are facts whatever we may wish or will concerning them. And if they were not thus establishable, we could not reliably guide an action in the light such factual knowledge gives. In the other, for an agent who knows how and *why* to use them in the right direction of his conduct, they are grounds for action. *That* this man is my brother I must find out, if there is any doubt about it, by impartial factual inquiry. But why, if he is my brother, I am obligated in a special way to be his "keeper" is something I must come to understand in a different way, as a responsible sharer in the distinctive goods of family life. "Brother" invokes at once this moral context, a context of shared understanding in which it has its distinctively moral use, while "male sibling" does not. And that is why we find practical significance in the notion of the brotherhood, but not in the siblinghood, of man. To change "Mother's Day" to "Female Parent's Day" would be a moral mistranslation, not just bad tactics from the advertisers' point of view.

The two uses are distinct, but they are also essentially related. Scientific inquiry as a practical activity has its own distinctive values not only in the good for scientists of finding out what is the case through the right observance of its own procedural requirements, but also in the information it supplies that can be a guide to further action. And it achieves this value precisely by being as factually accurate as possible. Practical judgment needs this kind of information, if it is to do its own work well. Where either is offered as a substitute for the other, neither can properly and without confusion be itself. *We* need both, and cannot be or do our human best without them. It is *because* they are thus different that they can, in this way, be intelligibly and fruitfully related. Once the smoke of dialectical controversy has cleared, the problem of the relation between facts and values becomes that of making this relation clear, and making the wisest use of it we can. This perhaps is not a philosophical problem in the way in which this task of philosophy is frequently conceived. But if philosophy is the love and pursuit of such wisdom as is possible to man, then it is in just such instances as this that it has a humanly rewarding work to do. This chapter is offered as a clearing of the ground for that kind of work.

CHAPTER **11** THE OBJECTIVITY
OF MORAL JUDGMENT
AND THE UNIVERSALITY
OF MORAL REASON

THERE IS, AS WE have seen, a sense in which all truth-seeking inquiry must be objective in its method and intent if it is properly to achieve its goal. No assertion is made true by our wishing, willing or believing it to be so. Such pro-attitudes may initiate changes in ourselves and our situations in which what we wished, willed or believed becomes a fact. I wanted very much to get the appointment and now, in large part through efforts that my wanting led to, I have got it. But that I now have it is not made true by my wanting it to be so; if I made my wants the arbiters of my judgment in this matter I should very often be deceived. And if my wants are to be intelligently directed to an attainable satisfaction, I must know not only what I want to be, but what is the case and what as such I have to reckon with. A wanting, willing or believing that gets in the way of such knowing and distorts my judgment accordingly has no proper place in any truth-seeking investigation. And if to be objective is to eliminate such distortion or bias from our estimate of truth, then objectivity is a requirement for right thinking as much in practical as in theoretical inquiry. If the answer to the question "why should I?" is to be a discoverably truthful answer, it must be warranted by the reasons that support it. My wishing or believing it to be thus warranted will not make it so and only what is so, not what is wished or believed to be, can serve in this way as a normatively cogent guide to action. *In this way,* the requirement for objectivity is as stringent in the case of moral judgments as in those of physics, for it is simply the requirement that we do our best to see things as they are or ought to be and to estimate their structure, their behavior or their worth accordingly. The notion of a merely subjective truth is essentially incoherent. So far as such a "truth" is merely an assertion about what a man wishes or wills or believes to be true it can, if it is sincere, tell us something about *him,* i.e., that he does thus wish or believe. If it did not aim at any further truth than this, if it were just an autobiographical confession, it would have no other truthful subject-matter than the "subjectivity" of the man who affirmed it. Of this, however, it would be "objectively" true, if it were true at all, as an authentic disclosure of what this "subjectivity" was, not of what he, or we, wished, or willed or believed it to be. What Kierkegaard, for example, tells us of the inwardness of his own existential situation often has a ring of authenticity about it, though sometimes it seems merely histrionic. But if this were the only truth at which it aimed, if it made no reference to a transcendent God and our right relationship to such a Being, it would not be the tortured and aspiring subjectivity it is. And the claim that this relationship is right cannot be made true by a sincere account of the subject's wishing or needing or affirming it to be so. If it could, the Christendom that Kierkegaard attacks would equally be "in the truth," and this is just what he is, "with the passion of the Infinite," concerned to deny. What the doctrine that, for man as a believer, "truth is subjectivity" does is not to redefine the nature of the judgment but to subject this subject-matter to that subjectivity in which a man's truth-seeking interest begins and ends in his own states of mind or agonies of soul. And this is for human purposes, including those of Kierkegaard, an impossible restriction.

But while in this sense all truth-seeking inquiry must be objective if it is to be genuinely a seeking of the truth, there is another sense in which practical inquiry is *not* "objective", and, from its nature, cannot be. It is not a "value-free" inquiry, for it is precisely about the authenticity or validity of "values" that it is its distinctive business to inquire. What is valuable or worth having cannot be determined in complete abstraction from what we want, or what ought to be done without regard to our practical commitments. The reasons that support a practical judgment, that show it to be objectively warranted are practical reasons, and only as engaged, with all his wanting, hoping, fearing, cooperative and contentious being, in a world that can in some ways confirm and in others thwart his purpose, has a man a practical reason for doing anything at all. His reasons, not his wants, must show him what he ought to do, but unless he had such wants he would have no reasons that could *in this way* show him anything at all. The reference to the subject here is not a negation of objectivity in moral judgment; it is a specification of the valuational structure of the situation in which the distinction between what is authentically warranted and what is only wished or willed or believed to be so can be significantly made out. An "objectivity", modelled on the pattern of the sciences, that on methodological grounds excludes this reference in effect rules out in advance the "why" of practical judgment as a subject for rational inquiry. If this is what it is to be "objective" then it takes no great wit to draw the conclusion that normative judgments cannot be objective but, if they are "judgments" at all, must be so in some quite different sense, as expressions of emotion, perhaps, or more or less disguised commands. The implications of that kind of analysis we have already seen.

How, then, *can* practical, and particularly moral, judgments—since it is about them that the hardest questions arise—be "objective"? Or to put the matter in a more useful way, how can we be objective in our search for and recognition of moral truth? This is a question of practical as well as theoretical importance. For while we are often told by the knowing that we *cannot* be objective about values, since a value judgment is itself the expression of a pro-attitude or bias, we are no less frequently exhorted by those whose concern is for right doing to be reasonable, fair and unbiased in our practical claims and judgments. "Bias" and "prejudice" as applied to moral attitudes and actions are terms not of analytic description merely but of reproach. But if our (or anybody's) estimate of what is desirable, honorable or just is itself the expression of a bias, what is a "prejudice" (where the question is not one of "value-free" information but of practical appraisal) but the expression of a bias that we happen not to like? The "fair" man who denounces such "prejudice" shows thereby only his bias against other peoples' biases. But would it not be meta-ethically naive to suppose that he can, by an appeal to right and justice as he sees them, show more than this? It is one of the ironies of contemporary thought that those who in their own political and moral attitudes are most vehement against "bias" are often also those who, in their theories, attempt to show that there is nothing else but bias for a moral judgment to express. The rest is name-calling. If our practical discussions are all too often reduced to this kind of abusive (or persuasive) name-calling, we have now, at least, a theory to explain that this is all that in such matters we could logically expect. To say that this is not a sound basis for the moral understanding on whose terms we can be reasonable in our dealings with each other is not, I think, an overstatement.

Here, then, we have another problem for moral philosophy, as we have come to understand it. Our procedure in dealing with it will be of a now familiar sort. The root of the trouble is to be found in a conceptual confusion that has serious consequences for the right (or wrong) direction of our conduct. We shall try to eliminate this confusion, not by inventing a logically purified language in which we may, with suitable stipulations and within the limits of our formal rules, say anything we please without fear of successful contradiction, but by so specifying the conceptual structure of the language we now use in practical discussion as to show that in its own intent and about its proper business it involves no such incoherence. And we shall further try to show how, by a right use of it, the "problems" of bias and prejudice with which *in practice* we are actually faced can have a rational solution. There is a sense in which moral judgments must be objective if moral right is to have normative cogency for action. And there is a sense in which they cannot be objective if they are to have a practical relevance and use. If to be "objective" in the first sense such judgments must also be objective in the second, our situation would be dark indeed— the kind of darkness that a too narrow rationalism can create and a willful irrationalism use for its obscurely edifying or distinctive purposes. But there is in fact no such necessity. On the contrary, it is by being objective in *their own* way—the way of practical reason—that moral judgments can give relevant and sometimes discoverably cogent answers to questions of the right or wrong of actions, and thus help to tell us what we should or should not do. What this way is we must now try more specifically to understand.

The basic problem here is evidently that of the relation and the distinction between wants and reasons in the work of practical justification. Wants are "subjective" in the sense that they are yours, or mine, or somebody's and it is a biological fact that what we want we go for, unless some counter-wants or organic disability or external obstacle impedes the natural course of our behavior. To call such a want a "bias" is no more than to say that it is a way of being for something and against that which gets in its way. About such wantings and the drives that they embody there is as such no question of right and wrong. They are as much natural facts as thunderstorms or earthquakes and can in principle be as "objectively" or impersonally described. There they are, and what, if anything, *should* be done about them is a further question.

Practical reasons, on the other hand, are in their intent never merely yours or mine. They (or those who use them) claim a cogency for action that any rational being ought to recognize and respect. That you want wine is no reason why I should do so, but that "wine is a mocker," if it is a reason at all for denying oneself the satisfaction of this want, is a consideration of which every practical agent should take account in the direction of his conduct. For the question here is not just of what we do, but of what we should go for, and this should claim a warranted validity for all concerned and competent to act in a reasonable way. A "biased" want is just a want, but a biased "reason" is a fake pretender to a justifying status that it cannot validly maintain. For here the question about right or wrong is the essence of the matter; it is in answer to that question that practical reasons are relevantly presented. There they are, indeed, but what we are to make of them as grounds for action is not a further question. It is the question of what, as reasons, and in *this* use they are. A want that is in some normative sense not a good want is nonetheless authentically a want. But a "reason" that is not a good reason is, *as* a reason, an impostor. It is just what someone wrongly takes to be or calls a reason. And it is in the work of practical justification, not in that of value-free description, that its status as a reason is relevantly appraised. The two uses, with the criteria appropriate to each, are so plainly different that it seems at first incredible that they should have been confused.

But the matter is more complicated than this contrast suggests, and with complication comes the opportunity for confusion. It does not just happen to be the case that men who give reasons for their actions have wants to satisfy. It is *as* wanting beings that they have such reasons, though their reasons are never merely the articulation of their wants. Smith's wanting to drink wine is not *as such* a reason why he should have it. But unless he wanted wine, or wanted something else which wine drinking helps him to achieve or unless someone else's wants were somehow brought to satisfaction by his drinking it, there would be no good in his drinking wine and no reason why he or we should so act as to maximize his opportunities to drink it. What practical sense would there be in such an action? And "wine is a mocker" would not be a practically relevant admonition if this mocking did not somehow frustrate the attainment of such a good. Even the most stringent moral requirements, as we have seen, are requirements for the right achievement of good, and in this good the satisfaction of man's nature as a wanting being is a basic and essential factor. There is much more than this to the normative cogency of good, but unless there is this *at least* there is no human good worth having. And in a democratic society in which everybody's wants are regarded as equally entitled to satisfaction, save where such satisfaction would impair the (quantitatively) greater satisfaction of others, it is easy to forget that it is an equalitarian moral ideal, not a value-free description of their biological occurrence as wants, that accords to them this title. We are then inclined to speak as if the wants *as such* made moral claims upon us and as if "I want it" or "he wants it" or, more insidiously, "most people want it," were itself the reason why an action should be done. Thus "in the end"—a dead end too easily reached in careless thinking—our reasons are just the articulation of what we want. And if our wants are different, how can our reasons be the same? On such a basis the way to justify an action is to persuade others (in a democracy, as many as possible) to want it, and by thus making everybody's wants as similar as possible, to achieve the generalized bias of a common good. Where this is not attainable and diverse wants lead to conflict, the recourse can only be to coercion—whether economic, psychological or military will depend upon the exigencies of the issue at hand. What most people want must be right, for what could right be "in the end" but just what most people want? Those who claim a higher authority or greater cogency for their own wants than they will acknowledge in those of others are, in principle, undemocratic. In such matters who's to judge, and how can anybody's judgment, if it is just the expression of his own wants, verbalized as reasons, be any better than that of anybody else?

This brings us to the heart of the matter. What would it be like to judge on such an issue? Wants do not judge anything or claim a right to satisfaction; it is only men as practical agents who do that. And for such an agent a *de facto* want, while it may supply the first word in an argument about claims and values, can never be the last. The whole picture of wants making claims which ought to have a right to be acknowledged as valid (by other wants?) is mythological, and no less fabulous for being drawn in terms that have a scientific look about them. Suppose that many other people want what I do not. What of it? Does the recognition of this fact cause me to want their want to be satisfied, even at the sacrifice of my own? If I have been appropriately conditioned, and am suitably suggestible it may do so, but sometimes it does not. People of "refined" tastes often find considerable satisfaction in not wanting what nearly everybody does. Are they somehow wrong in this? Is the fact that many (or most) people want something a *reason* why I should recognize their right to have it? How so? Are not their wants, though more numerous, just as subjective or biased as my own, and how can the summation of biases make an objective right or establish the truth of the judgment that more wants have a greater claim to satisfaction? The question here is not merely "who's to judge?" but rather how and on what grounds is anybody to judge anything about the *should* of action? The imposition of the moralistic language of equalitarian *rights* upon the subject-matter of *de facto* wants or interests does not answer this question; it simply compounds the confusion. Yet without a reasoned answer to it, there can be no justification of democracy that makes moral sense.

The first essential step in such an answer is to reaffirm the categorial distinction between wants and reasons and to show how, in practice, this distinction works. That other human beings, as well as I, have wants, that they are hard to get along with when the appeasement of these wants is frustrated, and that it is to my interest, where I can, to live at peace with them, are facts that in our society any fool can plainly see. And where they are people I am fond of, or about whose welfare I am in fact concerned, then even without this appeal to interest I normally want their wants to be satisfied. But it is also true that I can sometimes get what I want only by frustrating the wants of others and that, where I am not tied to them by bonds of loyalty or affection, my interest in their welfare is usually not great. In such a case what should I do? This question, wants do not ask, and cannot answer. But men sometimes ask it, not as *merely* wanting beings, though if they and others had no wants they would have no such problem, but as practical agents whose business in this status is to do not merely what they want but what they ought. It is here that the question of *claims* significantly arises. To understand another man's want, or my own, not just as an occurrence influencing behavior, but as a ground for claims upon right action, is to see it in another light, the light of practical justification. Why *should* my want have priority over his? Is it in some way more important? Of course, as *my* want, it has a special urgency for me, but what is this but the subjective bias of the want itself? No doubt his wants are just as urgent for him. As wants, they have a similar push for satisfaction in them. To judge fairly the merits of claims made in their behalf I must discount this subjective bias and try to weigh the issue on a scale in which no weight is given to my wanting as a reason for right doing that would not, in like circumstances, be registered for his. This is what it is to be objective in such judgments. And it is just here that the distinction between wants and reasons is of practical importance. My wanting influences my action in a way in which his, since it is not mine, does not. But if I am to be fair or practically unbiased, it should not so influence my judgment as to what is right. For it is here considered not as a causal push but as a ground for justifiable action. And a justifying reason *must* have equal cogency in all cases to which it has a relevant application if it is to be a valid reason.

This is a logical "must". The judgment that affirms it is analytic of the conceptual structure of any practice in which justification makes moral sense. It sets a minimum requirement for what it is to be reasonable in the adjudication of such issues. To offer a consideration as a justifying reason when it supports my cause and, in relevantly like circumstances, to refuse to recognize it when it supports yours, is just what it means to be arbitrary or unreasonable in the presentation of a moral claim. If my wanting something is a reason why you ought to respect my claim to it, then your wanting something is a reason why I should respect yours unless the two claims are different in some further morally relevant respect. And the fact that the one want is mine and the other yours cannot constitute such a difference. If it did, we should have no common grounds at all, and "I want" and "you shall" would be the final arbiters of moral right. And that is to say that, in the normative or justifying sense there would be no moral right. *This* "game" would not be played. This "must" is logically analytic, and it is by no means morally trivial. On the contrary, it sets a standard that is often very hard to meet. Our reasons must be common grounds if they are for the purposes of justification to be grounds at all. But how can they be? In any serious moral dispute, each side has its own claims to defend and its own interests to promote. It is as the partisan of such causes that its advocates make conflicting claims, and the reasons that they offer will naturally be those that support such claims and thus ideologically implement their push to make their side prevail. To ask me thus "engaged" to judge the issues fairly, to listen with an open mind to all morally relevant considerations, whether they count for their cause or against it, and to discount the urgency of their own partisan commitments in the "objective" recognition that subjective bias cannot be as such a ground for action, is to ask a great deal of contentious human nature. That is why, in the adjudication of legal right, we have a judge and jury, so selected as to be as free as possible from passional involvement in the dispute, to be the arbiters of justice between contending parties—the one on questions of law, the other on that of fact which specifies the relevance of the law in particular cases. If wanting were the norm of right, who could be a better judge than the defendant in a murder trial?

This is what Peirce meant, I think, when he held that "concrete reasonableness" is a case of "thirdness", not of "secondness", in human affairs. It takes only two to make a quarrel but (practically) it takes three to make a judgment, where the judge is the interpreter of the conflict in the light of reasons that represent not the clash (secondness) of the contending parties but the "habits" of rational procedure of the community to which, as justifiable, their claims are addressed. The "disinterested" third party is the judge of the merits of the case and it is to such a judge, or to any man in this concern and capacity to judge in this way, that the reasons are significantly addressed as grounds for action. Under the law a judge is disqualified, or disqualifies himself, where the suspicion of undue involvement or special interest has any color of justification, and a biased moral judgment is no less suspect. To be in this way objective is a practical requirement of which the logical requirement that the same reasons must in like circumstances have the same justifying cogency in all cases, articulates the formal structure.

In law this judging function is assigned to a disinterested third party. In morals there are cases where each man must be his own judge, must "give the law to himself," must decide for himself not merely what he wants but what is right or wrong and act in his own person for the right as thus established. This is what it is to be a moral self or person. That actual human beings *should* so think and act is not a logical or a causal but a moral "must"—it is a requirement *for* the achievement of that "realm of ends" or community of understanding in which a *common* good and right can have a practical cogency for action. Such personality is not a gift of nature or society; it is an achievement and humanly a great one. None of us ever wholly makes the grade. That is why it is so easy for a cynic to "unmask" ideologies and to caricature all justifying reasons as the imperfectly disguised expressions of a natural bias. But anyone who, in some area of practical activity and in the fulfilment of responsibilities that he can recognize as a *must* for conduct, has *tried* to be fair, impartial and morally discerning in his conduct knows what it is like to make this distinction and why, within the limits of his human capacities, he ought to do so. In this process he learns in hard experience the difference between wants and reasons and what it is, in consequence, to be objective in his estimate of the cogency of moral claims. If he cannot learn this, he will never know the meaning of a moral ought or achieve the stature of a moral agent.

It would be a serious mistake, however, to suppose that the objectivity thus precariously achieved is a mere detachment from the values and commitments involved in the conflict of wants and claims that gives rise to moral problems. The attitude of the judge is no more "value-free" than that of the litigants, nor is his judgment practically non-committal. His role in the transaction is to insure the maintenance of a procedure in which the values actually at stake can be authentically brought to light. For legal purposes, these are the limited values of law-abidingness within the community whose interest in law and order he represents. On moral issues a man who judges for himself speaks for the moral order of a community, however widely or narrowly he conceives it. The alternative here is not between commitment and no commitment, but between a commitment to a good that can in principle at least be that which men achieve in community and claims on good that cannot in this way be justified. His freedom from *undue* involvement is required for *this* involvement, for it is only by discounting biases irrelevant to the merits of the case that he can make a fair judgment as to what *is* warranted and should, as such, be done. Nor is the community for which he speaks a *mere* third party, external to the wants and concerns of the litigants themselves. Unless it is *their* community, too, in which their wants and concerns have, in like circumstances, as good a claim to satisfaction as any others, then it has no claim, in right, to their obedience. It is in the quest for morally sharable "values" that this question of objectivity arises, and it is for its sake that the work of practical reason is done. That is why it is at once so hard and so important to be reasonable in our practical affairs. That light travels with a finite velocity is a fact which everybody who has considered the evidence can agree, not only because the evidence is weighty but because nobody's ox is gored by its recognition. If it should turn out, by some odd chance, to be a fact which could be put to propaganda use by the Russians against us, or by us against the Russians, there would soon be thinkers eager to point out that it is really not a fact at all, but a questionable hypothesis and that those who offer theories that affirm it are ideologically not above reproach. In biology and anthropology we have, in the 20th century, had specimens of this sort of controversy.

We have so far spoken of good judgment *and* good will, as if these were distinguishable and separable elements in the work of practical reason. They are indeed distinguishable, and it is practically essential that they be distinguished. That to judge an action to be right is by no means the same as to do it for this reason we know from painful practical experience. But there is, nonetheless, an essential connection between them. The right act as thus judged is the one we would do *if* our moral concern and capacity were adequate to the requirements of our moral situation, and unless we had in fact some capacity to distinguish right from wrong and some concern to act in the light of such judgments we should have no will of which moral good and bad could significantly be predicated, for we should not be moral agents. On the side of judgment the connection is no less apparent. With the best will in the world we may still, if we are stupid, confused or ill-informed, make mistaken moral judgments. But without some measure of good will, as embodied in a willingness to be reasonable in our estimates of the relevance of "facts" to moral issues and to claim no cogency for *our* reasons that we would not in like circumstances accord to *theirs,* though "they" be men whose claims conflict with ours, we could not achieve that objectivity in judgment which is a prerequisite for the attainment of the truth our practical judgments seek. The competent judge in moral matters is not an unattached intellectual. He manifests his attachment *in* the objectivity of his judgment and such objectivity is itself to some degree a moral achievement, the self-mastery of a man who does not always want to see the truth but knows that he must take account of it if his wants are to be rightly satisfied within the structure of a moral order. Without this kind of good will we cannot practically have good judgment, and without such judgment "good will" would have no practical sense. If "will" and "reason" were independent faculties whose extrinsic connection somehow constituted practical reason this would be a puzzling situation. But for men whose thinking is itself a practical activity and whose doing needs a reason if it is to make practical sense, it is plain good sense. And that is just the kind of sense that we have tried to make of it.

Any reader familiar with the history of ethics will by this time have noted some important similarities between the account of moral objectivity here given and that of Kant in his *Foundations of the Metaphysics of Morals* and (with modifications) in his *Critique of Practical Reason*. This resemblance is not coincidental. For it was Kant who worked out the distinction between practical reasons and inclinations more thoroughly than any previous philosopher had done. The ethical theory he built on this foundation is a major contribution to our subject. We shall be well-advised, in this phase of our inquiry, to learn all we can from Kant. But to learn from him is not simply to expound and justify what he wrote. In some important respects, as we shall see, his account of practical reason is mistaken and the theory he derived from it quite incredible. Attempts to reinterpret, qualify and revise it, without correcting these mistakes, begun in Kant's own later writings and still continued by zealous commentators and/or apologists, have vastly complicated but have not substantially clarified the subject. Our own purpose is neither to bury Kant nor to praise him but to learn what we can, from both his insights and his errors, about the practical use of reason.

We shall begin with what is true and basic in his theory. That the "principles" that justify moral action, that show it to be right, must be universal in their normative application if our judgments are to have the objectivity essential to their rational cogency (what Kant calls their "necessity") is an a priori truth. A "principle" that did not meet this formal or conceptual requirement would not be a rational principle of moral action. If our subjective maxims, the rules according to which we do actually act, do not meet this requirement, they have no moral cogency at all, but are mere reflections of our wants. And a will that made such maxims, in their merely subjective status, sufficient grounds for action would not be a morally good will, for such willing would not embody a concern to discover and to do what is right. It would not, in this sense, be rational willing.

So much, if we take care not to misunderstand it, appears to be a minimal but essential requirement of practical reason. And important consequences seem to follow from it. A will that thus wills rationally cannot be "determined" merely by subjective wantings and desires, or by the hypothetical imperatives that guide such wants to a prudential satisfaction. The causes of wanting are not the becauses of willed action, they cannot serve in this status as common grounds for the determination of a right that is in principle the same for all. A man of good will is not a man whose inclinations cause him to act in conformity with moral rules, whether he does so out of fear, or a liking for such conformity, or a desire for some advantage to himself to be expected from it, or from a feeling of benevolence. He is a man who does right actions because he sees them (objectively) to be right. The capacity to act in this way is the autonomy of the will without which there could be no moral action and no moral worth of persons.

The intrinsic worth of men as moral persons (we need not say, with Kant, the only intrinsic worth of human beings) is the worth they manifest in such actions. Its goodness is not that of a means or instrument merely—it is an actualization of human excellence that is literally beyond price. (For what shall a man give in exchange for his soul?) As embodying this excellence men are ends in themselves and should be respected, and respect themselves, as such. In their mutual recognition of each other in this status, as freely giving laws to themselves which all alike can recognize as binding, they constitute a realm of ends which is the abstractly idealized version of what we have called a moral community. "Morality, therefore, consists in the relation of every action to that legislation through which alone a realm of ends is possible."[1]

In rational willing, thus categorized, lies the whole fulfilment of the moral law. Its rightness is its willed conformity to the rational necessity of law as such and its goodness the unqualified worth of a self that in such willing gives itself the law it follows not for the sake of satisfaction, advantage or any other consequence but simply because it is right, i.e., rational, to do so. The capacity for such willing, Kant maintains, lifts man above the world of sense with its categorial structure of space, time and causality and reveals him (though darkly) as an autonomous member of a noumenal reality in which reason rules by rational necessity and the ought of obligation is superseded by the *is* of transcendental freedom. Our acknowledgment of the moral law is our passport to this higher realm. And what is the moral law? Simply the categorical imperative that we be rational in our willing, that the will be determined "not by subjective causes but rather objectively, i.e., on grounds that are valid for every

---

[1] Immanuel Kant, *Foundations*, in *Critique of Practical Reason and Other Writings in Moral Philosophy*, trans. Lewis W. Beck (Chicago: The University of Chicago Press, 1949), p. 91.

rational being as such,"[2] "that the maxims of my action should hold as a universal law for myself as well as others."[3] Hence, "act only according to that maxim by which you can at the same time will that it become a universal law."[4] Rarely in the history of human thought has so much been got from so little by so formidable a process of reasoning.

It is time now to ask some questions. What is "rational" about morality as thus interpreted, and what is moral about it? Its imperative enjoins us to be rational in our willing. But does it enable us to understand what it is to be morally reasonable in our actions? That the rightness of an action should be determined "not by subjective causes but rather objectively, i.e., on grounds that are valid for every rational agent as such" is, as we have seen, the requirement of practical objectivity itself, without which there can be no moral reasons. And that a morally rational will is that of a man who does an action, of his own free will, because it is in this way right, is equally and analytically obvious. So far the Kantian doctrine is on solid and basic, if rather minimal, ground. But what Kant proceeds to do with these insights is another matter. What are the grounds of right action? In Kant's account they are "maxims", generalizations about kinds of action, which, applied as rules, bring the particular case under the "law" which the maxim articulates. It is in this way, that they serve as grounds for doing. They are subjectively valid when they are the rules a man does follow in his conduct. An objective maxim or principle or law is a rule that is in this way (i.e., subjectively) valid for a fully *rational* being, a principle that "would serve all rational beings subjectively as a practical principle of reason if reason had full power over the faculty of

---

[2] *Ibid.*, p. 73.
[3] *Ibid.*, p. 64.
[4] *Ibid.*, p. 8.

desire."[5] A rational will is one whose maxims can be thus willed as universal laws, and whose willing in conformity thereto is determined solely by the dictates of universal reason. What such reason dictates is universality in willing and nothing else. The "universality of the law as such" is the "sole content of the categorical imperative of reason." To this the maxims of our action should conform "and in effect this conformity alone is recognised in the imperative."[6] Thus you may will *anything* so long as you can thus will its maxim universally, for a maxim thus willed is objectively valid as a practical principle of reason and what is done willingly, in conformity to it is *eo ipso* right. If reason had full power over the faculty of desire this is what any rational man would will, i.e., for him it would be subjectively valid also. So far as we are not in this way fully rational but are also desiring, wanting beings in the world of sense, conformity to this principle is an ought, an imperative of duty which is not always (and Kant seems sometimes to doubt that it is ever) the subjective maxim of our conduct. But that it ought to be, that this is what it would be to will rationally, and that in willing in conformity to its dictates we should be acting as we ought, he claims to have proved.

Would such action be, in practice, reasonable action? If we follow Kant's specifications it is bound to be, for this, according to such specifications, is just what practically reasonable action *is*. But men were trying to be practically reasonable in their actions long before Kant's theory was invented to tell them what it was they were or should be doing, and our question concerns the adequacy of the theory offered to the normative requirements of this practice. Once the issue is put in this way, the Kantian theory presents itself in a rather different light. What, in the context of our concrete moral problems, *can* we thus "will"

---

[5] *Ibid.*, p. 62.
[6] *Ibid.*, p. 80.

rationally, and how, as responsible agents, can we deal rightly with our fellows on the terms it sets? Kant was not unmindful of such questions, and in the *Foundations* he gives instances to show how his imperative actually applies, to false promises and suicide, for example. The zeal and ingenuity that have been expended on the examination of these instances are impressive. But the point of the issue they involve is simple. You can no more get the blood and sweat and tears of an actual moral issue and its resolution out of Kant's categorical imperative than you can get blood out of a turnip, and it is vain to hope that any further dialectical tinkering at this late date will do the trick. Yet it is out of blood and sweat and tears, and the desires and hopes of men as well, that the operative structure of a moral order must be constructed. A rational will that could "determine" what is worth doing "independently of the faculty of desire" would have no practical reasons for doing anything. It might consistently and with moral purity follow any maxim it autonomously and quite groundlessly chose, if only it were so inflexible in its willing as to apply its rule as an ironclad directive for all cases (i.e., to universalize it) and to rule out all considerations of needs and consequences, of who would be helped or hindered by its actions, as morally irrelevant. It would have no moral dictates of its own willing but to conform to the universality of law as such and *any* rule thus ruthlessly or unconditionally applied, would be *in this way* universal. It might be very difficult for human beings, constituted as we are, to follow such a dictate, but that would have no bearing on the bindingness of the "ought" as thus "rationally" willed. On Kant's formula, this is what it would be like to follow "practical reason". In actual practice, however, it would be a way of being morally unreasonable, in a peculiarly arbitrary and self-righteous way.

In practice nobody but a fanatic really thinks and acts in this way. Kant did not, and his discussion of concrete ethical issues happily and, on his own grounds, "irrationally" deviates from it into good—and sometimes uncommonly good—moral sense. There, nonetheless, the theory stands, and, as it stands, it blocks the road to moral understanding. If this is what it would be like to follow "reason", then it is surely often better morally that we do not. For here indeed the heart has reasons that the categorical imperative will not let us comprehend. The road from Kantian reason leads straight to the "irrational". If this is what it would be like to be objective, "subjectivity" seems our only practical way of being human. Yet objectivity in our moral judgments is, as we have seen, and as Kant has rightly insisted, a requirement for the normative cogency of the *right* on which morality itself depends. Here again our theory and our practice fall apart and the one is empty and the other blind without that working connection which has here been rendered unintelligible. Can moral philosophy, as we have come to understand it, clarify this issue and, in so doing, clear the way for reasonable action? Let us see.

What does the rationality of objective moral judgment require of us? We learn the "rule" "thou shalt not lie" and we understand it as a moral maxim when we recognize it as a reason why we should or (as in this case) should not do a certain kind of action. That making a specific statement would be the telling of a lie is a reason why I should not make the statement. And if it is so in any case of this kind, it must be so in all, whether the lie be yours or mine and without regard to anybody's wanting or not wanting it to be told. To recognize this, and to conform our judgment to the rightness or wrongness of the act in question as "objectively" determinable by this use of reasons is a first essential step in being reasonable in our conduct. And a willing or voluntary doing that is guided by this recognition, that makes the right, as thus specified, its goal for action, is the action of a man of good will, a man who is performing well and wisely his function as a moral agent. So much is true, and without its practical acceptance there could be no moral truth.

Does this mean that, to be a moral reason, the maxim must be universalizable as an unconditional directive for actions to be performed, or not performed, in all cases, without regard for the further moral merits or demerits of the case in question? Of course not. No action, as we have seen, is ever *merely* the telling of a lie. It may also be the helping of a friend in need and this, other things being equal, is something that I ought to do. And if it is a reason for doing in any case then it must be so in all to which it relevantly applies—in which the action in question would be the helping of a friend. To rule out this claim in advance, to hold that the "rule" against lying is the *only* morally relevant consideration in the "objective" determination of the rightness or wrongness of an action, is not a way of being reasonable in our judgment on the case in question: it is the willful single mindedness of moral fanaticism. If this is what it means to universalize our maxims, then the less inclined we are to be in this way "rational" the better.

If the maxim against lying is not morally universalizable, is there perhaps some other rule that is, and that we ought in consequence to follow unconditionally in all cases? Kant thought he had found such a rule in his categorical (unconditional) imperative, a law that dictates for all rational beings the universality of law as such. But this, fairly obviously, will not do the job. This categorical imperative has no moral content of its own, it is a second order principle about maxims and their "rational" use. It tells us that only those that can themselves be thus universalized are practical principles of reason. It is such first order maxims, the rule against lying among them, that must be such that we can will them as universal laws if action in accordance with them is to be right. And if none *of them* can or should be thus willed, by a morally reasonable man, then the imperative to act in accordance with them only when they can be thus willed is a morally self-defeating principle. It justifies any maxim or none—any if we are morally simpleminded enough in this way to will it as an unconditional rule of action; none if we are mindful of the circumstances and conditions in which it can properly function as a moral rule, and so reject it, not in its own proper cogency as a reason but as thus inflated to the status of an ironclad directive for right conduct.

The basic trouble with Kant's whole conception of practical reason is that it sends us looking in the wrong direction for the reasonable use of "grounds" for action. It is not surprising that we return either empty-handed or with something that, in fact, is not a reason at all but a dictate or command. To call it a command of reason is at this point only to compound the confusion, for it is only a practically unreasonable "reason" that would in our moral situation issue universal dictates of this kind. That a statement is a lie is a good and, in many circumstances, a sufficient reason why we should not tell it. It is not a merely "subjective" reason or maxim; it is applicable *as a reason* to any case that would be the telling of a lie. It is by the right use of just such reasons that we can be objective in our moral judgments. But this use is not that of an unconditional law or command for action. To universalize it in that way is not to use it as a reason, to be weighed with others in right judgment on the merits of the case, but, as Kant says, as a dictate to be followed categorically, i.e., without regard for any further merits or demerits of the case than the one acknowledged in the rule to which, as a practical principle it dictates unqualified obedience. The "rationality" of such a dictate is determined solely by its form as "universal law", i.e., as an unconditional and unqualified directive, and a rational will is one that accepts it in this form as the maxim to which its action must conform. But a command does not become reasonable by being generalized, nor reason practically commanding by the inflexible application of general rules to instances in which their sufficiency can on rational grounds be questioned. That kind of generality is too frequently an excuse for the rule-bound stupidity that refuses to judge particular cases on their merits. Neither in administration, nor in morals, is there any rational substitute for such judgment. The attempt to find a general rule which, functioning as a command, will excuse us from its difficulties and responsibilities is both theoretically and practically misguided. *Of course* we should always do right actions, for the right, as justifying of moral action, is just what we should do. No command is needed to tell us this, nor could such a command add anything to the cogency of the right as reasonably established. The distinctive work of practical reason is that of enabling us to find out what in truth *is* right and what accordingly, as moral agents, we ought to do. Here reason functions, as it should, not as a dictator but as a discoverer of moral truth. The requirement of objectivity in moral judgment is a requirement *for* the use of normatively cogent procedures in this activity, not the imposition upon it of an imperative which decides by "rational" fiat what in general is to be done and commands our unconditional submission to its dictates.

When practical reasons are interpreted as the generalized commands of a will that, as rational, wills nothing but their unconditional or universal application (the universality of law as such) the concept of moral objectivity is correspondingly transformed. It can no longer be a discipline for finding out the merits of the case, so that we may deal justly with it. On the contrary, it becomes a way of emancipating us from all reference to the nature of the object or action willed in "determining" the right and wrong of action. The rational will is the autonomous will and

Autonomy of the will is that property of it by which it is a law to itself independently of any property of objects of volition.[7] The absolutely good will, the principle of which is a categorical imperative, is thus undetermined with reference to any objects. It contains only the form of volition in general, and this form is autonomy.[8]

Will what you will, so long as you will it universally—the form of the willing is all that counts and unconditional generality is this form. No foreign influences or considerations drawn from the nature of *what* is done, in what circumstances, and with what effect, can "determine" the formal purity of such willing and that, morally, is all that counts. Here the will quite literally has as its object "only itself considered as giving universal laws."[9] This is not objectivity at all, as we usually understand it. Rather it is the transcendental subjectivity of a self-centered willfulness that has become "rational" by making its own "rationality" the sole object of its practical concern. The objective necessity of the moral law for Kant is just its subjective necessity for a fully rational being; it is the "law" that all such beings would follow "if reason had full power over the faculty of desire." And the reason that would exercise this power would be that which found its whole rational fulfillment in the unconditional acceptance of its morally unqualified pronouncements. With respect to the merits of any concrete action it would be a supremely arbitrary will, but in its volitional self-righteousness it would be pure indeed.

Why should the dictates of such a will be obeyed? What is the objective necessity of the moral laws on which, for Kant, its imperatives are rationally grounded? For a fully rational will, as Kant defined it, such necessity is obvious, though hardly moral. As Paton observes, "the proposition that a rational agent as

---

[7] *Op. cit.,* p. 97.

[8] *Op. cit.,* p. 101.

[9] *Op. cit.,* p. 90.

such will necessarily act rationally seems to be analytic,"[10] for if such an agent did not thus act it would not (by definition) be a fully rational agent. This necessity is properly "a would that is valid for every rational agent provided reason is practical for him without hindrance."[11] But this necessity is not an *ought* at all, it is the transcendental *is* of "noumenal" freedom. A will *thus* rational would be a holy will: there is no place in its necessarily rational (and hence righteous) willing for imperatives, or obligations, or constraint. It wills rationally from the mere necessity of its nature, and this self-determination is its freedom. Here, as Kant says, the ought would be out of place.

> If reason infallibly directs the will, the actions which such a being recognises as objectively necessary are also subjectively necessary. . . . But if reason itself does not sufficiently determine the will and if the will is subjugated to subjective conditions (certain incentives) which do not always agree with objective conditions, in a word if the will is not in complete accord with reason (the actual case of man) then the actions that are recognized as objectively necessary are subjectively contingent, and the determination of such a will by objective laws is constraint. That is, the relation of objective laws to a will that is not completely good is conceived as the determination of the will of a rational being by principles of reason to which this will is not by nature necessarily obedient. The conception of an objective principle so far as it constrains a will is a command (of reason) and the formula of this command is called an imperative. All imperatives are expressed by an 'agent,' and thereby indicate the relation of an objective law to a will which is not in its subjective constitution necessarily determined by them. This relation is that of constraint.[12]

A holy (or wholly rational) will requires no such imperatives.

10 Paton, *The Categorical Imperative* (London: Hutchinson's University Library, 1948), p. 246.
11 "Foundations," *loc. cit.*, p. 104.
12 *Ibid.*, p. 72.

"The 'ought' is here out of place, for the volition of itself is necessarily in harmony with the law."[13] "The dependence of a will not absolutely good on the principle of autonomy (moral constraint) is obligation. Thus obligation cannot be applied to a holy will. The objective necessity of an action from obligation is called duty."[14]

When we recall that objectivity is the subjective necessity of the action *for* a wholly rational will, and that the will for which conformity to its mandates is a duty is one that is *not* in this way wholly rational, this would appear to mean that duty is the necessity of an action for an agent for whom it is not in this way a necessity. And what else but this, on Kant's theory, could it mean?

Something further must be added if we are to make any rational sense of this. For a "holy" will there is no ought, no obligation, and no moral imperative. For the "actual case of man" and *his* morality, these notions are, for Kant, the center of the matter. So far they have been described merely as constraints upon a will that subjectively is not inclined to respect them and need not, from the necessity of its own nature, do so. Why should it obey them? If this human will is also, in its own somewhat different way, a rational will, it will ask for a justification of such commands; it, or the agent whose will it is, will want to know *why* it *should* obey them. It will demand a justification of such categorical imperatives, that is not itself a mere constraint, nor a tautological necessity which, in the actual case of man, does not apply. What *reasons* can be given for obedience to such unconditional commands?

Here Paton summarizes Kant's thought neatly.

Kant attempts to justify the principle as a moral law and thereby to justify it as a categorical imperative: if it is a principle on which a fully rational agent would necessarily act, it must also be—on this

---

13 *Ibid.*, p. 73.
14 *Ibid.*, p. 96.

view—a principle on which an imperfectly rational agent *ought* to act, if he is tempted to do otherwise.[15]

What concerns us here is precisely the nature of this "ought". Is it an analytic necessity? Obviously not. Is it just another command or imperative now added to the others it is supposed to justify? If so, then some questions will rationally arise concerning it. It does not help at all to say that it is a command of reason that ought as such to be obeyed. For here the ought *is* just the command itself as constraining a will for which it is not, subjectively, a neccessity of reason, and reason has nothing to offer to the human will but such commands. Why should *we* be in this way rational, i.e., unconditionally obedient to such dictates? On penalty of contradicting our own willing natures? There is no contradiction whatever in an imperfectly rational will being imperfectly rational. Because the rational will is our own "real" will, which necessarily wills the moral law? So far as it is, in any world to which the moral law applies as a necessary law of "the causality of free agents," there is no obligation, ought or duty to obey it. So far as it is not, there is, for it, no such "objective" necessity. As an objective necessity it makes all commands out of place. As a command, in its relation to an imperfectly rational will, it has not this kind of objective necessity, and hence no rational cogency for such a will. It is just a command of reason which, as we have seen, is by no means to say that in our human situation it is a rational command. The ought of duty is here warranted not by the cogency of the reasons that support it, but by the unconditional dictates of a *will* whose rationality is not "determined" by such reasons but is rather the expression of its own subjectively autonomous and self-centered willfulness. Why should we conform our will to a "duty" thus imposed upon us as constraint? This question, in Kant's Ethics, both demands and cannot have a cogent answer.

---

[15] *Op. cit., p.* 193.

Thus, in interpreting moral reasons as generalized commands, Kant has deprived himself of the right to use them as reasons, as the grounds of obligation that justify an "ought" in its normative use, precisely where he needs them most. A super-moral reason, the *is* of noumenal freedom, he can give us, but this is a necessity only for a will for which the "ought" of obligation is out of place. And a sub-moral imperative which, to be morally cogent, would require a justification which no further imperative can give it, is much in evidence. Without such a justification the categorical imperative becomes, as Bergson has called it, the morality of the drill sergeant—"you must because you must." But the ought in moral obligation itself has no place in his system. This may seem a surprising thing to say since Kant is usually regarded as the philosopher of duty and of obligation par excellence. But if we follow out the implications of his own account of the rational *use* of moral maxims, this and nothing else is what we find. And we can see quite clearly why it must be so. A command of reason is a sad, infertile hybrid, for its "reason" has no moral cogency and its command, in consequence, no moral warrant. As rational, the law which a wholly "rational" (or holy) will would necessarily follow, it commands nothing, and as a command it justifies nothing, but shows its "rationality" only in the unconditional generality of its groundless edicts. A will *thus* rational is not the will to understand adequately, to judge responsibly what, in the light of all his obligations, a human agent ought to do, and to act accordingly. It is a will to maintain the unqualified "universality" of its own volitions in their self-determining and self-centered purity (it has only itself for its agent). Such a will may be "good" in some metaphysical sense, as an embodiment of noumenal autonomy, but this is not the goodness that we need and value in the conduct of men who, if they are to live well together, must respect each other, and each other's rights and interests in another and more human

way—must take rational account of them, in the contingent circumstances of their human existence, as grounds for valid claims
on conduct. In the case of man, at least, to be *morally* rational
we must be reasonable and this a morality of commands whose
"rationality" consists in the unconditional generality of their
autonomously willful application does not enable us to do. Hence
what Kant offers is not the practical reason that we seek.

This long excursus into Kantian ethics has been worth making
for two reasons. The first is negative. So firmly, in the academic
mind, at least, is the notion of practical reason linked with what
Kant had to say on this subject, that when an account of the
one is offered it is frequently supposed that it must be the other
that is really meant. It is therefore important to show explicitly,
for our own theory, both that and why this is not the case. In
defending practical reason we are not accepting and defending
Kant's account of it. On the contrary, if our theory is right on
quite fundamental points, Kant's must be wrong, and vice versa.
Our aim has been to specify those points in such a way that
there need be no misunderstanding about them.

The second is more positive. By showing just what kind of
"universality" for our practical reasons objectivity of moral
judgment does and does not require, we can clear the way for
further and essential work to be done. Such universality, while
necessary, is not sufficient to answer rightly any concrete moral
question. *Whatever* our practical reasons may be, they must, if
they are to be reasons at all, have equal cogency *as reasons* in
all instances to which they relevantly apply. But what good
reasons are, what they are good *for,* and when they are sufficient
to decide a specific issue on its merits are further questions to
which the "universality" requirement gives no answer. Taken as
a self-sufficient criterion for moral right, the formal "rationality"
of our procedure shuts us up in a self-righteous rectitude which
itself requires, and cannot of itself supply, a practically reason-

able justification. The trouble with it is not that it is too rational but that, for moral purposes, it is not reasonable enough. We must indeed have *grounds* more relative than this if we are to act well and wisely. Unless the moral law is a requirement for the right attainment of a good we seek, not as spaceless, timeless agents in a supersensuous realm of ends, but as creatively, conditioned beings with needs to be satisfied and responsibilities to meet that are by no means the expression of our own autonomous willing, it has no justifiable claim upon our conduct. A "good will" not thus grounded in and disciplined by the order of a world our thinking and our willing never made is, for human purposes, a practically arbitrary will. We must find out what, in such a world and under such conditions, we can, as moral agents, rightly do. It is in such finding out that the requirement for moral objectivity in the use of reasons has its practically cogent meaning. And it is in this way that we must understand and use it if it is to be a reliable guide to right conduct. The circumstances under which we act, where they are morally relevant to the right fulfillment of our desires and obligations, *are* our grounds for acting in one way rather than another. And it is inside, not in abstraction from, the situation they define that we are called upon, as men, to be morally reasonable. In one sense this limits the work of moral inquiry by focussing it on the human work we have to do. But in another it broadens it immeasurably. For it brings out of the airtight realm of "universal legislation" and into vital connection with the world in which things move and grow and sometimes, if we have the sense and will to do the job, grow better as we guide them rightly to a rewarding issue. For the conditions under which the action is thus done are also the connections that guarantee its practical linkage with this larger world. If our discovery of the moral sterility of an unreasonably rational ethics has brought us back to this essential and invigorating truth it has served, so far, a fruitful purpose.

CHAPTER 12

ULTIMATE GOOD
AND PRACTICAL REASON

WE HAVE SO FAR had little to say about what is traditionally regarded as the unique and essential contribution of moral philosophy to moral practice—the identification of the Good, or of the highest and ultimate good to whose attainment all our actions, insofar as they are rational, are "in the end" directed. No action is worth doing, and in that sense "practical", unless the end at which it aims is the achievement of a good worth having. To act rightly, therefore, we need a knowledge of the good, for it is only in the light of such knowledge that we can properly assess the import and the worth of actions whose goal is to attain it. What is this good? How are we to know it when we see it? And how, on the terms it sets, can the worth of anything in particular be determined?

Prima facie, there are many goods, and each, in its own way, is a norm for reasonable action in the practice in which the distinction between authentic worth and spurious pretenders to this status can reliably be made. A competent buyer knows a good bargain when he sees one; he can tell what goods are worth the price that is asked for them without resort to theories as to the ultimate nature of "the good". A discerning critic knows (or is supposed to know) a good play and can often tell us in an enlightening way why it is good or what is good about it. He need not be a philosopher to do his work well. Such an expert, in the field of his own competence, has a knowledge of good that is normatively cogent as a guide to any action in which the achievement of such good is our practical concern. *This* kind of good we have already taken full account of.

The problem here, however, is a different one, and those who raise it frequently become impatient if, like Socrates, we refer to the experience of artisans and craftsmen when we try to deal with it. "Good" of this kind is one thing; ultimate good is something of a higher and more general sort. There are times when it is not good to buy a good car, even though its mechanical superiority is recognized. And a good bargain may be one that it would, for other purposes than those of which the bargaining takes account, be bad to make. The Mad Hatter's justification for putting butter in his watch—that it was the best butter—does not show the rationality of his action even if, by the Department of Agriculture's tests, the butter can be proved to be the best. The point is, of course, that the practices in which such excellence is established are limited in their scope and purpose and when a practical decision must be made, *their* "good" may not be all we need to take account of. Perhaps, in some sections, "integration" now would lower the level of the education given in the public schools. Even if this were the case, it might still be good to integrate the schools in the interest of racial equality, or national unity, or the good will we should thus gain from countries whose votes we need in the United Nations. Whether or not this would be the case cannot be settled by showing (if it can be shown) that, in its actual content, such integrated education would be less good pedagogically than that a segregated school system now supplies. In this situation, there are different goods to be weighed against each other. Which, either by itself or in combination with others, is *more* good? To be rational here, we seem to need some common measure for such goods, or some hierarchy of values that will show us which, when all can not be had, are entitled to precedence over others.

This, clearly, is sometimes a practical problem. Is a good football team more important for a university than a good library (where the goodness of each, in its own kind, can be objectively judged)? That depends on what a university is for, and on this point the taxpayers, legislators, regents, and administrators who "in the end" control its policies seem not yet to have made up their minds. What is the good of a university, by reference to which the worth of its practical policies can be rightly judged? Thus, since a university is not a self-enclosed and self-justifying institution, what is the good of a good university for the community to whose larger good, in its own way, it should contribute? And what is the good of the community except the good of the individuals who, in their communal relations, constitute it? What is the good *for man,* the final or ultimate good, in whose terms all other goods must be measured if their comparative importance for practical action is to be rationally established? And, finally, how can we estimate the good for man without some adequate notion of what is ultimately good in the Universe, and of our own right relation to it? Without answers to these questions, we seem, in the end, to have no valid answer to the question of the comparative importance for practical action, of the goods whose worth we can establish by more familiar tests, and hence no rational ground for the preference we are often called upon to make among them. Provisional answers, based on unquestioned preconceptions, we can often give. In our society, at the present time, winning the cold war is almost universally accepted as a primary objective for right action and if a winning football team, or the learning of a foreign language, or more and better science teaching in the high schools or the integration of the schools can be shown to be a needed contribution to this cause, it gains thereby a priority in importance that would not otherwise be accorded to it. In practical decisions we must "put first things first." But winning the cold war is not our only or our final end. As Aristotle said, we make war (if we are rational) for the sake of peace and the kind of peace that this must be if men of many nations are to live well together on the terms it sets is a consideration also relevant to the wise direction of our present policies. And how can it be answered save by reference to the true and final good of man and the moral requirements for its right achievement? We may, for "practical" purposes, bypass such questions when something must be done and we still do not know, or are not agreed about, the answers to them. But unless they are faced somewhere, and rightly answered, how can any purpose "in the end" be practical?

It is in this way that the question about ultimate or final good does practically and quite genuinely arise. We shall be well advised, I think, to keep this fact in mind as we go on to consider what would be a relevant and reasonable way of dealing with it. For while it is a genuine and important, it is also a quite special kind of question. It is not the sort of question that we ask when we try to determine whether in its own way, and with reference to the aims and standards of the practice in which the question of its goodness is relevantly raised, a thing is good and in this way worth having, or an action well performed. The man who finds it necessary to refer to the ultimate end of man, or of the Universe, to determine whether a baseball player has pitched a good game is not likely to be a good judge of pitching. And unless some things were in this way good and some actions well done there would be no point in practical action. The question to which the reference to ultimate good is pertinent is a second order question. It is that of the comparative importance of goods thus established to some further end or ends. Good pitching is in its own way good, but what's the good of good pitching? It is not an isolated and self-contained activity, but has its place within a network of acceptances and "values" among which, when all can not be satisfied, we are practically obliged to choose. If all able-bodied men in the country should be contributing directly to the cold, or hot, war effort there may be times when we cannot afford good pitching. And if great poetry, as some Puritans have suspected, brings with it licentious living, perhaps the poets must be banished from a good society. This, even if it were the case, would in no way show that they were not good poets. The issue here is that of a right *ordering* of goods in relation to a higher, more ultimate, and hence rationally more authoritative standard. What could this standard be but "good" itself? If each of the alternatives for preferential action is, in its own way, good, which is *more* good, or the higher good, or the one more essential to the achievement of the true end of man? How could we tell unless we knew what this true end and final good really was? The primary business of moral philosophy, it is often held, is to supply us with this knowledge.

The same question can, and in our own inquiry has, been approached from a different angle, that of the apparent "conflict" of obligations. Where in terms of obligation, there are reasons both for and against the doing of a specific act—telling a helpful lie, for example—the question as to what, in the specific case, we should do remains so far unanswered. What could be more rational in such situations than to answer such a question by reference to the good of all concerned? If no one, including the teller, would be harmed by such a lie, while considerable good would come of it, the answer, save for the most rule-bound moralist, seems plain. And if there must be some good and some harm in either case, what can I rightly do but so act as to maximize the one and minimize the other? This is, of course, an over-simplification, since the question of *whose* good and *whose* harm would still need an answer. But would not this answer itself be in terms of good and harm on the whole, and with impartial regard for the interests of all concerned, and hence for the "larger" good? Here it is not the ordering of goods, but that of obligation, in their "bindingness" or urgency or importance that is the relevant issue, and the same reference to a more ultimate good, and, finally, to a final good, would seem to be required to answer it. What is this good? A rational account of duty, no less than that of worth, seems "in the end" to lead us to this question.

This, then, is the problem, in its time-honored form. How are we to deal with it? My thesis will be that in this time-honored form the question, from the standpoint of practical reason, has been wrongly put, and the answers given to it, in consequence, while often illuminating on particular points, have on the whole, created more difficulties than they have solved and have left us in confusion on just the points where understanding was most needed. It is no wonder that the question about ultimate good is one of the "perennial" or "enduring" problems of philosophy. It is *bound* to be perennial, or to keep coming up again, because there is, in the terms in which it is stated, no convincing way of answering it. For those who like unanswerable questions, this may add to its attraction. At least it makes it an inexhaustible theme for inconclusive argument. But, when its practical bearing is stressed, as it regularly is in emphasizing the importance of the subject, it is a right answer to it that is held to be important. And if no such answer can, with rational cogency, be given, the suspicion will actually arise that if a rational solution of our moral problems must wait upon such answers, there can "in the end" be no solution for them. Here once more a chasm separates a theory that is, in principle, practically inconclusive and a practice that without it must be rationally blind. Our aim has been to bridge such chasms by a better understanding of the use of practical reasons as justifying grounds for action. Our present task is to show, if we can, that this method is applicable and fruitful even in those lofty regions where ultimate good has its spiritual (or dialectical) home.

It is clear, at least, that before we can use this notion of ultimate good in the guidance and appraisal of our conduct, we must find out what it is that is in this way good. How are we to recognize the final end of action in this normative status when, or if, we see it? The criteria for its correct identification will evidently be of a different sort from those we use when we estimate the worth of ends and actions by the standards of the practices in which a good bargain, or poem, or performance is distinguished from those that lack such merit. For these latter, as we have seen, are all provisional and incomplete when it is ultimate good that is in question; it is just because they are so that recourse to it is made. Perhaps by noting more specifically what is incomplete in them we can see what it must be, if it is to have the normative finality for action that they lack.

One way of putting the matter is to say that while their good in the end is always for the sake of something else, this final good is for its own sake, and requires no further justification than that which its own intrinsic and ultimate goodness provides. Good pitching is in its own way good, no doubt, but it is not its own excuse for being. If no one wanted or enjoyed it, or the sport of which it is a part, what would be the good of it? And no sane man wants just *this* enjoyment standing quite alone. He has other and more basic wants and, if the good of good baseball can be had only by sacrificing them, he will reasonably hold that it is not good *enough* to justify this sacrifice. Those who praise baseball as our national sport emphasize its value for physical fitness, character building, and morale in a way of life in which, we are assured, it is as American as apple pie, and similarly to be commended. They place it, that is to say, within a larger framework of good to which, without undue cost, it makes a distinctive contribution. To hint of excellence in baseball as maintaining its normative status as a worthy end of action "quite alone" and without regard to other worthy ends whose attainment may be helped or hindered by it, as good *per se* and for its own sake merely, would be practically absurd. It is quite otherwise, however, with ultimate good. This *must* be worth having for its own sake merely and not for any farther good to which it contributes, for if it did not have this status it too would be provisional and require "in the end" a justification that carried us beyond itself. Nor can this be a merely partial good, or one among others, for if it were it would be improved on by the addition of something of a different sort, and this larger good would be a higher excellence to which its own importance would be normatively subordinate. Since final good, to be our final and self-justifying rational end of action, must thus be *per se,* self-sufficient and self-complete, it must be intrinsic to the object or objects that possess it, a good that would belong to them if they (or it) existed quite alone, in isolated grandeur. Any dependence on conditions or circumstances would deprive it of its unqualified and unconditional perseity and hence of its normative finality as "in the end" the measure of the provisional and conditional goodness of all other goods.

It seems, indeed, that the very considerations of which it would be reasonable to take account in estimating the importance of provisional goods are those from which we must rigorously abstract if ultimate good is to be rationally identified. This observation is not at this point presented as an objection. Perhaps the nature of the subject requires just this procedure. But the contrast indicates at least the very special nature of the problem with which we are here confronted.

So far, in dealing with it we have been confronted with a string of "musts". These lay down the ground rules for the search for ultimate good and provide what there is in the world (or out of it, as Kant would add) that meets the specifications thus laid down and is thereby qualified to serve as the final referent and standard for all the good we know. To consider all of even the most formidable of the contenders for this status would require a treatise of some magnitude. And to deal adequately with some of them a whole system of metaphysics and/or theology would be required. Fortunately for our purposes the most empirically modest of them—pleasure, or the various more refined derivatives: happiness, immediate value, "welfare" and, in general, "satisfaction", that are offered, under criticisms, as improvements on it—is a hardy perennial in this field and the Utilitarian theories based upon it will serve as well as any others as clear cases of what an ethical theory of this sort is like. In Britain and America, Utilitarianism in modern times has had more influence on non-philosophical writing and practice than any ethical theory, and while it is often refuted it never dies, nor does it wholly fade away, though its doctrines tend to become more tenuous as its advocates grow in philosophical sophistication. No moral philosophy that claims to be adequate to the facts of moral experience can afford to ignore its teachings and its influence. Let us see what we can make of them.

The line of reasoning that appears to lead straight to the conclusion that pleasure is "the good" is presented with beautiful simplicity by Socrates in Plato's *Protagoras*. It is agreed by Socrates and Protagoras that no man lives well who lives in pain and grief, but he who lives pleasantly to the end of his life will have lived well. Hence to live pleasantly is *a* good and to live unpleasantly an evil. Yes, replies Protagoras, if the pleasure be good and honorable. But Socrates is rather disposed to say that things are good insofar as they are pleasant, and evil insofar as they are painful, if they have no consequences of another sort. This would amount to saying not just that to live pleasantly is *a* good, but that pleasure is *the* good, and Protagoras is hesitant at first to put the matter "*in this unqualified manner.*" But Socrates is pushing for an ultimate standard. The thesis he presents is that pleasure is the *only* measure of good and pain of evil and this as he correctly notes would imply that pleasure is a good *in itself.* If some pleasant things are nonetheless judged to be evil it is on account of their evil (painful) consequences, and it is in a similar way only that unpleasant things can rationally be called good. Pleasure or the advance of pain are, as we should say, the *only* justifying reasons that can establish the worth of anything—the only standard that we look to when we call them good. And since no man would willingly choose evil in preference to good, if he knew what he was doing, the choice of evil must be due to ignorance, i.e., to a miscalculation of the aggregate consequences, in terms of pleasure and pain, of the action done. Immediate and remote pleasures, so far as good is concerned, differ only in pleasure and pain; there can be no other measure of them. The *more* of good the better, and the less the worse. And since it is always rational to choose more good, in preference to less, a man will always choose the greater pleasure or the lesser pain, *if* he knows what these are. The salvation of human life consists in the right choice of pleasures and pains—of the more or the fewer, and the greater and the less and the nearer and remoter—"moral arithmetic", as Bentham was later to call it. All this follows if we agree that "the pleasant is the good and painful evil," and that "all actions [are] honorable and useful [good] of which the tendency is to make life painless and pleasant."[1] To determine rightly, therefore, which acts are truly virtuous, all we have to do is to find out which are in fact pleasurable or pleasure producing, and which on the other hand are themselves painful or "end in pain." Right action

---

[1] *Protagoras,* Jowett translation, 358b.

is guided by knowledge of the good, and "the pleasant is the good and the painful evil."

In this quite simple form hedonism runs too sharply counter to our customary moral preconceptions to be widely accepted as an adequate moral philosophy. Almost endless qualifications and complications of its initially forthright doctrine are required to save the moral appearances. And in other dialogues the Platonic Socrates spends much effort and ingenuity in attempting to refute it. But the central structure of the reasoning remains the same. The good *is* (tautologously) what we should seek, and evil what we should avoid. (To "do good and avoid evil" is held to be a first principle of the moral law.) For "the good is the (rational) end of all our actions, and all our actions are to be done for the sake of the good and not the good for the sake of them." Hence, if pleasure is *the* good, it has in this status an ultimate rational authority, for it, and nothing else, will supply the final reason why an action should be done, and nothing that conflicts with it can be ultimately good. This does not mean, of course, as Moore was at great pains to point out, that "good" in this warranting or justifying use *means* the same as "pleasant". If it did we should have said no more when we said a pleasant thing was good than when we said that it was pleasant. The whole point of the argument is to claim that its being pleasant is not the same as, but is rather the final and self-sufficient reason for, its being good, where such goodness is a status that warrants us in making it, as such, the final goal of all our actions and their achievement of it the *only* "ultimate" measure or standard of their worth. This is by no means a tautology. It is an assertion about the salvation of human life, which is thus shown to consist in nothing but the right choice of pleasures and pains—a proposition many of us would wish, on moral grounds, to deny. It gives us one big reason for doing anything, a reason to which all others are subordinate, since other things are to be sought as good only insofar as they are pleasurable (or less painful than available alternatives) either in themselves or in their consequences. If claims to good conflict, the only arguable question is as to which is the *greater* good, since it stands to reason that the greater good is always rationally to be preferred to the lesser, and the greater good will be the greater pleasure. Other "goods" are not good *in themselves* at all; it is only as means to pleasure, or the avoidance of pain that it is rational to seek them. The question of means is an empirical question; it could in principle be answered by reliable prediction as to what agreeable or disagreeable experiences are likely to occur under assignable conditions. The normative question is answered once *the good* is identified, and there is no further need to argue about it. When we know what, on the whole, are the "felicific" consequences of segregation or desegregation, we know which social policy it is right for us to adopt. And for the purposes of rational action a good poem is a pleasure producing or pain avoiding poem. Thus our second order principle for a rational preference among goods becomes a first order principle for the calculation of pleasures. The standard we should appeal to "in the end" is in truth our only *normative* standard, and there is nothing left to "deliberate" about but the most effective means for the attainment of the single end it establishes as "the good" which as such we should always seek.

As a dialectical identification of such final good, hedonism has very considerable advantages. Pleasure and pain appear to be quite readily identifiable—everybody knows what pain is and all of us, at some times in our lives, have been pleased by something. And the practical relevance of such experiences is plain to any normal human being. That an action or its consequences would be painful is obviously a reason for not doing it; and that the fact that someone would be pleased by it is a reason why it should be done, is something any generously disposed man can understand. A society in which such considerations were not recognized as good reasons for or against an action would be one in which we could not live on terms of shared practical understanding with our fellows. If these are not good reasons, what would a good reason for doing anything be like? Moreover, they are, in one sense, quite *final* reasons. It makes no moral sense to ask *why* pain is evil, or pleasure good. A painful experience is bad (so far at least) just because it is painful, and to say that an experience is pleasant *is* to give a reason why it is "intrinsically" as such worth having. *In that sense,* pleasure is its own excuse for the being, and pain for the not being, of the experiences in which it is involved. This does not mean, of course, that pleasure and the avoidance of pain is or ought to be, the only *final* end of all our striving, but for the dialectician whose stock in trade is the neglect of relevant qualifications and distinctions this transition from the one use of "finality" to the other is a simple one to make.

Finally, the weighing of "felicific consequences" is *a* relevant consideration in the right ordering of the comparative importance of goods and bindingness of obligations. If one good, though "higher" of its kind, is accessible to but a few, or can be had only at the cost of pain to many, then there are times when we ought to sacrifice the higher to the lower in the interest of "more". The good of pleasure, in the humble and familiar sense of agreeable feeling, is a peculiarly democratic good. And while it may take discipline and training to judge what is bad about a cheaply sentimental poem, anyone can understand what is bad about a toothache. If these rudimentary and familiar goods and ills are made the final common measure of *all* good, we seem to have a universal standard that is also a least common denominator. This, of course, was never Socrates' intention, but it lends a considerable humanitarian glow to modern Utilitarian and "welfare" theories. There is indeed some moral ground for its equalitarian zeal. But to take that ground as the only final practical ground for anything—to say that "in the end" the worth of a good poem is its capacity to contribute to the "welfare" of mankind as an aggregate of such painless pleasures for an endlessly multiplying population—is a very different thing. It is by the identification of its good as final good, as finally the *only* good and hence "in the end" the measure of all other goods, these being now reduced to the status of means to its own unqualified and self-justifying goodness, that this difference is dialectically eliminated. By such devices we can be at once dialectically profound and practically simple-minded. It is no wonder that the procedure is perennially attractive.

As a moral philosophy, however, hedonism is a very dubious doctrine indeed. If the pleasure that is the ultimate good is to be identified with the agreeable feeling whose goodness "any fool can plainly see" then those who seriously espoused the theory were saying, as Anscombe has observed, that "something which they thought of as like a particular tickle or itch was obviously the point of doing anything whatsoever."[2]

Thus if pleasure is now broadened to include those spiritual satisfactions that were said by John Stuart Mill to be qualitatively higher (and in this way "more") we get a nobler but much vaguer view. For who's to gauge the height of pleasures and is it in terms of pleasure merely, as a "final" standard, that such discriminations are made? Mill's answers to both these questions were quite unconvincing. "Welfare" is the term now in common use as a substitute for pleasure, but this too frequently means, in practice, the pleasure that a "welfare" worker thinks you ought to have. Happiness is a more morally significant term, for it at least suggests that well-being and well-doing that is worthy of man and might even, as in Aristotle's ethics, be identified with virtuous activity. But how in hedonistic terms is

---

[2] G. E. M. Anscombe, *Intention* (Oxford: Basil Blackwell, 1957) pp. 77.

such worthiness to be assessed? "Ideal" Utilitarianism rises above all such particularities of content and affirms that it is just the good as such that is intrinsically worth having, and that more good is always better (more) than less. Which objects or experiences possess such final goodness as a quality or property, and which have more of it, is a further question. Since it is good *per se* that is here in question the answer can be provided only by an immediate apprehension, whether in sensory experience or in a supersensible intuition, of the presence or absence of the good or "value-property" that is the final reason for the worth of anything. All other rational assignment of worth depends on this and when we see it, all else is normatively made plain. What it is that is thus seen to have the "good" property and thus to be intrinsically good is a matter on which would-be seers gravely disagree. It has even been maintained that pleasure is not intrinsically good at all. How, save by looking very carefully and just seeing (or not seeing) could we tell? As a method for the rational resolution of disagreements about the importance of competing goods, this pretty clearly has its limitations. But it does at least assure us that more good, whatever it may be, is more than less and has as such a normative priority for preferential action. And that, surely, no rational man can deny.

There is, however, a further question to be dealt with before this rather meager insight can be put to use in practical judgment. Ought we so to act as to maximize "good" whosoever and whatever it may be? It may at first seem obvious that we should. With respect to "final good" at least, whether this be pleasure, or refined spiritual enjoyments of beauty and affection, or "welfare", or something other than all these, "if some's good, more's better" and the most attainable would be best of all. Our one ultimate good appears to carry with it normatively one ultimate obligation which, in the case of conflicts of conflicting claims, is entitled in all cases to priority. *Maximize good and minimize evil*, no matter whose, or when or where or how, if only in the final theological balance it is more (or in the case of evil, less). If to tell the truth would be an action that would, on the whole, do more harm than good, we ought not to tell the truth. And so for any other obligation short of this one. All alike are provisional in their cogency, though experience has shown that *as a rule* to act in conformity to their dictates does more good than harm and, *in the end,* all must be rationally qualified by the subordination to the one big obligation, which is simply and "universally" to do good. As compared with the rule-bound morality of traditional acceptances this seems a generous and enlightened doctrine, and that the considerations it stresses are in many cases relevant to the determination of the rightness of an action we have ourselves insisted in our criticism of Kant. It is no wonder that Utilitarianism in this large, loose and "universalistic" sense is the ideology of so many humanitarian liberals or reformers. For it rationalizes their generalized benevolence as the final and self-justifying principle for all right action and enables them to discredit, on principle, all claims to good and right that are not "in the end" subservient to it. Who but a selfish and/or snobbish rule-bound reactionary could deny the moral priority of the "larger" good? And what could the larger good be but "more" good, if not for *all* concerned then surely for the greatest number? In this form the Utilitarian doctrine is still, practically, very much with us, and requires a kind of rational scrutiny that its own adherents are, on principle, in no position to supply.

Since this theory holds that our only ultimate obligation is to do good, and that in consequence the right action is simply the good-enhancing action, it is sometimes said that it defines right in terms of good and thus reduces it to both a logically and a morally derivative position. In fact, however, it appeals to a quite ultimate principle of obligation of its own, and would make no moral sense without it. To say that more "good" is more than less is one thing. To say that we ought so to act in all cases as to produce more good is something else. It is only when "maximize good" is understood in this way that it has any cogency for moral action. The good-enhancing character of the action is here presented as ground for moral claims upon our conduct. And in the Utilitarian scheme it is a ground of quite ultimate and unconditional moral stringency. No other is ever entitled to prevail against it and it is only as a way of meeting its requirement that any other is entitled to prevail at all. Other moral rules are "defeasible" by reference to considerations of good and harm, but no deviation from it is ever morally justifiable, since it itself is the rule by which the legitimacy of all deviations must be judged. As such it is to be applied with strict impartiality. For

> the Utilitarian standard of what is right in conduct is not the agent's own happiness but that of all concerned. As between his own happiness and that of others Utilitarianism requires him to be as strictly impartial as a disinterested and impartial spectator.[3]

We may find that Utilitarianism morally leads us up the garden path, but it is certainly not the primrose path of laxity or self-indulgence. This is not a no-obligation theory. It is rather a one-obligation theory, whose single final dictate is so universally and unconditionally binding as in every instance to be morally inescapable. That, precisely, is what is ultimate about it.

The Utilitarian is to be as impartial in estimating the happiness of all concerned as a distinterested spectator. Who are "all concerned"? There has been some debate about this, but Henry Sidgwick, the most systematic and careful of the sect, is surely right in saying that from a genuinely universal point of view, "from the standpoint of the Universe," it can be nothing less than the whole sentient creation present and to come. If it is

---

[3] J. S. Mill, *Utilitarianism*, Chapter 2.

only ultimate "good" that ultimately counts (and Sidgwick still courageously identifies ultimate good as pleasure) then any pleasure anywhere at any time has equal weight with any other, save only when, as pleasure, it is more or less, and the maximum of pleasure thus achievable by action is the "impartial" norm for right conduct. "In the end" and from the standpoint of the Universe nothing but good (pleasure) counts, and this counts only in respect of more or less. This means not merely that we must claim no special favors for ourselves. It means that we should treat the claims of those who stand to us in the closest and most intimate relations only as candidates for such a share of generalized benevolence as, for the overall maximization of pleasure in the whole sentient creation, present and to come, it is, from the point of view of the Universe, right to bestow on them. It may be that we ought to be specially benevolent to those nearest to us—if such behavior leads us to maximize pleasure in the Universe such would be the case. It may be that we ought to be felicifically niggardly to those we care for, thus counteracting any natural bias in their favor, and particularly benevolent to those as remote as possible from our local loyalties and affections. And there is a kind of humanitarianism that appears to take this maxim as its guide. But which course of action is right can be determined only if we can tell which contributes most, on the whole, to total good (pleasure) in the Universe, no matter whose, where, when, or how achieved, if only it is more. Sidgwick asserts that conformity to the rules of accepted morality does on the whole thus contribute and that they should in consequence be followed save where, in exceptional instances, such conformity would clearly do more harm than good. From the standpoint of 19th century British morality this can plausibly be argued but from the standpoint of the Universe it appears more questionable. No doubt the observance of such rules helped to make Britain strong and law-abiding. It was men thus disciplined who built the British Empire. Perhaps it would have been better (more felicific on the whole) from the standpoint of the colonies if the Empire had not been built. A moral laxity that made the British less inclined to serve queen and country, from this point of view, might have been a contribution to the larger good. After all, there were more of the colonized than of the colonizers and hence, from the point of view of the Universe, their pleasures, being more, would have the greater claim to consideration. There are the feelings of the animals to be considered, too, and the germs destroyed by modern sanitation doubtless also have their feelings. And beyond that, there are from the standpoint of the Universe, the as yet wholly unapparent consequences of present action to be weighed impartially, i.e., equally, on the scale. The Universe, or those competent to speak for it, may know where "in the end" the felicific balance stands, but the plain fact is that we do not. And if the valuation of our more proximate judgments of right and wrong must wait upon such knowledge, it will for practical purposes, never be achieved. This kind of generality is as morally rootless as Kant's Categorical Imperative and for a similar reason. It has generalized itself clear out of the human situation, while it is *in* this situation and subject to its limitations that rationally cogent judgments must be made.

To this kind of criticism of his theory the Utilitarian has a two-fold reply. First he observes that it is not fair to emphasize such difficulties merely in the case of his own theory. *Any* estimate of right and good that is prepared to take account of consequences in its judgment of the merits of particular actions is in a similar position. To a large extent we are ignorant at the time of action of the long run effects of what we do and hence of what on the whole is best, but must nonetheless do the best we can. The "principle of utility" tells us in principle what this best would be and provides an empirical method by which, within the limits of our knowledge, we can calculate, in its terms, the merits of specific actions. More than this cannot reasonably be required of it. And, in the second place, it is said, the difficulties have been overstated. For the Utilitarian, like the rest of us, does not start from sheer ignorance in these matters. The accepted rules of society sum up the funded experience of the past with respect to those kinds of action that are good-producing on the whole and those that are not. They are empirical generalizations about such actions supported on the whole by the moral experience of mankind. Only when these rules conflict or are, under changing circumstances, inapplicable to the requirements of present action, need the principle of utility be invoked to reach a "final" estimate of what we ought to do. And, in such cases, it is the *only* principle that will do the job "objectively"— in the light, so far as we have it, of a factually accurate and morally impartial estimate of all the "final" or intrinsic good involved. A reasonable Utilitarian does not claim more for his theory than this, and a reasonable man cannot be satisfied with less.

To see why these answers will not do will bring us to the center of the issue about "ultimate" good. In the first place, the Utilitarian, if he is faithful to his theory and does not deviate from it with practical goodness, is *not* in the same situation as the rest of us in the estimate of the morally relevant consequences of an action. In one way his problem is simpler than ours, in another it is incalculably more complex. The *only* consequences of which "in the end" he needs to take account are those that produce pleasure or pain (or whatever in the way of intrinsic good and evil he has substituted for these) no matter whose, or how achieved, or when or where, if only in the Universe at large they are more. But only as in this way "more" has the good, to which our actions *should* be directed, any normative cogency at all for right conduct. We cannot even say that one play is better than another, where its betterness is offered as a ground for preferential action, except by reference to the total felicific (or intrinsic good-producing) balance that such action would achieve. A good knife, for the purpose of right action, is a happiness-producing knife, and a good man a happiness-producing man. And this happiness, considered from the point of view of the impartial spectator, is that net felicific balance in the Universe on which, for normative purposes, all else depends. To say that one of the essential moral requirements for such happiness, at least, is that it be that of good men, rightly enjoyed, would be of no help here, for until we know what this balance is we cannot know what men are good (happiness-producing) or what kind of enjoyment is right. Perhaps, as some Utilitarians have argued, "enlightened" selfishness is more productive of such good than benevolence, and should therefore be ranked higher in a moral ordering of the virtues. And perhaps "bad" plays produce more happiness than those the critics have called "good", and should be prized accordingly. With the whole sentient creation and all future time to consider, how are we to judge?

This brings us to the second point. It is quite true that a reasonable man will normally rely in his normative judgments on the more provisional standards accepted in our practice for the right guidance of his preferential action. But the Utilitarian is in no position in such matters to be a reasonable man. For, on his reckoning, these standards have as such *no* normative cogency at all. They are merely empirical rules of calculation that sum up past experience in these matters. Past experience of what? Of what has been found to maximize felicity from the standpoint of the Universe at large and in its total history? By no means. It is within the working practices of a way of life that some objects are found good and some ways of acting right and these have never had the net balance of felicity in the Universe as their point and purpose. Whether, by the standard of the Universe, what they approve as good is "really" so, is something that experience in their successful use cannot reliably tell us. For its standard is not theirs, and when judgments reached by means of them are interpreted as guesses at what would best meet its requirements they become profoundly problematic. What was offered as a principle for the right ordering of their normative claims *inter se* is here a first order principle for the calculation of a good that is not their good, but an ulterior end to which their achievement can make, at best, an instrumental contribution. It is the final end alone that justifies the means and without such justification, we are not warranted in claiming for the goodness they establish any normative significance. Rather, we should strip our minds of any "biased" preconceptions in their favor if we are "objectively" to estimate the final good that, as desirable *per se,* we "rationally" seek.

But how, thus stripped, are we to estimate it reasonably? Are we in any position to do so? The standpoint of the Universe, if it has one, is not that of our moral situation. *We* have commitments of a less cosmic order. We are citizens and sons and brothers, and, in the shared responsibilities of a common way of life, have discovered goods that make that life worth living. It is in the moral order thus achieved or achievable that good and right have, for us, an examinable sense. *Of course* we value pleasures, where they can be fairly had and decently enjoyed, and condemn the affliction of needless pain. But what pains are needless and what pleasures decent we estimate not by reference to the maximization of "good" in general, no matter whose or how achieved or when or where, if only it be more, but by what these practices, in such a way of life, have taught us to respect. The good that justifies right action is itself a morally structured good, and this structure is that of a community in which the claims of "right" and "good", as we already in some measure understand them, can be adequately fulfilled. We can no more moralize at large than we can live at large. It is not surprising that those who attempt to do so lose their bearings and are "in the end" unable to tell us, morally, which way is up. For it is only from a local standpoint that this judgment can significantly be made. It depends on where you are.

In fact, of course, the Utilitarians, in their own practical judgments, make no such "ultimate" abstraction. The "moral arithmetic" of Utilitarian calculation is applied by Bentham not from the standpoint of the Universe at large but from that of a reforming Englishman of the later 19th and early 20th century (1832-1904). As Leslie Stephen noted:

> Bentham's man is not the colorless unit of a priori writing nor the noble savage of Rousseau, but the respectable citizen with a policeman round the corner. Such a man may well hold that honesty is the best policy; he has enough sympathy to be kind to his old mother, and help a friend in distress; but the need of romantic and elevated conduct rarely occurs to him and the heroic, if he meets it, appears to him an exception not far removed from the silly. He does not reflect—especially if he cares nothing for history—how even the society in which he is a contented unit has been built up, and how much loyalty and heroism has been needed for the work; nor even, to do him justice, what unsuspected capacities may lurk in his own commonplace character.[4]

For such a man, and in a community thus constituted, the principle of Utility makes moral sense. For the pleasures to be maximized are those of men who are, or under the sanctions of law and education will become, *intelligently* self-interested, industrious and well-behaved. And the pains to be eliminated are those produced by a legal and penal system whose needlessness for the true ends of a good government any sensible man can plainly see. In such a context to identify pain as *the* evil and

---

[4] Leslie Stephen, *The English Utilitarians* (London: Duckworth and Co., 1900), I, 314f.

pleasure as *the* good is to present a moral ideal of what a good life and a good society should be that has a reforming point for practical action. To say that such pains and pleasures are to be given equal consideration, if they are of equal amount, no matter whose they are, is to embody the ideal of social justice in a democratic program of reform. The "philosophical radicals" used this ideal as a ground both for the criticism of existing institutions and for proposals for their rational reconstruction—they proposed to rear the fabric of felicity. In this use there is much to be said for their philosophy.

Our question is whether their work was made more reasonable or less so by their identification of ultimate good and evil with pleasure and pain, and of right with pleasure-producing (or pain-avoiding) actions, all other considerations of rights, loyalty, and sympathy being subordinated as mere means to the attainment of a maximum of this unqualified and unconditional good. This, in effect, was a way of saying not just that pleasure and pain count and that everybody's pain and pleasure *as such* counts alike within the area of the agent's responsible action, but that "in the end" nothing else counts and no normative claims are entitled to a hearing on any other ground but this. Put in this form the question is not difficult to answer. *Of course,* where other things are equal, pleasures should be maximized and pains if possible eliminated. But where established rights, or the special ties that bind a man to his own family, or cause or country, are involved, or where the greater pleasure to be gained is in unworthy or degrading objects, other things are not valuationally equal, and no community that conducted its practical business on the assumption that they were could long maintain the structure in which even the appeal to hedonistic good and right makes moral sense. The way in which Universalistic Hedonism solves the problem is by asserting that "in the end" they are all equal, since nothing but the obligation to produce pleasure ultimately counts and all else is to be reckoned merely as a means to this. It thus projects the initial conflict onto the unarguable plane of "ultimate" good—you just "see" that pleasure is the only final good (if you are "rational") or else (if you are irrational) you don't. And once this is seen all further normative problems are settled in advance, since claims whose cogency is not calculable on this morally simple-minded and empirically problematic basis are ruled out a priori as ultimately groundless. In its doctrinaire application—in the reform of the "poor laws" for example—in its Benthamite philistinism ("quantities of pleasure being equal, pushpin is as good as poetry") and above all, in its meager ideal of human nature and the goods to which it is appropriately addressed, Utilitarianism as a moral philosophy showed clearly in its fruits where this kind of "ultimacy" leads. John Stuart Mill saw its moral defects but could find no rational way, within the limits of the Principle of Utility, of correcting them. The result was, as it has been in much of later Utilitarianism, a well-intentioned confusion, an earnest attempt to disavow in practice the implications of a doctrine that the believer feels bound, on principle, to accept. And that, given its philosophical procedure, is precisely what we should expect. A one-obligation theory of right can be made to cover the complexities of our actual moral situation only if it ceases in the process to be a one-obligation theory—if, in other words, it is torn apart. The attempt to patch together the resulting fragments is a work of ideological rationalization, of "saving the appearances" not of morally determinable right and wrong but of a theory that has shown its incapacity to do justice to them. What a Utilitarian must say if he is to protect his theory against damagingly relevant criticism is one thing. What we must say if we are to judge rightly the comparative importance of competing claims to right and good is all too often something else. Here theory and practice do indeed part company and the gulf between them is a formidable one.

But we should know by this time how such gulfs are made and what to do about them.

It is often said that a moral philosophy that stops short of "the ultimate" is rationally but half-hearted and half-thought-out. And it is quite true that a theory that leaves us with no rational means for handling the problems to which the recourse to ultimate good and right was offered as an answer is an inadequate and incomplete philosophy. We shall have this problem on our hands and must do our best to deal rationally with it. But, as a necessary first step in this undertaking, and as a way of clearing traditional obstacles from our path, we have now, I think, seen how and why it is that a moral philosophy that stops *with* "the ultimate" as thus identified is morally wrong-headed and must, *on principle,* remain but half-thought-out. For what it does is not to place "goods" and "rights" each in *its own way* normatively cogent in a perspective in which their comparative importance and urgency for action in specific moral situations can be reasonably assessed, but rather to project their competing claims onto a level of unconditional generality and unarguable finality on which only one among them is "in the end" to count at all. And it is to such an end that it instructs us to refer all problems of this sort. This enables us to be high-minded in theory and high-handed in practice and to import into practical discussion an unqualified finality against which the very nature of the problem should have warned us in advance. In ideological warfare it obviously has its uses. If ultimate good and right are with us who but knaves and/or fools can be against us? And what considerations can count morally against the righteousness of our cause? But as a way of finding out what specifically is *the* good and *the* right of the normatively complex situations in which we are called on to *be* reasonable in our actions it is a one-way street that leads to a dead end. That "ultimate ends" thus invoked and justified are in this way dead ends for constructive practical inquiry and that a problem "settled" on their terms is still for moral purposes profoundly problematic is what in this chapter I have tried to prove. So far from being too good for the work of practical reason, they are rationally (i.e., as normatively cogent guides to action) not good enough.

The selection of Utilitarianism as a target for this kind of crticism is not meant as an invidious attack upon this venerable doctrine. On the contrary, it is a moral philosophy worth examining because the Utilitarians have tried to be clear-headed about what they were doing and to apply their principle consistently to issues of practical importance. It is not at its worst but at its best that the appeal to "final" good can most adequately be judged. And Utilitarianism, so far, has been, for our purposes, just about its best. The esoteric goods of more speculative philosophies would have been more obvious targets. And the current liberal substitute of "welfare", where the content of such welfare is borrowed from the liberals' own moral preconceptions and benevolently spread abroad as generalized concern for the "liberation" of men's capacities on the confident assumption that the liberated will, of course, be liberals and the moral unity of mankind the sociological consequence of the indiscriminate aggregation of their "enlightened" interests, deserves a special treatment for which this is not the place. Our concern is with the best that can be said for "ultimate good" as the final rational answer to our practical problems. If this best is not good enough we must go further. And we are now, I think, in a position to do so.

CHAPTER 13

MORAL DIVERSITY
AND ETHICAL ABSOLUTISM

WE MUST HAVE GROUNDS more relative than this. The notion that concrete issues of better and worse, right and wrong, can be settled by a "rational" reference to good in general, from the point of view of the universe, which our own "reason" somehow "dictates" that we follow is at once pretentious and equivocal. *Our* reasons are not, and should not be, of this morally rootless and disembodied sort. They are the considerations we learned to understand and honor as obligations in the family, the community, the nation into which we were born, and in whose shared life we have become such moral agents as we are. And these were not universal communities; they have a local habitation and a name. The freedom that, in America we have learned to value, has Concord Bridge in it, and Walden Pond, and the life and work of old Abe Lincoln who came out of the wilderness, down in Illinois, and is buried now in Springfield, and Davy Crockett and the Alamo. If we ever so far forget the worth of this birthright and the local goods it represents as to trade it in for a mess of universalistic pottage in which its commitments of individual self-respect and self-reliance are lost in indiscriminate benevolence, we shall have done more than merely make a wrong decision; we shall have betrayed a trust. We have commitments *where we are* that are less than global, and more, for they are the commitments that have made us what we are as moral agents, and without them we should not be ourselves. "The idiot who praises in enthusiastic tone all centuries but this and every country but his own," would have been no happier there than here; he could, in fact, take root nowhere. His good in general is not of this world; but it is inside this world, and *where we are* that we must achieve such human good as is possible to us. And in this work, what is too good for this world is, for practical and moral purposes, not good enough. It is, as we have now amply seen, an evasion, not an effective answer, to our actual problems.

So much we can, I think, now take as definitely established. But it leads at once to a difficulty which, in ethical theory, has been regarded as very formidable indeed. If our reasons are *merely* local and parochial, how can they, in the proper sense, be reasons at all, or do the work of reason in the achievement of a common understanding with those whose local background and traditions are, naturally, quite different from our own? *Must* not the cogency of reasons transcend all local standpoints if it is to do the mediating and justifying work of reason? And if the possibility of this is denied, are we not in consistency obliged to admit that our *own* reasons are not "really" reasons at all, but merely verbalized appetites, local prejudices of our own?

Justice Holmes saw this implication clearly and cheerfully embraced it.

> What we most love and revere generally is determined by early associations. I love granite rocks and barberry bushes, no doubt because they were my earliest joys that reach back through the past eternity of my life. But while one's experience thus makes certain preferences dogmatic for oneself, recognition of how they came to be so leaves one able to see that others, poor souls, may be equally dogmatic

about something else. And this, again, means scepticism. Not that one's belief or love does not remain. Not that we would not fight and die for it if important—we all, whether we know it or not are fighting to make the kind of world that we should like—but . . . we have learned that others will fight and die to make a different world, with equal sincerity or belief. Deep-seated preferences cannot be argued about—you cannot argue a man into liking a glass of beer—and therefore, where differences are sufficiently far-reaching, we try to kill the other man rather than let him have his way. But that is perfectly consistent with admitting that, so far as appears, his grounds are just as good as ours.[1]

And again: "it is true that beliefs and wishes have a transcendental basis in the sense that their foundation is arbitrary. You cannot help entertaining and feeling them and there is an end of it."[2]

In the times in which this was written it had a genial, generous sound, and many "liberals" heard it gladly. What could be at once more tolerant and, in contrast to the narrow-minded morality of the day, less demanding? "Relativism" or "Skepticism" thus defined was surely the truly *moral* (in the *broad* sense of morality) answer to our moral problems. A generation later the climate of opinion had changed. With Naziism to face and Communism just over the horizon, serious and angry men felt that a sterner moral standard was required. "Relativism" became a term of reproach again in ethical theory, and the defenders of all respectable ethical theories were anxious to disclaim it. To refute relativism and skepticism was the first task of any ethical theory that could hope to win the approval of *TIME* (Incorporated), the Ford Foundation, the Catholic Church, the Communist Party and other major contenders in the spiritual revival of the 1930's. Dr. Mortimer J. Adler presented a notable specimen of such refutation in an essay "The Dialectic of Morals." He identi-

---

[1] "Natural Law," *Harvard Law Review,* 32 (1918), 41.
[2] *Ibid.*

fied the enemy in terms that any disciple of Holmesian "liberalism" or Jamesian pragmatism could recognize.

> The position of the moral skeptic can, therefore, be summarized as follows. He says that about moral matters (good and bad, right and wrong, in the actions of individuals or groups) there is only opinion, not knowledge. Or he says that moral judgments are entirely subjective, i.e., having truth or meaning only for the individual who makes them. Or he says that moral judgments are relative to the customs of a given community, at a given time or place, in which case, although the judgments of a given community may be measured in terms of their conformity to the *mores* of the group, the *mores* themselves have no truth or meaning except for the group that instituted them. Or he says that all norms or standards are entirely conventional, whether instituted by the will of the community or by the will of individuals, and this amounts to saying that moral judgments are ultimately willful prejudices, expressions of emotional bias or temperamental predilection. That these several statements all come to the same thing can be seen by the fact that in every case the same thing is being denied. Namely, the possibility of making moral judgments that are true for all men everywhere, unaffected not only by their individual differences but also by the divinity of the culture under which they live.[3]

"The issue is quite clear," Dr. Adler goes on to say. But is it? The difference in answers and animosity between Holmes and Adler does indeed seem clear enough. But the most striking thing about the controversy is their basic philosophical agreement, and this, ironically, Dr. Adler seems wholly to have failed to note. What makes Holmes and Adler brothers under the skin, though Holmes, at least, would hardly have welcomed the relationship, is their joint assumption that a local reason, rooted in preferences and folkways, is not a reason at all, but a mere preference, bias or temperamental predilection—like a taste for barberry bushes or for beer. *Of course,* where there is diversity

---

[3] Published in *The Review of Politics* (1941) 9f.

in such preference, his *grounds* are as good as ours; for neither party to the argument has any "grounds" at all that could be rationally good or bad and neither side has so far offered any reasons why we should both *do* anything rather than anything else. The absolutist is quite right in calling such a position moral skepticism, for what it does is to deny the possibility of any cogent moral claims at all. You cannot help entertaining and feeling such "beliefs" and wishes, but it is merely as your (or ours) that they have this status "and there is an end of it."

But of course, in the procedures of practical reasonableness, that is *not* the end. We do feel the need of *justifying* our preferences, not as ours merely, but as grounds for action in which others may fairly be asked to unite for a common good. As Sir Frederick Pollock wrote, in reply to Holmes, "If you deny that any principles of conduct are at all common to and admitted by all men who try to behave reasonably . . . well I do not see how you can have any ethics or any ethical background for law."[4]

By all men who try to behave reasonably. But what is it to behave reasonably in a situation in which moral diversity is a fact to reckon with and we do *not* initially agree in our grounds for action? Here the Absolutist merely accepts the relativist's initial mistake and compounds it. There *must*, he says, be moral judgments that are true for all men everywhere, unaffected by their individual differences and the culture under which they live, for if there were not, we should be driven to moral skepticism. And *only* what is thus "unaffected" and hence true universally and "for" all men is objective truth or knowledge. The rest is merely particular, local and "subjective". There is no reasonableness *in it* at all. What we find if, with Dr. Adler, we follow the quest for such great universal "truths" as "do good

---

[4] In a letter to Holmes dated Dec. 20, 1918. Marke DeWolfe Howe (ed.) *Holmes—Pollock Letters* (Cambridge, Mass.: The Belknap Press, Harvard University, 1961), p. 275.

and avoid evil" and "more good is better (more) than less", are tautologies as empty as they are pretentious, plus an appeal to a human nature whose "rational" outlines were laid down by Aristotle, Aquinas and, more recently, Drs. Hutchins and Adler themselves. And this, of course, in respect of its particular structures of approvals, rights and duties, is just as "relative" as any other moral code. The difference is that by *claiming* universal authority for it, the absolutist has claimed a finality for it that puts its pretensions to universal truth beyond the reach of argument. He has reached the same point as Justice Holmes—where we fight and die for our "ultimate" predilections, less honestly and with greater bombast and without the respect for the opinions of others that made relativism seem, by comparison, at least the code of a gentleman.

Mr. Santayana saw the difference with his usual honesty of mind, and stated the case for the *reasonableness* of moral skepticism as well as anybody ever has.

> I cannot help thinking that a consciousness of the relativity of values, if it became prevalent, would tend to render people more truly social than would a belief that things have intrinsic and unchangeable values, no matter what the attitude of anyone to them may be. If we say that goods, including the right disposition of goods, are relative to specific natures, moral conflict could continue but not with poisoned arrows. Our private sense of justice would be acknowledged to have but a relative authority, and while we could not have a higher duty than to follow it, we should seek to meet those whose aims were incompatible with it as we meet things physically inconvenient, without insulting them as if they were morally vile or logically contemptible . . . Policy, hypnotisation and even surgery can be practiced without exorcisms or anathemas. When a man has decided on a course of action, it is a vain indulgence in expletives to declare that he is sure that course is absolutely right. His moral dogma expresses its natural origin all the more clearly the more hotly it is pro-

claimed, and ethical absolutism, being a mental grimace of passion, refutes what it says by what it is.[5]

This is finely said and there is surely much truth in it. In the half-century since *Winds of Doctrine* was written, we have had ample opportunity to see in action the kind of absolutism that Santayana well described and its mental grimace of passion has become a familiar part of that "image" with which the representatives of rival absolutes confront each other in what is held to be a battle of principles or ideals. And yet there is something wrong, and radically wrong, with it. The language is moral, and on a highly rational level, but the sense of what is affirmed is not. What is a *private* sense of justice? Is it, too, a "mental grimace of passion" and, if so, how can it be our highest *duty* to follow it, treating those who get in our way as "things physically inconvenient," on whom surgery may appropriately be practiced, though without anathemas? Moral truth, like any truth, is public, and a "private sense of justice" has not even relative moral authority, for it has none at all. It is in the process of trying to be reasonable, to come to an understanding with others whom we treat not as "things physically inconvenient" but as men whose estimates of right and wrong are as much entitled to respectful consideration as our own, that such truth is authentically achieved. In other words, it is only on the assumption that there is a potentially common truth which would be true not *for* us merely, or *for* them, or for all men, since there will always be those who could be led in no circumstances to accept it, but *for* (as shared understanding) those who are jointly trying to be reasonable and to judge the moral import of their mutual concerns on its basis, that our talk of justice here makes rational sense. And in such a shared activity

---

[5] George Santayana, "Hypostatic Ethics," in *Winds of Doctrine* (New York: Charles Scribner's Sons, 1926), pp. 151f.

there can no more be private justice than there can be private reasons. As he made clear in *The Realm of Truth,* Santayana did not believe that there was any such truth, and this is what it properly means to say that he was a moral skeptic. But what Adler offers as an alternative is not at all a solution of this problem. It is merely skepticism on stilts, affirming the "universality" of a moral truth that could be the same for all men everywhere only so long as it had nothing in particular to say, and that in fact proclaims its own parochial origin and limitations in the vehemence of its claim to universal truth. It is on this common disrespect for the reasons that we have and use that these allegedly competing theories build "isms", each of which is right only in its exposure of the errors of the other, and both, in fact, are equally and in the same way false.

If we are to return to sanity in these matters from the overheated battle of the "isms", the primary questions we must ask are simply these: When does the fact of moral diversity, which no man who has observed the world around him with a candid eye can honestly deny, become a moral problem? And, when it does, what kind of problem is it, and what, if we could get it, would be a reasonable solution? If once we are clear on these basic matters, we shall be in a position to say with some chance of point and cogency, what we can rationally do about it.

First of all we must be clear that the diversity we are here concerned about is *moral* diversity. This is a difference not in "predilections" merely, but in judgment as to what is right and wrong and what ought, in consequence, to be done. Where one group calls an action "right", and another "wrong", each, if its verdict is more than mere name-calling, has its own reasons for the verdict that it gives. These are in some measure local reasons; they reflect the *ordering* of worth and merit in a society in whose "way of life" not everything is of equal value and importance. "Why", in terms of causal conditions and social conditioning, some will honor chastity and others not, "why" some are, by long habit, men of peace where others are endlessly aggressive is something that the social scientist, if he can, must tell us. But "why" within the given forms of life they approve some actions and condemn others is a question not of its causal antecedents, but of the moral structure, of the light in which they can make sense of their own conduct and can understand (within limits) that of others. With those who acknowledge the same reasons they can live in some degree of mutual understanding and respect. Those who differ radically on such matters are natural objects of suspicion and hostility. They seem by their very existence to present a threat to the moral order with which their own integrity and that of all they value is bound up. Queen Elizabeth was simply not interested in "the nasty customs of the heathen," as reported from America, but the missionaries went to work at once to produce the uniformity that would make the red man a spiritual duplicate (though, of course, in a subordinate status) of the white, and the army was soon there, also, to promote their spiritual claims.

This, as an occurrence, is the most natural fact in the world. We should be surprised if it were not the case. But for whom, and in what connection, does it present a *moral* problem? There is, of course, an epistemological problem. If diverse groups disagree in their judgment as to what, in the way of specific action, is *really* right, someone, if there is "objective" truth at all, must be really wrong, and there is great spiritual satisfaction in proving that it is those whose judgment disagrees with ours who stand in this invidious position. But so far, on the moral level, there may in fact be no disagreement. If the poor Indian, judging what is right for him, concludes that, as a loyal member of his tribe, he should act for time-honored reasons which would certainly not bind me, does this mean that *he* is wrong in so judging? On the contrary, it is a matter of quite minimal fairness or moral objectivity to recognize that he may quite well be right. And this is a truth that I, though I do not share his predilections, can quite well recognize and respect. Nor does it in any way contravene the morally tautologous principle of universality which in a careless statement affirms right for one: right for all. For that principle, as we have seen, must be qualified to read, "in like circumstances." If I were in his circumstances, it would be right to act as he does. But I am not in his circumstances. And a major part of the relevant diversity consists just in the fact that I do not share the commitments that bind him, in all that is most moral in his training as a man, to just this way of acting. Each of us may and should be right here in his *own* way. To recognize and respect this is the beginning of moral wisdom.

Who then is to judge of what is right in such a case? The answer surely is, as it has always been, that the best that each of us can do is to judge for himself, according "to his lights" which are not merely private lights but the embodiment of his own way of being moral, and act accordingly. Where his ways are markedly different from ours, and we can find but little common ground on which to stand with him in shared experience, the maxim of justice clearly is "Judge not, that ye be not judged"—in terms as morally impertinent as your own. Some of the allegedly "deepest" problems of "ultimate" right could practically be solved if moral busy-bodies, intent on rating all men's values on a scale that presupposes the preferential finality of their own, would mind their own business and let others solve, in their own way, the problems which are theirs, not ours. To make moral judgments at large about the Universe, or the ancient Greeks (*should* Antigone have buried her brother?) or the folkways of the Samoans, is for the most part simply not our business. The "decisions" *we* are called upon to make are those that concern what we must do, where we are, and with the moral equipment which our own loyalties and reasons have supplied us.

There is enough, and more, to keep us busy here. Moral diversity *becomes* moral disagreement only when the diversity itself is made a moral issue. And in nine cases out of ten, the part of plain good sense is *not* to make a moral issue of it. But the tenth case remains to plague us and, in our times, it has unhappily become the model for all the rest. There are authentic practical conflicts that cannot in this way be resolved and the issues involved in them may become a source of moral conflict also. If I have a predilection for keeping pigs and my neighbor peacocks, our customs are indeed diverse, but so far hardly of an ideological nature, especially if the spaces between us are broad and there is but little occasion for either to be outraged by the nasty, or snobbish, customs of the other. If, however, the screeching of his peacocks disturbs my slumbers, while my pigs become in other ways offensive to him, we have a problem, and it is not a merely physical one. My addiction to pig-keeping may well be linked with a "way of life" brought over from the old country and maintained in the new with stubborn pride, and even with religious sanctions, while his peacocks represent the snobbish amenities of a culture of which I, and those with whom by preference I associate, regard with deep suspicion. What *right* has he to try to impose such "values" on a community whose natural and democratic hoggishness is offended by them? And he, for his part, will naturally see the matter in a somewhat different light. Our conflict, if not controlled by any reasonable concern to mediate our differences in the interest of public sanity and order, may reach the point at which I am not merely ready but eager to fight to make, at his expense, the kind of world that I should like. Nor will it be much help to remember, with Justice Holmes, when I am shooting his peacocks, that his "right" to poison my pigs has as much, and as little, ground to support it as mine to behave as I am doing, since that means in effect that both are equally groundless, and that force must be the arbiter between us. When the warfare over pigs and peacocks becomes a battle between rival absolutes, this is the sort of thing that it becomes. And each side will have its own philosophers, defending as inviolable and self-evident first principles the "reasons" that confirm me in self-righteous antagonism to him, and him to me. In such a battle there can be no neutrals; those who are not with us are against us, for the issue, though local in its origins, is global in values—the very structure of the moral order in which men can live together in mutual respect and good will. If they do not love someone as we do, how can we love our fellow men or share with them a common way of life? Who would not laugh if such a war there be? Who would not weep if he saw his own country take the lead in it?

Our present questions are less controversial. How, in the name of reason, does such a conflict arise, and what, as reasonable men, can we do about it? To the first question the answer is plain enough. There *is* a problem about keeping pigs and peacocks side by side in a community that includes groups of men strongly addicted to the one practice or the other. It is not a situation in which either side can be allowed to follow its own "private sense" of right without regard to the claims and interests of the other. It looks, at the start, to be a problem of mutual accommodation in which each, in the interests of an effectively common good, may fairly be asked to surrender something of the intransigence of its initial claims. But as tempers rise and philosophers get to work on it, it soon ceases to be that. It becomes instead the question: which is *really* right? Is the pig-keeping or the peacock breeding way of life the one that is truly ours, and that in moral righteousness we must ultimately cleave to at all costs? To any loyal pig-keeper the answer to this question will be self-evident, and those who fail to recognize it as such must be exposed as lesser breeds without the law—the *moral* law of righteous pig-keeping—to which all good men in their hearts, or at least after proper indoctrination, will assent, and any dissent from it, however qualified, will be in principle subversive. There can be, we are told, no charity or compromise among *ideas*, for here the issue is one of principle, and can be adjudicated only by appeal to those universal first principles which all reasonable men *should* see, but only those on our side, and after suitable instruction, ever really do. If our principles, for example, are Christian principles, who but a holder of the true faith could be expected to see them for what they are? And by whom, save the appropriate authorities, is the true faith to be identified? We may well be grateful to E. Gilson, a scholastic, for the explicitness with which he states this issue.

> ... it cannot be mere coincidence that the great masters of our natural theology are found to be at the same time the great masters of revealed theology. . . . Besides it is not doubtless any more of a coincidence that what natural reason can know with certitude, many a natural reason does not so know, or even doubts, when it doesn't go so far as to deny it. For it is no longer a question here of ignorance, or lack of leisure, or intellectual ineptitude. The professionals of scientific and philosophical thought, whose natural reason denies God in the name of the principles of reason, ought to be naturally capable of perceiving the compulsive force of proofs such as those St. Thomas uses in his *Summa Theologica*. They are given five ways of going to God; they refuse them all, and yet we know that reason alone can know God with certitude. Why does theirs not know him? Why, to put it bluntly, is the philosophical world divided into two groups; those who have evidence of the existence of a transcendental being and who believe in Him, and those who, not believing in Him, judge such proofs to be impossible? To put the same question rather rudely, for which I beg to be excused: why is the philosophy called Scholastic true only for Catholics, taught, when it is taught, only by Catholics, and absent, because unknown, misunderstood or denied, whenever Catholicism is absent? Experience, to be sure, suffers some exceptions, the number of which I do not know, but it is quite sufficiently general to give one pause. . . . The old theological argument, 'by the contradictions of the philosophers,' is

not without its lessons for the philosopher himself, which is that reason can hope for a relative unity which will save it from disorder, only when the perfect unity of faith is reflected in it.[7]

In the midst of the mealy-mouthed talk about "universal moral truth" in which all men of good will, of whatever faith and creed, can freely unite, such plain speaking clears the air. It tells us where we stand, and how a parochial "reason" is prepared in fact to support its claim to ultimate "rational" authority.

Catholicism is, of course, not the only faith that presents its claims in this manner. As Monsignor Fulton Sheen pointed out in 1948, it is in this at one with Communism, and the two make common cause against the degenerate liberalism of decadent Western thought. "A little-known fact is that communism and the Catholic Church are at one in their opposition to historical liberalism, but for very different reasons."[8] Both stand for absolutes, and demand the unconditional adherence of those who accept their faith. They face each other as competing absolutes, and there can be no ideological common ground between them save in their shared antagonism toward those who still look for such a common ground. Between them, so Monsignor Sheen affirms, they will divide the loyalties of the new era upon which we are now entering.

> The new era into which we are entering is what might be called the religious phase of human history. By *religious,* we do not mean that men will turn to God, but rather that the indifference to the absolute which has characterized the liberal phase of civilization will be succeeded by a passion for an absolute. From now on the struggle will not be for the colonies and national rights, but for the souls of men. There will be no more half-drawn swords, no divided loyalties, no broad strokes of sophomoric tolerance; there will not even be any

---

[7] E. Gilson, *Christianity and Philosophy,* trans. R. MacDonald (New York and London: Sheed and Ward, 1939), pp. 78f.

[8] Fulton Sheen, *Communism and the Conscience of the West* (New York: The Bobbs-Merrill Co., 1948), Preface, p. 4.

more great heresies, for heresies are based on a partial acceptance of truth. . . . From now on men will divide themselves into two religions—understood again as a surrender to an absolute.[9]

No sordid compromises nor carrying water on both shoulders will see us through. Those who have the faith had better keep in a state of grace, and those who have neither had better find out what they mean, for in the coming age there will be only one way to stop trembling knees and that will be to get down on them and pray.[10]

Communism and the Conscience of the West was published in 1948, the year of the first fine flowering of McCarthyism in America, and the state of mind that it portrays and glorifies goes far toward explaining what happened, in the ensuing ugly years, to that consensus of moral decency and mutual trust which had been the hard-won basis for rational political action in America. The ironical fact was that this return to divisive absolutes was advertised and praised in intellectual circles, and not least among philosophers, as a return from relativism to Reason, to first principles and final, "universal" truth. On a certain level what they said made sense. Was not logic, the logic of "ethical systems", on their side? Must not Reason be universal, unconditional and ultimate in its claims if it is to maintain its normative authority? And where can loyal, frightened and embattled men find such Reasons except in the "truths" that their tradition, or their church, or their party has taught them to respect? These, surely, are our ultimate commitments, since it is on their terms alone that any "final" justification of anything can be ultimately given. And what common ground *can* there be with those who deny their unqualified finality? The only terms for a *moral* agreement here would seem to be those of the unconditional ideological surrender of the enemy. For on issues of principle there can be no "sordid" compromise, and where our ultimate

---

[9] *Ibid.*, p. 22.
[10] *Ibid.*, p. 46.

spiritual commitment is at stake *any* compromise would be "sordid". He who is not with us is against us.

There could hardly be a clearer instance of the concrete difference between being "rational" and being reasonable in human affairs. *In theory* the appeal to universal truth is an appeal to common principles that all men can understand on equal terms. *In practice,* it is a divisive instrument for exacerbating conflict and arbitrarily restricting the range of action in which there can, among men of diverse faiths and loyalties, be shared understanding and mutual respect. A truth that is discernable as such only by Catholics or by Communists or by the members of some other appropriately indoctrinated sect is a truth that one must become a Catholic or a Communist to "see", surrendering his own prior loyalties in the process, and his right to use his own judgment in estimating what *he* can estimate, see to be reasonable and right. It narrows the range of possible moral community to those thus indoctrinated. It ranges Christians against atheists, West versus East, free world against slaves, and calls for a holy war against those who will not see the light. It is a good fighting faith for which to die, but it does not provide a working basis on which men can live together in any sort of community. And in a world in which men must *learn* to live together if they are not to destroy each other and themselves, it is a formula and excuse for being unreasonable, for short-circuiting the development of those habits of mutual accomodation that might in fact, if given a chance, provide that working basis for a *modus vivendi* (which is also, in a manner of speaking, a way of life) which *are* practical reasonableness in operation, and which have their fruits in human understanding. The issue between the two rival senses of "practical reason", whose meanings we have traced in this volume, here itself has practical implications of a quite explicit kind.

This is where we stand today. The age of the absolutes has come and, let us hope, has gone, as sanity and self-respect have supplanted trembling knees and moral prostration in the ordered affairs of men who still place a high value on their freedom. But the basic problem still remains. The differences between "east" and "west" remain, and unless common grounds for their mediation can be found there will "in the end" be war, though this time both sides know in advance that such a war will be the end, in grim reality, of the very things that they profess to value. How *can* there be such common grounds, when their initial loyalties and their reasons are not ours, and yet unless there are such grounds, what place or room is there for reason? This is our old question about the local grounds and the universal pretensions over again. But we have made some progress, nonetheless. For when it is thus put in the context in which, as a practical issue, it actually arises, we know at least what sort of problem it is, what the conditions for an adequate solution are, and what would constitute an adequate solution if we could get it. We know, in other words, what we are looking for and how to go about our work and this, in philosophy, as in any other respectable sort of inquiry, is at least half the battle. How *can* we be reasonable in the reconciliation of moral diversities where these, if left unreconciled, would jeopardize the moral order of a livable community? This is what the absolutism-relativism issue comes to in terms of the effective work of practical reasonableness, and it is on these terms that we propose, from now on, to deal with it.

We began with a homely illustration about pigs and peacocks, and it is time for us now to take a closer look at it. For there will be those who will want at once to object to it, on the ground that our devotion in America to ideals of freedom is not at all like pig-keeping, while the peacocks of our enemies are the sheer embodiment of spiritual evil. About pigs and peacocks we might be tolerant, but about right and wrong, never. And our ideals of freedom claim a cogency that should prevail not by local habit merely, but of right. And this right is in principle the same for all men. We agree. Indeed, it is just this difference that we wish particularly to stress. But first it is essential to see in what, more precisely, it consists.

Our American ideal of freedom, to which we rightly appeal as a ground and justification for political freedom, was never merely traditional, nor merely ours. It was presented in the Declaration of Independence, "with a decent respect for the opinions of mankind," as a reasoned ground for action. The truths *we* held to be self-evident were the inherited preconceptions of a natural rights philosophy. They were in fact the commonly shared convictions of most enlightened men of the time, and could therefore serve as common ground for the presentation of political claims. But Jefferson would have been the last man in the world to claim a theological, let alone ecclesiastical, purpose, or to hold that they were truths that only those already committed to our side and its "faith" could be expected to see. If they had been, they would have been of no use for his justifying purpose in their use. And the fact was that the philosophy of political freedom that they were used to warrant, that government derives its just powers from the consent of the governed and must justify its claim of authority to them as rational creatures if it was to deserve and win such consent—did in this way win the free assent of many men of many nations whose faiths and traditions were quite different from ours. The promise of American life, as thus defined, was one in whose fulfillment they too could freely share. The spiritual greatness of America lay in the fact that over many years, and in the hard development of free institutions, that promise though often betrayed or forgotten has on the whole been kept. It is the keeping of that promise and not our wealth or power or comfortably cushioned "way of life" that makes it to this day a great thing to say, "I am an American."

Yet it was nonetheless a very local and limited freedom for which the Founding Fathers spoke—the rights of embattled farmers and merchants, *as Englishmen,* to representation in any legislative body that claimed the authority to tax them. The rights of slaves, if any, did not for many years come into the question at all. Nor were the implications of a universality of right at any point pushed further than the claim for American political independence required. There was practical good sense in this. We solve our problems piece-meal, as we must, and if one good thing can be accomplished at a time, it is a great achievement. But the implications of universality were there from the start and long after the language of natural rights had become obsolete—an obsolescence from which theologizing lawyers are now trying rather ludicrously to revive it—the ideals of the Declaration still did their work. What that work was Abraham Lincoln finely said in his 1857 speech at Springfield on the Dred Scott Decision.

> They [the authors of the Declaration] meant to set up a standard maxim for free society, which should be familiar to all and revered by all; constantly looked to, constantly labored for and although never perfectly attained, constantly approximated and thereby constantly spreading and deepening its influence and augmenting the happiness and value of life of all men everywhere.

That is the way an ideal works when it functions *as* an ideal, and the nation that is prepared to live by it is like a city set on a hill, whose light cannot be hid, and is by no means reserved for those who wait with trembling knees inside its walls to "defend" its esoteric glow against "alien" subversion.

Our "reasons", in happy cases like these, show themselves to be good in the actual achievement of that community of understanding which, from the start, it was their business to achieve. *Of course* they are ours, and we are committed to them, but they need not be merely ours for there is in essence nothing private or esoteric about them. They can be understood in public by all who have a mind to share with us in the great enterprise that our commitment, *as ideal,* defines. Without this fulfillment they remain, as practical reasons, morally incomplete, for they aimed at a truth that lay in part beyond the limits and conditions of their initial statement. In some measure we have still to learn what "freedom" as "a standard maxim for a free society" that is not *merely* "ours" can rightly mean in the kind of world in which we live today. It would be surprising if their initial ultimacy "for us," in the form in which we learned them, were *not* qualified and corrected in this process. If we are to *learn* the meaning of our freedom we must grow in understanding and such growth is bound to carry us beyond its starting point. Yet it is in just this growth that concrete reasonableness is actually achieved in human affairs, not all at once or melodramatically but line upon line, precept upon precept, here a little and there a little as human need and human wisdom find a larger use for it. The process of rational inquiry is a self-correcting process and its "ultimates" are found neither in initial preconceptions or final self-evident disclosures, but precisely in this learning process itself and the values that are attained through its reliable and constructive operation. What else could we reasonably expect, and how else vindicate our "values" than in the process in which, in sharable and communicable experience, their claims are *made* good in the use we make of them? This is the way in which the spiritual claims of an ideology are defended if they are worth defending. In the past and in America, we were not afraid to submit our ideals to this test.

In stressing the potential universality of our ideals in their use as justifying grounds or reasons, however, we must not fall into the complementary error of imagining them to be rootless or unconditional in their cogency and use. The freedom that concerned them was for and in the American community, and as such to be preserved and defended. Others might share in it, if they would, or profit by its example, but it was not our national business to shape the world to an American "image" or to impose our moral patterns upon others whose habits and traditions differed substantially from our own. A hundred years of isolationism testify on the whole to our lack of proselyting zeal on any moral issues other than those that concerned us in the Western Hemisphere and in the pursuit of our own proper interests. The universality of reasons was to be applied *within this community* and as providing common grounds for concerted action *here*. It is community, not universality, that is the fundamental notion here. For and in such a community there must be common reasons if there is to be a common good, and no reasons can be common that do not in like circumstances apply with equal cogency to all. The range and limits of such community are determined by the maintenance of a form of life within which such community is more than a mere ideal aspiration, where it is in fact a working *modus vivendi* of mutually acknowledged rights, responsibilities and self-imposed restraints. To talk of operative common reasons where there is and can be no such common life is to invite the sort of pious platitude that becomes in abstract ethical theory a substitute for thought. So long as the oceans served to separate us effectively from the entanglements of the larger world, we saw but little need to proselytize for freedom, though we were glad to welcome to our shores those who wished to share *in* ours with us.

If this ideological situation has changed, it is not through any shift in the eternal verities, or as a result of a new revelation as to their essential nature. It is the result, rather, of a drastic change in our means of spatial locomotion and capacity to menace and destroy each other at long range. What is happening in Moscow, or Southeast Asia, or the Congo has *become* a matter of our unhappy concern because we cannot get away from it. The pigs and peacocks of diverse cultures must live together within hearing and smell of each other, and if their local conjunction is found intolerable, one or the other must be eliminated. And for this we have as yet no adequate "ideal" equipment. Some sort of *modus vivendi,* some way of getting on together in mutual tolerance and forbearance, is the only discoverable alternative to another battle of the Absolutes, but we have not got the conceptual structure for a moral order in which the reasons that could in truth be practical principles for such an order can be adequately articulated and made clear. Instead we have that frantic clutching at first principles and last analyses that, by assuring us of the "ultimacy" of our starting point, assures us that since our traditional faith is ultimately right, anyone who disagrees must be wrong, and that there can be no compromise with evil. Just where accommodation and understanding are needed, it sets the stage for new demands for unconditional surrender. And it calls this procedure an appeal to rational first principles.

There is nothing in principle new about this sort of situation. Our traditional ideals have come up against requirements for reasonable action with which they are not, in their present form, sufficiently flexible to cope. Hence, on their terms, we find the moral world with which we have to deal a chaos. And so indeed it is, for us, if we can make no better sense of it than this. "These fragments I have shored against my ruins." And if our mental and moral powers remain inadequate to master the physical environment we have created for ourselves, this may indeed be, for us, the last analysis in the human enterprise of moral understanding. For there will be no one left with even the rudimentary mastery of moral categories required to make a new one. This game will no longer by played. But it need not be the last analysis. There is nothing in the nature of human reason that requires it. On the contrary, there *is* something in the nature of practical reasonableness that rejects it, as a violation of its own primary function and intent. The choice between being "rational" and being reasonable in our dealings with our fellow men is a choice of one of these alternatives against another. In the mental and moral confusion of our time, it is a choice that can make a substantial difference in the way we think and act.

Our analogy with pigs and peacocks, though over-simplified, was by no means wholly without point. The problem was, in the first instance, the physical proximity of customs or "ways of life" which are not merely physically but morally obnoxious to each other. Pride and peacocks go together, as do pigs and plebeian virtue. Each, in its own fashion, has something good about it and is in an important way bound up with other values that those who honor it have learned to cherish, as we are alleged to cherish apple pie and Coca Cola and that Revlon look which marks off the well-dressed American female tourist from all others in the world. And, in our zeal to propagate the "American image", to make all men love us and our "way of life", we sometimes contemplate this image with that unwholesome kind of national Narcissism that is frequently our national surrogate for patriotism. Verily, we are the people. And it is then surprising and even disconcerting to realize that those with other "ways of life" feel much the same way about their "images" which, like us, they sometimes unwisely confuse with their essential ideas. When such images conflict, and each side maintains the unqualified authority of its own, something has to give. But an image is by no means the same as an idea, in its reasonable use, and it is with this use that we are, in this book, concerned. The use of an idea here would be not to exacerbate but to mediate this conflict; to stand as common ground on which men who value pigs and peacocks may live together within a community whose common good is achieved, not by the imposition of a single pattern on all alike, but by the maintenance of those habits of self-controlled behavior in which men may pursue their diverse ways with some degree of mutual forbearance and regard. If our ideal of freedom is justifiable by this standard, it is as a contribution to this common form of life from which neither pigs nor peacocks are arbitrarily excluded—though a zoning law may be required to keep their owners out of each other's way—but each can be itself in a moral world that is large enough in principle to include them both. Such an order is possible only for those who are trying to be reasonable in their mutual relations; and to make good this attempt, to make it concrete, specific and relevant in a world peopled today by moral monsters of each other's diseased imaginings is not an easy task. It is, in any case, the task of a moral philosophy that knows and does its business, and it will be in the sanity, courage and integrity of the way it does it that its own claim to rational credence can be made good.

CHAPTER 14

THE RATIONAL COMPARISON
OF GOODS AND RIGHTS

WE ARE NOW IN a position to deal affirmatively with the basic problem of the normative use of practical reason. It is, as we have seen, a quite familiar problem and no man of moral maturity has failed to encounter and, in his own way, to deal with it. It arises from the familiar and forbidding fact that sometimes moral problems are not simple—that there are situations in which we are called on to think if we are rightly to determine what we ought to do. If asserting what I know to be false would be, in some circumstances, a helpful act, then I have a reason why I should make that assertion. But it would also be a lie, and we all learned long ago that lies should not be told. This action, however, would be both at once; and its rightness and wrongness can equally be deduced from principles whose cogency, as they stand, no right-thinking man would wish to question. There is here a plural relevance of reasons beyond the scope of moral simple-mindedness and deductive demonstration that seems to call for a kind of practical good sense or judgment of a different sort. How "rationally" are we to deal with it? The classical systems of ethics are all, in their several ways, attempts to meet this problem, and what they call "practical reason" is their answer to it. All, as we have seen, are attempts to reintroduce the original simple-minded situation on a "higher" level—to find in the end, or in the last analysis, some one big, all-inclusive reason on whose terms the competing claims of more proximate goods and rights upon our wills can be "finally" adjudicated. Sidgwick has been our model on this kind, but the pattern is by this time painfully familiar. In the light of its ultimate authority, all lesser claims are reduced to the merely relative and conditional status and "reason", following its own supremely simple-minded "dicates", can in general tell us absolutely what we ought to do. What this one big reason, whether "good", or "law", may be and how in their turn its claims to rational finality are reasonably substantiated are further questions, of course. But that there must *be* such a Reason if the conflicts of our moral life are to be rationally resolved and that our business is somehow to discern and use it in our practical affairs is the shared dogma of those who claim, in ethical theory, to speak for Reason. How else could we ever make a judgment of comparative worth or value? And if their final Reason is not the same as ours, how can we ever practically understand each other?

We have seen the impasse to which the attempt to retain this higher simple-mindedness in the face of a world of moral diversity has brought us, and there is no need to comment on it further here. But we have also seen, though in the first instance by contrast mainly, what it would be like to *be* practically reasonable on such issues. There is, happily, nothing unfamiliar or esoteric about this process. Sensible and responsible people are continually called upon to make judgments of the sort required, and frequently do so with remarkable discernment. It is in such judgment that our presently limited supply of moral understanding works effectively as a basis for cooperative action, and on the promise of a better use of it that our hopes for a moral order not as yet attained but greatly needed are based. Since, however, it has been endlessly misinterpreted and misunderstood, it will be well to set down once more, as clearly and responsibly as we can, the requirements and the nature of a reasonable solution to the "problem" of competing "rights" and "values".

Unless each of the claims made had some moral cogency *of its own,* unless each, as it stands, had a reason and, other things being equal, a good one to support it, there could be no problem of a moral issue between them. The sheer conflict of good and evil—if it even occurs—is not a moral problem but only of the mobilization of the power to make righteousness prevail. These reasons are drawn from the experience of our common lives and have, in their normal use, an authority which *is,* so far, that of moral justification. To be merely indifferent to them, to be openminded or non-committal with respect to their claims upon our conduct until some higher "reason" has certified their merely relative and derivative cogency would be to fail, so far, to make moral sense of them at all. Where they do their justifying work they *are* the moral "why" of conduct and unless they did for the most part work in the unquestioned acceptance of those in whose learned behavior moral action is a going concern, there would be no moral problems, for there would be no morality as the normative structure of the form of life in which a justifying "why?" makes practical sense for conduct. This "game" would not be played. And it is inside this game that we have moral problems and "rights" that *need* a "higher" reconciliation because *each* is in the first instance and in its own way right. It is such proximate, conditioned, and, in their own way, quite "ultimate" rights that are the ground and basis of morality and we can no more make moral judgments without them than we can breathe without oxygen. However high we may soar into the interstellar spaces, we must carry our own supply with us from the earth or we shall be as dead on arrival as are the ethical theories that seek to perform a similar abstraction in the world of speculation.

Moreover, as they stand, these "rights" do not conflict. Which of the two obligations should I honor in my conduct? The answer is, *in general,* clearly "both". A kindly man should be honest, and an honest man benevolent. *On this level,* the problem of their conflict does not arise at all. And so we should, of course, always choose *more* "good" to less, for what we want, surely, is as much "good" as possible. The difficulty arises in a different place. If the particular action is one that ought to be *both* truth-affirming and kind but cannot be one save at the cost of the other, *then* a hard choice must be made, and we need grounds for making it in one way rather than another. Nor will it help to say that being honest is in general more important than being kind, or vice versa. There are cases where the claim of kindliness is plain for all to see, which the violation of truth required to meet it would be trivial and peripheral. Only such a fanatic as Jeannie Deans (immortalized by Sir Walter Scott and T. H. Green) would prefer the sacrifice of a human life to the telling of a lie which was, in the particular instance, less misleading than the truth. And yet a flabby morality of *mere* kindliness, in which candor was always rightly sacrificed to a concern for the sensitive feelings of others, would show as little respect for the personality of those with whom we have to deal as, in much "broad" or "liberal" morality, we find today. Which of the two is more important? There is no answer in general here to a question that does not arise in general, but where specific discriminations of worth and importance must be made in complex cases. For this we need good judgment, and sound judgment is not learned, or exhibited in the mindless following of general rules. The fruit of such discriminating judgment is that of the rational comparison of the normative cogency of *generally* valid reasons in their application to instances to which all are relevant but none, by itself, sufficient to adjudicate. And where our problem is, there may we sensibly expect to find our answer also.

The answer, evidently, will in general be couched in terms of relative importance and expendibility. Which matters more here and which, if we have to, can we at least cost do without? On the level of ethical loose talk this is the opening wedge, as we have seen, for that whole string of "musts" that are the stock in trade of the "higher" rationalism. If there is relative importance, *must* there not be something that is absolutely important—*the* End or goal, for the sake of which all else is done? And if there is a right we cannot rightly surrender, even for kindliness, say, or mutual good feeling, *must* there not be something *ultimate* that we cannot rightly surrender at any cost, an inviolable "ought" that is in no conceivable circumstances to be infringed? Until we know what is absolutely important, how *can* we say what is relatively so? And what but an incorrigible first principle could rationally serve as the standard by which anything *else* could be morally qualified or corrected? And so we are off again, on the same old "final" round to the same dead end—that "end of the endless journey to no end, conclusion of all that is inconclusible" in which T. S. Eliot, among others, has found the goal, in moral prostration, of human striving.

But all this is based, in fact, on a quite elementary blunder. The *standard* by which we can properly judge of relative importance is not an *End* to which, and for the sake of which, all that is worth doing is "reasonably" done. Suppose we say, with Aristotle, that the End is happiness, and that this alone will justify and fulfill the virtues in whose exercise he holds such happiness (for man) to consist. Then "in the end," we estimate all relative importance in terms of contributions to "happiness". But it is not *any* sort of "happiness" that will serve us as a standard. It must be that which a good man can achieve in the "satisfaction" of that which is *best* in him, i.e., his reason. "For reason in each of us chooses what is best for itself and the good man obeys his reason." This turns out, of course, to be theoretical and not practical reason, the "wisdom" of the philosopher whose satisfaction is found in his contemplation of that which is most divine in himself and in the universe at large, which is just *Reason* itself in its eternal finality. Thus our standard of ultimate practical importance in human affairs turns out to be, in the select few who are capable of it, that rather special kind of satisfaction or fulfilment that was actually of most importance for Aristotle himself and some, at least, of his disciples. What else but this *could* be the true end of man as a rational animal, and in where but in what the wise man chooses can we find a final goal for all our striving?

   That philosophical wisdom, thus identified, was a proper human goal for Aristotle and his associates, an ultimate good *for them,* and that in the exercise of this intellectual virtue they found a measure of fulfilment that made sense of all the rest, need not be denied. But that it could serve as a standard of ultimate good for all men, and that all claims to relative importance could or should be measured in its terms was preposterously false. And it is just as false when some other candidate for such finality, whether it be *Virtue, Pleasure, God,* or general welfare that is cast in this unplayable role. Our "ultimate" ends, the things for which we personally, and those who share a way of life with us, would gladly live and die, are often the most relative, local and limited of excellences. They mean the world *to us,* and we should be false to ourselves if we were to compromise or to surrender them—*this* family, *this* plot of earth, *this* quest for truth. A higher good that did not find a place for them, and for our preferential addiction to them, would not be a good in which we could honorably share. But to make *their* importance the measure of a good that can take just account of what means the world to others also, though we cannot see why they should, is moral arrogance of a common but inexcusable sort. It is rather just insofar as we can treat them as *not* thus final or ultimate that we can be reasonable *about* them, and this kind of reasonableness is the goal of the shared understanding that we seek when we can no longer treat what is initially obvious to us as a final measure of moral truth but must weigh the relevance of diverse "ultimates" to the determination of a *common* good.

By comparison with the goods that are, and ought to be, for us of primary importance, such a comparative good must be a rather minimal and meager good. It is by no means a highest good in whose self-sufficient finality all others are impartially embraced or an end to whose achievement they have worth as means only. Unless these proximate and personal goods were good on their own account and as such *worth* preserving, there would be no good in that order of shared forbearances and responsibilities which makes their *joint* achievement possible. If we are to survive we must have peace. For only on the terms of mutual security and self-control that it maintains can we enjoy the further goods that make life *for us* worth living. But to call peace our final good, and to say of everything else that it has a moral claim upon our conduct only as it conduces to "peace", or to the rather schematic world order which is thought of as its political guarantee, would be preposterous. For we do not want peace unconditionally, or at any price. Only a peace that would maintain and respect the freedoms without which we cannot honorably live is one that we can decently accept. It must be, as always in this world, not the peace that passeth understanding, but a peace that *we* can accept and use as a ground of common understanding, and in terms that we respect. That means that it must include and build on the structure of goods and obligations that makes our present society to some degree a moral order. It would indeed be a mistake to make this minimal requirement the final goal of moral order. But unless we had it as a morally structured starting point, a *requirement* for common good, not merely a means to something of a higher order, we should have no foundations on which to build. The problem is precisely to discover how these requirements can, without losing their cogency in the cases to which they obviously apply, be so combined with others that the resulting moral order will be one that will be neither "ours" nor "theirs" alone, but one in which all who must accept and live with it can find a *modus vivendi* that is "common" not because in it all things are uniform, or average, or alike, but because it constitutes, for those who share in it, a common *ground* for the composition of difference, and the pursuit, in mutual forbearance and respect, often of divergent but not, as thus composed, conflicting ends. That is what practical reasons are *for,* when they function *as reasons,* not as isolated bits of self-evident and final truth, in the achievement of a mutual understanding. And here and nowhere else we must look for what, in that use, they can tell us that is normatively relevant to the right conduct of our lives.

What would we expect to learn by the use of reason that would be relevant to a practical decision between comparative rights or goods? In one sense, as we have seen, we already have our reasons, ready-made. We ought to tell the truth, and that this statement would be a truthful answer to a question rationally asked is, so far, a reason for making it. But the truth *in this case* would cause suffering to a friend, and it would be a kindness not to tell it—to lie, if need be, to conceal a painful fact. And it is self-evident, surely, that it is never right to cause "gratuitous" suffering. But so our suffering would not be "gratuitous" if it were required for the maintenance of a standard of honesty which is essential to our integrity as persons. And is our integrity as persons worth having if it must be purchased at the cost of other people's suffering? Once this line of argument is started we can, as we have seen, go on indefinitely. Our "reasons" are in conflict and there seems to be no way of reconciling their claims save by an appeal to one big Reason that "in the end" will override all others. Is this end "virtue", to be maintained by truth-telling at all costs, or "happiness", to whose attainment all moral rectitude is but an expendable means? Who is to say? And until we can say, how can Reason render final judgment on the specific issue that confronts us? And when—and if— it does, what is there to do but follow its "dictate" to a now predetermined conclusion and maintain it at whatever cost in practical humanity and good sense?

It is not, of course, in this way that any man who was trying to be reasonable would actually proceed. His first question of either alternative would be, and ought to be, how much will it cost? What difference will it make in our whole scheme of moral acceptances and practices if we compromise our principles in order to be kind, or insist upon them at the cost of suffering which may be a small price comparatively, to pay, for their uncompromising preservation? To whom will it make a differ- ence? Whose business is it, and who is in fact concerned and responsible for the maintenance of a right order? And how *im- portant* is that difference, not just in this instance, or here and now, but in the whole structure of our preferences and valuings that constitute our common stock of moral understanding? Some compromises are sheer matters of good sense that have ceased to be dogmatic or doctrinaire. Others we could not rightly make at any cost, since our integrity as moral agents—without which there could be no *sense* in practical reasons, would be surrendered in them. Men of practical good judgment do not come to such questions empty-handed or with only moral platitudes to guide them. They have had some experience in these matters; the values of their community are bred into them and they do not have to stop to choose between one "way of life" or another, for it is within their own way of life that they have the responsibility for acting wisely. Neither, however, are they blind to the complexities and qualifications of the practical requirements of specific situations. They know that in human situations moral truth is never simple, that there are *many* claims and interests of which account must be taken, and that the harmony that holds a community together is at best a working *modus vivendi* of mutual accommodations in which people get along together, not on ideal terms, but on those on which experience has shown that they can live. Only a fanatic would deny the beneficent and leavening influence of kindliness in such a mixture. Only a fool would suppose that it can be maintained except at the cost of facing hard truths, when there is need of it, no matter who is pleased or discommoded by them. When is there need of it? Is *this* such a case? That is the question for practical judgment, and there is no general formula or categorical imperative by which it can be answered in advance. This is perhaps the most unpleasant truth of all for the morally immature to face. They can understand a reasonable judgment only as the deductive conclusion of a syllogism whose major premise is a "first principle" they need not think to follow and to understand. But the reasonableness of concrete moral judgment, in fact, is not at all like that. Pascal made the right point about it long ago when he distinguished between the mathematical and the intuitive judgment. In the latter case,

> the principles rest on common experience and all eyes can see them. We have only to look; it requires no effort. It is only a question of good eyesight, but we must have that. For the principles are so common and numerous that it is almost impossible not to miss some of them. Now the omission of a single principle leads to error. We must be very clear-sighted, therefore, to see them all, and we must have

very accurate minds also not to draw false conclusions from known principles.[1]

The term "intuitive" is unfortunate here, since Pascal makes it plain that this is a matter not of feeling but intelligence, and it is intelligence that, in right judgment, reaches its goal, "but it does so silently, naturally, and without technical rules."[2] Pascal adds, perhaps too pessimistically, "It is beyond any man to explain this reasoning and only a few are sensitive to it."[3] What he calls "principles" here are what we have called reasons, as relevant considerations bearing on the adjudication of specific issues. The turn of the mathematical mind, as applied to such issues, is that of the very simple-mindedness which makes it so powerful an instrument of theoretical generalization. It misses some of them and deduces morally inept conclusions from premises that do not cover adequately the case at issue. Hence it ends—Lord Russell is an example—in irresponsible folly or fanaticism. To keep one's eye on the specific case and the adequacy of the "reasons" offered to *its* resolution is not easy, though here there is nothing esoteric, or occult, or hidden but it is the way, and the only right way, to face this sort of problem.

Wittgenstein makes a similar point in a somewhat different context.

Is there such a thing as 'expert judgment' about the genuineness of expressions of feeling?—Even here, there are those whose judgment is 'better' and those whose judgment is 'worse'.

Correcter prognoses will generally issue from the judgments of those with better knowledge of mankind.

Can one learn this knowledge? Yes; some can. Not, however, by taking a course in it, but through '*experience*'.—Can someone else be

---

[1] Blaise Pascal, *The Pensées*, trans. J. M. Cohen (Baltimore: Penguin Books, 1961), p. 32.

[2] *Ibid.*

[3] *Ibid.*

a man's teacher in this? Certainly. From time to time he gives him the right *tip*.—This is what 'learning' and 'teaching' are like here.— What one acquires here is not a technique; one learns correct judgments. There are also rules, but they do not form a system, and only experienced people can apply them right. Unlike calculation rules.

What is most difficult here is to put this indefiniteness, correctly and unfalsified, into words.[4]

To be content with a philosophy that is *in this way* indefinite is not easy for a simple mind. We want to know how to tell whether truth-telling is more important than kindliness, and so far no plain "yes" or "no" answer has been given. And, of course, none can be. It all depends on what the traffic will bear, and that depends, in its turn, on the nature and volume of the traffic. We are just now learning, the hard way, the sort of terms on which those with different "value" standards can so compose their "reasons" as to *be* reasonable in their common life. To offer in advance a philosophical blueprint of the "world order" which would be the final (and self-evident) answer to such problems and demand, in the name of "Reason", that all men follow this would be the height of folly, though there are some who have proposed it. What a sound moral philosophy can do is to help us to see the problem when we do face it, in a proper *light*; to understand what kind of problem it is, what considerations would be relevant to a solution, and what a right or justifiable solution would be, if we could get it. It can teach us something of the moral temper and practical habit of mind in which men of good will can seek such solutions in common, and know how to live with them when they have found them. Universal wisdom is not available to us in our professional capacity as philosophers —there is simply too much that we do not know, or whose prac-

---

[4] Ludwig Wittgenstein, *Philosophical Investigations*, trans. G. E. M. Anscombe (New York: The Macmillan Co., 1953), p. 227e.

tical import we lack the experience to measure in our class-rooms. But if we are true to the example of Socrates, and we know what it is like to *seek* wisdom here, and why it is important, practically to be wise—if we can communicate some grasp of what *being* reasonable thus requires—it may be that we can explain this reasoning at least far enough to make others sensitive to its claim upon us. For reasonableness in this sense is not the privileged possession of a cultural elite, it is the daily bread that nourishes our common life where in fact we live together in our aims and purposes, and not in mere angry physical proximity. And without it we are today morally starved, in the midst of what is offered to us as "spiritual" plentitude of our own self-righteousness.

The philosophical danger here is that we shall be tempted to take refuge from the complexities of concrete practical judgment in a new over-simplification—to say that "judgment" of this sort is really just a matter of feeling what is right, with an "inner" eye, perhaps, and that it is, as such, *essentially* in-communicable—an affair of the heart and not of the head. Pascal himself moved disastrously in this direction and his clarifying work is chiefly used today to justify obscurantism by multiplying "mysteries" where none need in fact exist. And there are traces, at least, of a similar obscurantism in Wittgenstein. But there is nothing in the situation itself to justify such a move. *All* practical reasons are in one sense reasons of the heart, as we have seen. They can be understood and used as grounds for action only by those who share responsibly in the concerns in which their relevance to effective doing has a point. We must *learn* their meaning and cogency in this use, if we are to make sense of the demand for justification to which they can supply a reasoned answer.

This process of learning, however, is a *public* process. There is nothing private or esoteric about it. Rather it provides the basis for that community of understanding in which moral reasons *can* be public and as such the shared foundation for a common good. In this process each consideration understood as relevant to the work of justification must be recognizable *as,* so far as it goes, a valid ground for action in the case of all alike, and not merely in his own. To understand them thus, and to maintain that objectivity *of judgment* in which the merits of the case are thus specified, not the inner feelings or private illumination of that agent, is a moral achievement; it is what it is to *be* reasonable in the conduct of our practical affairs, and there is no place in it for the "subjective" self-complacency that fishes from its inner feelings a "final" mandate that its own "decision" validates as sound. Moral truth is public, and must maintain itself as such if we are rightly to respect it.

If our traditional reasons are inadequate to achieve this end, what we are to look for is not something that "transcends" in principle the reasons we already know and, in practice, live by, but better reasons—"better" in the sense that they do provide a working common ground for action for all who are concerned and willing to be reasonable, not merely those of our side, or sect, or party. What such reasons can be we do not know in advance but must *find out* as the enterprise of co-operative living and the exigencies of joint action disclose new responsibilities and new opportunities in the fulfilment of a common task. To be *willing* in this way to learn, to maintain these habits of inquiring and self-controlled belief in which we no longer make our own preconceptions the final boundaries of possible moral understanding, is an essential part of what it is to be reasonable in practical affairs. And this attitude is the polar opposite of that "subjectivity" which looks to the "heart" merely, not the head, for the solution of hard moral problems. There is room here for endless spontaneity, and imaginative "leaping", and creative innovation that will extend the range and depth of our understanding of the possibilities for good attainable in the world that now alarmingly confronts us. "The light that puts out our eyes is darkness to us. Only that day dawns to which we are awake." If we have not been thrown completely off our balance by the menace of the world within the atom, and in our own hearts when we use its still incalculable energies for divisive ends, we may still have the courage to say, with Thoreau, "There is more day to dawn." But we must have our eyes and our minds and our hearts open when we say it, or we shall end not in the better world we seek, but in something like the dreadful behaviorist Utopia of *Walden Two*, which was all that Professor B. F. Skinner could make of the promise of Thoreau. We must, in other words, be practically reasonable men.

And, above all else, we must *go on* being reasonable. For, as Wittgenstein puts the matter, the "game" does not *end* with the making of decisions. We have to live with them, and with their consequences, and with others on the terms they set, in a world in which some moral ventures, no matter how well intended, will turn out to be mistakes. And unless we can recognize and learn from such mistakes and *change* our minds accordingly, the new day that dawns for us will be disastrous indeed. This, again, is an essential part of what it is to be reasonable, for the work of practical judgment is a continuing and self-correcting process and a mind mired in self-luminous "first principles" will never learn to master it.

'The genuineness of an expression cannot be proved; one has to feel it.'—Very well,—but what does one go on to do with this recognition of genuineness? . . . does the game *end* with one person's relishing what another does not?[5]

The "game" of moral understanding does not and cannot end in this way. We must be able to use the "insights" of the heart as

---

[5] *Op. cit.*, p. 228e.

grounds for public understanding, that all alike can live by in the light of common day, for it is in this light that we live our days in common. To be able in this way to *go on* is the essential *mark* of understanding here, and it is in the answering assent of others who are concerned and competent to share this work with us that we show when and how far we *have* understood and that the confusions that blocked the road to understanding have in fact been removed. There is no inner illumination, or private relish, or in-group self-admiration that can compare with this in normative cogency. For this is what it *is* to justify our moral claims. Nothing more is needed; nothing less will suffice. And it is in the continuing work of practical reason that it is sometimes quite publicly and conclusively achieved, never "finally" or once and for all, since new problems will always face us as we live and learn, but in the steady maintenance of that consensus in which problems can be solved, as they arise, with some regard for common good and the achievement in this process, of those qualities of mind and character in which man, as a self or moral agent, achieves his own appropriate fulfilment.

These, however, are not the qualities most usually manifest in the discussion of moral issues. Where the love of argument has supplanted the love of wisdom, and the determination that our side shall be proved right in every controversy in which its interests are involved has become our governing consideration, we use a very different procedure—one in which acceptable conclusions are deduced from principles whose cogency any fool, who shares our antecedent predilections, can plainly see, and are used as bludgeons against an antagonist who is in the same manner assaulting us. It is an oddly inconclusive warfare, since neither side seems sensitive to the verbal wounds thus inflicted on it and nothing suffers but the chance for some sort of communicable understanding between them. The work of moral inquiry is not like this. Its business is not to win a battle, either academic or ideological, but to find grounds for a working under-standing on which all concerned may *go on* together to the resolution of their common problems. Among the qualities of mind and character it calls for are constructive imagination in grasping possibilities of accommodation so far missed; tact and ingenuity in bringing diverse interests to a public meeting-ground and persuading them to speak a common language; clear-headed firmness in holding to essentials that must not be com-promised and good sense in surrendering what comparatively does not matter; courage to *hold on* to the right as thus deter-mined against the clamor, not only of evil, but of opinionated and self-righteous men; and an enduring commitment to the maintenance of those processes of public order and fair dealing in which this right can be authentically discerned. For this, and nothing less, is what it is to *be* reasonable in judgment on the *specific* merits of an issue of conflicting rights and values. There is nothing logically peculiar about this way of being reason-able. Where textbook logic and semantic elucidation come with it, they do so in a quite usual way. A contradiction makes no more sense in practical than in theoretical reasoning—i.e., it makes no sense at all—and an undistributed middle is as much of a blemish on a moral as on any other argument. And here, as always, we must watch our language and not let ourselves be deceived by *mere* words. But, as we have seen, our language is here used for a quite distinctive purpose and in a somewhat larger undertaking than that of either sub- or meta-ethics. And it is in its use in this great enterprise that its practical significance is properly to be assessed.

This is what it would be like to follow reason in its practical use. But why should we follow reason? By what *right* have its dictates taken precedence over the demands of other and "deep-er" sides of our nature? Why should we do what our reason wants, when our hearts are set on something else? The answer is by this time obvious, but perhaps, in the murky atmosphere of contemporary thought, will bear repeating. "Reason" as such has no "right" to dictate anything, and it is never by dictation that it does its proper moral work. The right for which it speaks is a right it *finds* by honest searching, and if it is not thus findable by all who will *in this way* seek it, then it has no justifiable claim upon our hearts and wills. Nor has practical reason any axe of its own to grind in this discovery. It is not its *want* that that should prevail, for it is not one want among others but the concern that *all* wants shall be satisfied so far as this is possible within the structure of a moral order which all men of good will can accept as one in which *their* wants can be reasonably fulfilled. The question is not what *Reason* wants but what a man can rightly *will* as a responsible moral agent, as a self. It is only in this capacity that for him the question of right arises at all, and it is in these terms alone that a "should" has normative or justifying cogency. If you did not expect this kind of an answer, why did you ask the question? What else but this would *be* a relevant answer to it and only for a man in fact concerned to act rightly, i.e., reasonably, could such an answer have practical relevance or point. Is such action to his advantage? That depends, of course, on how he reckons his advantage. There is no guarantee that it will always give him what he wanted, and he would be a fool to expect it. Nor is it certified to satisfy all sides and levels of his "nature", for there is much in his nature that resists the requirements of moral order—as Freud has frequently insisted. It is what will satisfy him *as a self* or responsible agent and the only happiness it guarantees is that which *on these terms* is possible to him. And it sets the conditions on which he can live honorably with others in the shared enjoyment of a common and communicable good. To live in this way as a self is, as we have seen, not a gift of nature; it is a hard-won achievement, to be sustained with vigilance, and sometimes against great odds in a world not wholly friendly to the best in man. The time may come when we shall no longer care enough to pay this cost, when this "game" no longer will be played. And then the word "justification", if still uttered, will have a different meaning, for it will have some other use. Those who spoke the language would never know the answer to a question as to why they *should* be reasonable. They would have no means of understanding the question. In our present moral situation we are not such men. We do understand the question, and are concerned to offer a right answer to it. It is to such men thus concerned that this inquiry is relevantly addressed.

We may reasonably hope, I think, that this moral concern will prove itself deeply rooted in our nature. The moral interest is but one among many and, taken by itself, not a very strong one. Its strength lies in the fact that it does not exist, and cannot properly be "taken" by itself. Its business is to discern a way in which other interests which, taken by themselves, are not concerned with righteousness at all but for food, love, power and social recognition, may be jointly pursued in such a way that none is arbitrarily frustrated, defeated or denied. When they are *in this way* satisfied, then its "demands" are satisfied, and unless they are *thus* satisfied then the men whose wants they are will not be satisfied as selves in their enjoyment of them. Concrete reasonableness, as Peirce maintained, is a way of bringing things together and it is only as *thus* together that they can grow to the level of their humanly appropriate fulfilment. The man who fails to achieve this synthesis—the sick soul—is, as we have noted, properly described as all to pieces. And what is often called the "sickness" of our society, especially on the international level, is this same sort of fragmentation "writ large," as Plato would have said. Whether we have the spiritual resources to pull ourselves together is still an unsettled question. Assuredly, it will not be easy. But at least we know what these resources are: for they are those of practical reason in its appropriate concrete use. And it is by no means assured that we shall fail. "Fair is the prize, and the hope great." No man of courage would in these days ask a better guarantee than this for success in the work he has to do.

Stated abstractly and schematically and therefore, of necessity, inadequately, our "solution" of the problem of the comparison of the moral claims of competing rights and values comes to this. The relative weight of moral reasons in inherently problematic cases is measured by their comparative place and function in a moral order, a *community* of rights and goods, that on the whole and in its essential structure and purposes can be maintained, in mutual confidence and understanding, as a going concern. Each right has some placement, and each good, some normative claim on our allegiance and respect. If what they represent were not *in its own way* right and good, they could not relevantly serve as grounds for moral claims. In fact they are, in their proximate and familiar cogency, the familiar and substantial groundwork of the only moral world we know, or could rightly live in. A "higher" good or right that was not in some way the fulfilment of *their* meaning and intent would make no normatively authoritative contact with the only world of good and right we know. Yet, taken as each in itself a sufficient and incorrigible ground for action in all instances to which it relevantly applies, each may exclude others which are also relevant to the case in hand, and in this exclusion, stand as a competing claim to final truth for which, as it stands, there is no warrant. In this way a plurality or diversity of justifying reasons becomes a conflict that cannot be rationally adjudicated on the terms that any, taken by itself, provides—for there is now no longer any common ground for the judgment that would appraise their relative cogency and importance. When such conflicting claims become the slogans of competing groups, each with its own urge to justify, on moral grounds, the unique and final righteousness of its cause, the conflict may become overt, and moral "principles" the divisive instruments of social intransigence that defines their ideological use as weapons. It is to this unhappy outcome that the "ultimate" appeal to justifying reasons has, in our time, discoverably led.

But so to understand and use them was from the start a misunderstanding and misuse. It is not as "finally" divisive slogans nor as self-evident grounds for their own moral self-sufficiency that they have normative cogency in any case. Only a fool or a fanatic is simple-minded enough to suppose that the obligation to tell the truth makes practical sense in itself and as existing "quite alone", or that the easy satisfactions of kindliness, purchased at any cost in lies, evasion and self-deception, are morally worth having. We want to be both agreeable and honest, but we must draw the line somewhere. Where in particular cases we should draw it is an issue to be determined partly by the moral habits of the particular community, which must not be "gratuitously" offended. Some groups, Nietzsche's "masters" for example, set a high value on personal honor and a low one on indiscriminate benevolence. Our own "liberal" democracy has gone a dangerously long way in the opposite direction. The question of how much mendacity is compatible with personal and national honor is one that might well be soberly considered today by indoctrinating educators and by propagandists who seek to "sell" our "image" to the world at large by practicing a judicious reticence with respect to those aspects of our character and history which do not conveniently fit the image. There is room here for serious heart-searching and honest thinking. Yet there remain for all decent men some lies that must not be told at any cost, and some that it would be sheer fanaticism to condemn, since the pain they cause is out of all proportion to any good that, in this instance, truth could do. The problem for practical judgment is to determine where, between these limits, a working adjustment can be reached that will serve on the whole to satisfy the *reasonable* claims of both truth and kindness. It takes tact and sympathy, as well as "firmness in the right as God gives us to see the right," to do this responsibly and well. But it *is* done all the time, and our existing supply of good sense in dealing with conflicting "rights" which, if we were not prepared to be thus reasonable, would be ultimately irreconcilable, is the best evidence we could have of the working, over-all success, with which this work is done. We do not normally have moral crises about such issues. We can take them in our stride. And that is precisely because we have learned how to *go on,* to use the reasons that we have not as ultimate finalities but *as* grounds for concerted action in which, in mutual respect and understanding, we pursue a common good. When the issues that divide us are not those that arise between fellow-citizens and neighbors, but become "global" in their scope, the strains put upon our capacities for such understanding are far greater, and the temptation to take refuge in the initial finalities that were taught us long ago by those for whom such problems had not yet effectively arisen, is very great. But the right way to deal with them does not change when it becomes more difficult to follow. We have still, as has been said, *to find out* here what composition of rights and goods is possible, not in the abstract or in general, but for suspicious, stubborn and envious men who cherish their own institutions, which often seem incongruous or even odious to us, with the tenacious loyalty that makes accomodation to "alien" ideas so difficult in principle to achieve. It will not in fact be achieved in the first instance at least "in principle". On the ultimates of our personal and national loyalties we must—and this is natural and appropriate—agree to differ. But it can sometimes be achieved in practice on issues that are negotiable precisely because they are *not* in this way "ultimate", but within the range of relative comparison and bargaining. The *modus vivendi* thus achieved, which can serve as a *common* ground for "reasonable" action will at the start be a morally meager sort of order—a minimal condition for the common life of a community that may one day achieve a fuller and a richer life. The great thing is that where habits of reasonable procedure are thus established a community can *grow*. It is, as Peirce held long ago, the essential nature of concrete reasonableness, order or thirdness, that it grows and in its growth can bring together things that in themselves (firstness) are as sheer occurrent facts (secondness) poles apart. It is this enterprise, and nothing less, in which we are reasonably engaged when we weigh the claims of competing groups and nations from the standpoint of a moral order, adequate to our present human situation, to which they can, as thus ordered, jointly and without conflict contribute.

It would, perhaps, be prudent to stop here, for this in substance is what we have to say. But it is all too easy to anticipate the misinterpretation to which our account will at once be subjected by those intent on understanding it as something else with which, since their early college days at least, they have been familiar and believe they know, in consequence, how to handle. And since their error is, with their antecedent training, a natural one to make, it may be well at this point to take brief account of it. We have said, have we not, that the point of the comparison of claims to right and worth is to maintain the moral order of "the community", in which the harmonious reconciliation of all claims will then constitute a highest good whose rational authority provides the standard in whose light all lesser claims are judged. The *true* good is what is good not for the special interests involved but for the community as a whole, to which all lesser goods are of course and in principle subordinate. If this good is that of Plato's ideal justice, which only the Reason of philosophers is competent to discern, we have a clear case for the rational authoritarianism by which those capable of such esoteric insight are licensed to rule the state. If "reason" has become, as in Hegel, the institutionalized embodiment of "objective" authority by which the actual state exercises its final coercive "right" over the lives and minds of those who must submit to it, we have a somewhat different picture. But again it is the "community" whose supreme right is entitled in all instances *de jure* as, in Hegel's account it does "in the end" *de facto*. And the dialectical embodiment of this power in secular affairs is the incarnation of the Absolute or God, the *Logos* made of the flesh of institutionally licensed officialdom, in the only actually moral order that we know. Or, in a more general instance, we may recall Royce's reverence for the "great community," the truly final referent of all our loyalties, on whose service our obligation to the moral law is wholly and adequately fulfilled. This loyalty is nothing less than the love of a community as if it were a person, though in the greatness of its object it far transcends any love of merely human persons.

> It is the State, the Social Order [later broadened to become the Great Community] that is divine. We are all but dust, save as this social order gives us life. When we think it our instrument, our plaything, and make our private fortunes the one object, this social order rapidly becomes vile to us: we call it sordid, degraded, corrupt, unspiritual, and ask how we may escape from it forever. But if we turn again and serve the social order, and not merely ourselves, we soon find that what we are serving is merely our own spiritual destiny in bodily form. It is never truly sordid, or corrupt or unspiritual: it is only we that are so when we neglect our duty.[6]

It is to such heights as this that a moralist of the social order can soar when the spirit moves him. And have not we ourselves made "social order" the *final* measure for all claims to right and good? Or, finally, we may be recognized, to our great moral peril, by

---

[6] Josiah Royce, *California* (Boston: Houghton Mifflin, 1886), p. 501.

the sociologists as blood brothers. What are we saying "in the end" but that social agreement is the point of all accommodation of competing claims to right and good, and that what everybody will agree to, as a working *modus vivendi,* is the final measure of the social acceptability of moral claims. And this, too, is something that we seem to have heard before, and that surely has been more scientifically stated in standard social science texts.

The answer is, of course, that we have said none of these things, and want, in fact, no part of them.

> 'So you are saying that human agreement decides what is true and what is false?'—It is what human beings *say* that is true and false; and they agree in the *language* they use. That is not agreement in opinions but in form of life.[7]

And Wittgenstein goes on to say that for language to be a means of communication, there must be agreement not in opinions but in judgment, as, e.g., "what we call 'measuring' is partly determined by a certain constancy in results of measurement."[8] This, of course, is the essential point. To agree in the language that we use, most obviously if it is a normative cogency we have in mind, *is* to share the common standards which make *rational* agreement, or agreement not in opinions but in judgment, possible. And this can be achieved in fact only in the more basic "agreement" that constitutes a form of life. "What has to be accepted, the given, is—so one could say—*forms of life.*"[9] And that is why "If a lion could talk, we could not understand him."[10] Our present problem is that this form of life is still in the making, and within it those who are trying to be reasonable,

---

7 Wittgenstein, *Op. cit.,* 241, p. 88e.
8 *Ibid.,* 242, p. 88e.
9 *Ibid.,* p. 226e.
10 *Ibid.,* p. 223e.

seek the agreement in judgments of others who will share this enterprise and achieve the communication in terms that have a morally common meaning. And hence the enterprise of shared understanding, if it is to meet our present needs, must carry us beyond its given starting point if we are to "find our feet" with those with whom on some terms or other we must live. We do not expect everyone to agree with us—"Woe unto you when all men praise you." Our goal is not mass agreement or conformity but that agreement in use of the language of communicably justifying reasons by which those who have a mind for it can *judge* in common the moral truth or falsity, which is to say, the normative cogency of what they say and work together in the light of the truth thus achieved. The only moral world in which we are concerned is our actual world of human affairs, understood in this light, and it is its requirements, thus discerned and measured, not the agreement of the many, or the "wise"—unless it is in this way ascertained and measured—that is the proper standard for our judgments of comparative worth.

With the "claims" of the community as the final end and standard for all right action we can deal more briefly. "Community" in this sense is a myth, and in some instances a rather ugly one. There are no communities save as actual men in social groups are so related as to share in rights and goods that *in common* they can recognize as their own. It is as persons or moral agents that they can be thus related. The moral order, insofar as it is moral at all, is not something imposed on them by a "higher" authority; it is the order *they* maintain in their mutual relations through their own willed action, and it is a harmony so far as these purposes can be reasonably combined. To say that Reason must govern such a harmony is only to say that the judgment as to what is required for the preservation of this kind of order must be reasonably substantiated, if it is to have the normative cogency which is the "because" of moral action. A higher speculative reason, reflecting only a concern for the ideal order of a timeless truth, is not a reliable guide for the contingencies of the composition of moral differences in the world of practical affairs. And as a legitimation of the claims of self-selected individuals, groups or classes to rule the state in the name of a common good which only they can understand, there is even less to be said for it. The description in Book X of Plato's *Laws* of the fate assigned to those who are unwilling to accept the theology of the rulers as a doctrinal ground for public action is ample evidence of what, in practice, such a use of "reason" would entail. It is, like all such authoritarian doctrines, "rational" in its pretensions but highly arbitrary and exclusive in the actual imposition of its power. Its "Reason" is not reasonable, nor its procedures wise. *This* is by no stretch of the imagination the moral order we should seek, in righteous action, to preserve.

Nor can the institutionalized social order of the Hegelian state provide such a standard. For while, with Hegel's guidance, its dialectical necessity can "show" us—in a manner of speaking— why things ought metaphysically to be as they are, it cannot enable us to judge reliably when morally they are as they ought to be. It is in fact an attempt to disguise the *de facto* social order as a moral order by portraying it (as the incarnation of the Absolute) as an object of speculative and religious veneration, with which the individual must achieve a higher reconciliation if he is to find his duly ordered place in ultimate Reality. That, as Bradley duly noted, requires "in the end" the prostration of morality before religion. Such prostration is not a posture in which the worth of things and the right of action can be reliably discerned.

The reference to a "Great Community" looks more liberal, but in fact helps not at all. For such community would in fact be just one society among others and, for our human purposes, a painfully thin and schematic one. Its minimal requirements set limits for the composition of differences whose opposition might otherwise be destructive of *all* social order but in themselves or as a final good for all cooperative action do not comprise the substance of a shared and livable form of life. It is not in *this* way that its claims upon us have rational authority.

The mistake in all such theories has already been discussed. The relative measure of importance in the adjudication of social conflict is by no means the final and self-justifying *end* or goal of all rational action. Its requirements set conditions within which the quest for more rewarding and specific goods can go on, and are in *this* way final, when such accommodation is the point at issue. But they by no means constitute that good nor *by themselves* do they define a community in which we could live well together. Their claim is derivative and conditional. We compare goods only when there are goods to compare, and our goal, if we are reasonable, is the better realization of *these* goods under those conditions of mutual restraint in which none need be attained through the arbitrary deprivation of others. Where the question asked concerns the relative weight of rights and goods in the preservation of a moral order, *then* the standard they supply provides the relevant answer to it. But the preservation of such order is itself a means to the fulfilment of the shared ways of life that would not be possible without it and has a practical point in this use only. In our reference to "the community" we are as far as ever from an ultimate end that in itself and for itself alone can provide the rational goal of all our striving. The simple-mindedness of ethical theorizing has here returned at just the place at which, in the relative, contingent and exploratory order of comparative right and good there is least excuse for it. That we are now, perhaps, in a position to see this error clearly is, on the whole, a mark of progress. What we have found, in the moral order is not a final resting place for tired minds but a light in which we can *judge,* in hard cases, the minimal requirements for a common life. This and no other is the use that in this chapter we have made of it.

CHAPTER 15 DECISIONS OF PRINCIPLE

THERE IS NO TERM more widely and enthusiastically used in current philosophical discussion, or less adequately understood, than "decision". It has a tone of earnestness and urgency about it, and it is clearly practical in its implications. Men of action are decisive men. They do not merely cogitate and balance reasons; they determine on their own responsibility what shall be done and give their "reasons", if they think of any, afterward, according to the principles that their own normative decision sets. Those who would rise in the world, especially to positions of executive responsibility, are urged to follow this example. And yet, in this age of advanced research, we are reluctant to believe that this decision-making process has not some inner rationale of its own. Courses are offered and books written on techniques for decision-making and logical calculi devised for the "programming" of "correct" decisions by rules that any well set up machine can then follow "without a thought"—since its thinking is just its efficiency in the implementation of the program thus devised. For those who find this "objective" handling of the matter spiritually alien and superficial, there remains the deeper problem of the more ultimate commitment of *the*

Will by which this whole machinery is ontologically set in motion. To be obliged to make such existential decisons in an alien world of mindless machinery and, in the process, to create, on our own responsibility, the standards by which alone they could be justified, is the dreadful freedom by which a generation of disoriented thinkers has been at once charmed and terrified. Much of what is now called moral philosophy is concerned with the decision problems of the existing individual, as thus somewhat melodramatically portrayed in a blend of Kierkegaard and Karloff that has its own peculiar charm in the theater and church and on television, as well as in the more advanced classroom. For ours, we are told, is a time for great decisions, and if we are to be in step with it, we must in some way make them for ourselves.

Has the theory so far presented in this book anything of rational relevance to say about such "problems"? Indeed it has and the discerning reader will already know in substance what it is. To summarize it here will be, in one sense, to go over ground already covered. Yet to reaffirm it in specific contrast to so much that now passes in our time for deep thinking on ultimate issues may nonetheless be illuminating. And in the darkness of this time, we need all the light that we can get.

What, then, is a moral decision, and on what grounds, if any, is it rightly made? R. M. Hare's statement of the problem in *The Language of Morals* has set the pattern for its academic discussion in the past decade and will serve us here as a working model for our own. With the more exciting and popular aspects of the problem, as presented notably by Sartre, we shall later deal. Hare starts, as most ethical theorists do, with the traditional pattern of practical reasoning. In the making of any decision to do something, he tells us, two factors may be involved: a major premise which is a principle of conduct, e.g., never say what is false, and a minor premise which is a factual, and so far as possible, valuationally neutral statement of what we should be doing if we acted in one way or another in the particular situation, e.g., that the utterance of this assertion would in fact be saying something false. In deciding not to make this statement *because* it would be false I am acting on a principle of which the action in question is an instance. And this is what it is to have grounds for a decision.[1] My principle is my ground and, as a major premise, it specifies univocally the moral right of cases that are factually certifiable as falling under it. We have heard this sort of thing before and know by this time what to think of it. For Hare, however, it is only a beginning. For the unique character of "decision" does not adequately appear in this decision to act, or not to act, on moral grounds.

Suppose, now, I am not satisfied to let the matter rest at this point. This statement would indeed be false, and to eschew false statements is my principle. But, nonetheless, I *decide* in this instance to make the statement. Here a further "decision" is required. For I decide now *not* to apply my principle or "reason" or so to qualify it that it allows exceptions of specific kinds. This does not make my principle more loose.[2] On the contrary, with the allowable exceptions specified the general rule is tighter than before. And Hare, who clearly is a Kantian at heart, is all for tightness. But the decision to alter the principle in this way is one I make on my own responsibility. There is, presumably, no "principle" for it, or none that I have not, by a prior decision, legislated for myself. Thus we are confronted, not merely with decisons to do one thing rather than another, for a reason, but "decisions of principle" about the grounds or reasons I will follow in deciding, in the more familiar sense, to act in one way rather than another. It is important, I think, to

---

[1] R. M. Hare, *The Language of Morals* (Oxford: The Clarendon Press, 1952). See pp. 56f.

[2] *Ibid.*, p. 93.

note the difference between these two sorts of decision, though Hare does not do so. The former is clearly present in all voluntary action, which just is the doing, so far as it is unimpeded, of what in such action I decide to do. The latter is a horse of another color. It is not the doing of something for a reason, but a pure choosing or "deciding" of the reasons for which anything should be done. For the one I have reasons—those that, presumably I have in this instance chosen to accept as principles. For the other, what reasons or justification could I have? Any justification would be itself a reason which by prior decision I had chosen to accept. And by what reason would this choice be justified? Here finally, as Hare affirms, we must simply *decide,* presumably without a justification, and accept the responsibility for so doing. It is, he holds, the part of moral maturity to recognize this hard fact. A decision *of* principle cannot be made *on* principle, but requires a groundless fiat of the will. This fiat is the morally unique and ultimate decision which traditional ethical theories have neglected—"a factor which is the very essence of morals."[3] We must "learn to use 'ought'-sentences in the realization that they can only be verified by reference to a standard or set of principles which we have by our own decision accepted and made our own."[4] *This* is the "decision" whose "justification" is not presented to us as at once a tragedy, a problem and a task. We must try to see what sense we can make of it.

Hare's own way of dealing with the "problem" is well known. If asked to justify a decision completely, we have to give a complete specification of the way of life of which it is a part (of both the "principles" in it, by which decisions are made in it, and a full account of their observable consequences in conduct). This it is in practice impossible to do.

---

3 *Ibid.,* p. 54.
4 *Ibid.,* p. 78.

Suppose, however, that we can give it. If the inquirer still goes on asking, But why *should* I live like that? then there is no further answer to give him because we have already *ex hypothesi* said everything that could be included in this further answer. We can only ask him to make up his own mind which way he ought to live; for in the end everything rests on a decision of principle. He has to decide whether to accept the way of life or not; if he accepts it then we can proceed to justify the decisions that are based upon it; if he does not accept it, then let him accept some other, and try to live by it. The sting is in the last clause.To describe such ultimate decisions as arbitrary, because *ex hypothesi* everything that could be used to justify them is already included in the decision, would be like saying that a complete description of the universe would be utterly unfounded, because no further fact could be called upon to corroborate it. Far from being arbitrary, such a decision would be the most well-founded of decisions, because it would be based upon a consideration of everything upon which it could possibly be founded.[5]

Evidently Mr. Hare has here forgotten a distinction that, a few pages earlier, he took pains to make. He there imagined the case of a man who has a peculiar kind of clairvoyance such that he can know everything about all the effects of all the alternative actions open to him. But he has (has decided to accept) no principles of conduct. Would his choice of one alternative rather than another be arbitrary? If asked to say why, in this full knowledge, he made this choice he "might say 'I can't give any reasons; I just felt like deciding that way; another time, faced with the same choice, I might decide differently.' "[6]

Hare asserts that in such a case we should "in a certain sense of that word" call his action arbitrary. So, evidently, this is a way in which we used the word sometimes. And the decision he describes in "choosing" a way of life is arbitrary in just this sense. Its "justification" would include a *statement* of all relevant

---

[5] *Ibid.*, p. 69. Reprinted by permission of The Clarendon Press, Oxford.
[6] *Ibid.*, p. 58.

facts, including the fact that certain principles are actually accepted in it. "This is what *we* do." But this so far, as he should be the first to insist, gives no practical reason and hence no justification for choosing anything at all. It lacks the imperative which, as he holds, is the essence of all value judgments. The inquirer, if he had not wholly lost his wits, might well reply: I quite see that these are the principles that those who share your way of life have chosen to accept. But how is that a reason for me to do so? A complete *description* of the universe is still practically and morally incomplete—it gives no ground for choosing one thing rather than another. And it was for this, presumably, that the inquirer was asking when he asked for a justification. Hence, this ultimate decision of principle, on which all else depends, *is* arbitrary, in the quite simple sense that it is practically and morally groundless. All other justifying "whys" lead up to it, but for it there is no "why"; we must decide on our own responsibility—which is to say without a reason. All ultimate moral choices in the end are unjustifiable.

And yet the "problem" is so stated that a justification appears to be required. For the "choice" is presented as a moral choice, and even as a *judgment* that one way of "life" ought to be chosen in preference to another. For when I choose a *principle* I legislate its rightness not only for myself but for all men. "To ask whether I ought to do A in these circumstances is (to borrow Kantian language with a small but important modification) to ask whether I will that doing A in such circumstances should become a universal law."[7] The rational universality of principles (and, in "decisions of principle", that is what I choose) required nothing less than this. But the relativity of the normative cogency of such principles to a decision for which there is nothing better "in the end" to be said for it than "I have spoken" or "I just felt

---

[7] *Ibid.,* p. 70.

388   The Theory of Practical Reason

like deciding that way," or "in our way of life this is what we do"
makes the claim intolerably pretentious.

Such a decision is not merely groundless in the sense in
which a dog is speechless or a stone dead; it is morally arbitrary
to legislate my own *de facto* preferences into the status of a
universal norm of right. As such, we are by this time sufficiently
familiar with it. And to speak of such a "decision" as a judgment
is to talk mere nonsense. Arbitrary decisions we know well
enough, but a groundless *judgment,* claiming for itself a rational
authority it could no more possess than a sneeze could be well
founded is both theoretically and practically absurd. That there
are those prepared to embrace this absurdity as the "final"
warrant for all moral truth is a significant indication of the
extent and depth of our current ethical confusion.

For this next step, however, we must leave Oxford for the
sidewalk cafes of Paris, and the philosophical reflections of Jean
Paul Sartre. The logical pattern of the discussion does not change
—all the familiar ingredients are there—but the dramatic overtones and undertones are heightened, and the spectacle is
presented on what purports to be an ontological scale. We are
again presented with what purports to be a realistic, and is more
properly a cynical, account of human "decisions" and are invited to consider in all honesty the tragic "facts" of man's
existential situation as a moral being. But Sartre is actually not
much interested in the rationale of our practical decisions. The
"choice" involved in doing one thing rather than another, where
reasons can be given for it, appears to be determined by our
nature or character as already formed. Sartre describes it, where
he has occasion to mention it at all, in quite crudely deterministic
terms.[8] What does concern him deeply is the ontological pre-choice

---

8 Jean-Paul Sartre, *Being and Nothingness,* trans. H. E. Barnes (New York:
Philosophical Library, 1956), pp. 445-452.

behind all such choices—the spontaneous irruption, here called freedom, of a "will" that is not yet a self and chooses, in a world which so far has no value, the "value" that will thereafter—or until some new ontological irruption of freedom shall occur— determine its choices as a moral self, and thus the kind of self it is to be.

> [B]y the word 'will' we generally mean a conscious decision, which is subsequent to what we have already made of ourselves. I may want to belong to a political party, write a book, get married; but all that is only a manifestation of an earlier, more spontaneous choice, that is called 'will.' But if existence really does precede essence, man is responsible for what he is. Thus existentialism's first move is to make man aware of what he is and make the full responsibility of his existence rest on him. And when we say that a man is responsible for himself, we do not only mean that he is responsible for his own individuality, but that he is responsible for all men.[9]

Why responsible? Because in this ontological pre-choice he has decided, groundlessly, to be what as a moral agent he is, and all his subsequent "choices" are determined by this irretrievable involvement. Responsible for what? For deciding *rightly* or as he ought? But on this account there is no right or wrong for him but what he makes so by his own by thus deciding. Responsible to whom? To others who can judge the merits of his choice? But for him there are no others in this position but those who, by his own decision, he recognizes as such. He is responsible *for* all men, in the sense that his decision *claims* to be of universal validity for all men, but so does theirs *for him*, and in the arbitrariness of their unconditioned freedom they may, and often do, "decide" quite otherwise. We can well understand here the remark of one of Sartre's characters in *No Exit*: "Hell is other people." It is the only appropriate con-

---

[9] Jean-Paul Sartre, *Extisentialism,* trans. B. Frechtman (New York: Philosophical Library, 1947), pp. 19-20.

clusion for an existentialist ethics, and from the moral cul-de-sac to which it leads there is indeed no exit.

Yet Sartre is quite logical in his presentation of the issue. If there is such a pre-choice in which in ultimate subjective arbitrariness the universal principles of moral action are willfully legislated "for all men," what else but this could it be? Such a choice, in its moral pretensions, *needs* a justification, if it is in any way to serve as a ground for common understanding, and from the nature of the case it cannot have one. Yet such a decision must be made if the will that is not yet a self is to make a *moral* choice at all, for which as a self it could reasonably be held responsible. Faced with this desperate situation, what can the free individual do but recognize his guilt? And this recognition is anguish. "Anguish is constant in the sense that my original choice is a constant thing. In fact, anguish, as I see it, is the concurrence of complete absence of justification and responsibility toward others."[10] This is the anguish that Sartre invites us to share with him, and there are many who have been glad to do so.

This philosophy is often said to be very deep and hard to understand. It seems to me, on the contrary, that for anyone acquainted with the history of modern philosophy, of which Sartre himself has expert knowledge, its plausibility is remarkably easy not merely to see, but to see through. The will that legislates itself into moral selfhood is nothing but our old acquaintance, the dislocated "act of volition" cut off from its roots in the concrete world of responsible human selfhood and operating on the loose on what, in the Kantian tradition, is still called noumenal freedom. From Kant to Sartre this will has lost its reason, but it had much beyond its formal pretension to universal authority from the start, and, since it still maintains

---

10 *Ibid.*, pp. 65f.

the intransigence of its claims, the omission of the machinery of transcendental justification will seem a gain in "realism" rather than a defect. When a moral nonentity (the will that has still to create its "self" *ex nihilo*) attempts to justify its "values" in a moral vacuum, what can it expect to find? Nothing. And this is just what Sartre does find, and offers as a metaphysical disclosure of the first importance. Since all that could give the situation moral sense had been abstracted in advance, there was nothing else to be found. And if this encounter with nothingness—the ultimate practical senselessness or "absurdity" of a world we try to understand in this false light—is less universally significant as ontology than the existentialists would make it, it does at least describe an authentic human experience.

What Sartre in fact has offered is a brilliant *reductio ad absurdum* of philosophical voluntarism as an account of human freedom. The initially surprising fact is that he asks us to take this reduction seriously and to adopt it as a way of life. That is indeed absurd, and the absurd, as he assures us, is at the root of his philosophy. So far we could not agree with him more. Our only serious objection to it is that the result is stated in mis-leadingly portentous and pseudo-moral terms. If this pre-choice is what he tells us, what else could it be but exactly what he says it is? There is no more profundity in calling such a "choice" unjustified than in calling a tree "speechless" or a stone "dead". What else could it be? And to speak of being responsible in any moral sense for the "decision" or to feel guilt about it is an absurdity that must stand high on even Sartre's preferential scale. How, if right is what I make it, could I possibly decide wrongly? I legislate the norms for my decision along with the decision itself and how, save by the sheerest intellectual in-coherence, could they *fail* to agree? Others may legislate the contrary course, but as a "free" man, that is not my concern. *I* take the responsibility for all men, and what I make of it is wholly my own affair. There *are* for me no values but those which my pre-self created, and to these my conscious self is tied until a new inception of ontological spontaneity, a new thrust toward existence, changes my direction. The use of normatively moral language to characterize such freedom is more than just absurd; it is downright silly. For the philosophy in which this language now occurs has systematically robbed such terms in this new ontological meaning of all moral sense. What we may properly object to in Sartre is not the amazing cynicism of his parody of human nature but the moral overtones of edification he tries to inject into it. Is he himself really serious about it? Sometimes, as the royalties from America roll in, one seems to detect a slight Gallic leer behind his comments on the world. He seems too clever a man to be wholly imposed on by what he says. But there are clearly others who have been imposed on by it. The existential attitudes of a considerable section of the clergy, as well as of the "humanists", and the manner in which they have embraced the opportunity it offers to be quite intensely earnest about nothing in particular is an unedifying spectacle. It reflects the moral rootlessness of a generation that wants intensely to be in earnest *about something* but, in its unhappy subjectivity, has no firm standards by which it can distinguish anguish from responsibility or willfulness from sustained coherent purpose. And for this at least it deserves to be remembered.

We shall be told, however, that this existentialist nightmare of existence is no mere figment of a cynical imagination. It *fits* the moral disorder of the social world in which, for the past two generations, we have lived. The clash of the unteachable and groundless wills of conflicting groups and leaders is what freedom comes to in the end, or when the moral order of a community cannot sustain the pressures brought against it by the ungovernable pretensions of willful men. Hitler's Germany, and its Fuehrer most of all, were a *reductio ad absurdum* of the doctrine of the "primacy of the will" in Western culture, but they happened nonetheless and for a time our free society seemed helpless before them. And the ideological cold war that followed has elements in it of comparable absurdity. Yet these are the realities of our contemporary world, and is it not the part of common honesty to face them? It is indeed, but face them *how?* At what level and within what range of understanding? Surely not by cynical acquiescence in "new waves" of the future. The situation that the "voluntarist" describes *can* happen, and we have now seen enough of it to know what and when and how it happens and what it portends. The triumph of the unconditioned will is magnificently described by Ulysses in Shakespeare's *Troilus and Cressida*:

> Take but degree away, untune that string
> And hark, what discord follows. Each thing meets
> In sheer oppugnancy . . .
> Force should be right, or rather right and wrong
> (Between whose endless jar justice resides)
> Should lose their names; and so should justice, too.
> Then everything includes itself in power.
> Power into will, will into appetite;
> And appetite, a universal wolf,
> So doubly seconded with will and power,
> Must make perforce a universal prey
> And last, eat up himself.

This dreadful freedom *can* be the "ultimate", the last analysis, of the nature of our moral world if we choose to make it so. Take but degree away, rational composition of competing values in the structure of a common good, and this is what is left of human nature. And of it Spengler was right when he said, "Man is a beast of prey." But we know now that it need not be. There are those who in the past have stood against it, as Britain stood in 1940, and over many centuries we owe the best of what we are and have to them. They too were men of decision, and of great strength of will and moral tenacity. But they were also men who knew what they were doing, and the worth of it. Their wills followed their understanding, not at all in the sense of being enslaved to antecedent preconceptions, for they were builders of a better world than the one they found, in which to understand is rightly to assess the worth of things and men, and to go forward in its light, justifying in their achievement their claims to rational authority in the government of men. That is what the justification of the normative cogency of moral reasons amounts to when we really have it, and we too can have it if, not as mindless unconditional volitions, but as responsible selves, we will. As Mr. Hare would say, *that* decision is for us to make.

But first of all we must see, as he does not, that the nightmare of "ultimate" and groundless choosing is a nightmare, the misbegotten product of a logical confusion of decision with subjective willfulness, and that the only "truth" involved in it is only the distortion that bad delusions too frequently produce. The "decision" to create *ex nihilo* a world of "values" on our responsibility is, fortunately, one that, as moral agents, we are never called upon to make. We are required to justify our decisions to *do* one thing rather than another, and we do this understandably when we give our reasons for so doing. Here it is the action, not the reason, that is the appropriate object of willed or decisive action, and it is *this* "decision", made often in the face of great obstacles and strong temptations, that is the appropriate object of rational justification. We do not, in such situations, choose our reasons. We are morally in no position to do so. The reasons we have learned to use in the whole course of our moral training are the very structure of our own moral being as agents or deciders; they constitute the normative order of the *Lebensform,* or form of life, in which the practice of moral justification has a normative authority as a guide for conduct. Where there is a question of the adequacy of a particular reason or "principle" to the issues of concrete action, we can refer, as Hare rightly notes, from such a "principle" to its quali- fication within the network of related principles which constitute the pattern of our "form of life". But to talk of deciding for a way of life in general and *in vacuo* is a sheer absurdity. We do not in this sense choose our way of life: we are stuck with it. Its "principles", not as social habits merely, into which we happen to have been born, but as normatively cogent grounds for right action, are the very fibre of our being *as* responsible selves or moral agents, and we could no more get outside them to decide, in value-free and unconditioned independence, what "values" are, than we could speak English without using the syntax of the language to express our thoughts. We may, of course, rebel against the standards we have learned and look elsewhere than to the family, the church or the nation into which we were born to find a worthy object for our ultimate allegiance. But if our rebellion is not merely aimless and blind, we have grounds for it and those grounds are produced by those very factors *in* our form of life which have taught us to be discontented with its presently inadequate acceptances and procedures. We could have no other ground than this on which to stand. The free thinker who turns against the church, and has good grounds for doing so, has learned the meaning of the freedom that he cherishes in a community that is, in its pretensions at least, a Christian society. And it is in the name of a truth which he there learned to value, a truth whose knowledge can genuinely make men free, that he justifies the shift in his allegiance. And the rebel who, like Henry Miller at Mycenae, finds his spiritual home in an Heroic Greece of his own imagining, a Greece which, since he has not read Homer he is free to imagine as he will, carries with him into the picture all the old unreconciled negations and antagonisms of his rebel- lion against Brooklyn long ago. What Greece was, when we dis- count the magnificence of his language and reflect on its sense, is largely what the "air-conditioned nightmare" he has to leave behind him should have been and lamentably was not.[11]

What neither he nor we can do is to drown our own moral roots and still make value judgments. We carry our moral past and its traditions with us, if not as a spiritual resource, then as a scar. There is no way that we can judge or justify anything save *on* the ground that it initially provides. We are not uncommitted shoppers in a world of *morally* possible alternative value-systems who may quite groundlessly "choose" one or another to our taste and *then* proceed to live with it. We do not choose our reasons when we choose to act for a reason. This prior "choice" calls for no justification, for it is never made. It would be in truth a moral absurdity, for it would *call* for a justification that could not be itself a justifying ground for action until, by a "responsible" but unjustifiable choice we ourselves had made it so. To see that a morally disembodied will thus legislating for itself and for all mankind is an absurdity is so far a gain in analytic understanding. But to accept the result as a fair account of our actual human situation is to show, I think, a rather cynically twisted sense of humor. Or, to put the whole matter in a form with which the reader should by this time be familiar, morally normative communications are significantly addressed to the concerned and competent, for only they would understand or know what to do with them. This understanding, hardly won through centuries of funded moral experience, *is* the ground for rational decision, the solid substance of our moral world, and for better or for worse, we and our moral responsibilities are *inside* it. Santayana once judiciously observed that "we cannot cease to think, and still continue to know." It is no less the case that we cannot stand outside the categorial structure of the practice in which "responsibility" makes sense, and still make moral judg-

---

[11] Cf. *The Colossus of Maroussi*, passim.

ments. Only a morally uprooted and disoriented thinker could seriously suppose that in this way he was morally free to choose his "values" without prior moral standards. And he, however much he might have to say about "ultimate decisions", could not make a moral judgment of the justification, i.e., the rightness, of decisions that require such justification in the shared work of our common life. He would have nothing to judge with. His freedom would indeed be "dreadful," but it would also be inane. It is this inanity, now discovered as a fact of "subjective" experience itself, with which existentialism confronts us.

But we do, nonetheless, change our moral standards, and we do this, at least in part, by our own decision. Of course we do, and while we sometimes do so blindly and irrationally indeed, we also sometimes do it for good reasons. It is that kind of change that is often called moral progress and in the early years of the present century we heard a good deal about it. The "immoral moralist," the value-innovator who breaks the old tablets of the law and would impose a new and better "order" on society, was the intellectual hero of the 1910's and '20's. Mencken's Americanized version of Nietzsche, Shaw on *Ibsenism* and the cynical idealism of Veblen's *Theory of the Leisure Class* were required reading for emancipated minds (and there are those who read them still) and Bergson's *Two Sources of Morality and Religion,* a moral classic not as well known as it should be in America and Britain, summed up the gospel in its classic form. Morton White's *Social Thought in America,* gives an excellent account of the indebtedness of the "progressive" movement to this kind of iconoclasm. Its rationale is neatly stated by George Bernard Shaw in *The Quintessence of Ibsenism.*

> The statement that Ibsen's plays have an immoral tendency is, in the sense in which it is used, quite true. Immorality does not necessarily imply mischievous conduct: it implies conduct, mischievous or not, that does not conform to current ideals. All religions begin with a

revolt against morality, and perish when morality conquers them and stamps out such words as grace and sin, substituting for them morality or immorality. ... He [Ibsen] is on the side of the prophets in shewing that the spirit or will of Man is constantly outgrowing the ideals, and that therefore thoughtless conformity to them is constantly producing results no less tragic than those that follow thoughtless violation of them. ... He protests against the ordinary assumption that there are certain moral institutions that justify all means used to attain them, and insists that the supreme end shall be the inspired, eternal, evergrowing one, not the external unchanging artificial one; not the letter but the spirit; not the contract but the object of the contract; not the abstract law but the living will. And because the will to change our habits and thus defy morality arises before the intellect can reason out any socially beneficent purpose in the changes, there is always a period during which the individual can say no more than that he wants to behave immorally because he likes, and because he will feel constrained and unhappy if he acts otherwise.[12]

He holds further that a conversion to the open-minded vigilance of Ibsen "must at once greatly deepen the sense of moral responsibility."[13] And he holds that a realism that could recognize this fact would be "a most desirable step forward in public morals."[14]

Shaw himself, as we have long since discovered, is a tireless and incorrigible moralist and it is in behalf of public morals, though also with the support of a new "Life Force" religion, that his varied panaceas for humanity are advanced. His anticipation, in the passage quoted, of the major doctrines of Bergson's *Two Sources* is very striking. What interests us here, however, is his description of the stage in moral change at which accepted institutions have lost their moral cogency, for advanced minds at

---

12 *The Quintessence of Ibsenism* (New York: Hill and Wang, 1957), pp. 152f.
13 *Ibid.*, p. 54.
14 *Ibid.*, p. 155.

least, while for the new morality that would give more adequate expression to the "eternal spirit of mankind", no socially beneficent purpose has *yet* been reasoned out that would justify this change. In this transitional stage the "creative" will is morally on the loose; it has divorced itself from one allegiance and found *as yet* no reason that would warrant what it blindly feels it wants to do, and would feel constrained if it were hindered in what, so far, can appear to the righteous only as the willful self-assertion of "deviant" or aberrant individuals. The situation, more dismally described by Matthew Arnold, is that in which the emancipated individual stands perplexed between two worlds, one dead, the other powerless to be save as its own unreasoned affirmation shall establish it. This was the favorite cultural malady of humanists in the 1920's and almost everybody with refined feelings and advanced ideas suffered from it. In its extremer form, it was expressed in the exploits of the "lost generation", disillusioned, presumably, by the first world war, and of Gertrude Stein who went to Paris to be alone with English, an encounter which has left that language not quite what it was before.

Is this, perhaps, what those who speak of a pre-choice of "values" have in mind, this transitional dislocation of the moral will, still very much in earnest about its own "open-minded" responsibilities, from its traditional loyalties, this willful adherence to a new "good" whose justification has still to be made out? It is, in its way, a groundless choice, an affirmation of "the will" beyond the accepted limits of the understanding, an urge, so far without a justification, toward goals not seen as yet but somehow felt as "higher" than the customary standards it rejects. If so, it is a quite familiar phenomenon, and there is, in principle, no mystery about it. But *if* this is what is meant, then the existential account of it in terms of a pre-choice made unconditionally and in a moral vacuum is a peculiarly inept account of it.

For the whole point of the account is that *this* sort of will-fulness is not ultimate. It is *essentially* a stage in a transition from something *to* something else, and it would make no sort of moral sense if it were not. It is one stage in a movement *from* something previously accepted, and the iconoclast is throughout parasitic on the moral order he reacts *against* for the pertinence of his moral indignation, and *toward* something, a new and discoverably *better* order in which the will can again be fulfilled in an understanding adequate to its now inchoate though somehow "creative" purpose. How could the "new" morality thus "chosen" be significantly described as higher" than the old unless it were in some way not merely the negation but also the fulfilment of that out of which it grew? Before we can judge our movement as a "progress" we must know at least which way is up. And this a morality of "ultimate" decisions could never tell us. It is precisely what is *not* ultimate in it as it stands but the expression of an aspiration in which the good in what we already know and honor can be better and more adequately achieved that makes sense of any claim to "justification" that can here significantly be made. And it is within the world in which we already have commitments and responsibilities, not adequately articulated in the reasons we have traditionally been taught to treat as "final" that this sort of growth can sometimes fruitfully occur. This capacity of such "better" reasons *is* their justification as principles or reasons, the ground for the "choice" that, however "blindly" *at the start,* we are now, as moral agents, responsible for making.

In this work there is ample room for seers and prophets, the "seers" of a better life for man whose creative inspiration sometimes enables us to see all things in a new light and to guide us in our purpose to achievement. He who has the gift of prophecy, let him prophesy, and, if he knows what he is doing, we shall all be the better for what he has to tell us. We can hardly be grateful enough to those who, by their insight and their example, have thus broadened the range of our capacity to grasp the creative possibilities of human life, and to direct our faith to goals not seen as yet, but nonetheless the evidence of things hoped for. "And I, if I be lifted up, will draw all men unto me." The spiritual truth in these words is an abiding truth and our moral world would not be what it is today without the light that it has given us.

The classic instance of this sort of ethical theory is Bergson's *Two Sources of Morality and Religion*.[15] The reader will recall its drastic distinction between two sorts of morality, neither of which, however, Bergson holds, can actually exist in isolation from the other.[16] The one is the closed morality of obligation, social habit, which links us with the ants and bees. Its authority is wholly that of social pressure and its final answer to the "why" of moral obligation is just "You must because you must," the "reason," Bergson holds, at once of the drill sergeant and the categorical imperative. The other is the open morality of creative emotion which is all aspiration and love. It is embodied in devotion to the person of a charismatic leader in whose service pressure wholly yields to inspiration and to love. It has no rules or commandments; its ultimate injunction is simply "Love and do as you please." The individuals who can inspire this devotion are truly supermen. In them the creative impetus, which had previously been arrested at the level of social habit and routine, breaks through to new and superhuman heights of "vital" expression. And for it there are no barriers that its all-embracing love can not surmount. "Let no one speak of material

---

[15] Henri Bergson, *Two Sources of Morality and Religion*, trans. R. Ashley Andra and Clondesley Brereton (New York: Henry Holt and Co. 1935.) [Reprinted in 1954 by Doubleday and Co., Inc., Garden City, New York.] All page references are to the latter edition. Permission to cite passages here has been granted by the owners of the copyright, Holt, Rinehart, and Winston, Inc.

[16] *Op. cit.*, p. 51.

obstacles to a soul thus freed."[17] It does not need the faith that removes mountains. Rather for it there *are* no mountains, and neither matter nor society is any longer a barrier to its "free" spiritual self-affimation in its higher union with the creative force of Life itself. Bergson's favorite example of such supermen is the Christian mystics, of whom he writes with great sympathy. Static religion is the deposit that this dynamic faith has left in social institutions, and "closed" morality owes what is spiritual in it to its faint reminiscence of their inspiration.

All this is eloquently said, but leaves us with some unsolved problems. The open morality of emotional inspiration is an esoteric achievement of the privileged few who in their own persons or by direct association with the charismatic leader can make such love the law of their still mundane lives. For the rest of us it is available only at second hand and on the credit which their inspiration gives it. *We* must go on living, for the most part, on that plane of human action on which the only "why" is a *must* of social pressure. How then are we to share in it, or even understand its meaning? What reasons can it give *us* for the "higher" life to which its inspiration calls? Bergson's answer to this question is not as clear as we might well wish it to be. Here, evidently, enthusiasm is not enough, and "love" which can exist in morally equivocal forms, requires a spiritual director for right action.

> True, it has been given only to a chosen few to dig down, first beneath the strata of the acquired, then beneath nature, and so get back into the very impetus of life. If such an effort could be made general, the impetus would not have stopped short at the closed society, ... as if before a blank wall. It is none the less true that these privileged ones would fain draw humanity after them; since they cannot communicate to the world at large the deepest elements of their spiritual condition, they transpose it superficially; they seek a

---

17 *Ibid.*, p. 53.

transposition of the dynamic into the static which society can accept and stabilize by education.[18]

It is thus that we have achieved the kind of half-way spiritual order, that blend of pressure and of inspiration that, in Christian civilization, and especially in the Catholic Church, toward which Bergson moved markedly in his later years, can actually move or "motivate" our wills. Here, as he puts it in another place, the static has added to the dynamic something of its pressure, discpline and drill, while the dynamic diffuses over the static something of its perfume.[19]

Or as an unkind critic might express it, spiritual regimention plus incense. Where Bergson remains vague as to how this basically impossible "transposition" of the incommunicable into the static terms of authoritarian pressure takes place, his disciple, Toynbee, has been quite sufficiently specific. The answer, for the spiritually underprivileged, is discipline and drill, faintly illuminated by the emotional afterglow of a second-hand inspiration. Love and do as you are told. The elite who share at first hand in this inspiration will know intuitively that the direction in which they are going is forward. " 'Progress' and 'advance,' moreover, are in this case indistinguishable from the enthusiasm itself."[20]

And if even there are definite obstacles to their material advance, they will not see them. But, again, the rest of us must seek a more objective and external guide. There have been many collective inspirations which, under the influence of those who were beyond the ordinary limitations of humanity, have spread through mankind like a conflagration. By no means all of them were "creative" by any moral standard we can recognize as

[18] *Ibid.*, pp. 273f.
[19] *Ibid.*, p. 51.
[20] *Ibid.*, p. 51.

normatively sound. And when men are gathered together in drilled devotion to a leader they thus blindly follow, the aroma that is diffused among them is not always that of sanctity. How are we to tell? How is an essentially esoteric inspiration to justify itself in communicable understanding? The "dynamic" can give no reasons to the static, for it is not in terms of public reasons but of private inspiration that its claims are made good. And the static, as Bergson describes it, being all pressure and social habit, would not know what to make of such reasons if it had them. The two remain essentially incommensurable and there simply *is* no common ground on which to stand when we try to bring them into any sort of justifiable relation. Yet it is the distinctive business of morality to establish just such a relation within the world of our common life. There is a shrewd point in Maritain's observation that Bergson's ethics preserves "all of morals but morality itself."[21] For the morality of ants and super-men he can find at least some sort of communicable "why," but for that of human beings who must understand the good of what they are doing before they are of their own will to do it, none at all.

Evidently, what is left out here is precisely *judgment* as a factor in the creative process that Bergson so persuasively describes. And it is its omission that makes all the difference. Faced with a decision between an open morality which is so far all will and emotion and a closed morality to which we are "bound" only by social training, habit and routine, what justification can we have for the one choice or the other? For the mystic there is here no problem, the surge of his emotion carries all before it and moves the will to follow blindly. For the routine-bound disciple there is equally none. He simply does as he is told and, if his training has been spiritual, perhaps feels "good" about it. There is no sense here in the idea of justification. In what com-

---

21 *Ransoming the Time* (New York: Charles Scribner's Sons, 1941), p. 95.

municable terms could it be stated? But there is equally no
sense in "responsibility". Such men do not decide anything on
their own responsibility, or at all—they are simply pulled or
pushed, and though the description gets overtones of edification
when the pull is called an inspiration, or the push creative, no
grounds are or can be given that would *warrant* such a designation. It is ironical that, in spite of all his talk of human freedom,
Bergson's own account of the way in which motives "get a hold
upon the will" and "set it in motion" is quite simple-mindedly
deterministic. There is no place at all in it for moral agency, as
we have come to understand it. And within the terms of reference
of his romanticized biology, there could be none.

We have done our best to find, within experience itself, some
discoverable equivalent for the groundless, but nonetheless responsible decision which is supposed to be the "final" ground
for all our value judgments. None has been found, and it should
by this time be apparent that none can be. For the notion is itself
a normative absurdity—it exists only as the fruit of the disordered imaginings of morally disoriented men. The human
predicament they parody is by this time plain enough. There
are situations in which our available supply of understanding,
the funded reasons of our traditional allegiances, proves inadequate to satisfy the requirements of moral order which now,
as moral agents, it is our responsibility to meet. Our "creative"
purpose, where it is authentically constructive, here moves beyond the scope of our existing acceptances, and we act for ends
that, in the only terms that yet have normative authority, we
cannot justify or "rationally" explain. The "will" can no longer
"follow" an understanding that at this point blocks the road to
just that *better* understanding that we seek and the reformer
must appear as an iconoclast, a breaker of the old laws, in their
traditional finality, if he is to speak for a *better* good, not seen
as yet but nonetheless, through his constructive effort, in the

making. There is need here for decisions of a difficult and sometimes daring sort and those who have the courage *and* the intelligence to make them rightly earn the right to be regarded as the moral leaders of mankind.

But such decisions, if they are to be authentically constructive can by no means be groundless, arbitrary or blind. The reformer who knows what he is doing does not create *ex nihilo* or in a moral vacuum. He draws instead on those forces in the accepted moral world which are in this way capable of growth and of expansion. He comes, as the great prophets have always claimed, not to destroy but to fulfil, and unless what he has to offer can be seen to be such a fulfilment it can in no way be recognized as good. The possibilities of growth on which he pins his faith must be *real* possibilities, not for an ideal world of his own imagining, but *in* the actual world in which *we* live, with all our creaturely limitations, and must somehow work together. It is for the preservation *and* development of a moral order in *this* world that as a moral agent he is responsible, and if this is to be an order of shared purpose, not the esoteric imposition of his own incommunicable inspiration upon others, he must justify the promise of this better order to the answering judgment of those who are asked to share in both its burdens and rewards. That means that he must *find* the better reasons on whose terms his inspiration can be thus understood by those he is concerned to reach, and to preserve a livable understanding and build his case upon them. The "will" that goes beyond the understanding must *find* its justification in the discoverably better order for which such reasons can provide the normative structure. This *is* the justification of the reasons that he chooses here to follow, and it is for making *this* decision rightly that, in deciding, he makes himself responsible. The risk indeed is great, but it is basically the risk involved in *all* moral judgment which, as we have seen, is *never* merely a deductively certified conclusion formed from accepted principles, but rather an assessment, on the ground of all morally relevant considerations—including some whose relevance traditional acceptances ignored—to the merits of the specific case in which "decisions" must now be made. We may in such cases, and with the best intentions, decide wrongly, but unless there were a discoverable distinction between right and wrong which our wills as moral do not create by their own groundless fiat but must learn in the mature exercise of responsible judgment, there would be no sense or seriousness in the whole undertaking. It is this judgment, and the decision responsibly based on it, which the existentialist account parodies in its talk of "decisions of principle." And we can agree with them that, rightly understood, it is of basic practical significance.

The "game" in which such decisions are made does not end with the making or imposing of decisions. It goes on, in the continuing work of being practically reasonable which is the shared basis of our common life. What is in this way decided *needs* a justification and unless it can find and maintain it in the way that, in its light, we live and work together, it will not long retain its hold upon the minds and wills of men who know what they are doing. A reason that can maintain its cogency in this way shows itself in the process to be adequate to its task. This is its only, and its sufficient, justification. What other was to be expected or would morally make sense? Our reasons justify themselves *as* reasons in this normatively cogent use and our practical decisions are justified when they are in this way reasonable and just. The truth is "in the end" as plain *and* as complex, in its practical application, as that, though the morally simple-minded will never find it so. And we have seen now, at sufficient length, I think, that in the demanding world in which we live today it is not wise to be morally simple-minded. But suppose our justifications give out *before* a moral understanding has been reached—there would, of course, be no point in continuing them beyond that point. This does sometimes happen, and the resulting chaos is the appropriate reward of moral failure. It may happen now and here—there have been times in the last two generations when we have come perilously close to it. There is no external guarantee that we shall not fail, just as there is no fool-proof safeguard against error in our practical judgments. But there is a way of learning not to be fools, and there is a way of so behaving that our reasons will not give out. That is the way of practical reasonableness and by this time we should know at once its dangers and its worth. By all that is best in our own tradition, which is that of rational consent to "rules" that all who will share responsibly in this great undertaking can accept as just, we are committed to it. Is this itself a rational statement? In the only sense in which a reason could be significantly asked for, *yes*, it is indeed. For there is reason in it, and this reason is the only justification that a moral commitment needs or could require. And it was about the grounds of moral justification that the questioner, presumably, inquired. If this is what he seeks, then here he has it, and to ask for more would merely be to manifest a failure to understand the import of his own inquiry. If it is something else that he is looking for, then he must look elsewhere for it and perhaps, as the existentialists have done, find Nothing. And if he claims for his findings a relevance or cogency that makes practical or moral sense, we shall now know what to think of him. Meanwhile we have our own work to do and it is time for us to return to the main theme of our inquiry.

CHAPTER 16
BEYOND REASONABLE DOUBT

BUT WHAT DOES ALL this come to "in the end"? Where, if anywhere, in all this talk of relativities, opportunities and finalities, do we reach a *final* truth? Where are our "last ditch data" and our "ultimates" of incorrigible assurance? Assuredly we have not found them. Yet how, except as based on them, can any moral truth be "really" true? If what is true "in the end" is doubtful, must not everything be insecure and doubtful "in the end"? We have now reached "the end", or as near to it as, in this inquiry, we shall get, and as philosophers we must face this question, which is very "philosophical" indeed, and, if we can, give a reasoned answer to it. In so doing there will be an opportunity to restate and, perhaps, further clarify much that at the start may well have seemed irrelevant or evasive to the "ethical theorist" who looked to us for at least an attempted solution of his problem.

In a memorable sentence in his widely influential book, *Perception*, H. H. Price observes: "When I see a tomato, there is much that I can doubt."[1] Indeed there is, and some such doubts are of considerable importance. His, however, are of a rather

[1] *Perception* (London: Methuen & Co., Ltd., 1932), p. 3.

special sort. He wants so to "see" it that he can be sure at once about all angles and all aspects of it in a single and all-comprehending act of vision that would leave no theoretical ground for questioning the "reality" of what appears, as we look at, grasp and taste it, to be *really* a tomato—to see it, that is to say, outside the limitations of the human standpoint, from which in fact we do actually observe tomatoes, and sometimes recognize them for what as objects of human use and nourishment, they discoverably are. And when he finds that, like the rest of us, he cannot thus incorrigibly "see" them—we sometimes do make mistakes about tomatoes—he invents a sense of "seeing" in which a very special sort of objects which are not tomatoes but "families of sense-data" can, in sequence, be infallibly seen, and tries to build on this unshakable foundation our knowledge of the world that we perceive. This turns out to be of little help in confirming our more usual judgments about tomatoes; they remain as questionable as ever, since we never know for sure that the sense-datum we now take to be a member of such a family is *really* a member of the family and not a mere appearance. But it gives rise to a whole family of new "problems" more "ultimate," and thus ostensibly more profound, in which the whole *ground* of our perceptual knowledge of the world in which we live and move and find tomatoes, can significantly be called in question. *This* doubt is in principle unappeasable, for there is no way of answering it for tomatoes or any other objects in the world around us that would meet the requirements for "seeing" that the doubter sets. Perhaps, though this is not Price's line, we ought to say that on strict analysis, there is really no such world at all, but just a network of "families" of private, incorrigible and incommunicable "data", among which the "mind" and "body" of the doubter are somehow to be included, though this has so far, in actual epistemological description, proved very hard to do in any remotely plausible way. Perhaps.

And perhaps what we need to get out of the predicament in which we have involved ourselves is a "leap of faith" which will carry us beyond tomatoes, which at this point tend to disappear from the discussion, and on to some still higher object of our willful aspiration. Since nothing here is *certain,* anyway, why not believe anything we please? What in this process we leap *over,* for our philosophy has now no place for them, are just those criteria for reasonable or *justifiable* belief on whose terms a "true" tomato is reliably distinguished from a questionable pretender by those whose business it is to make this distinction. These, of course, are not criteria for "ultimate reality", and this humble vegetable might make but a poor showing on the "deeper" terms it sets. But, for tomatoes, they are indispensable. Perhaps what I see darkly as a tomato is really a colony of spirits, timelessly united in eternal love. "When I see a tomato there is much that I can doubt." But it is questionable at least that the sort of doubt that inspired Professor Price when he thus contemplated them is reasonable or judicious in its context.

It is *this* question, as the reader will have guessed, that I propose to raise about the skeptic's ultimate ethical dubieties. A moral judgment is, of course, a far nobler thing than an estimate of the authenticity of what *appear* to be tomatoes— but who can ever really *know?*—but there are important resemblances between them from which, if we will pay attention to it, we may well learn something useful. The first and most "fundamental" is simply this. If we are to make sense of their rational cogency we must be willing to accept the conceptual structure of the language of their tested use in making thus such distinctions, on its own terms—not impose those of some epistemologically more eligible use upon it. Our estimate of the "reality" of objects seen and smelled and eaten is confirmed or disconfirmed by what, as finite and sometimes uncritical observers, we see. Further, we see things as they look, and there is, for us, no other way of seeing them. And it is not families of sense-data that we devour when we eat them and later conclude from the observable effects of such consumption that they were not what they seemed. For better or for worse, perceptual observation as a ground for reasonable belief *is* a fallible *and* corrigible business and no verbal magic can give us any "ultimate" security about it, beyond that which its own reliable use warrants and sustains. And for the purposes of such belief, what looks and tastes and digests like a tomato, and can observably maintain this status under chemical tests which, not merely in the end but at every step, are confirmable in perceptual observation *is* a tomato. "There is nothing hidden."

The reader may recall John Wisdom's amusing instance of the man whose doubt of cheese was unappeasable because, though he could see and touch and eat it, he was somehow never able to "see cheese face to face." His metaphysical thirst was indeed insatiable, but was the sense of it? Was he, perhaps, expecting something else and on what grounds did he expect it? His doubt here is not grounded in the situation which ostensibly gave rise to it, but is rather the expression of his "ultimate" dissatisfaction with that whole way of looking at the world in which cheese can in fact be seen. He wants to "know" cheese as he might "know" a personal and private datum that was "his" alone and that no one else could possibly see. And when he finds he cannot do it, he invents a sense of "see" that would meet this requirement and asks us to show him how, in its terms, perceptual objects are *really* seen. He cannot feel finally secure without it. His state of mind is understandable, but it is not wise. And if he imagines that any juggling with "families" of sense data will meet *this* need, he is indeed deceived. He will have to turn his attention instead to the contemplation of his own frustrated subjectivity and brood in private (though not failing to write books about it) on the emptiness of a world which his understanding has refused to meet on the terms appropriate to its publicly discoverable nature. There are philosophers of this sort, and, as we know, there are those who hear them gladly.

My thesis will be that what passes for profundity in "final" philosophic doubt is basically a refusal of a comparable kind— a refusal to accept the limitations and opportunities of the human situation in which moral judgments are responsibly made or to respect the categorial structure of the language in which a justification of their claims can significantly be given. This brings with it also a refusal to take seriously the relativities, conditions and concrete possibilities for action in which grounds can reliably be found for preferring one such action to another. *Of course* those who look for an "ultimate" validation of the grounds of moral action *outside* the considerations that *make* one course of action better, for human purposes, than another will never find it. Their thirst for reassurance is inherently insatiable, for nothing that would *be* a normatively cogent answer to a moral question could appease it. And if they fool themselves, or us, by *calling* "final" those "ultimates" which, in their own incorrigible preferences, show themselves in their working to be thus final only for themselves, neither they nor we will "in the end" be the wiser for it. Their doubts are "ultimate" indeed, but they are morally irresponsible and philosophically inane. To treat the discovery of this inanity as an exposé of the final meaninglessness of "merely human" values is an understandable mistake, but an error nonetheless.

In a morally problematic situation there is indeed much that we can doubt—if there were not there would be no occasion or opportunity for critical reflection, and no constructive use to which it could be put. But it is well to remind ourselves that in such a situation not everything is morally problematic. Unless we had some common grounds for action not themselves "problematic" in the situation in which we base our claims upon them, we should have no reasons for doing anything at all. Before our reasons can conflict, there must first of all *be* reasons, and these must be understood and used as such in the situation in which appeal is made to them. These are categorical "musts", and as such basic to the normative structure of the situation in which we appeal to them. A groundless claim requires and can have no justification.

We do not need to make up such reasons for ourselves, and we do *not* do *this* on our own responsibility. We learn them as we learn to act *as* moral agents in the communities in which we become responsible selves or moral persons. There can be no ethically non-committal or "value-free" moral judgments. And *for the most part* there is substantial agreement as to their proper use. If there were not such agreement, as the conceptual framework for our moral problems, *this* game would not in practical actuality be played, and it is *inside* the game that we significantly have such problems. The extent of this agreement is too frequently ignored. Moral conflicts are news. The continuing understanding that is the basis of the preservation of the common human decencies is ordinarily simply "taken for granted." And it is just because we do take it for granted, and in so many *unproblematic* cases accept and act on, "as a matter of course", the judgments unquestioningly based upon them, that the instances that fail to fit them can present for us a moral problem—a choice that calls for adjudication on its merits. Those morally we do *not* "choose"; we simply understand and act. And this is not because in such cases we do not have a reason, but because it is so obvious that there is simply no occasion to express it. In the shared activities of decent men its cogency is recognized as a matter of course.

A general doubt of the validity of such reasons, in their normal use, would be a merely groundless doubt. If in specific cases, we are reasonably called on, as we well may be, to defend their adequacy in the use we make of them, there must be grounds for this demand. And these must themselves be presented and maintain themselves *as reasons,* as considerations of moral relevance to a judgment of the over-all merits of the situation in which a choice between alternatives is made. If we are not prepared so to consider them, they can have for us no moral bearing on the moral merits of the case, and that is what, in responsible judgment, we are trying to find out. That someone else objects to what I propose to do, or will fight me if I do it, is *so far* no reason why I should not do it. There are occasions, surely, when we *ought* to fight for the things we know to be good, and the opposition of willful men to any action that meets hard moral requirements is to be expected. Unless there is some reason to support moral claims, there is none why we should take account of them in our estimates of right, save as obstacles to be overcome or wickedness to be conquered. The reduction of conflicting claims to this level of sheer arbitrary opposition is, as we have seen, the *reductio ad absurdum* to which the current war of ideologies appears, on "ultimate" issues, to have brought us. And moral objectivity, on the other hand, where it can be attained, is the concern and capacity to understand and appraise the adequacy of the reasons that support such claims and to reach a verdict, not for "their" side or for ours, but on the merits of the case. This is a difficult and too often, in our time, a rare achievement. But all rational assignment of moral excellence depends upon it.

In such an adjudication the reasons that should rightly prevail are *better* reasons, "better" not in general or in the abstract, but in their capacity to specify a livable solution for just this problem. Most usually, they will not be *either* "ours" or "theirs" as initially presented but that composition of the two with *other* morally considerable claims will here provide a working basis for

continued action in which nobody will merely lose or win but all
alike, though with some discipline in mutual forbearance and
respect, can find a common good.

For hard and unfamiliar cases we do not know in advance what
this solution will be. It must be found out, worked out with pa-
tience, prayer and ingenuity for the case in hand. To draw up
advance blueprints for a final federation of the world is generally
a waste of time, though some vague inspiration may be derived
from it. But we do not come to such decisions empty-headed.
The more we know of past history, present population trends
and human nature, about what in human relations the traffic
will bear and what without cynicism or illusion can plausibly be
expected of the *kind* of human beings with whom, just here, we
have to deal, the wiser, other things being equal, we can be in
making it. And we have our own deep rooted moral traditions
that we cannot and would not disavow. The essential truth in
them we must abide by at all costs. But equally we must not
claim that their truth is the only truth there is. To learn how
that truth, and those who honor it, can live with others not
made or remakable in our "image" is what it is to be reasonable
in practice. And while, as we have seen, there are in such matters
no general rules for judgment on such issues, there is a way of
being judicious and responsible in the way we make them.
More than this is fairly asked of no man. But nothing less or
easier will suffice. And any man of practical good judgment who
has put away the childishness of moral simple-mindedness knows
this.

The man who makes such judgment is responsible in his
decision to the community for which he makes it. All judgments
are personal, for it is men as selves who make them "on their
own responsibility." But none are merely private, for they claim
a rational warrant and there can be no private reasons. Here as
always, truth is public. A responsible judgment is addressed to

those concerned and competent in the situation in which all alike are morally involved. Unless it can be justified *to them* in terms which they can understand and practically accept, not as a fulfilment of their private wishes but as meeting on the whole the over-all requirements of their common moral life, it has no public warrant. To retain this is a long, hard job. But we cannot do without it. For this is the consent from which derive the just powers of all governments, and all others who claim to act in our behalf with normative authority. If our own tradition has not taught us this, then indeed we have been inattentive pupils.

And finally such judgments and the decisions that they warrant must maintain their cogency in the long, hard run of subsequent experience. If they are accepted we shall have to live with them, and take their consequences—whose full moral import is often not apparent at the time when they are made. The man who judges fairly and acts honorably "according to his lights," if he has taken full advantage of the light available when he makes his decision, has done his best "according to his lights." But his best may not be good enough to solve the problem set him by the situation. This, again, is something to be found out. The work of practical reason is a continuing and a self-correcting work. We cannot fairly blame a man for mistakes that in his situation he could hardly have avoided. But unless we and he as well can recognize them *as* mistakes when more light *is* available, there can be no rational learning from experience. A reasonable man can live honorably with others and learn from them, and from his own growing experience, what the authentic moral import of his actions is. Only so, indeed, can he live adequately with himself. For thus to live and learn, and to act accordingly, is in practice what it is to be a moral self.

The point of this summary of a familiar process for our present purposes will by now be obvious. The right decision on a moral issue is the reasonable decision and the right reasons to support it are those that reliably establish it in this status. Where our familiarly accepted reasons adequately do this job within the area of agreement that makes moral action possible, they are not merely good but sufficient for the purpose, and there is, within this situation, no ground to doubt the cogency of the judgment unquestioningly based upon them. Where they are not sufficient, and better reasons are required, it is in just this way that they must be better if they are here to do the work required of them. If they do it adequately, if initially competing claims can be reasonably composed within the normative structure of the moral order that their shared acceptance defines, then the problem to which they were addressed is solved, and there is no further ground, in this situation, for doubt about their cogency. This doubt would itself require a reason *not* thus included and nonetheless entitled to reasonable consideration. And here, *ex hypothesi,* there is none. So long as there are such reasons our moral problem has not adequately been solved and doubt of the finality of conclusions irreconcilable with them is a reasonable doubt. We may well expect that in the imperfect world in which we live there will always be such problems. But *some* problems can be in this way solved—our existing moral order is the embodiment of this solution—and the understanding thus achieved is the working basis for our hope that we can successfully *go on* to deal with others. It is our good fortune that not all such problems are of equal urgency and not all are in the same way our concern. We are not called on to legislate for humanity at large in all times and ages, or to play God in the final judgment of the world. We, and our reasons, are *inside* the world we judge about and morally as well as perceptually we "see" it only from where we are and in the conceptual terms of our quite limited moral understanding. For us the point of wisdom is to mind our own business and to adjudicate only those issues in which we, as practical agents, are called upon to make a responsible decision. Future generations must be left to handle their own problems as they arise. The best that we can do is to maintain in our own time, and develop where we can, that continuing consensus of due process and moral order on whose terms specific problems, as they arise, can in their turn be rationally solved. Within this process there is much that we can doubt. And here also there are grounds for doubt and grounds also for its removal. Such doubting is essential to all rational inquiry. But for a merely groundless doubt, not in this way resolvable in the continuing work of such inquiry, there can (tautologically but conclusively) be no ground, i.e., no reason, at all. Such doubt is unreasonable doubt and in the right conduct of his affairs no reasonable man need or should take account of it.

How do we really know that the reasons that we offer in such cases are here indeed sufficient reasons? By showing in their use their adequacy to do this work. How do we *know* that we are capable of reliable judgment in such matters? How do we *know* that we can speak the English language? By speaking and being understood. It is in the answering judgment of those who do in this way understand, and the life we live together on the terms this understanding sets, that our reasonable doubts have their sufficient answer. The reasons that in this way show their justifying cogency are good and sufficient reasons. This is what is good about them; it is what they are good for. What in this way looks and acts and works like a sufficient reason *is* a sufficient reason; its discoverable adequacy leaves no ground for doubt of the validity of its normative claim upon us. This *is* its justification *as* a practical reason and it is as such that we must understand it if we are to estimate its cogency *as* a ground for moral action. If the reasons so far offered do not do the job, then we must go on looking for the better reasons that will more adequately meet this need. It is in this *going on* that moral inquiry, as a rational procedure, has its distinctive use. Nothing more is needed; nothing less will suffice. If this is what we asked for when we asked that a sufficient ground for action be given, then here we have it, beyond reasonable doubt. If it is something else the "ultimate" doubter wants when he asks for final reassurance of the truth of moral judgment then, of course, he must look elsewhere for it.

We can by this time see quite clearly that it is something else. The doubter's quest for final reassurance is insatiable, within the universe of moral discourse, precisely because he refuses to accept the concepts and the categories of this discourse as a "final" measure of the truth he seeks. He "sees", in one sense, all the reasons that we offer, and can often make shrewd use of them in the conduct of his practical affairs. But for philosophical purposes of "ultimate" analysis he will not let them count as reasons without some sort of external support that, as we quite agree with him, is not here to be found. His doubt is thus not practical but philosophical, in a sense of that term of which Wittgenstein has made considerable use. He is, in fact, our old associate the ethical theorist on the job again, demanding that the moral world should fit the pattern he proposes to impose on it and, when he finds that it does not, expressing in this way his own ultimate dissatisfaction with its nature. The truth that he seeks is not in it.

Wittgenstein's analysis of this attitude seems to me essentially correct, though sometimes too invidiously expressed. It is here a picture that holds us captive, a picture deeply imbedded in a language still inadequately understood, and so long as we are fascinated by this picture we cannot see through or beyond it to the facts that would authentically solve our problem. In these facts themselves there is nothing hidden; they are the daily bread, the substance of our common moral life. But we shall only see them if we look, and for this a directness and integrity of understanding is required from which the "demands" of our own preconceptions shut us off. The blue glasses on our nose show everything as blue. And because we cannot imagine what it would be like to "see" without them, we *will* not take them off.[2] We should feel insecure and lost in a world in which we were obliged to *look and see* for ourselves, and to judge accordingly.

There is nothing "unnatural" in such an attitude. It is, on the contrary, the normal starting point of moral learning. The spectacles that we wear are those fitted to us by early training, emphatically and authoritatively given, and the world we see through them is of one color and one price throughout. To move confidently about in it, we have only to follow our noses. It is all quite simple and, as Kierkegaard has said, blessed are the single-minded (those who only will one thing—"the good") for theirs is purity of heart.[3] It is not surprising that there are those who cling to it through life, and at any cost.

The cost, however, can be great. For most of us soon find that our moral world in which we have to live is not in fact that simple. To discover this, and to learn to live with it is basic and essential learning; it is, or can be at least, the beginning of wisdom. To adjust our judgment to "the facts of life" and at the same time to retain, "in principle" at least, the simple-mindedness with which we began is a considerable feat. We have followed its tortuous development to the very heights of ethical theory and have found that the goal it seeks is "in principle" and in practice a dead end. But this, for earnest and opinionated men, is a hard truth to admit. It is easier to try one more reshuffle of the old, worn counters of the dialectical game and dimly hope that "finally" we shall win, if not on rational, then on supra-rational terms. And while this game is played, in classrooms, pulpits,

---

[2] *Op. Cit.*, p. 45e.
[3] Cf. his *Purity of Heart, passim.*

public platforms and sometimes, with disastrous effect, in the parochial absolutism which is its practical embodiment, the world goes on about its wisdom none the wiser for our effort. This no longer seriously surprises us. As C. D. Broad has said, "salvation is not everything; and to try to understand in outline what one solves *ambulando* in detail is quite good fun for those people who like that sort of thing."[4]

But even in this case the recognition that the "rules" of such "understanding" are in fact inadequate *in principle* to the actual cogency of the solution offered *ambulando* somewhat spoils the fun. The game seems to lose its point. The current gap between an understanding thus impractical and a practice thus unenlightened was the starting point of our inquiry. It is appropriate that at its conclusion we should survey it again—now, perhaps with greater understanding.

Are we, here, confronted with a final choice between ultimate attitudes, each in itself quite groundless, and each stipulating for itself the grounds on which the game of moral justification is to be played? By no means. For the two "attitudes" are not of equal human urgency and importance. In the "game" of practically reasonable and responsible action we are inextricably involved as selves or persons. For it is not an optional game. Our integrity as moral agents is bound up with our roles and function in it; this indeed is what it is to be "bound" or obligated all. And, if we are to play it responsibly, we must follow "rules", not of our own arbitrary preference, but of public right and common good. Nor is the "game" of ethical theorizing wholly independent of it. Its dialectical inquiry begins with *our* moral problems. Its categories are parasitic for their normative significance on an understanding of the moral cogency of such notions as "obliga-

---

[4] *Five Types of Ethical Theory* (London: Routledge and Keagan Paul, Ltd., 1930), p. 285.

tion", "worth", and "right", which, in their own terms they cannot even in principle supply. And its ingenious conclusions are supposed to be "directives" that can relevantly tell us how to live well, not in the world of its own analytic or dialectical construction but in that of common earth and air and light and, we may add with a backward look, of authentically discoverable tomatoes. Unless this meaning is imported into ethical theorizing then, as we have seen, it makes no moral sense at all and has no right to be called the theory of our moral life.

Our thesis is that this meaning, which is its only rational stock in trade, is illegitimately imported by a systematic misinterpretation of the conceptual structure of the language of practical action. Given the initial standpoint, the misinterpretation was to be expected, and it has been carried out with a dialectical skill that is worthy of a better cause. But it remains a misinterpretation nonetheless, and until we free ourselves from it we shall never understand the basic categories of practical thought or know how, in hard and complicated cases, to make a proper use of them. And it is this use that in our own time particularly is our most urgent human business.

And since our sickness here is a confusion and failure of understanding, it is by a better understanding, for those who are not altogether beyond the reach of rational inquiry, that it can at least in more fortunate cases be cured. Wittgenstein has sometimes spoken of philosophy as a kind of linguistic cramp for which a cure is needed. He has not always been at pains to emphasize that the cure for such misunderstanding is a *better* understanding, and thus a better philosophy, the kind of philosophy, in fact, that his own *Philosophical Investigations* have notably helped to teach us to pursue. This better understanding will perhaps not be philosophy as it is practiced in some classrooms or even at some sessions of the American Philosophical Association. But it is that embodiment of the love and quest for wisdom in whose light we can most adequately understand each other and ourselves for our own human purposes. These purposes, if we have even begun to be wise, are hard and deep. Nothing human need or should be alien to them. If religious experience and/or authority can bring us authentic tidings of a better world in which we personally shall one day live, that is good news indeed, and it is the part of wisdom to take full practical account of it in our behavior. But unless the God for whom religion speaks is at least a person we can love and understand as such, he is not worthy of our worship, whatever rewards or punishments may be promised for our faith in him. "Just are the ways of God, and justifiable to man." There is no more basic tenet than this in any faith that can rightly claim our practical allegiance. So it is, of course, and tautologically with any justifiable claim upon the human will; and of unjustifiable claims we know by this time what to think.

A proper use of the categories of practical understanding does not provide an adequate answer to the riddle of the Universe, if there is a riddle, or tell us what is Being or whether sense-data have unobservable backsides. On any reckoning man is a late comer in the world and even his most cosmic decisions so far cause but little stir in interstellar space. There is nothing you can properly do with the language of normative appraisal but make right normative appraisals with it. There is no other right way of doing this and for our human purposes we cannot do without it. In this way, and in this way only, the "attitude" of practical reasonableness is *for us* quite ultimate and inescapable, and the attempt to discount or transcend it in a higher truth that still makes moral sense is bound to be self-stultifying. It is no wonder that the "ultimate" doubter cannot find in the procedures of practical reasonableness the "final" truth he seeks. On his own terms he could not recognize such truth if, through his spectacles, he "saw" it.

There is one final truth of practical reason on which before all others we would stake our case:

Gentleness, virtue, wisdom and endurance,
These are the seals of that most firm assurance
That bars the pit over destruction's strength.
And if, with infirm hands, Eternity,
Mother of many acts and hours, should set free
The Serpent that would clasp her in his length,
These are the spells by which to reassume
An empire or the disentangled doom.

So Shelley grandly states it in *Prometheus Unbound*. The setting is melodramatic but what is stated is minimal practical truth, and it is true beyond all reasonable doubt. Judge Learned Hand comes at the same point from a more prosaic angle. Speaking at the high tide of McCarthyism in America, he said:

I believe that the community is already in process of dissolution when each man begins to eye his neighbor as a possible enemy; where nonconformity with the accepted creed, political as well as religious, is a mark of disaffection; where denunciation without backing takes the place of evidence; where orthodoxy chokes freedom of dissent; where faith in the eventual supremacy of reason has become so timid that we dare not enter our convictions in the open tests, to win or lose. Such fears as these are the solvents that can eat out the cement that binds the stones together; they may in the end subject us to a despotism as evil as any that we dread; and they can be allayed only in so far as we refuse to proceed on suspicion and trust each other until we have tangible ground for misgiving. The mutual confidence on which all else depends can be maintained only by an open mind and a brave reliance upon free discussion.[5]

"The mutual confidence on which all else depends." This is in sober truth the foundation for any community in which men can live fully and responsibly together. And the condition for

---

[5] Irving Dilliard (ed.), *The Spirit of Liberty; Papers and Addresses of Learned Hand* (3rd ed.; New York: Alfred A. Knopf, Inc., 1960), pp. 274f.

its maintenance is the exercise of not just "virtue" in general but of that continued use of practical reason through which all good things can show their worth and imposters be reliably exposed. And this truth, too, is beyond reasonable doubt. It does not solve all our political problems. There is room for reasonable disagreement as to its proper application in specific cases. But it sets the rational conditions for the right operation of the process in which, for the purposes of common action, such disagreements can be resolved, not to the unqualified satisfaction, but with the reasonable consent, of those who share responsibly in the form of life whose moral structure it defines. In this sense and no other it is for us a final truth, and there is no "security" that we could buy with its denial that could possibly repay us for its loss. On it today, as in the past, we are prepared to stake our lives, our fortunes and our sacred honor.

"It often happens that we only become aware of the important *facts,* if we suppress the question 'why?'; and then in the course of our investigations these facts lead us to an answer."[6] Our own experience in this book has been of this sort, though here, as is frequently the case, Wittgenstein's remark, as it stands, is too cryptic to make the precise point clear. The "why?" that we "suppressed" at the start has not now been answered. On the contrary, our continuing aim throughout has been to show that it was a mistake to ask for it.

To look for a *why* of moral reasons outside and independent of the categorical structure of their practical use is wrong-headedly to look away from the "why" that is in them *in* their own appropriate use and which is in fact the only and sufficient justification of that use. In Part I our aim was to look squarely and independently at these facts, and to try to understand them as they are. And to do this, we have throughout

---

[6] Ludwig Wittgenstein, *Philosophical Investigations* (New York: The Macmillan Co., 1953), p. 134e.

maintained, they must be understood as *moral* facts. Their normative cogency is *in* them from the start; they make no sense as practical reasons without it. No analysis which ignores this fact or fails to build upon it can make sense of the cogency and the point of moral judgment. It is not surprising, therefore, that it has so frequently made nonsense of it.

In tracing out the normative requirements for *being* practically reasonable we, too, have found a kind of answer to the doubts of moral skeptics, for we have found a truth that we can build on with our eyes open and in the reasonable assurance that in the right use of it we shall not be morally defeated or deceived. It is a truth that we can take our stand on and live by and with—without cynicism and without illusion. But it is not the answer to the question asked. It tells us rather something else—what Wittgenstein has elsewhere described as "the importance of being justified." It shows us the essential place of "this very special pattern in the weave of our lives"[7] and why it is that nothing that is important to us can "in the end" make justifying sense without it. And this *is,* though in a somewhat different sense, *its* justification—the only sort that can be significantly asked of it. We cannot get outside of it to legislate impartially for the universe. Our moral roots are in it and without it we should not be the moral agents that we are. And it is as such agents that we are called upon to make, and to justify, our moral judgments. To recognize this fact is to accept the limits and responsibilities of humanity; to consent to be, in our own persons, neither more nor less than men. There are still those for whom this is difficult to do, and they will not hear us gladly. But the truth is there, for those who have a mind to see, and the proposal of this book is simply that we build our moral philosophy upon it.

The moral rules we follow are in one sense arbitrary and con-

---

[7] *Op. cit.,* p. 229e.

tingent. In a different sort of world, or for a different sort of creature, they would no longer be required. Ants and bees seem to get on very well without them, and the superman who supposes himself to have "transcended the limitations of the human species" will naturally refuse to be "bound" by them with consequences we have recently had occasion to observe. In a radically different sort of world this "game" would not be played; and it is only in it, and as expressing *its* requirements, that the rules of morality make justifying sense. Yet *for us*, it is not arbitrary, or rather, it is so only in the sense that, "The rules of grammar may be called 'arbitrary' if that is to mean that the *aim* of the grammar is nothing but that of the language."[8] The aim of the language is here the achievement and maintenance of a certain kind of understanding and, in its light, of the goods that only its right use makes humanly attainable, while they make no normative sense save on the terms it sets for their right attainment. And so it is, with the "grammar" of practical reason. In the fulfillment of this aim, through its sustained and self-correcting use, it finds *raison d' être* and its vindication. And here, once more and now quite finally, "nothing more is needed; nothing less will suffice."

It is *because* the starting point of reason is thus relative and conditional that *growth* in understanding is both possible and essential. Our given reasons, in their rational pretensions, are morally incomplete so long as only those on our side can "see" and understand them. The justification they purport to offer must answer to and find confimation in the judgment of *all* reasonably concerned to reach an understanding with each other in the moral requirements of their common life. Men of ill will refuse to see it and those whose tenacity of belief exceeds their capacity to recognize and correct mistakes will remain too stubborn or too blind to see. Our reasonable hope for better under-

---

[8] Wittgenstein, *op. cit.*, p. 138e.

standing is based on the conviction that the resources in human nature on which it could be built are not yet exhausted and that in our own time and beyond it men of steady purpose and good will can put them to constructive use. *This* choice is for us to make, and much depends on how we make it.

Philosophy can contribute to this work by the removal of misunderstandings that have led us to look in the wrong place for the kind of reasons that, in this constructive work, we need. The business of "conceptual analysis" is the clarification of meaning; its point is the elimination of misunderstanding—not any that might conceivably arise but such as do in fact arise and stand between us and the proper doing of the work that we are in. Philosophy in this use has no esoteric information of its own to contribute on the metaphysical insides of electrons or the axiological priorities among eternal values. All it can offer is a sort of light—the light of common day, indeed, for it is the light in which, at our best, we live our days in common. In that sense only I would wish this book to be considered as a contribution to philosophy. It is addressed to those by whom, in this way, it may be found. The justification it claims or would desire will be found, if at all, in the answering judgment of the reader who will say, "I understand. Now I can go on," and who makes good what he says in what he does.

INDEX